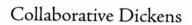

Collaborative Dickens

Series in Victorian Studies

Series editors: Joseph McLaughlin and Elizabeth Carolyn Miller

COLLABORATIVE DICKENS

Authorship and
Victorian Christmas
Periodicals

Melisa Klimaszewski

OHIO UNIVERSITY PRESS   ATHENS

Ohio University Press, Athens, Ohio 45701
ohioswallow.com
© 2019 by Ohio University Press
All rights reserved

Printed in the United States of America
Ohio University Press books are printed on acid-free paper ⊗ ™

29 28 27 26 25 24 23 22 21 20 19   5 4 3 2 1

Library of Congress Cataloging-in-Publication Data
Names: Klimaszewski, Melisa, author.
Title: Collaborative Dickens : authorship and Victorian Christmas periodicals
  / Melisa Klimaszewski.
Description: Athens : Ohio University Press, [2019] | Series: Series in
  Victorian studies | Includes bibliographical references and index.
Identifiers: LCCN 2019004319| ISBN 9780821423653 (hc : alk. paper) | ISBN
  9780821446737 (pdf)
Subjects: LCSH: Dickens, Charles, 1812-1870--Authorship--Collaboration. |
  Christmas stories, English--History and criticism.
Classification: LCC PR4586 .K55 2019 | DDC 823/.8--dc23
LC record available at https://lccn.loc.gov/2019004319

This book is dedicated lovingly to Rose Cuschieri, Adam Klimaszewski, and Daniel Klimaszewski for their unwavering support, compassion, and encouragement through countless stumbles.

~Inhobbok hafna

Contents

Illustrations

Acknowledgments

The idea to begin researching Dickens's Christmas numbers stemmed from my participation in a 2004 National Endowment for the Humanities Seminar at the Dickens Project in Santa Cruz, California. Thanks to the seminar participants and to leader John Bowen for being part of the beginning, and thanks to the Dickens Project for decades of generously supporting my intellectual development. Collaborating with Melissa Valiska Gregory led to my first editorial work on the Christmas numbers, and I am grateful to her for inspiring ideas that spawned this monograph and for being a steadfast friend. Holly Furneaux provided essential help at various stages of writing and crucial sustenance in the form of olives.

Special spaces and special people have enabled me to press forward through all sorts of obstacles. Shout out to Ritual Cafe, the Rare Books Reading Room at the British Library, The Lamb in Bloomsbury, and my front porch. Love and thanks to all the people who inspire and sustain me, including Christine Klimaszewski, Alice Reinke, Benjamin Gardner, Amy O'Shaughnessy, Ted Lyddon-Hatten, Mariella Theuma, Karl Kaufman, Barbara Klimaszewski, and the mighty Sofia Turnbull. Warm gratitude to Craig Owens, Erik Siwak, Mazz Swift, Angelica Saintignon, John Jordan, Bill Ingram, Emily Miranda, and my dear nephew, Wolf Miranda Klimaszewski, who indulges my desire to tell stories and who gives me hope. Forever thanks to Carlton Floyd, who helped my brain to grow at a key stage and who affected my core in ways that continue to benefit all aspects of my life. To the Coalition of Black Students and inaugural Crew Scholars at Drake University, thanks for all the years of walking together.

In a book focused on Dickens and the Victorian periodical press, the notes and bibliography will express my engagement with and implicit gratitude toward scholars in those fields. I must also acknowledge this book's and my own debt to writers and thinkers whose focus does not fall directly on the primary sources I discuss but whose work has shaped my thinking. Once one has read James Baldwin, Toni Morrison, or Eve Sedgwick or listened to *Songs in the Key of Life*, one simply does not think the same way again. I am as intellectually indebted to Steve Biko, Mamphela Ramphele, and Zakes Mda as I am to Sandra Gilbert and Susan Gubar.

Several grants from Drake University provided critical funding for research travel, research time, and conference attendance, which enabled me to develop ideas central to this book. Without the material support of Drake's Center for the Humanities, the College of Arts and Sciences (presided over by Dean Joseph Lenz), Drake International, and the Office of the Provost, this book would not have made its way into print. For valuable research and proofreading help, my thanks to the following student workers: Erin Mercurio, Jon Heggestad, Yvonne Gildemaster, Nicole Margheim, and Dominic Adduci. Thanks also to the Interlibrary Loan staff at Drake University, the librarians at the Forster Collection of the National Art Library in the Victoria and Albert Museum, and the patient workers in the British Library Manuscripts and Rare Books Rooms. The Dickens Museum in London, especially Louisa Price, has graciously provided archival access and photographs while on a tight schedule. An earlier version of the portion of chapter 4 that discusses *The Wreck of the Golden Mary* is reprinted here with kind permission from *SEL Studies in English Literature 1500–1900* 54, 4 (Autumn 2014).

Finally, deep thanks to the doctors and nurses at the Mayo Clinic in Rochester, Minnesota, and John Stoddard Cancer Center in Des Moines, Iowa, for spending a great deal of time saving my life while I completed this manuscript. Their expertise has enabled me to hold this book in my hands. To Dr. Boughey and Dr. Nguyen, who gracefully agreed to play Stevie Wonder in the operating room, my insides are forever grateful. Onward we dance.

Introduction

For those who think of Charles Dickens as a professional and personal bully, the phrase "collaborative Dickens" may sound like an oxymoron or an overly generous fantasy. For those who associate only *A Christmas Carol* with the phrase "Dickens and Christmas," the phrase "Dickens's Christmas numbers" may act as a reminder of the seemingly infinite number of *Carol* adaptations. There is, however, a whole cache of Dickens Christmas literature that has little to do with Ebenezer Scrooge and is indeed collaborative. Readers and scholars do not usually regard Dickens as a famous writer who placed his voice in conversation with and sometimes on a level with fairly unknown writers. And yet this Dickens, a significant collaborative presence in the Victorian period, is one that I have found repeatedly while editing and studying the literature he produced for Christmas.

Between 1850 and 1867, Dickens released a special annual issue, or number, of his journal shortly before Christmas. Enormously successful, these numbers eventually sold upwards of 200,000 copies: "[I]n Britain and America, the most popular single issues of *All the Year Round* remained, as with *Household Words*, the annual Extra Christmas Numbers. These . . . had the highest circulation of any of Dickens's serial or periodical writings."[1] The special Christmas issues contained stories written by Dickens in addition to work from friends and colleagues he invited to contribute. For each one, Dickens would work fictional prose and verse (only the first two contain some nonfiction) from other writers into a frame concept he devised. The title of one of the early numbers, *A Round of Stories by the Christmas Fire* (1852), describes a basic frame: people sharing tales as they sit around a fire. Dickens soon made the structures more elaborate, as for *Somebody's Luggage* (1862), which features a waiter discovering manuscripts tucked away inside various pieces of travel gear.

Collaborative Dickens is the first comprehensive study of these Christmas numbers, which are some of the most fascinating works Dickens produced. Restoring links between stories from as many as nine different writers in a given year, this book shows that a respect for the Christmas numbers' plural authorship and intertextuality results in a new view of the complexities of collaboration in the Victorian periodical press and a new appreciation for some of Dickens's most popular texts. Examining the complete numbers reveals Dickens to have been an editor who, rather than ceaselessly bullying his contributors, sometimes accommodated contrary opinions and depended on multivocal narratives for his own success. As often as Dickens was defensive or controlling, he was playful and self-conscious in collaboration. Reevaluating all eighteen Christmas collections leads to an understanding of Dickens as a variable collaborator and illustrates more broadly that collaborative texts require a flexible definition of authorship. Tracing the connections among and between the stories uncovers ongoing conversations between the works of Dickens and those of his collaborators, and some Christmas collections emerge as texts that enact their own fraught origins.

Eagerly anticipated and broadly appealing, the annual numbers quickly spawned imitations from other publishers, but those texts were not emulating Dickens alone. For all issues of *Household Words*, Dickens called himself the periodical's "conductor" and, with rare exceptions for serialized novels, included no individual bylines for authors. The practice of anonymous publication was not unusual for periodicals whose editors generally saw bylines as impediments to a journal's creation of a unified voice. Some authors disliked anonymity, and Douglass Jerrold reportedly remarked that Dickens's journal was "mononymous" rather than anonymous because every page header of the regular issues announced, "Conducted by Charles Dickens."[2] Kelly Mays points out that anonymity or the use of pseudonyms also contributed to "the corporate character of the periodical text."[3] Whether reacting to his journals as entities or to Dickens as an individual, not all authors resented anonymity. Dickens's unique conducting metaphor at once acknowledged and subordinated other creative talents. In an orchestral conducting context, without skilled musicians, a conductor's wand would fail to impress; successful conducting requires deep familiarity with each individual's aptitude and savvy coordination of styles. Other readings of the metaphor, which consider railway conducting or material objects that conduct electricity and energy, likewise reference scenarios in which interactions are crucial to achieving a desired effect. Alexis Easley further contends that a byline for women writers could act as "a barrier to those who relied upon anonymity as a means of separating their private and public identities" and wished to address "conventionally masculine subject matter in their work."[4] And Joanne Shattock notes that Dickens's celebrity was profitable even for unnamed contributors: "None of the other eponymous journals had a 'Conductor' with such pulling power. . . . Writers wanted to be published in Dickens's journal, and then to republish their essays, stories and articles, as having been 'first published in *Household Words.*'"[5] Thanks to the survival of the *Household Words* Office Book (see figures I.1–I.3) and other records, we can identify the nearly forty collaborators who contributed to Christmas issues, but constructing a careful methodology for the study of those collaborative relationships is a much more difficult task.

Despite the complexity of the conducting metaphor, the dominant critical tendency has been to characterize Dickens as an inflexible editorial bully. Edgar Johnson's dated yet still frequently cited biography claims, "Dickens maintained a vigorous, a dictatorial control over every detail. . . . His hand was everywhere," and Ruth Glancy concludes, "*Household Words* achieved its vision through Dickens's powerful editorial control. . . . Dickens edited every item."[6] Lillian Nayder's *Unequal Partners*, as its title indicates, emphasizes power struggles in the only full-length book study of

Figure I.1. *Household Words* Office Book, cover. Morris L. Parrish Collection of Victorian Novelists (C0171), Manuscripts Division, Department of Rare Books and Special Collections, Princeton University Library.

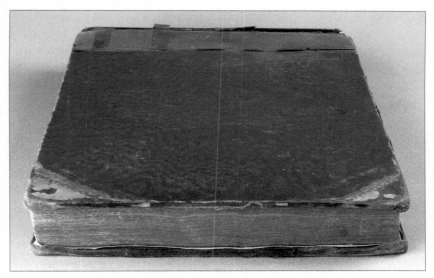

Figure I.2. *Household Words* Office Book, side view. Morris L. Parrish Collection of Victorian Novelists (C0171), Manuscripts Division, Department of Rare Books and Special Collections, Princeton University Library.

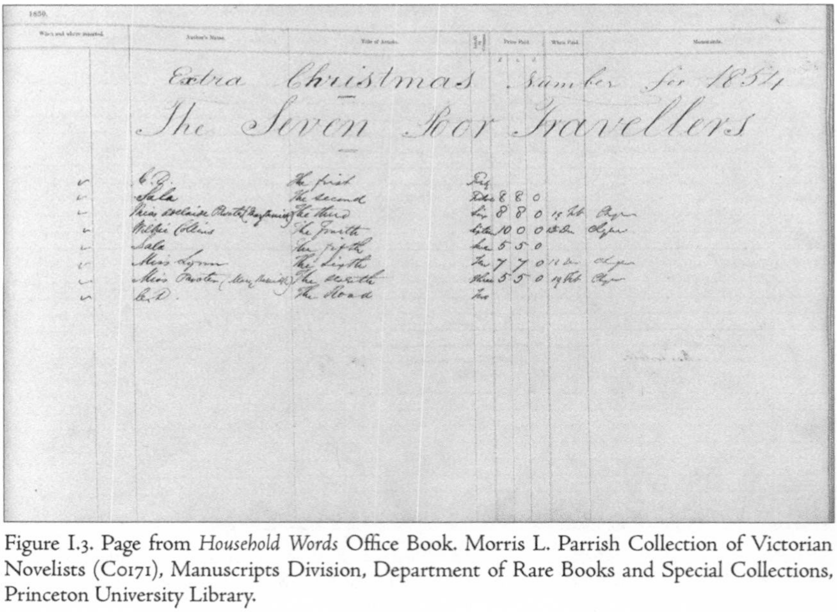

1850.

Extra Christmas Number for 1854

The Seven Poor Travellers

When and where inserted.	Author's Name.	Title of Article.	Length	Price Paid. £	s.	d.	When Paid.	Memoranda.
	C.D.	The first						
	Sala	The second		8	8	0		
	Miss Adelaide Procter (Mary Berwick)	The third		8	8	0	19 Feb	
	Wilkie Collins	The fourth		10	0	0		
	Sala	The fifth		5	5	0		
	Miss Lynn	The sixth		7	7	0		
	Miss Procter (Mary Berwick)	The seventh		5	5	0	19 Feb	
	C.D.	The Road						

Figure I.3. Page from *Household Words* Office Book. Morris L. Parrish Collection of Victorian Novelists (C0171), Manuscripts Division, Department of Rare Books and Special Collections, Princeton University Library.

Dickens's work with Wilkie Collins. Nayder posits that contributors "were forced to submit to the editorial authority of Dickens" and goes so far as to state that Collins sometimes saw himself "as a wage slave" to Dickens.[7] Such critical presentations of Dickens as a domineering editorial force who never actually collaborated with his contributors are not borne out by examination of the complete Christmas numbers. Nayder's work brought important attention to collaboration but has skewed critical discourse further toward hierarchy and contention as the central aspects of Dickens's joint works. Misdirection toward competition ignores the fact that the Christmas numbers repeatedly include dissonant or contradictory voices comfortably. As Melissa Valiska Gregory states, "The scholarly emphasis on Dickens's efforts to establish his supremacy over the very authors that he invited to work with him obscures some of the intriguing tonal nuances, weird internal friction, and peculiar crossbreeding effects that animate his collaborative work and make it a dynamic reading experience."[8]

Still, deep irony accompanies Dickens's desire to present a collective, unified voice in his journal given his self-donned nickname. John Drew remarks, "This from a writer who styled himself 'The Inimitable' clearly raises some complex issues for the study of literary distinction, editorial approach and collaborative authorship."[9] As I probe such complexities, I am aware that my work pushes against a scholarly trend that has accepted the "inimitable" designation without considering other voices that were part of it. Those other voices at times provided a robust (if friendly) undermining of Dickens's inimitability. Catherine Waters demonstrates that "while Dickens exercised tight editorial control and even rewrote contributions to *Household Words,* the journal's form is nevertheless dialogic, with differing lights being cast on a given topic, and the individual voices of such writers as George Augustus Sala, Harriet Martineau, Wilkie Collins, and of course Dickens himself, readily distinguishable to the avid reader despite the policy of anonymity."[10] As we shall see, the thematic and stylistic tendencies of these contributors also emerge recognizably in their fiction for the Christmas numbers, and many Christmas stories that have come to be regarded as characteristically Dickensian did not come from Dickens at all.

Perhaps the figure at *Household Words* and *All the Year Round* that has been overlooked most severely is William H. Wills. Dickens used the term *sub-editor* for Wills, but *coeditor* is a more accurate term for his duties.[11] Wills and Dickens were in nearly constant communication about almost every issue of the journals, and when Dickens was unable to read contributions or galley proofs, Wills made final decisions himself. Working with Wills,

Dickens was constantly functioning in a collaborative mode, and extant letters document a fluctuating relationship between the men. At least once, Dickens calls Wills "my other self in *Household Words*."[12] Focusing strictly on Dickens's egotism, one might at first glance categorize this statement as an example of Dickens appropriating another's work or subsuming it into his own identity. A slower approach enables one also to see that, as a collaborator, Dickens was willing to open his "self" up to include other people and their ideas. Sometimes, Wills exercised more control over a Christmas number than did Dickens, and other times, Dickens's ideas controlled a text to its detriment. As the chapters ahead demonstrate, reading the complete numbers exposes a plethora of such surprising details. Dickens printed endings he did not like under his own name, asked another person to co-write more than one frame story, allowed yet another person to decide the ordering of stories, and included a poem that approves of cannibalism in stark contrast to his other published work on the subject.

In most cases, with the notable exception of Wilkie Collins, the Christmas contributors did not spend time together discussing a plan for the stories. Dickens sporadically provided direction or a frame concept via letters of invitation that Wills usually distributed. Unless one belonged to Dickens's circle of close friends or conversed with him consistently, a writer did not know who the other contributors might be or what they would write. Dickens famously (or infamously) burned his correspondence in an 1860 bonfire and subsequent smaller conflagrations, and the low number of his contributors' surviving letters compounds the difficulty of forming definitive conclusions about the editorial process. It is also important to avoid overgeneralization. Dickens produced Christmas issues for nearly two decades, and his creative processes did not stagnate over such a long period of time. Some writers submitted work for multiple numbers and seem to have figured out what Dickens desired, while others contributed only once, and most contributors do not appear to have corresponded directly with others about Christmas content. We do not know how routinely these individuals may have crossed paths in London's bustling literary scene or in contexts having little to do with Dickens, but the stories for the Christmas numbers were submitted in response to instructions that did not require or even encourage such contact.

Regardless of the format of the original *Household Words* and *All the Year Round* issues, dominant scholarly practice has broken the Christmas numbers apart, separating each writer's contribution from its host compilation. Since at least 1964, when Ada Nisbet complained about critical neglect of

Dickens's short stories, other scholars have echoed the call.[13] Harry Stone first investigated the Christmas numbers in detail, and his *Charles Dickens's Uncollected Writings* tries to identify and reprint exactly which words Dickens wrote in his periodicals, proposing that the genius of his prose will be evident in isolation from the rest of the texts. Regularly cited as an attributive authority, Stone's work is in fact highly speculative. Taking the 1854 number as an illustrative case, Stone writes, "Dickens probably wrote the introductory passages to the stories of the Second, Fourth, Sixth, and Seventh Poor Travellers."[14] Already qualifying claims with "probably," Stone further hesitates: "Dickens may also have written or modified the introduction to the story of the Fifth Poor Traveller."[15] Stone's tentativeness when attributing sections to Dickens is essential; more frustrating is that Stone does not provide reasoning for attributing only some linking passages to Dickens, and the criteria are usually missing. After making a brief case for the subjective use of "internal" evidence, such as "allusions, imagery, structure, division, ideas, diction, syntax, and the like," when Stone uses "general internal evidence" to make an attribution, only conclusions appear, "not the analysis itself."[16] The lack of grounding for certain choices and the lack of comment on others leads back to the initial "probably" that moderates Stone's assertions so importantly. I do not dispute that Dickens "probably" wrote some of these passages, but realizing how uncertain the attributions must remain, we learn the most by using the speculative information, perhaps paradoxically, to take emphasis off of attribution and place it onto collaboration.[17]

More recently, Dickens Journals Online, *The Dent Uniform Edition of Dickens' Journalism*, a 2011 issue of *Victorian Periodicals Review* titled "Victorian Networks and the Periodical Press," and various monographs centered on major figures testify to consistent and growing interest in journalistic work that was often collaborative.[18] Even as the Christmas numbers gain notice, however, critical stress has remained on Dickens and high-profile contributors like Wilkie Collins, not on the complete versions of the collaborative texts. To explain such choices, scholars tend to note that contributors republished their pieces outside the Christmas number frames and cite the fact that Dickens himself extracted pieces from seven numbers to form the "Christmas stories" volume of the 1867 Diamond Edition of his works, which includes a prefatory statement declaring that his stories "were originally so constructed as they might express and explain themselves when republished alone."[19] Evaluating Dickens's claim, we do well to keep in mind Robert L. Patten's lucid readings of several prefaces in which Dickens's statements are misleading or blatantly false: "For well over a hundred years, Dickens has with considerable success controlled how we read him. In the manuscripts and biographical materials John Forster preserved, in the thousands of letters that the Pilgrim editors have annotated, even in the memoirs of Dickens's agents, publishers, family, and friends, he has to a rare degree fashioned his public image."[20] When it comes to the topic of collaboration, this type of retrospective shaping of Dickens's authorial persona has also existed because scholars have been willing to let Dickens have such control, interrogating his own statements about his co-writers less rigorously than, for instance, his statements about his wife. In the Christmas numbers, one discovers a much more varied Dickens than he himself describes.

Furthermore, when Dickens published his extractions as "Christmas stories" for the Diamond Edition, his selections make for "a sometimes bewildering collection of dislocated pieces."[21] As Jack Stillinger points out, "The fact is that authors themselves are among the most ardent believers in the myth of single authorship."[22] Dickens's perpetuation of the myth does damage to the legacy of the Christmas collections, and the existence of selective reprints does not justify anticollaborative critical stances. Such an either/or formulation unnecessarily simplifies the realities of the Victorian publishing marketplace in which texts could circulate in various forms simultaneously. Novels might be printed in volume form before the final serial installments had been issued, and stage adaptations overlapped with ongoing periodical publications. Fran Baker usefully refers to Elizabeth Gaskell's "The Ghost in the Garden Room" for the 1859 Christmas number having a "double life," as it appeared in the collaborative collection and then independently.[23] Exploration of such textual double lives has been eclipsed by interest in particularized textuality. One of the central lines of inquiry this book pursues, then, is: what happens when we reinsert all of the collaborative voices into our discussion of these numbers?

What happens when we read not only Dickens's contributions but also stories by the likes of George Sala, who also wrote pornography? To study the Christmas numbers completely, one must consider Dickens alongside writers like Wilkie Collins and Elizabeth Gaskell, whose other works were commercially successful. One must also consider Dickens alongside writers such as Eliza Griffiths and the Reverend James White, whose names have not endured or whose works never earned fame. Julia Cecilia Stretton, for instance, wrote domestic novels featuring idealized heroines with titles like *Margaret and Her Bridesmaids* (1856), which was a best seller in England and America, but few think about her as a collaborator of Dickens.[24] Then there is Reverend Edmund Saul Dixon, a man of the cloth who wrote a famous "Chicken Book," which really is all about poultry.[25] Quality questions arise quickly when one stops excising such collaborators. In restoring conversation between their pieces and Dickens's contributions, what if their voices make for an irritating conversation? No answer will please all. Just as readers might disagree over whether Oliver Twist's virtues and proclivity for fainting are cloying or whether *A Tale of Two Cities* is overly sentimental, so too there are stories in the Christmas numbers that some find abysmal and others call brilliant (or at least no worse than Dickens's other misfires). As the following chapters demonstrate, Dickens's stories might be the weakest in a collection while writers like Charles Collins, who contributed for seven years straight, consistently share storytelling gems. Regardless of whether we like all of the stories or whether Dickens ultimately liked them, they were part of what "Dickens" signified in the 1850s and '60s, and we are remiss if we excise them from our notion of what counts as "Dickensian" now. For most of the collections, Dickens is far outnumbered by his collaborators (see appendices), and some of their stories were misattributed to him for several decades, further justifying their inclusion in critical assessments of the Christmas canon.

I aim to persuade readers to do three overlapping things: to read collaborative texts in their complete forms, to complicate hierarchical models of collaboration, and to acknowledge the powerful polyvocal potential of periodical forms such as the Christmas number. To achieve those aims, I provide an examination of all eighteen Christmas numbers in their entirety, analyzing the textual dynamics and relationships between Dickens's narrators and those of his collaborators in the most comprehensive treatment to date. I also illustrate how my analysis of the numbers reenvisions Dickens as a collaborator and suggests new ways of thinking about nuanced literary collaboration, particularly in Victorian periodicals. In one volume, I hope to provide a sense of grounding for all the Christmas numbers, to give readers a sense of this body of work with a critical eye that spotlights collaborative textual dynamics. Those dynamics shift, morph, repeat, and change across years as the Christmas numbers exhibit multiple modes of collaboration and reveal a complex subgenre of the Victorian periodical press.

Several methodological questions challenge studies of extended collaborative relationships, particularly when it comes to the thorny issue of how to balance biographical information (or a lack of it) with the author function. Rosemarie Bodenheimer's pathbreaking study *Knowing Dickens* reshapes the options for how biographical inquiry and literary analysis might work in tandem. Bodenheimer investigates not only what Dickens may have known and the various ways he knew things but also the ways in which studying his works leads to fruitful questioning of our own ways of knowing. Juxtaposing several genres, including letters, journalism, and novels, Bodenheimer's approach reminds critics that any sense of biography as "the life" is mythical if it does not acknowledge that all understandings of Dickens's life and Dickens's relationships with others stem from readings of texts: "We cannot go back and forth between life and work because we do not have a life; everything we know is on a written page. To juxtapose letters and fiction, as I am doing, is to read one kind of text alongside another. Neither has explanatory power over the other; all we can do is observe, make connections and interpretive suggestions."[26] In agreement with Bodenheimer, in the chapters that follow I treat letters as representations, regarding them as the performances they are. Remaining cognizant of the self-fashioning maneuvers the genre of letter writing invites, I also realize that these texts nevertheless provide us with information. Letters simultaneously serve as evidence and as textual performance requiring careful interpretation.

Dickens's friendship with his closest collaborator, Wilkie Collins, provides an ideal example of how intertwined questions of biography and collaboration become. The two men engaged in moustache-growing contests, used aliases, acted together on stage, had secret love affairs, used opium, may have suffered from sexually transmitted diseases, co-wrote in the same room and from afar, cruised London's entertainment districts, and parodied themselves in fiction. When it comes to the Collins-Dickens friendship, the foregoing list only begins to gesture toward how much biographical information might be brought to bear on the many texts that they coauthored, performed, coedited, or read and reviewed for each other. There is no other writer with whom Dickens collaborated so frequently. The two men offered to finish each other's works when one or the other fell ill, and they seem to have shared an understanding that, even as each one published successful and unique novels in his own voice, their voices might also be interchangeable. In 1862, Dickens offered to finish the novel *No Name* for an ailing Wilkie Collins. He proposed reading and talking over Collins's notes, promising to write in a style "so like you as that no one should find out the difference."[27] As I discuss further in chapter 4, Dickens also sought to reassure Collins by reminding him of their previous collaborations: "Think it a Xmas No., an *Idle apprentice*, a *Lighthouse*, a *Frozen Deep*."[28] To be sure, Dickens worried about halting the publication of a novel appearing in his own journal, but his letter is concerned primarily with calming Collins (who finished the book after all). Most interestingly, Dickens rearranges many elements of the author function. Citing several genres across several years, he implies that collaborations create a joint voice and also enable the writers to ventriloquize each other.

Thinking of Dickens's voice as indistinguishable from Collins's voice challenges the idea that writers and their works can be separated discretely from each other, and most scholars and fans of Dickens are unaccustomed to fusing notions of "Dickens the great novelist" with "Dickens the collaborator." Jack Stillinger's *Multiple Authorship and the Myth of Solitary Genius* deals with texts quite different from the Christmas numbers but is interested in similar questions about how readers and critics dismiss or outright erase the presence of "other" authors alongside treasured, famous ones. Stillinger makes the astute point that the theoretical poles invested in killing the author or in insisting upon "the author's life holding the key to all textual meaning" share the presumption that the author is singular. Instead, Stillinger urges us to consider "*how many* authors are being banished from a text."[29] Reevaluating the complete Christmas numbers to reverse such banishment destabilizes some of the basic critical approaches that underpin scholarship on Dickens and on collaboration in the Victorian periodical press. Discussing the late nineteenth century and corporate authorship, Rachel Sagner Buurma faults critical debates following Michel Foucault's and Roland Barthes's interrogations of the concept of the author for positioning Victorians inaccurately: "[O]ver the past forty years, theorists writing specifically about authorship have developed ever more specific critical accounts of the incoherence or complexity of the author-function. Because of the way historical changes in authorship tend to be periodized, the Victorians are often unfairly blamed for their seemingly oversimplified notions of the author. . . . [L]iterary authority in Victorian England was much more contingent, variable, and contested than has previously been thought."[30] The critical tendency has been to view Dickens as always threatened, unsettled, or driven to autocratically control the variability Buurma describes. The Christmas numbers not only bear out Buurma's claim but also reveal that the contingencies and contestations enabled by collaboration often result in unique aesthetics.

Even within studies of collaboration, scholars tend to look at collaborative pairs rather than more pluralistic collaborative endeavors. Samuel Taylor Coleridge and William Wordsworth or Katherine Harris Bradley and Edith Emma Cooper (Michael Field) produced texts that raise fascinating questions about how joint imaginative productions take shape. Scholars such as Bette London, Holly Laird, and Jill Ehnenn have increased attention to women who collaborate but still favor pairs, or "author-dyads" for Ehnenn, over less tidy groupings.[31] For many critics, trying to advance theories of collaboration while also working with texts that extend past two or three authors introduces an unmanageable amount of complication, or the inclusion of such groupings is outside the scope of a delimited study. Laird, for example, explains that *Women Coauthors* will "only occasionally guess at what differences it makes when the number of coauthors increases" past two.[32] With great respect for the studies above, I aim to fill this gap, moving into the territory of previously guessed-at excitement and attempting to advance our collective curiosity about what happens when a cluster of people produce a text. Wayne Koestenbaum notes that texts "with two authors are specimens of a relation, and show writing to be a quality of motion and exchange, not a fixed thing."[33] Narratives with six or nine authors, then, present an even less stable set of relations whose fluid relationships merit investigation.

I do sympathize with the need to draw parameters around one's study. In highlighting the full Christmas numbers and the neglected collaborative dynamics in that group of writers—five to nine in a given year and as many as fifteen when frame concepts carry over from one year to the next—I include a broad range of texts but must sacrifice in-depth analysis to every pairing. The vitality of all of those voices singing in chorus but also ringing out in solos shapes the unique brilliance of the collaborative text and challenges us to reconceptualize the energies of collaborative authorship. When dealing with forty writers in total across eighteen numbers, tracing the contact points between Dickens and each collaborator or between all possible combinations of the collaborators becomes unwieldy. To keep the scope of this study manageable, in most cases, textual dynamics trump biographical detective work, as I am more interested in overlapping narrators and speakers than whether Dickens ever had tea with the elusive Eliza Griffiths.[34] I also lack space to consider the plethora of ways in which these same writers participated in collaborative relationships in the regular issues of Dickens's journals and in other publications. My hope is that this study will help to catalyze and motivate continued work in those directions.

The actual or possible sexual aspects of joint literary work is another focal point of much previous scholarship, as evidenced in the titles of Koestenbaum's *Double Talk: The Erotics of Male Literary Collaboration*, Ehnenn's *Women's Literary Collaboration, Queerness, and Late-Victorian Culture*, Jeffrey Masten's *Textual Intercourse*, and others.[35] Some of the Christmas numbers I examine require one to ponder the degree to which sexuality or queer intimacy arises as an important textual element. When particular stories or relationships intuitively lead in this direction (as in chapter 3), I pursue it. I also acknowledge that there is much work left to be done on the overlapping trajectories of queer studies and studies of collaboration and that such work must recognize that experiences of collaboration are as varied as experiences of individual authorship.

As is already apparent, I use the term *collaboration* to refer to multiple ways of writers producing texts together. In practice, collaboration includes all sorts of interactions that extend past two people sitting in a room together while one of them writes ideas down on a page. Seth Whidden's work takes nineteenth-century French literature as its subject and provides useful grounding concepts. Whidden separates intertextuality from collaboration and takes care to point out that agency is associated with the latter but not the former: "Collaboration refers specifically to the relationship between two or more agents at some point during the creation of a literary text, whereas intertextuality refers to the relationship between two or more texts; the former emphasizes the process, the latter the results."[36] One of the most fascinating aspects of these Christmas numbers is the way in which they inconsistently interweave both collaboration and intertextuality. In a given issue, Dickens (and others) might participate in conversations affecting the text or have no direct communication at all. One contributor, for instance, might talk to Dickens about the frame narrative or the content of a particular story, while another contributor sends in a submission and hears nothing further. Or Dickens may send in stories from afar while Wills has conversations with others about the number's shape. In the analyses that follow, I show that one must allow for the operation of both models and, most importantly, read from the text outward rather than imposing a strict model a priori based on unstable biographical evidence or unquestioned critical norms. In most scenarios, a critic can expect to be able to differentiate instances of what Whidden calls "collaboration *in praesentia*," when writers are together physically during the creative act, from "collaboration *in absentia*," when the writers are physically apart.[37] The Christmas numbers, however, force readers to consider both modes simultaneously.

Laird's work on feminist modes of collaboration suggests new paradigms that are helpful in thinking about collaboration that happens in multi-gendered groups. Especially useful to this study is a "model of coauthorship as distinct from both solitary genius and an authorless textuality. In this model a large range of different kinds of coauthorship includes, surrounds, and renders anomalous the idea of the autonomous, original author."[38] To address this variation in collaborative method, we must accept both "partial collaborations, in which full mutually acknowledged coauthorship does not occur" and "full collaborations," and we must avoid viewing full collaborations as "necessarily more balanced, more equitable, or more mutually rewarding than partial or 'approximate' . . . collaborations between authors and editors, speakers and writers."[39] Granting legitimacy to varying degrees and types of coauthorship means that one can no longer disqualify a text from the "collaborative" category based only on a printed byline or lack thereof. In part because I am persuaded by Laird's argument against "authorless textuality," my suggestions for how to rethink Dickens as a collaborative entity sometimes echo Marjorie Stone's and Judith Thompson's formulation of the author as heterotext without adopting their stance completely. Although Stone and Thompson intend to return "hetero" to its "older root," which includes meanings such as "mixed," I am not convinced that the prefix lends itself to the kind of intermittent blending evidenced in the Christmas numbers or that it avoids obliterating human agency.[40] In the case of an editorial authorial presence such as Dickens, the texts he published at times fit into a heterotextual model of mixture but at other times are unable to achieve narrative coherence. Therefore, rather than pursuing a theory of collaboration as heterotext, I am more compelled by extending and expanding the notion of collaboration as conversation.

To envision collaboration as conversational enables one to accommodate the fact that the Christmas numbers Dickens produced changed over the years, undulating in format, style, and number of voices in response to various factors. To converse is, in its most basic definition, "to communicate or interchange ideas (*with* any one) by speech or writing or otherwise."[41] A conversational model of analysis, then, can account for and examine verbal exchanges between writers, written correspondence about a text under construction, and narrative exchanges between the fictional voices created by each collaborator. Conversation also importantly honors the verbal or written exchanges that influence a creative team regardless of which collaborator's hand puts pen to paper to create a manuscript. Yet another advantage to the conversational model is that it complements Dickens's conducting metaphor: emphasizing conversation does not elide conducting, and conducting does not drown out conversation. Conversations can be conducted, and conducting requires conversation, whether metaphorically between instrument and wand or literally between composer, conductor, and/or musician as assorted creative visions converge. A conversational model upsets the more usual mode of tracing who influenced whom with the goal of determining which author should receive "credit" for passages or ideas. Instead, it listens to the dialogue inherent in literary texts written in an atmosphere of consistent creative exchange. This interpretive approach also enables one to see how texts communicate back and forth across space and time. My insistence is not that we abandon discussions of attribution or exploitation altogether but rather that we avoid relying on them as primary methodologies when reconstituting collaborative texts such as the Christmas numbers.

Within periodical studies, there is precedent for reading some types of Victorian literature from this more holistic position. Robert L. Patten, Laurel Brake, and others have pointed out that scholars should be aware of the conversations between part sellers and purchasers; between author, typesetter, and publisher; between writers and illustrators;[42] and between each installment and the advertisements or other articles surrounding it. Jerome McGann includes editors, printers, publishers, and readers in his formulations and warns that approaches focusing too intensely on the individuality of authors result in literary works being "divorced from the social relationships which gave them their lives."[43] Delving into the crisscrossings of major figures at the center of London's literary marketplace on Wellington Street, Mary Shannon's recent work importantly includes consideration of how "writers and editors represented their readers as active participants in a network" that also extended to imperial streets.[44] Such critics have illustrated that rich interpretive possibilities arise from studying advertisements, individual issues or entire runs of periodicals, logistics, geographical locations, and the simultaneous existence of a text in different forms. Examining Christmas numbers in their entirety, then, would seem to be an already common approach, but it is exceedingly rare.

By isolating Dickens's Christmas numbers, I do not attempt a systematic study of the Victorian press. As Joanne Shattock and Michael Wolff have put it, "The sheer bulk and range of the Victorian press seem to make it so unwieldy as to defy systematic and general study."[45] What this book offers is a new view of a small section of the massive whole that might serve as a microcosm for collaborative dynamics that also appear elsewhere. If John Plunkett and Andrew King are correct that "it is more helpful to conceptualize nineteenth-century authorship in terms of the existence of a range of what Foucault called author-functions,"[46] then it is also helpful to explore the overlapping of those author functions in texts that confuse the lines between editor, author, contributor, and creator. Drew has called the Christmas collections a "remarkable fusion of occasional journalism and communal storytelling," and we must persist in the challenging task of conceptualizing that "communal" aspect.[47]

The structure of this book follows the chronological publication order of the stories in the Christmas numbers. In part, this choice is dictated by the fact that *Collaborative Dickens* is the first study of its kind. To shift crit-ical practice away from the arbitrary isolation of stories and toward the collaborative context in which the stories first appeared, this book must es-tablish a foundation that values the numbers as whole texts. In the chap-ters that follow, each story does not receive the same amount of attention, and some I mention only briefly, but each story surfaces in its proper place as my argument about the collaborative dynamics of these texts emerges. To skip over stories whose quality I determine to be low would invalidate this book's premise that all of the stories constituting the Christmas num-bers remain instructive parts of the collaborative oeuvre. Fortuitously, many of the usually overlooked stories offer surprising moments of suspense or narrative complexity that exemplify the value of a comprehensive approach. Each chapter below begins with a brief forecasting section, which helps to orient readers seeking an in-depth treatment of just one year's Christmas number. This study is not organized as a casebook, and each chapter's ar-gument relates to the others, but time-restricted readers investigating one Christmas collection should be able to use this book's introduction and con-clusion alongside any of its individual chapters to understand its essential argument. The reference list of each number's contents and contributors in appendix A also enables one to place each story in context quickly and to explore additional connections between and across numbers. Readers might notice that, to avoid excessive and jarring verb tense changes in the chapters that follow, I often use the present tense to discuss not just literary texts but also Dickens's choices, authorial presence, and actions. Rather than, for instance, referring to what "Dickens wrote," I often refer to what "Dickens writes," which decreases historical distance and places emphasis on the ways in which Dickens's actions continue to influence critical assessment of his texts.

My first two chapters show how Dickens moves from producing Christ-mas collections that reflect upon the various ways that people around the world celebrate the holiday to crafting Christmas numbers with narrative frames that are enhanced by collaboration. Chapter 1 elucidates the ways in which the special issues for 1850 and 1851 link celebrations of Christmas to colonial ideologies that pervade the rest of the numbers. Chapter 2 argues that, drawing on oral storytelling modes in *A Round of Stories by the Christ-mas Fire* and *Another Round of Stories by the Christmas Fire*, Dickens creates a narrative atmosphere in which collaboration exists as part of a repetitive, polyphonic form. Chapter 3 demonstrates that, in contrast to the preceding *Rounds*, the numbers for 1854 and 1855 move from circularity to more linear structures. Limiting the type of mixing that characterizes the *Rounds, The Seven Poor Travellers* and *The Holly-Tree Inn* develop lacing structures that enable the stories to cohere. With Dickens's narrator organizing fictional travellers, the stories weave close male bonds and varied imperial visions into Christmas celebrations while revealing the importance of collaborative contexts to the emergence of detective fiction.

Chapter 4 argues that, as the 1856 and 1857 Christmas issues engage directly with questions of empire building and fortune seeking, collaboration is crucial to the ways in which the collections continue to explore the foundational ideologies laid out in the first two numbers. Restoring connections between the narrative parts of *The Wreck of the Golden Mary*, I recuperate the neglected dialogic aspects of the original text to assert that the interpolated stories of the middle section are essential to the success of the frame story and to one's comprehension of the links between trauma and storytelling. *The Perils of Certain English Prisoners* is the first number for which Dickens collaborates with only one other author, Wilkie Collins, and I demonstrate that their voices blend much more thoroughly than critics have been willing to acknowledge, even at the text's most racist moments. Collins's and Dickens's jointly created narrative device in *The Perils* routes their voices through an illiterate man who is unable to present his own voice in print and thus explores narrative impotence as a parallel to social inferiority in the face of colonial and racial violence. Chapter 5 reveals the range of outcomes exhibited in collaborative work as Collins and Dickens move from success to disappointment in *A House to Let*, the number that comes closest to collaborative failure. Dickens navigates personal crisis from 1858 to 1859, and collaboration enables him to experiment with representations that blur the boundaries between reality and fiction. As the frame concept unfolds in *The Haunted House*, Dickens weaves together commentary not only on the psychological dynamics of perceiving a thing, or place, to be haunted but also on storytelling, trauma, and the interpersonal dynamics of collaboration.

Three collections that revel in the chaos of collaborative storytelling form the focus of chapter 6. Spotlighting a poem in *A Message from the Sea* that depicts cannibalism and race in a manner that most scholars identify as antithetical to Dickens's usual aims, I continue to build a case for the necessity of constantly reading the numbers with attention to multivocal authorship. I also note the number's questioning of generic distinctions between pieces to excavate its ironic stance toward the storytelling its characters are trying to accomplish. *Tom Tiddler's Ground* comingles Dickens's real and fictional personas and further indulges irony by showing how storytelling can fail to have any positive effect on an audience. An especially strong example of how collaborative texts can volunteer responses to the very questions they raise, *Somebody's Luggage* is the most playful and entertaining in its meta-textuality as its narrative framing simultaneously insists on and deconstructs textual divisions.

Chapter 7 proposes that the use of kindly adoptive parental figures in frame narratives enables *Mrs. Lirriper's Lodgings, Mrs. Lirriper's Legacy,* and *Doctor Marigold's Prescriptions* to present collaborative storytelling as an act of cross-generational love. I argue that collaboration and story gathering are crucial aspects of how these collections validate non-biological family structures and advocate for working-class characters. The figures of Mrs. Lirriper, Major Jemmy Jackman, and Doctor Marigold were extremely popular, and their collecting of texts as a legacy-making act assumes a moral weight equivalent to their rescuing of children. Chapter 8 examines the final two Christmas numbers to show that as Dickens concludes the Christmas collaborations, he introduces major changes to the format but maintains other collaborative traditions as he identifies other authors in print for the first time, then returns to crafting a narrative solely with Wilkie Collins. *Mugby Junction,* a seemingly misordered set of contributions, is disjointed but nevertheless develops hitherto overlooked themes across stories that profoundly impact attempts at biographical readings of Dickens's fictionalized responses to trauma. *No Thoroughfare* mixes authorial voices seamlessly and reverts to a reinforcement of English identity in opposition to less pure others. The final Christmas number also illustrates a further new direction in scholarship that *Collaborative Dickens* makes possible: an investigation of how the collaborative conversations of Collins and Dickens persist in their joint works from the years of the Christmas numbers through to Dickens's unfinished novel, *The Mystery of Edwin Drood,* and Collins's best seller *The Moonstone.*

The range, skill, and complexity of the Christmas numbers, which have been overlooked in academic studies and popular accounts of Dickens and Christmas, illuminate an annual event in the nineteenth-century periodical press that involved readers in engaging, multivocal experiments. Evaluating the Christmas collections in their polyvocal completeness forces one to regard Dickens as a collaborator whose working methods and interactions with his colleagues shifted productively over nearly two decades and leads to a fresh awareness of Dickens as a multigendered and multimodal authorial voice. The Christmas collaborations also reveal that the idealized Englishness of what has come to be regarded as a typical Christmas is linked to a chorus of voices articulating sometimes conflicting racial and imperial ideologies. Accounting for the polyphonic nature of the complete Christmas numbers inspires a more comprehensive understanding of plural authorship in the nineteenth-century periodical press that prompts us to reconceptualize "Dickens."

1

Writing Christmas with "a Bunch of People"
(1850–51)

The standard practice of *Household Words* and many other Victorian journals was to print the work of contributors without naming them. In the absence of bylines, editors in chief hoped their journals would construct distinct, unified voices of their own, and the practice of publishing contributions anonymously "prevailed almost universally until the late 1860s and 1870s."[1] Dickens published his first pieces anonymously in the 1830s.[2] By midcentury, readers were familiar with the fact that Dickens and other editors did not write every column that appeared in their journals' pages but that each piece nonetheless publicly held the editor's stamp of approval. As Catherine Waters notes, there is a kind of inherent dialogism in this periodical form that resists easy categorization, in part because the texts that constitute *Household Words* simultaneously exist as the words of Dickens and the words of others.[3] Many writers were honored to have their work appear under Dickens's name, as after only a couple of years of publication, "Dickens's journal had a readership and a kind of glamour no other journal had."[4] *Household Words* also paid well at one guinea or more per page for a Christmas number contribution, making it an attractive venue. For the first two Christmas issues, a fair amount of scholarship exists on the pieces Dickens authored as they relate to his personal conceptions of Christmas and youth, but few scholars have viewed them alongside the contributors' pieces. The first Christmas number establishes important precedents, particularly in regard to contested imperial ideologies, that are visible only when the number is read in its entirety. In building a definition of acceptable English Christmas celebrations, the 1850 issue functions as a foundation for future years. The 1851 number continues to draw upon that base while also demonstrating that Dickens and Wills stumble in their second attempt as they learn how to sustain the Christmas numbers. Rather than showcasing a smooth progression of the form, the second number's repetitive missteps illustrate the need for the stronger framing apparatuses that appear in subsequent years.

Until 1866, the Christmas issues of *Household Words* eschewed bylines, following the same practice as the regular issues, and the unprinted name most crucial to the success of both the regular issues and the Christmas numbers is that of William H. Wills, Dickens's coeditor. Wills tended to the details of every *Household Words* issue as he communicated with printers and contributors, corrected galley proofs, reviewed more contributions than Dickens did, coauthored essays and stories, and arranged business matters such as payments and contracts. As John Drew points out, "Often portrayed as the anchor and engine of the editorial team, punctual, steady, unimaginative—Charlie Watts to Dickens's Jagger—Wills was a hugely versatile and skilled literary craftsman."[5] Shu Fang Lai also persuasively argues that Wills's role has been inaccurately diminished in most critical treatments of Dickens's editorship. Lai charts a perplexing resistance to acknowledging Wills as an instrumental component of Dickens's journalistic success even in the wake of persuasive studies from well-respected critics such as Drew.[6] Although I agree with Lai's assessment, Lai persistently draws Dickens as an editor who always wished for greater control and evaluates the Wills/Dickens relationship with an emphasis on contention rather than collaboration. Dickens often sent blunt instructions to Wills but also frequently needed his advice. In a letter about whether to publish poems eulogizing the Duke of Wellington in an issue that would coincide with his funeral, for example, Dickens writes, "I can't quite decide. What do *you* think?"[7] An earlier exchange between the two editors shows that when they disagree, Wills does not hesitate to challenge Dickens. Just a few months after the launch of *Household Words*, Dickens complains about a title Wills suggested, declaring, "I don't think there could be a worse one within the range of the human understanding," and then chastises Wills: "[D]on't touch my articles without consulting me."[8]

In a lengthy reply, Wills stakes out his position as a coeditor who will not accept provocative or unfair criticism without argument: "I hope you will understand what I endeavour always to intimate:—that when I make an objection to *any* article I do it suggestively."⁹ Wills makes clear that Dickens's consternation is a result of his own misunderstanding, not a mistake on Wills's part, and that Dickens's articles do not exist in a special zone exempt from comment. Explaining his editorial choices, Wills also snaps, "I did not suppose you would wish me to consult you upon so simple a matter of mechanical convenience." Drawing upon years of experience at both *Punch* and *Chambers's Edinburgh Journal* to put Dickens's presumption in check, Wills retorts (in regard to the title), "I am *sure* it is not the worst one within the range of human understanding. Forgive me for claiming for my worst suggestion a *locus* within that pale."¹⁰ Wills's teasing tone again shifts from the merits or shortcomings of his suggestion to Dickens's hyperbolic reaction, which contributes to an atmosphere of robust, collaborative friendship rather than hostile attack. The letter closes with Wills telling Dickens that he plans to take a couple of days off—obviously the comment of a man secure in his position. Wills kept a copy of this missive in his book of letters, perhaps to record his own strong voice for posterity in anticipation of a legacy that would cast him in a submissive role. In revising critical perspectives to account consistently for Wills's coeditorship, we must also regard him as a constant, influential presence in the Christmas numbers. As we shall see, his involvement in some years is even more determinant of the final outcome than Dickens's input, and his is one of a plethora of voices that speaks back to Dickens's own consistently.

The Christmas Number

The first Christmas issue of *Household Words*, called simply "The Christmas Number," was published as a regular issue on Saturday, December 21, 1850. The issue includes no table of contents, no passages linking the pieces, and no frame concept; the naming of "Christmas" in the title constitutes its strongest gesture toward commonality of theme. One senses that Dickens was still figuring out how he wanted to shape the Christmas number, blurring the lines between fiction and nonfiction without fully indulging either and including Christmas carols while avoiding the sheet music and visual art of literary annuals.¹¹ In many ways, the 1850 number is a collection of random musings about a holiday, but consideration of the number in its entirety reveals a coherence that has less to do with Dickens's request for essays on the Christmas theme and more to do with midcentury imaginings of empire.

The voices Dickens conducts advocate for England's "civilizing" mission and self-consciously defend the English citizenry's demand for the materials that make an idyllic English Christmas possible. The stories do not ignore the human costs behind the production of materials such as spices and fruits but rather justify them as part of an appropriate and beneficial system of global commerce that maintains English superiority. Whether the Franklin Expedition explorers or the "Genius of the Sugar," who "is a freed Negro," the figures dominating these stories collectively call for the preservation of imperial ideology alongside the preservation of plums.[12] The collection of nine stories, all written by men, depicts Christmas through various objects, with various types of people, and in various locations. In all of these contexts, the privileged consumer must not forget that each ornament, decoration, and taste of Christmas should be experienced as a conscious enactment of a specifically English Christian joy.

Dickens's "A Christmas Tree" begins the number: "I have been looking on, this evening, at a merry company of children assembled round that pretty German toy, a Christmas Tree" (289). Just two years earlier, a published sketch of Queen Victoria and Prince Albert celebrating around a Christmas tree raised the profile of the tradition and lent the authority of the monarch to the anglicized adoption of the custom.[13] Calling the tree a "pretty German toy" in the first sentence immediately indicates that English Christmas, from childhood on, includes the navigation and appropriation of things, traditions, and people whose origins remain identified as non-English. Delivering a long list of everything on and around the tree, the story "describes such a cornucopia of toys and gifts in its reminiscences about Christmases past, that it anticipates the growing commercialization of the festival."[14] The narrator is an unidentified man watching a group of children, and he returns home in a reverie of childhood memories of Christmas, imagining years as branches on the tree. He recalls books, plays, songs, and toys that are diverting or terrifying enough to cause nightmares. Some details, such as reading the *Arabian Nights* and enjoying a toy theatre, correlate with Dickens's accounts of parts of his childhood, but the story makes broader points about nostalgia and tradition rather than acting as an autobiographical essay.[15] The narrator's recollection of several "Winter Stories," or ghost stories, told "round the Christmas fire" foresees the frame concept Dickens develops two years later and embeds the supernatural in his delineation of Christmas festivities (293). Although the narrator's recollections span the varied nature of childhood experience, he nonetheless idealizes his memories: "Encircled by the social thoughts of Christmas time, still let the benignant figure of my childhood stand unchanged!" (295). This insistence on childhood as a fixed period of time with unchangeable memories is more intriguing than the story's final line (in which the narrator hears Jesus's voice whispering through the "leaves" of a pine-needled Christmas tree) because it links "social thoughts" to both the holiday of Christmas and the enshrining of romanticized individual experience (295). Combined with the narrator's opening observation of other people's children around a Christmas tree, which could be pleasantly nostalgic or creepily voyeuristic, the story's conclusion lends an air of performance to the holiday; celebrants in homes or outdoors will be watched by others who will judge their rituals. If observers use what they see as a springboard to their own memories, then all individual Christmas festivities also become communal, which increases pressure to celebrate in socially accepted ways.

"Christmas in Lodgings" hones in on this point about socially sanctioned attitudes toward celebration as William Blanchard Jerrold and W. H. Wills tell the story of a bachelor in a first-person voice that differs from the opening narrator. Because the bachelor's friends all reside "in Scotland, where Christmas is no festival," he has no plans to leave for the holiday, but his landlady needs to use his room for a party (296). The bachelor turns sour in his loneliness as others prepare for the celebration, treats a servant rudely, refuses all pleasant advances, and mockingly describes how his landlady's pity infuriates him. In this second story of the number, collaborative conversation is already evident as Jerrold and Wills seem to riff on two Dickens texts. The bachelor's nasty responses to the landlady's generosity on Christmas Day echo Scrooge's rejection of his nephew Fred's advances in *A Christmas Carol*, and the story's emphasis on social approval of one's Christmas rituals picks up a thread from Dickens's opening story. Both a landlady and a servant observe and criticize the bachelor as he rejects decorative greenery and pudding, and their scorn has a lasting impact when, after his marriage, the man insists on rushing out of another lodging house before a Christmas can transpire there.

The bachelor's most intense moments of loneliness come when he sits alone at a fire in his landlady's parlor, and the third story continues that motif as James Hannay's "Christmas in the Navy" features another Christmas fire into which the narrator gazes. The short piece carries a general message: even though some nautical Christmases are difficult, particularly if one lands in a Spanish jail, one also "may have a very pleasant Christmas at Sea" (300). The key is for sailors to remember the beauty of the homeland because, if they speak of England, think of "pretty cousins," sing songs, and drink rum, the holiday can authenticate their true English values (300). Whether on a merchant ship or a naval vessel, Christmas at sea becomes a literal way of advancing the imperial interests that sustain Christmas celebrations at home.

Much more complex in its advocating for English supremacy is Charles Knight's "A Christmas Pudding," in which Mr. Oldknow contemplates "the mercantile history of the various substances of which that pudding was composed" (301). Inspired by his reading of travel literature, Oldknow dreams of faraway places and encounters the genii, or guarding spirits, associated with various ingredients.[16] Defending Christmas pudding as an "emblem of our commercial eminence" against the Genius of the Raisin's complaint that England is depriving Spanish and Mediterranean lands of "grapes which ought to be reserved for the unfermented wine which the Prophet delighted to drink," Oldknow retorts that the demand created by English consumers is what causes the raisins to exist in the first place (301). Elevating an item's market value, in this view, is a viable defense for unequal distribution of resources, cultural indifference, and disparities in labor conditions. Paul Young argues that "to Oldknow's mind the Raisin represents Islamic irrationality and stagnation."[17] Oldknow's insistence that the Genius of the Raisin should simply be grateful for English patronage is an approach exemplified by the Genius of the Currant, a "little freetrader," and the Genius of the Nutmeg, an interspecies mix of contrite Dutchman and wood pigeon who thanks the English for leading him to renounce monopoly-protecting colonial violence (302–3).[18]

Illustrating how profoundly the standard Christmas rhetoric (and fare) is enmeshed in racial ideologies that glorify empire at the expense of humanity, the most problematic spirit is Sugar:

> A West Indian sugar plantation is now mirrored—with its canes ripening under a tropical sun, and its mills with their machinery of cylinders and boilers. THE GENIUS OF SUGAR is a freed Negro. It was said that in freedom he would not work; he has vindicated his privileges in his industry and his obedience. The grand experiment has succeeded in all moral effects. But the nation that demanded cheap corn would not be content with dear sugar. We must buy our sugar wherever the cane ripens. We use seven hundred millions of pounds of sugar annually, which yield a duty of four millions sterling. Mr. Oldknow thought about this, but was silent, when he saw the negro sitting under his own fig-tree; for the political questions which his freedom involved were somewhat complicated. He would trust to the ultimate power of a noble example, and in the meantime rejoice that the great body of the British people could buy their sugar at half the price that their fathers paid.

> Mr. Oldknow, being somewhat at fault upon the sugar
> question, grew confused as new forms flitted before him. (303)

Through Oldknow's confusion about the "complicated" postslavery questions embodied in the Genius of the Sugar, the story at once sidesteps and acknowledges the moral consequences of sugar production. Sugar's form, however, is not combined with an animal, nor is he a fairy hybrid, like the others. He is a dark-skinned human being who has been enslaved, and the story takes great care to identify him as freed. He also differs from the previously presented genii in having no voice.

Given that Sugar occupies the most ethically fraught position, casting him as the first genius to be denied direct speech severely impairs the critique of industrial capitalism that Young locates in the figure of the Raisin. Noting its publication just five months before the Great Exhibition at the Crystal Palace, which advocated for free trade on a grand scale, Young sees "A Christmas Pudding" as a contrary text whose dialogue "works to destabilise Oldknow's position as the voice of a pacific commercial rationale" but pays no attention to the other pieces in the Christmas number.[19] Once the dialogism Young mentions is expanded to include those voices, the number's stance clearly depicts British imperialism and its attendant white supremacy as contested and perhaps even contradictory but never fundamentally challenged as an ideological course preferable to all others. Although Oldknow is aware of his "fault" in uncritically joining the masses who blithely "rejoice" in the purchase of cheap sugar, he does not struggle to move quickly past the uncomfortable questions. Oldknow's thoughts move to the next genius, an Irish egg collector, whose complicated role in the trade markets he responds to in a manner similar to how he reacts to the black man: by lamenting previous suffering, wishing for "just masters and wise rulers," urging the Irish to forswear "agitation" in favor of working hard, and declining to grant the Irish woman a voice (303).[20] At the climactic moment of pudding lighting, all the spirits dance around a giant bowl, and Oldknow's song about the imaginary "social bands" forged by free trade creates a utopian vision that attempts to assuage the story's concerns about inequity:

> Britain, to peaceful arts inclined,
> > Where commerce opens all her stores,
> In social bands shall league mankind,
> > And join the sea-divided shores.
>
> > > > > (304)

This fantasy of mercantile domination that benevolently unites the globe, glossing over exploitative or outright abusive relationships to maintain a vision of Britain as "peaceful," is an integral part of the Christmas number's formulation of what it means to celebrate the holiday.

The second longest in the collection, Knight's story exalts England, and the next piece, Frederick Hunt's "Christmas among the London Poor and Sick," abruptly changes that vision by documenting how much deprivation continues to exist in the country's metropolis. Hunt lists the numbers of poor who eat at parish workhouses and hospitals on Christmas but delivers little social commentary beyond noting that a festive indulgence in any kind of excess tends to worsen the condition of sick people (304–5). Concluding with a sketch of drunken men whose condition is difficult to differentiate from apoplexy, Hunt's contribution contrasts the idealized view of England underpinning the stories that surround it. Thus, reading the number in its entirety reveals an ongoing conversation among the pieces that makes each one less definitive than it appears in isolation.

Following Hunt's contribution, "Christmas in India" by Joachim Heyward Siddons returns to extreme vaunting of English Christianity as a civilizing force. Siddons's essay bounces off of the idea that Christmas in a land associated with Hinduism and Islam (denigrated as "idolatrous" and "rude") is not a ridiculous concept. The projects of "zealous missionaries" and others have succeeded in transforming India so that "the tide of European conquest, and, better still, the tide of European civilisation, has carried to the benighted land knowledge, and a large spirit of toleration" (305). Ignoring the violence of conquest and imperialism, the speaker then explains how Indian culinary traditions and decorative plants are repurposed to enhance Christmas celebrations. In another linking of the Irish to racialized others, rural Indians' worshipful offerings "resemble the contributions of the Irish peasantry to Father Luke or Father Brady" (306). The strength of the colonial rulers in this setting is so profound that they can even affect the experience of climate in Calcutta, where English households light Christmas fires and "there is a wintry *feel* about the atmosphere; and as the chairs are drawn round the fire-place, and the whiskey-punch is brewed, the cherished idea of *home* on Christmas Day is suitably and completely realised" (306). Siddons's idyllic domestic fireside forecasts the frame concept Dickens develops for 1852 and reduces the materials necessary to create such an atmosphere to chairs, a fireplace, and some whiskey. The emphasis on "home" as both private and public, as a space for family celebrations as well as the achievement of England's national dominance, also resonates with the voyeurism of the number's opening piece, in which Christmas celebrations are surveyed to ensure that celebrants exhibit an appropriate level of cheer and introspection.

Dialogism continues to characterize the 1850 number as the imperial project moves from hot to cold in Robert McCormick's and Dickens's "Christmas in the Frozen Regions," which relates an episode pertinent to an 1841 polar expedition. McCormick joined an expedition that explored the South Pole in the same two ships John Franklin would take on the ill-fated 1845 expedition in search of the Northwest Passage. The level of fictionalization in McCormick's piece is unclear, particularly since Dickens is listed as a collaborator. The story is important to the Christmas canon in at least two ways: first, as part of the premier Christmas number's endorsement of imperial dominance as part of the holiday's significance; and second, as the journal's first Christmastime reference to the Franklin Expedition, which Dickens later defended passionately and alluded to in many future Christmas stories. McCormick's story is about how the men celebrate Christmas in 1841 with "the usual old English fare[,] Roast beef . . . followed by the homely never-to-be-forgotten plum-pudding" (307). Surrounded by icebergs, the crew carves a ballroom into the ice for New Year and sculpts a snow woman complete with "a profusion of ringlets" about her head (307–8). The story closes with an insistence that the missing members of the Franklin Expedition may still be alive (a Christmas wish disappointed years later as news of the expedition's demise spread).[21]

McCormick and Dickens weave storytelling and exploration together to maintain English Christmas traditions, and Samuel Sidney's "Christmas Day in the Bush" continues those themes in Australia. Two men living a sparse life at a "new station" in the bush take a shortcut through the countryside "guided by Bushman's signs and instincts" to crash a gentleman's Christmas party (309). True to the tropes of transformation that undergird colonial dreams, the host states in his toast that he had been "a beggar and an outcast" at home in Devon (310). The story augments the others by encouraging continued use of colonial lands for the reformation of those who fail in the home country. A happy ending reinforces that point as one of the visitors marries the pretty woman whose presence had drawn him to the party, and they pass "every succeeding Christmas Day under his own roof in the Bush" (310).

The number's concluding piece, Richard H. Horne's "Household Christmas Carols," lacks strong thematic connections to the preceding stories, indicating that Wills and Dickens explore the possibilities of the Christmas number genre without a map dictating how the pieces fit together. Still, the mix of voices in the carol form and the collaboration inherent in group song-making draw out the conversational dynamics that run through the collection. Horne's piece is one long carol with distinct verses spoken in the first-person voices of ailing children. "The Lame Child's Carol" is followed by verses (all with the same chorus) for children who are "deaf," "deformed," "deaf and dumb," "blind," and "sick." The final verse from a "healthy" child includes the aforementioned ill friends in his winter play, and each verse firmly links the patient, hopeful endurance of children to Christian love (310–12).

In addition to delineating subjects deemed appropriate for Christmastime, the first number's formal qualities embed dialogue in the genre. Considering Knight's story of the Christmas pudding, Waters notes that "dialogism is . . . a defining feature of the periodical context of the story," which holds true in varying degrees for each piece in the collection.[22] The implicit conversation between the stories validates and reinforces the necessity for specifically English customs to determine proper celebration of the holiday. As Sabine Clemm remarks, "*Household Words* frequently shows itself aware of the arbitrariness of national characteristics and its own struggle to define these. However, even the most astute writers never quite abandon the assumption that an essential Englishness does exist, even though *Household Words*' definitions of it are usually fairly feeble."[23] The Christmas numbers will continue to construct, respond to, and sometimes fetishize this "essential Englishness." The 1850 number concludes without remarking that a tradition of holiday writing has begun, but the following year's publication takes steps to distinguish the Christmas issue as special.

Extra Number for Christmas of *Household Words*

The 1851 issue, called the "Extra Number for Christmas of *Household Words*," is the first to be designated an "extra." An advertisement declares that it will please readers by "Showing What Christmas Is to Everybody,"[24] and six of the nine titles indeed begin with "What Christmas Is. . . ." Lacking a mission strong enough to sustain interest for twenty-four pages, the collection's repetitive traits emerge in multiple descriptions of Christmas, exposing a need for the type of frame concept that Dickens develops the following year. Each piece displays a different angle from which one might glorify an English Christmas, but the reappearance of domestic fires, trees, festive foods, and principles of charity signals a lack of originality and creativity. Even giving voice to usually mute symbols, such as tree branches, fails to provide relief from the abundance of holiday clichés that plague the number. Some of the stories touch on an occasional unpleasant experience, but such moments are sandwiched by joyous recollections, and, on the whole, one can stomach only so many mentions of redemptive currants.

Still, the number's common focus, "What Christmas Is," suggests that the stories reinforce one another and that no individual speaker is alone in believing that Christmas merits pondering in print. Dickens begins with "What Christmas Is as We Grow Older," a rumination on the role of memory and regret in celebration that continues to build a foundational Christmas vision. The piece defines "the Christmas spirit" as "the spirit of active usefulness, perseverance, cheerful discharge of duty, kindness, and forbearance" (1). Outgrowing romantic fantasies of life, one should place hope in future generations and encourage dreams in children rather than turning bitter and regretful. The piece also insists on a particular type of remembrance of the dead, barring grief and tears while insisting that residents of "the City of the Dead" be welcomed in the celebration (2). Recounting the sad deaths of individuals ranging from young children to sailors, the narrator commands, "You shall hold your cherished places in our Christmas hearts, and by our Christmas fires; and in the season of immortal hope, and on the birthday of immortal mercy, we will shut out Nothing!" (2). Leading up to the framing concept for 1852, the joining of people around the Christmas fire is crucial to this vision, and one is struck by the insistent tone that sanctions only one type of mourning.

Following Dickens's piece, neither Richard H. Horne's, Edmund Ollier's, nor Harriet Martineau's contribution offers insight that moves beyond nostalgia or clichéd observation. Rather, they are noteworthy because Dickens and Wills were astute enough to recognize these contributions as the type the Christmas collections needed to depart from in order to become consistently successful. Horne's "What Christmas Is to a Bunch of People" is no more complex than its title, commenting on the hopes and concerns of two comfortable households. Community members—including the beadle, postman, publican, and shepherd—feature in the story's contemplations of Christmas perspectives, and the shopkeeping class appears, but the upper ranks of the working classes merit attention only as their points of view relate to serving wealthier customers. No lower servants or factory workers are granted perspective, and the most stressful outburst from any of the included figures is the pastry cook's "Sugar-frost and whitening!" when confection-induced anxiety startles him out of a deep sleep (6). The story ends with a brief recognition of kitchen labor, but once the cook serves a perfect Christmas dinner, she "loves all mankind; and retires to rest, after a small glass of cordial, at peace with herself and all the world" (7). Ollier's "An

Idyll for Christmas Indoors" shifts from human to plant voices. On Christmas Eve, a Sylvan Spirit sits atop the greenery decorating a sitting room, and the poem grants the spirits of holly, laurel, and mistletoe one stanza each before they speak together. The voice of the holly describes birds dying and a climate so cold as to kill its natural residents, which causes the sprig to gloat about its warm position indoors, where laurel affirms that it feels like a "glowing household June" (7–8). Ironically, natural items from outdoors accentuate the unnatural traits of idyllic domestic Christmas atmospheres. In "What Christmas Is in Country Places," Martineau locates "the good old Christmas—the traditional Christmas—of Old England" in strictly rural locales (8).[25] Noting variations in local customs, the speaker explains that some regions believe good luck will grace a family if "a dark man" is the first to enter their home on New Year's Day (10–11). Therefore, "it is a serious thing to have a swarthy complexion and black hair" because such men are compelled to enter so many people's houses early in the morning (for a fee if the man is poor) (11). One senses possible danger for dark-skinned residents as their neighbors demand human good luck charms, and Martineau's piece explicitly reveals the role of racialized identities in popular visions of "Old England" and its Christmas traditions. The story nevertheless concludes with another idealization of the rural scene "sheeted with snow," producing a "social glow which spreads from heart to heart" (11).

Exemplifying how contributors' voices became Dickens's public voice and the entwining of collaborators' styles, George A. Sala's "What Christmas Is in the Company of John Doe" was reprinted in *Harper's* with Dickens identified as its author, and as late as 1971, the *New York Times* printed it as "Christmas with John Doe" by Charles Dickens.[26] The story contrasts its predecessors with a refreshingly bleak declaration at its opening: "I have kept (amongst a store of jovial, genial, heart-stirring returns of the season) some very dismal Christmases" (11). Thomas Prupper then recounts terrible situations that have accompanied the holiday and details the year when he was arrested for debt on Christmas Eve. Although the prison inmates celebrate with traditional fare, Prupper cannot enjoy eating in such a hopeless place: "But what were beef and beer, what was unlimited tobacco, or even the plum pudding, when made from prison plums, boiled in a prison copper, and eaten in a prison dining-room?" (15). Once released, Prupper spends New Year's Day with "a pretty cousin" who becomes his wife, and he concludes the story by demonstrating that the legacy of his brief incarceration brings no shame; rather, he jokes openly about not naming their first child after the prison (16). Sala's vision may have shaped Dickens's imagination, as the dismal atmosphere of prison saturating Prupper's mindset resonates with Arthur Clennam's experience in Dickens's *Little Dorrit* (1855–57), whose title character is not named for a prison but is born in one. The story of John Doe takes on even greater significance in beginning to treat serious or distressing situations as appropriate Christmas topics.

Depicting the least nostalgic Christmas experience of the collection, Miss Eliza Griffiths's "The Orphan's Dream of Christmas" moves the number toward the types of pieces that characterize future Christmas numbers as Dickens abandons the concept of using stories simply to list "What Christmas Is" and approaches storytelling as a communal act that unites readers, listeners, and tellers even across boundaries of life and death. Sala's story maintains a cheerful, sometimes self-mocking tone that leads to a happy ending, but Griffiths's verse does not find its way to uplifting cheer. The poem opens with a solitary, weeping eight-year-old girl looking out of a workhouse window on Christmas Eve (16). Her parents and siblings have all died, and she dreams of death, Heaven, and Jesus—only to die herself at some point during the night. This verse indirectly challenges Dickens's opening formulation of welcoming denizens of "the City of the Dead" to the fireside in "What Christmas Is as We Grow Older" by describing the Christmas of a family who is not fortunate enough to age at all.

Focusing on another orphan, Samuel Sidney's "What Christmas Is After a Long Absence" changes the number's tone yet again with a tale of emigration to South Australia that harkens back to the colonial emphasis of the first Christmas number. Facing greater obstacles than anticipated in the unfamiliar landscape, Charles imagines himself "constantly in danger from savage blacks" (17). He lists indigenous human beings alongside animals such as dingoes, uses "rude words, and even blows" to discipline his workers, and fears "the wild mountainous songs of the fierce aborigines, as they danced their corrobberies, and acted dramas representing the slaughter of the white man, and the plunder of his cattle" (18). Reinforcing the idyllically white "country" places of Martineau's contribution, Charles is lonely when Christmas comes around and comforts himself with memories of "the Christmas time of dear old England" (18). Sixteen years later, having made the natives "tame" in his part of the bush colony, Charles returns home to search for a wife (19). Welcomed heartily, he glories especially in the "delicate-complexioned" women, appreciating a "fair white face" above all else and in contrast to his own suntanned skin (18–19). Returning to Australia with a new wife and about twenty relations, the Christmas visit enables Charles to expand the imperial project while escaping the class snobbery of England (20).

Pretension remains identified as a national flaw in Theodore Buckley's "What Christmas Is If You Outgrow It," but the lack of framing continues to challenge the 1851 number's pace right up to its conclusion. Buckley's story presents a plot that future Christmas number stories will repeat: an ungrateful son rises in social stature above his parents, then disloyally takes them for granted. Horace DeLisle, son of a respected country parson, becomes increasingly arrogant while away at school as he falls into debt and neglects his studies. His debauched character manifests most hurtfully when he leaves home before Christmas to resume carousing with friends. The story does not follow Horace to his implicit demise, ending instead with the general caution, "You may be quite sure that you have grown too fast, when you find that you have outgrown Christmas. It is a very bad sign indeed" (23). The number then concludes with another contribution from Horne, "The Round Game of the Christmas Bowl," which comes "originally, from Fairy-Land" (23). Players convene to toss symbols of pride into a huge bowl of ice, which liberates them from troubles, and as they dance and sing, "the heat of the Christmas hearts outside causes the Offering which each has thrown in, to warm to such a genial glow, that the heat thus collectively generated, melts the ice" (24). The stress on communal offerings and the effect of the collaboratively produced heat then shifts suddenly (and rather mind-bendingly) back to the individual as the melted water transports participants home to the beds in which they dream (24).

So ends the 1851 Christmas number in a vision of individual Christmas happiness enabled by communal endeavor. Although the 1851 number is, as a collection, fairly weak in quality because of the redundant Christmas fantasies, this concluding story connects directly to the opening piece for 1850, which links individual memories of childhood to the notion that a stranger may be observing and judging one's Christmastime recollections. The 1850 number establishes important foundations and traditions from which the future numbers consistently draw but that the 1851 number does not necessarily enhance, leading one to feel a keen need for the kind of narrative organization that Dickens devises for 1852. Had the numbers stagnated as loose assemblages of fairly random thoughts about Christmas, their future would probably have been limited and unimpressive. Beginning in 1852, however, the framing that emerges significantly advances what the multivocal collections are able to accomplish.

2

Reading in Circles: From Numbers to Rounds (1852–53)

A Round of Stories by the Christmas Fire (1852) and *Another Round of Stories by the Christmas Fire* (1853) are the first Christmas numbers for which Dickens uses a loose concept to hold the contributions together. Although the Christmas fire acts as a reliably familiar symbol, the relationships of the people telling tales around it and the stories of the *Rounds* are fraught with complication. The contributions for the two *Rounds*, which come from thirteen authors, range from parables to ghost stories to poems of intense loss. Each piece bears the title of its teller: the host, the guest, the schoolboy, and Uncle George, for instance. In drawing upon oral storytelling modes with the round structure, Dickens creates a narrative atmosphere in which collaboration exists as part of a repetitive, polyphonic form.

Attention to the complicated narrative structure of these numbers reveals a Dickens whose contributors' voices often destabilize his own. Considering the vocal qualities of the round as a form illuminates a new interpretive angle for the musical metaphor in Dickens's role as the "conductor" of *Household Words*. Calling the 1852 and 1853 collections *Rounds* also implies a circular form that links each segment to the others through the others; this circle has a center, but its top changes depending on the tilt of one's ear. Laurel Brake speaks of the periodical press "articulating eloquently . . . a cacophony of presence and absence."[1] The sometimes-jarring juxtapositions of tales in these collections can certainly feel cacophonous, and the loudest voices in the din sometimes come from the unnamed contributors. Those names may have been absent from the title page, but the noise that they make, and their existence as part of the "Dickens" of the Christmas numbers, prompts one to reconsider the pitch of that iconic voice.

A Round of Stories by the Christmas Fire

The first Christmas number to have a unique title, the 1852 compilation suggests that a blaze for the holiday might differ uniquely from other fires, but for its content, Dickens seems to have realized that the previous numbers had exhausted the numbers' ability to keep specifically Christmas-themed writing interesting. In a letter to Reverend James White, Dickens shares his plan for the 1852 issue: "I propose to give the number some fireside name, and to make it consist entirely of short stories supposed to be told by a family sitting round the fire. I don't care about their referring to Christmas at all; nor do I design to connect them together, otherwise than by their names."[2] Dickens's declaration that he does not aim to "connect" the stories beyond the names might nudge future readers (and scholars) who value the intentionality of an author away from a cohesive approach to the text. That the writers did not discuss a shared strategy for their stories can lead to a view of the numbers as miscellanies—bits of discrete fiction that one can easily pluck apart. Dickens had edited *Bentley's Miscellany* from its launch in January 1837 to February 1839 and fostered a much more unified vision for *Household Words,* but even he might seem to have encouraged a fragmented approach to the Christmas collections when he republished some of his own pieces without all of their original counterparts.[3] The form itself, however, and the mandate of the collection titles lead in a different direction; threads of connection between and across all nineteen stories in the two *Rounds* are abundant. Closely examining the linkages between the stories not only results in stronger textual interpretations but also subverts the notion that Dickens is a figure with a single, stable voice.

Nine authors contribute to *A Round of Stories by the Christmas Fire,* and each title locates a speaker around the fire while isolating an identifying characteristic. The titles are more complicated than what Dickens describes to White and include nonrelatives, such as the deaf playmate, which evidences a flexible editor adjusting the frame in response to the contributions he receives. The finalized titles also signal that the assembled speakers are not complete strangers without explaining each relationship precisely. Even after some of the narrators address one another, the narrative revels in the

ambiguity of this set of relationships. The number's aesthetic lies partly
in its awareness of the rich potentialities embedded in the titles, and the
Round even teases its own frame with the broadly titled "Somebody's Story."
The musical aspect of the collection's title resonates with the structuring of
Dickens's phenomenally popular *A Christmas Carol* (1843), whose chapters
are called staves, but nine years after the *Carol,* Dickens imagines singing that
is both individual and communal in place of a single song. The initial speaker
in a round may contribute an individual voice, but each part in a round can
also be sung by the group, and the structure is decidedly circular.[4] The fact
that voices in a choral round literally overlap encourages readers to break out
of a linear mode of reading and invites them to hear the story's converse.[5]

The *Round*'s opening paragraphs immediately draw attention to complicated narrative positioning. "The Poor Relation's Story" begins:

> He was very reluctant to take precedence of so many respected
> members of the family, by beginning the round of stories they
> were to relate as they sat in a goodly circle by the Christmas
> fire; and he modestly suggested that it would be more correct
> if "John our esteemed host" (whose health he begged to drink)
> would have the kindness to begin. For, as to himself, he said,
> he was so little used to lead the way, that really—But as they
> all cried out here, that he must begin, and agreed with one
> voice that he might, could, would, and should begin, he left
> off rubbing his hands, and took his legs out from under his
> armchair, and did begin. (1)

This narrator's speech temporarily but conspicuously bridges class divisions
within the family as the "poor relation" humbly addresses his wealthier
relatives and sets up a model for cross-class storytelling from other speakers.
More significantly, the listeners encourage him "with one voice," increasing
the feeling of intimacy and closeness among the future narrators and establishing immediately that their voices will overlap. "The Poor Relation's
Story," written by Dickens, also shows Dickens enlisting his contributors
as cheerleaders; he makes them responsible for his narrator being the one
to start the round, casting himself in a modest role that hardly matches his
confidence as an artist and as an editor.

Shifting into a first-person voice, Michael (the poor relation) continues
to reference "the assembled members of our family," and understanding the
possible relationships between those members becomes increasingly complicated as the round continues (1). The aged poor relation shares a tale in

which he fantasizes about the life he might have lived if various people had not treated him poorly. A gullible and benevolent man, Michael loses his professional and personal well-being when his wealthy uncle disowns him for proposing marriage to a woman with no fortune. She marries a rich man instead, and Michael's business partner takes advantage of his trust to force him out. An opposite trajectory of events constitutes his fantasy, and the tale concludes with the disheartening reality that John, the host, provides Michael's actual financial support. Moving immediately to another contribution from Dickens that continues to develop family bonds among the storytellers, "The Child's Story" presents a version of the parable of the seven ages via a traveller who experiences all phases of life in a single compressed day.[6] The short piece features no real climax, but its conclusion reminds one of the relationships between listeners. The fictional traveller is surrounded at the end of his journey by the people he has lost to death, and their respectful love for one another leads the child to speculate, "I think the traveller must be yourself, dear Grandfather, because this is what you do to us, and what we do to you" (7). Forecasting his grandfather's death, the naïve child also makes clear that even the cliché-driven stories in the collection pertain specifically to the family around this particular fire.

The number does not, however, settle into a consistent depiction of those family relationships, as William Moy Thomas's "Somebody's Story" remains deliberately vague. Adding to the confusion about which "somebody" tells the story, it is set in Germany with no recognizable characters from the frame. Successful, loyal, and strong, Carl is an apprentice cask maker who must travel to earn enough money to marry Margaret. After building his fortune in a distant town, Carl temporarily loses it when he hides gold pieces in his lucky hammer, which a comedic, monkey-like hired boy drops in the river (10). Carl's homecoming is therefore subdued, but his luck returns when the gold-filled hammer appears in the river behind Margaret's house and he is feted for having inadvertently discovered the source of the River Klar. The story's message—that people should not doubt the honest intentions of hardworking young men with bad luck and that those young men should not rush the pursuit of their dreams—suits the mood of a family gathering at which people of various ages visit. Still, with no articulated link to the family around the fire, one might begin to suspect that the collection's cohesion is weak, but Elizabeth Gaskell's "The Old Nurse's Story" potently brings the frame back to the fore.[7]

Given the scandalous nature of the family events the nurse relates, questions of relationality add to the story's mysterious Gothic atmosphere.

The nursemaid begins, "You know, my dears, that your mother was an orphan, and an only child; and I dare say you have heard that your grandfather was a clergyman up in Westmoreland, where I come from" (11). The mother to whom the nurse refers is Miss Rosamond, just a girl in the story, but we do not know for which people present she is a mother. The nurse, Hester, tends to the orphaned Rosamond in a household with the elderly Grace Furnivall and a few servants. Hester immediately senses the danger of the place when she hears booming music emanating from a broken organ, and Rosamond subsequently disappears during a heavy snowfall. Hester finds a shepherd carrying the child's almost frozen body and learns from the revived Rosamond that another little girl tempts her outside then takes her to a weeping woman beneath a holly tree, where that woman lulls her to sleep (15–16). These figures are the ghosts of Grace's sister (Maude) and her daughter, who froze to death when the former Lord Furnivall cast Maude from the house after discovering from her envious sister that she secretly married a "foreign musician" and had been hiding their child (17–18). Hester learns this history "not long before Christmas Day" (17) when she herself sees the spectre of the child, and at the end of the story, the ghosts of Lord Furnivall, Maude, and the girl appear to the entire household, reenacting the scene of Maude's banishment. When Grace sees her own "phantom" take shape, "stony and deadly serene" in youth, shock and shame send her to her deathbed, muttering the story's final words: "What is done in youth can never be undone in age!" (20).

The story's account of bad behavior on the parts of both sisters and Lord Furnivall raises questions about the nurse's motive and tone as she exposes this family history around the fireside in the company of outsiders ("The Guest," for instance). Is she exposing a piece of shameful knowledge or resisting stigma by speaking truth and refusing to obscure family history? Does she speak in order to humiliate the main actors in the story, warn future generations to avoid certain behaviors, or advocate for the semifallen woman? Told from the perspective of a servant, her story's indictment of the unyielding Lord Furnivall for his stern parenting stances also rebukes the more privileged classes of her social "superiors." The narrator's position significantly influences one's interpretation of the story's message, making its context crucial to complete readings. The original timing of the number in anticipation of the Christmas holiday, with its attendant emphasis on forgiveness and generosity, may also impact one's assessment of the story's moral lessons. The appearance of "The Old Nurse's Story" in anthologies, sometimes without any reference to its original publication in the Christmas number, limits these fruitful interpretive possibilities.[8]

If the "Old Nurse" has told a story about the mother of some of the people sitting around the fire, then we must also wonder how this contribution relates to the collection's final piece: "The Mother's Story" by Eliza Griffiths. Readers certainly could envision Miss Rosamond, the little girl from Gaskell's tale, growing up to be the one telling Griffiths's story, as the nursemaid has already identified Rosamond as the mother of some of those present. Within the structure of the round, if the timing were such that Gaskell's story and Griffiths's poem overlapped, the story of the Furnivall woman dying in the snow with her child would be interwoven with Griffiths's poem about a mixed-race woman who collapses in the snow just before reuniting with her son after having endured twenty years of slavery away from her children. Repeated imagery of this sort helps to explain how a collection of tales that might seem randomly collected sometimes exhibits an organic cohesiveness. In the conglomeration of narrative voices, individual writers' voices often become indistinguishable, and even though Dickens is the "conductor," he does not always control the combined effect of the voices he conducts.

Edmund Ollier's "The Host's Story," following Gaskell's piece, is in verse form and adds unexpected irony to the collection as it relates the adventure of a greedy travelling merchant setting his host's palace aflame. Sneaking through the palace as the household sleeps, the merchant "fills a bag with jewels and with gold," sets a fire that nearly traps him, then escapes by jumping out of a window, leaving his treasure behind. Again, a contributor's piece adds rich possibilities to the relationships between the storytellers in the frame. The poor relation presents John as a generous and modest host, noting that John does not want the group to dwell on the fact that he supports the poor relation financially. Considering Ollier's piece, however, we might question whether a cautionary tale warning against taking advantage of hospitality shows the host to be less content in his role. The irony in Ollier's poem, if it undercuts the credibility of Dickens's narrator in the first story, may pose a challenge to Dickens's authority that one would expect him to have put in check, but his correspondence with Gaskell and others displays more flexible editorial behavior than most critics allow.

Already the successful author of *Mary Barton*, Gaskell was a writer whom Dickens esteemed highly and whose authorial voice, from the very first issue of *Household Words*, sometimes melded with the public voice of Dickens. He was thrilled when she agreed to write a multipart story to help launch the periodical.[9] As Linda Hughes and Michael Lund point out, "When ['Lizzie Leigh'] appeared without attribution in *Household Words*, many inferred that the story was Dickens's own, given its prominent place in the first number. And the story was first published in the United States under Dickens's name."[10] By December 1851, Gaskell's *Cranford* series had also begun appearing in the journal, which sparked some sparring between Dickens and Gaskell over the sketches' references to Dickens's *Pickwick Papers*.[11] In regard to "The Old Nurse's Story," Dickens was confident enough to try to persuade Gaskell to change its conclusion. After complimenting the "wonderfully managed" writing and suggesting that Gaskell alter the ending so that the child sees more ghosts than the adults do, Dickens asks, "What do you say to this? If you don't quite and entirely approve, it shall stand as it does."[12] Gaskell immediately makes it known that she did not "entirely approve." A few days later, Dickens persists in trying to change her mind: "What I would propose to do, is, to leave the story just as it stands for a week or ten days—then to come to it afresh—alter it myself—and send you the proof of the whole, and the manuscript (your original manuscript) of the altered part; so that if you should prefer the original to the alteration, or any part of the original to any part of the alteration, you may slash accordingly."[13] The process Dickens describes is not one in which he bullies Gaskell into accepting his revisions. Rather, she is the one who may "slash," and his proposal includes a creative cooling-off period that places his "alteration" on a level equal (not superior) to hers, as he is careful not to discard her "original" brusquely. These interactions force one to reevaluate Harry Stone's assertion that Dickens's usual practice with the Christmas number contributions is to "edit them with his usual freedom."[14] To the contrary, with the print deadline approaching, Dickens repeatedly asks Gaskell for her permission before making permanent changes to her text, and their correspondence points to a stimulating collaborative relationship.[15]

Gaskell left the ending as originally written, and Dickens printed the story as she wished, knowing that readers might think the story was his own.[16] His letters to her then mix defensiveness with reassurance: "I have no doubt, according to every principle of art that is known to me from Shakespeare downwards, that you weaken the terror of the story by making them all see the phantoms at the end. And I feel a perfect conviction that the best readers will be the most certain to make this discovery. Nous verrons. But it is greatly improved, and in making up the Xmas No. finally today, I shall of course be careful to preserve the New Ending, exactly as you have written it."[17] Even while placing himself in a direct line of descent from the Bard to defend his vision, Dickens concedes to Gaskell, demonstrating that their disagreement does not nullify the act of collaboration. As if to reinforce their status as creative allies, two days later he adds, "Pray don't, in any corner cupboard of your mind, put away the least doubt or disparagement of the story. I read it carefully on Saturday (when I made up the Number finally) and did so with the greatest interest and admiration."[18] Dickens almost apologizes for having voiced his opinion so emphatically. He does not simply pay lip service to the idea of having an open mind when it comes to his collaborators' choices but revisits their work and sometimes changes his valuation of it.

Once the number is published, Gaskell sends Dickens compliments on the stories she (correctly) guesses are his, while Dickens again contradicts his previous opinion: "I don't claim for my ending of the Nurse's Story that it would have made it a bit better. All I can urge in its behalf, is, that it is what I should have done myself."[19] The Dickens/Gaskell exchange bears out Rachel Sagner Buurma's view that "literary authority in Victorian England was much more contingent, variable, and contested than has previously been thought."[20] In this case, the critical binary between anonymous authors as either exploited or subversive does not do justice to the original collaborative texts. Dickens strives to present work that accomplishes his storytelling goals and also allows the Christmas *Rounds* to tell the stories of his contributors with respect for their artistic integrity. The issue's "conductor" listens, calibrating final decisions with consideration for the wishes of his talent.

James White's "The Grandfather's Story" again shows Dickens changing his mind about what he deems acceptable for the number, as he initially rejects a story that he ultimately prints. In his letter to White about the number's frame, Dickens specifies the types of characters and plot that he desires: "The grandfather might very well be old enough to have lived in the days of the highwaymen. Do you feel disposed, from fact, fancy, or both, to do a good winter-hearth story of a highwayman?"[21] White obliged, and his narrator speaks of his days as a bank clerk when he and a colleague, Tom Ruddle, are robbed while delivering gold to the bank's clients on Christmas Eve. Pursuing a thief who has slit a full bag but taken only three guineas, Ruddle and the grandfather become sympathetic toward the criminal because he is motivated only by trying to keep his wife and baby from starvation after having been swindled (25). They let the man celebrate Christmas freely and offer to loan him more money, which seems to embody the generosity of the holiday that Dickens often prizes, but he sends remarks of dissatisfaction to White: "You know what the spirit of the Christmas number is. When I suggested the stories being about a highwayman, I got hold of that idea as being an adventurous one, including various kinds of wrong, expressing a state of society no longer existing among us, and pleasant to hear (therefore) from an old man. Now, your highwayman not being a real highwayman after all, the kind of suitable Christmas interest I meant to awaken in the story is not in it."[22] What is the "spirit" that Dickens feels should characterize this number so strongly? Dickens's piece for the 1851 Christmas issue defines it as "the spirit of active usefulness, perseverance, cheerful discharge of duty, kindness, and forbearance" (1). Alternatively, he could be referencing the "Carol philosophy": his idea that compassion for others should guide people's interactions all year long and the belief that drawing upon memories, even sorrowful ones, will restore proper moral principles.[23] Apparently, White either did not understand why his story—which indeed exhibits kindness, forbearance, and traits of the "Carol philosophy"—failed to meet expectations, or he did not care to exemplify his understanding with a new tale. The story Dickens claims is a poor fit is the one that he prints, allowing the visions of others to continue shaping the "spirit" of the numbers.

The relationships among storytellers continue to join the Round's pieces in circular fashion as Edmund Saul Dixon's "The Charwoman's Story" begins with a servant figure complaining about her inclusion: "A person is flustered by being had up into the dining-room for to drink merry Christmases and them (though wishing, I am sure, to every party present as many as would be agreeable to their own selves), and it an't easy rightly to remember at a moment's notice what a person did see in the ghostly way" (25). Displaced from her usual position downstairs, the charwoman does not regard inclusion in the family circle as an honor but rather as an anxiety-producing burden because she is expected to wish people she serves a merry Christmas and to perform for them "at a moment's notice." Put on the spot with the imperative of telling a ghost story, the charwoman blames the "Nurse" for telling the "ladies" that she is in possession of such an account, creating tension between the two servant figures (who act as the fourth and seventh narrators) and reminding readers that both stories associated with servants deal with supernatural topics (25). The charwoman's brief ghost story tells of how her colleague Thomas accurately foretells their employer's death when he hears an alderman's distinct step at what they later learn was the moment the alderman died several miles away. More poignant than the idea of the haunting, however, is the way in which Dixon's story about the jarring quality of a noise dovetails into Harriet Martineau's story, which explores hearing from a much different perspective.

In a collection whose title alludes to overlapping voices, whose genre almost demands cacophony, Martineau's "The Deaf Playmate's Story" forces one to ponder the absence of voices. As a child struggles to understand that he is losing his hearing, thinking that others are suddenly treating him meanly for no reason that he can perceive, he acts out violently and loses his friends. Even the adults in his life fail to realize that he is becoming deaf. The speaker of Martineau's story is that child, never named and therefore identified primarily by his lack of hearing.[24] The deaf boy is the playmate of Charley Felkin, but because he never addresses Charley directly and identifies Charley as well as his own family with third-person references, the playmate does not seem to be in the presence of those people. The family around the fire, then, is not the Felkin family, nor is it the family of the deaf playmate, so we do not know why the deaf child spends time with the other narrators; the reader is left to wonder whether the deaf boy is in the company of strangers, extended family, the doctor who treats him kindly in the story, or friends. That ambiguity about the child's location not only heightens his potential vulnerability as a narrator but also forces readers to continue puzzling over the relationships among the storytellers.

The most difficult questions the story raises pertain to the way one should comprehend a deaf child's role in a verbal round. Up to this point, the round structure has suggested that each speaker may overlap with the previous one(s) and that something or someone gives a cue to commence. When a story begins without comment on the transition between narrators, the round structure invites the reader to imagine a head nod, eye contact, or some other nonverbal gesture to indicate which person will speak next. Those gestures would reach the deaf playmate, but the content of the previous narrators' stories would not. Storytellers in a round might adjust the beginning of a tale depending on how the previous speaker has concluded, or a particular detail might suddenly seem humorous when juxtaposed with an earlier tale and merit an altered style of delivery. For the deaf playmate, however, even if he understands nonverbal cues passing among the fireside company, none of the interactions pertaining to events narrated in previous stories would reach him. His first words to the assembled group boldly declare, "I don't know how you have all managed, or what you have been telling" (27). One speaker explicitly acknowledging his exclusion from the conversational nature of the round might raise doubts about whether the previous stories really do have any significance. The import of "The Deaf Playmate's Story" lies in its raising of this question rather than in proposed answers, and Dickens may have been especially comfortable with such questions given his own inclusion of "the deaf gentleman" as a key member of the storytelling group in *Master Humphrey's Clock* more than a decade earlier.[25] The deaf playmate suffers as much from the ignorance of adults as from his inability to hear. Early in his experiences of deafness, before he understands what is happening, the playmate reacts aggressively to changes in his hearing and kills an innocent dove, spotlighting the high stakes involved in suiting one's method of communication to one's audience. That point resonates strongly with a group of storytellers as the child becomes a source of wisdom. "The Deaf Playmate's Story" holds as much weight as the stories narrated by adults, forcing the adults to reflect upon how exactly they decode the signs of others and lending a self-reflexive layer to the *Round*.

Reinforcing communal feeling around the fire and his sense of acceptance, the deaf boy concludes, "How you all nod, and agree with me!," and the lack of transition to the next story makes "the guest" seem less integrated into the group (30). Samuel Sidney's "The Guest's Story" abruptly begins, "About twenty years ago, I was articled clerk in the small seaport town of Muddleborough" (30). The guest then explains how a one-handed Irishman, Peter, cons the entire town out of its money by promising to use their investments to go to Portugal and retrieve a buried treasure (31–32). After Peter disappears, misery and regret ensue, but justice catches up to Peter when he tries to take advantage of an American, who shoots him (33). Only by looking at the collection as a whole does one notice the connection between "The Guest's Story" and "The Host's Story." The host warns against taking advantage of hospitality, while the guest's tale stresses misplaced confidence and the penalty of death for those who scheme in the face of generosity. Seeing the link not only adds interest to each story but also uncovers a conversation that is audible only in the original context of collaboration.

Concluding the collection, Eliza Griffiths's "The Mother's Story" continues to complicate questions of narrative voice and challenges the primacy of the text's "conductor."[26] Griffiths's poem depicts an interracial romance sympathetically, criticizing racial persecution and the destruction of family bonds in South America. Leena, the protagonist, is the orphan of an indigenous woman and a white hunter. Her solicitous care of Claude d'Estrelle, a Frenchman she discovers dying in the forest, leads to their marriage, but once Claude dies, his relatives mistreat her. The poem simultaneously emphasizes a highly idealized maternal love and Leena's color, comparing her "brown cheek" to a "crimson streak" and taking Dickens's voices across geographic, racial, and gender boundaries (34). That this is "The Mother's Story" aligns Griffiths with the immediate speaker in the round. The "Mother" repeats a tale that an old male traveller, who also appears in the story, told her by this very same fireside. She thus appropriates a man's voice that has already appropriated a woman's. The entire poem is spoken in the "I" voice, and with the exception of the introductory stanza, that "I" is the male traveller even though Leena's trials, not those of the traveller, guide the plot. Leena never controls her own story; it is the presumably white-identified mother around the fireside in England who has chosen the story of a racially mixed character to represent the pinnacle of maternity, which is not a vision one would usually associate with Dickens.

Yet Griffiths's voice is both the "Mother's" and Dickens's, and her piece strategically essentializes maternity in a manner that advocates for cross-racial female solidarity and condemns oppressive men. When Leena seeks shelter with Claude's brother, he insists that she leave the children with him so that they can "outgrow" and forget the shame he associates with their indigenous heritage (34). The uncle steals the children from a resistant Leena and bribes a tribe to enslave her. Most striking is the fact that the poem's portrayal of the maternal takes place in the complete absence of white-identified women in the story, focusing on the experiences of multiracial women and other women of color. Leena is able to escape enslavement when maternal solidarity leads an indigenous woman to liberate her, but Claude's brother sends her back into slavery on a "wild plantation" (35) in Africa from which it takes her twenty years to flee.[27] Upon returning home, Leena cannot track down her son, but she finds her daughter wedded to a wealthy white man. The melodramatic conclusion of the number revolves around this extremely troubled reunion. Whether Leena's daughter understands herself to be multiracial is unclear. Once she recognizes her mother, their interaction is strained and truncated because they hear the footfall of her husband, a man she truly loves but whom she, "Fair" and with "auburn hair," has married as a white woman (35). The young woman knows that her husband's "title high / Would ne'er to Indian blood ally" (35), so she tells her mother that they may never meet again. Leena departs in fear and, true to the strained coincidences of nineteenth-century sensation fiction, discovers (after two nights of sleeping in the snow) a house of worship where her son is preaching about undying maternal love. Before the concluding tableaux of Leena and her grandchildren appears, Leena's regretful daughter sends for her, and their deathbed reunion shows that the path to heaven lies with other women of color. The cost of not having seen that truth kills Leena's daughter, and the poem's final lines nearly deify Leena: "A very presence from above, / That simple woman's faith and love" (36).

What do we make of the fact that the number closes with Griffiths's words? Initially, Dickens had considered Martineau's piece about the deaf boy to be the ideal final story, telling Wills, "For the last story in the Xmas

No. it will be great. I couldn't wish for a better."[28] At that date, Dickens had not yet read Gaskell's story, and we do not know whether he had read Griffiths's contribution. He may have decided at a later date that Griffiths's story was an even better concluding piece than Martineau's, or, especially if Wills disagreed about the placement of Martineau's story, Dickens may have changed his mind. Whatever the decision-making process, Griffiths's poet's voice assumes the authority to conclude the number as a whole, and readers must ponder the negotiation of power between this nearly anonymous woman writer, her fictionalized woman of color, and the white men publishing a journal that builds its audience with the story. I do not see an articulated set of points in Griffiths's piece that Dickens would have found repulsive, but this story's take on matters of race differs from Dickens's often-hostile depictions of racially othered groups.[29] Although we know almost nothing about the relationship between Griffiths and Dickens, the collaborative practices of *Household Words* as a literary enterprise establish that, in Griffiths's case, the voices of women collaborators become Dickens's own voice even if he does not like what they say. And as the histories of Gaskell's and White's stories for this same number demonstrate, Dickens does not always use the Christmas number as a place to insist on his will over all others. In these ways, Dickens's editing, collating, and framing are also a form of collaborative authorship—a form that he simultaneously controls and to which he submits. This model of collaboration differs distinctly from the type that has been delineated in most scholarship on Dickens's collaborative ventures, and it continues in the following year.

Another Round of Stories by the Christmas Fire

Dickens is so pleased with the effect of the 1852 *Round* that he writes to Elizabeth Gaskell on April 13, 1853, to let her know that he has already decided to structure the next number "on the plan of the last" and to solicit her work for it.[30] *Another Round of Stories by the Christmas Fire* both acknowledges an existing audience from the 1852 number and informs new readers of its predecessor's existence. The second *Round* contains pieces named for the following speakers: the schoolboy, the old lady, the angel, the squire, Uncle George, the Colonel, the scholar, nobody, and "over the way," a nickname for the person living at that location. Sharing the first *Round*'s potentialities for cross-speaking within a single number, *Another Round* consistently includes family bonds that extend beyond the biological. The interpretive possibilities expand even further when one views the two collections in relation to each other. A complicated chorus exists within each *Round*, and those choruses subsequently combine in endlessly rich pairings. "Somebody's Story" in the first *Round* is answered by "Nobody's Story" in the second, but they do not occupy the same position in each. The title of "The Old Lady's Story" echoes "The Old Nurse's Story," and their themes are somewhat similar in treating women whose deaths are caused by seductive "foreign" men. "The Angel's Story," rather than hovering above them all, exists on the same terrestrial plane as "The Charwoman's Story," and the threshold crossings are not only narrative or temporal when one attempts to imagine the ordering of the two *Rounds*. The interconnections between speakers cut across the landed aristocracy and the serving classes; spiritual and earthly realms; and military and civilian life. Such a levelling of speakers implicitly claims that a servant's voice merits as much attention as a squire's. This range of perspective, speech, and experience comes together in the authorial identity of "Dickens," which, in the context of the two *Rounds*, becomes as much a concept as an individual identity.

The first story illustrates how narrative threads crisscross between the two years' collections as *Another Round* begins not with an explanation of who is sitting around the fire or why and how they come to tell stories but rather with the first speaker launching right into "The Schoolboy's Story." The framing fundamentals of the first *Round* therefore carry over as the journal, *Household Words*, binds the two numbers and provides a rationale for readers to presume that the same household from 1852 hosts the second storytelling round in 1853.[31] The schoolboy recalls not Dickens's opening narrator of the first *Round* but rather Martineau's deaf playmate, who likewise recounts his school days. This entertaining account, however, is much more cheerful in its childlike tone: "However, beef and Old Cheeseman are two different things. So is beer. It was Old Cheeseman I meant to tell about" (1). Living his entire life at the school as an orphan and enduring the ridicule of boys who label him a "traitor" for having turned from pupil to Latin master, Cheeseman shocks them by disappearing suddenly then returning with an inherited fortune (2). Having anticipated that Cheeseman would reappear with an avenging "prizefighter," the boys prepare for battle by stockpiling stones in their desks only to find that, instead of warfare, the school fills with "sobbing and crying" when they take leave of their old friend (3).

The direct address of the schoolboy so early in the number also reminds readers that each speaker is sitting in the presence of others at a fictional fireside and positions readers as possible family members. Just before the story ends, the speaker suddenly commands, "Don't look at the next story-teller, for there's more yet," then shares surprising twists: Cheeseman marries

Jane, the school's servant, and the schoolboy does not meet them until they take him home for Christmas well after the events he has been relating (5). The schoolboy reminds his audience, "[I]t was the year when you were all away; and rather low I was about it, I can tell you" (5). Not until the end of the story do we understand that the schoolboy is speaking to his family members—although, as in the first *Round*, we do not know precisely which other speakers are his kin. One's curiosity continues to forge links across the numbers and to keep the narrators connected: for instance, the deaf playmate from the first *Round* could be this speaker's friend, making the schoolboy Charley Felkin. The boy clearly shames his family for abandoning him at Christmas, and his report of having a grand time at Cheeseman's hints that the Cheeseman family may provide better company than his own (5). The schoolboy's insecurity about holding the attention of the adults at the fireside prepares readers for the pending narrative shift and suggests that the old lady of the next story hovers impatiently, waiting for the boy to finish.

"The Old Lady's Story" from Eliza Lynn[32] continues to develop family relationships in the group before describing a most extreme sacrifice as it begins, "I have never told you my secret, my dear nieces" (5). Noticeably, she does not speak directly to the schoolboy, who has just warned her off. Lizzie, the old lady, tells of her youthful infatuation with Mr. Felix, a "foreign man" who moves into the neighborhood with a retinue of servants whose darkness adds to his mystery: "Hindoos, or Lascars, or Negros; dark-coloured, strange-looking people" (6–7). Mr. Felix's presence poses a racial threat, and the Orientalized description of the estate that he transforms into a "fairy palace" full of velvets and "foreign smells" accounts for how he is able to cast a seductive spell over Lizzie (7). She defies her father and neglects her sister, Lucy, whose concern for Lizzie has made her gravely ill. Lucy dies at the moment she stops Lizzie from eloping, and guilt prevents Lizzie from ever marrying (8–9). The story's warning against allowing foreign charms to enchant vulnerable English girls is one that Lizzie shares because she anticipates dying soon, and it reinforces the undercurrent of imperial anxiety that runs through the Christmas numbers. Exactly to whom Lizzie issues the caution is unclear because she mentions no siblings beyond the dead Lucy in her tale, and the other speakers offer no clarification of how an unmarried, siblingless woman would come to have nieces. The most likely explanation seems to be that the aunt/ niece relationship is one of endearment, with Lizzie as an "adopted" aunt of a family, allowing the collection to advocate for non–biological family bonds.[33] The reader's inclusion in such a circle increases the text's intimacy and justifies the next speaker, a neighbor who is included in the family grouping.

George A. Sala's "Over the Way's Story" brings fairy-tale tropes into the number and speaks back not just to the other narrators but also to Dickens. Barnard Braddlescroggs, called "the Beast," is a grumpy merchant with a rigid attitude who runs a profitable warehouse (10). A clerk, Simcox, becomes the focus of the story, and his resemblance to Mr. Micawber, a character famous for always being in debt in *David Copperfield* (1849–50), is one reason that some identify the story as Dickensian. Simcox is a good-hearted man whose debt stems from his inability to control his drinking and the spending of his wife, who is characterized in a sudden and sharp emergence of the number's underlying racism as a woman who is "of all domestic or household duties considerably more ignorant than a Zooloo Kaffir" (12). Ridiculing the idea of a black South African woman running an English household reinforces the notion that whiteness is synonymous with the idealized domestic hearth in the imaginary space of the number. Simcox compounds his family's trouble by borrowing ten pounds from petty cash without permission, and when Braddlescroggs discovers the embezzlement, he plans to jail or transport the entire family. Bessy, Simcox's ailing daughter, saves the day by accepting Braddlescroggs's offer of employment as a housekeeper at the warehouse, where he forbids her from speaking to her father, and Bessy's meekness in that role slowly softens Braddlescroggs's character. The story invokes fairy tales in its characterization of Bessy, who occupies "an analogous position to that of the celebrated Cinderella" (13) in her own family but then becomes the heroine of a *Beauty and the Beast* transformation plot in the Braddlescroggs family: "So Beauty was married. Not to the Beast, but to the Beast's son" (17).

Substituting "scrogg" for "scrooge," Braddlescroggs's name riffs on Ebenezer Scrooge, and the story's plot converses with *A Christmas Carol*. Philip Collins and others have noted that Sala's essays regularly feature him "out-Dickensing Dickens" with ease.[34] The unreformed Braddlescroggs dampens his son's generous spirit in the same way that Scrooge curtails the cheer of his nephew Fred, and, like Scrooge, Braddlescroggs's "compeers, fell away from him on 'Change" (11). For Braddlescroggs, a young girl whose patient duty to her alcoholic father threatens her health takes the place of the uncomplaining disabled boy who inspires Scrooge. The result for both protagonists is an excessive and buoyant generosity. Without published bylines to identify authors but with the common knowledge that Dickens "conducted" his contributors, readers could legitimately read this piece in numerous ways. With Dickens as the author, the story comes across as self-parody or an example of Dickens unoriginally repeating his own story lines.

Speculating that someone else is the author, a contributor like Sala may be offering a tribute to the conductor via imitation or, alternatively, making fun of him. The unique collaborative context makes any or all of these readings feasible, and the plethora of possibilities attests to the rich interpretive arena that attention to collaboration opens.

Following Sala's piece, Adelaide A. Procter's "The Angel's Story" brings the collection back to a more traditional Christmas setting, but decoding its message about death continues to illustrate the indeterminacy that the collection's form enables. The poem takes one to a wealthy household as it endures the loss of a child. At the moment of death, an angel flies away with the boy then tells him the story of a poverty-stricken orphan who also used to dwell in London. That boy, in low health, wanders up to the garden gate of a rich family, and when the servants send him away with a little money because they are "tired of seeing / His pale face of want and woe," the young boy living in the house takes pity on his poor counterpart and shares a handful of blooming roses (18). The roses comfort the orphan as he dies the next day, and he turns into the angel that now bears the wealthier boy to his own death while adorning him with the same red roses. Although the story initially appears to sanctify children's solidarity across class lines as their pure souls console each other in heaven, a more disturbing interpretation emerges when one recognizes that the children also act as catalysts for death. The poor child is ill when he first meets the rose-bearing boy, and their encounter seems to speed up his decline. As an angel, he tells the wealthy boy,

> Ere your tender, loving spirit
> Sin and the hard world defiled,
> Mercy gave me leave to seek you;—
> I was that little child!

(19)

These closing words of the poem yoke the wealthy boy's death to a vision of his corrupt future, making the angel an agent of death who takes the life of the generous boy as a means of proactive "mercy." The wealthy boy, however, has already proven himself to be more compassionate than his servants even when living in luxury. The angel's appearance pessimistically implies that humanity's sin is too strong for even the most righteous children to withstand.[35] Crucially, we do not know who narrates "The Angel's Story" at the fireside, information that could assist in determining its tone and message. The poem shifts from an unidentified third-person speaker to the voice of the angel, and its title does not match the others in the collection unless readers believe that an actual angel joins the assembled family. Gill Gregory, one of the only scholars to situate an analysis of a Christmas number story in relation to those of other collaborators, notes that the placement of Procter's piece after Sala's potentially creates a tension between those two contributors, as Sala's emphasis on "essentially generous" qualities of children contrasts with the image of children as fatal deliverers of retributive justice.[36]

The number moves quickly from the celestial realm back to worldly interests in Elizabeth Gaskell's "The Squire's Story," and Dickens's correspondence with her again reveals an excessively complimentary editor, perhaps anxious to be sure that she will contribute to the collection despite Dickens's vociferous attempts to get her to change her story the previous year. In September, after Gaskell asks for more specificity about the frame concept, Dickens replies, "No. I won't give any outline. Because anything that you like to write in the way of story-telling, when you come out of that tea-leaf condition will please me. All I say, is, it is supposed to be told by somebody at the Xmas Fireside, as before. And it need *not* be about Xmas and winter, and it need *not* have a moral, and it only needs to be done by you to be well done, and if you don't believe that—I can't help it."[37] Countering Gaskell's wish for more information with a playful but firm insistence on his vision, Dickens stresses her talent and creative vision rather than his own, declining to insist upon a theme or "moral" for her story. The setting—being "told by somebody at the Xmas Fireside"—Dickens finds important enough to mention, which associates the domestic hearth with appropriate subject matter. Given that the deadline for contributors to submit their pieces was not until early December,[38] Dickens may also have declined to send more details simply because he did not yet know how the number would shape up. Set in 1769, Gaskell's story follows Dickens's vague instructions by shying away from Christmas themes in its depiction of a sadistic thief who deceives an entire small village by masquerading as a respectable gentleman. The periodic absences of Mr. Higgins, necessary for "collecting his rents" in another region, are the times when he commits highway robbery (22). Eventually, he is caught and hanged after murdering an old woman in Bath who had reputedly been hiding a fortune. The story is fairly anticlimactic because it is so obvious from the start that Higgins is a sadistic, suspicious man. More surprising than his criminality are the story's odd details; Higgins, for instance, is a kind husband with mysterious health-preservation habits that might contribute to the couple's childlessness. The squire concludes by asking the listeners at the fireside if they would like to join the hunt for the fortune

Higgins is rumored to have stashed in the house he rented: "Will any of you become tenants, and try to find out this mysterious closet? I can furnish the exact address to any applicant who wishes for it" (25). Listeners, then, are invited to participate actively in what could become a sequel to the squire's tale as the stories in *Another Round* continue to unfold in circular patterns.

Treating a different aspect of criminality, "Uncle George's Story," by W. H. Wills and Edmund Saul Dixon, emerges from multiple layers of collaboration and shows the number again endorsing non–biological family bonds. George shares the story of his adventurous wedding day when his bride, Charlotte, stands alone at the altar because George has fallen into a shaft on unstable cliffs. George's rescuer, the outcast Richard Leroy, explains that the town's reason for ostracizing him stems from his work as a smuggler, which accounts for his familiarity with the hidden tunnel and exposes the previous occupation of George's father. After Leroy becomes a close friend and stops smuggling, the families hope that their children might marry. The story evidences collaboration so thorough that no awkward transitions or recognizable marks of distinct voices diminish its delivery. Wills was clearly able to move between creating and editing with success, yet the story raises more unanswered questions about the frame. George is uncle to someone around the fire, which means that a grandfather figure for some people around the fire was a smuggler. This grandfather, however, must be different from the one who narrates "The Grandfather's Story" because that speaker is a bank clerk. The criminality of a patriarch would certainly affect one's reading of the other stories in the collection that touch upon illegal activities, such as Gaskell's tale of the highwayman. At the same time, as with Linton's aunt character, one cannot be sure whether the family relationships of the story titles are biological or metaphorical. George has no siblings, nor are any siblings of Charlotte's mentioned in the story, but they have joined a kin group so completely that they fill familial roles and are comfortable enough to discuss their family's criminal past. Overcoming such social hurdles in a celebration of Christmas camaraderie lends an enhanced sense of togetherness—because it is so purposeful—to the storytelling gathering.

The adoptive family story in Samuel Sidney's "The Colonel's Story" is not so uplifting. Orphaned, the Colonel is a teenager when his uncle adopts him and funds an indulgent lifestyle but forbids him to marry anyone who is not wealthy. After falling in love with a young widow, the young man marries her secretly then discovers that she is a spendthrift who is slightly mad and prone to violent quarrels. On the way home from visiting her at a remote cottage, the young lover falls from his horse, and when he wakes up, the blood covering him is taken as proof that he murdered his wife, whose dead body is discovered not long after he leaves her. Acquitted once the real murderer is found, the Colonel now enjoys the sharing of stories with the extended family at the fireside, but readers never learn whether the Colonel is a member of the host's family or an honored guest.

The scholar's position in the family is likewise unclear, but Elizabeth and William Gaskell's "The Scholar's Story" presents a more complicated scenario of collaboration. William Gaskell translated the ballad from Théodore Hersart de La Villemarqué's *Barzaz-Breiz* (1845), a text based on ancient Breton oral folk tradition.[39] The letter in which Dickens first asks Elizabeth Gaskell to keep the Christmas number in mind also brings William Gaskell into the collaborative relationship: "I receive you, ever, (if Mr Gaskell will allow me to say so) with open arms."[40] Asking Mr. Gaskell's permission to violate a social code (wrapping metaphorical arms around another man's wife) after he has already expressed that desire lessens the respect the letter might communicate, and one can further criticize Dickens for treating an immensely successful contributor as if she is an underling of her husband's.[41] In light of the ongoing professional relationship between Dickens and Mrs. Gaskell, who published under exactly that name, it is also possible to view the inclusion of her husband as a way Dickens expands the collaborative circle. William published another ballad from *Barzaz-Breiz* in the October 22, 1853, issue of *Household Words* and was involved in later negotiations surrounding the publication of Elizabeth's novel *North and South*. All three individuals seem to have expected to interact through various pairings and triangulated communications. The Gaskell text appearing in *Another Round* is a translation of a translation, but the filtering does not stop there. Elizabeth writes the introductory paragraphs to the verse that William translates, and her preliminary note states that the scholar character hears the story from the mother of the woman who originally told it. Two layers of oral telling, one involving a fictional character, precede the written translations, and Elizabeth Gaskell, not Dickens in his role as conductor, is the one who massages all of these tellings and translations into the frame concept with impressive wit.[42]

The scholar opens the story with a defensive maneuver that unsettles the harmony of the round and further questions authorial dynamics: "I perceive a general fear on the part of this pleasant company, that I am going to burst into black-letter, and beguile the time by being as dry as ashes. No, there is no such fear, you can assure me? I am glad to hear it; but I thought there was" (32). Since Dickens would provide Gaskell with no outline or list of speakers, it is likely that Gaskell herself decided to insert a scholar into the fireside circle as a means of introducing her husband's translated poem. Her nursemaid narrator for the first round addresses the group, and she would have observed the other speakers delivering comments that bounce off of other characters. Given that Wills decided on the final ordering of the stories for 1853, his involvement as a collaborator is also crucial to this dynamic. The scholar's resistance to an idealized fireside image skillfully balances congenial teasing with hostility, and his desire to avoid boring his companions with too learned of a story recalls the schoolboy's worries that the assembled group will move too quickly away from him. Wills very well could have placed this joint piece late in the number so that its setup would tie back to the first story. Both he and Gaskell would have been aware of the way in which her opening for the story deftly points out that Dickens is not the only writer who can exploit the fire puns, and her narrative framing demonstrates that contributors sometimes pull Dickens's voice into theirs rather than vice versa.

Far from pedantic, the verse the scholar shares is gripping in its portrayal of a young wife who is tormented then killed as a result of male jealousy, and this second violent story from Gaskell reminds one that Dickens's emphasis on the setting of the domestic fireside never excludes gruesome topics from the Christmas season. Count Mathieu departs to fight in the crusades, leaving his wife and infant son under the protection of a cousin who serves him as a clerk. The wife, never named, maintains devotion to her husband but must lock herself in her room to hide from the psychotic cousin, who badgers her with declarations of love. To provoke the couple, the madman kills his master's dog and horse, sending letters each time that blame their deaths on the negligent wife, whom he also reproaches for entertaining suitors at glamorous balls. Count Mathieu finally takes the bait after the cousin murders the family's infant son and accuses the lady of having cavalierly left the baby near a giant, hungry sow. Oblivious to the improbability of such a scenario, the lord arrives in a rage, slays his cousin for not taking better care of his family, kills his wife before she can speak a word, and is left to regret the horror of his own ignorant brutality.[43] The ballad's final lines describe a priest who sees the spirits of the hound, the steed, the wife, and the infant comforting each other in a churchyard, but they offer little relief from the deranged behavior that makes the verse so haunting.

The deeds that need amending in "Nobody's Story" are not nearly as bloody, as Dickens closes the *Round* with his own prose in a tribute to workingmen. His story allegorically indicts the ruling classes for blaming societal ills on workers without funding infrastructures that would empower laborers to live more comfortably. The Bigwig family represents the wealthy classes while Nobody speaks for "the rank and file of the earth" who are ignored in monuments while the feats of less industrious noblemen are commemorated (36). As Nobody's life advances, his children fall into immoral habits because they lack schooling while the Bigwigs debate educational policy, and his family dies from preventable disease that the Bigwigs care about only when their own families risk contagion (35–36). The final words of *Another Round of Stories by the Christmas Fire* implicate the reader directly in these dilemmas as Nobody implores, "O! Let us think of them this year at the Christmas fire, and not forget them when it is burnt out" (36). This plea for compassion addresses not only readers but also the fictional narrators of both *Rounds* with an inclusive "us" around the Christmas fire. The call brings all of the voices together and places the conductor's baton firmly back in Dickens's hand as he transforms it into a sort of poker to extinguish the fire that, for two years, has helped to create a polyvocal space where Dickens loosens his conductor's grip and enjoys the music for a bit.

Dickens's lack of autocratic control is even more apparent when we pay close attention to his correspondence with Wills. Dickens was traveling in Europe from October to early December when the 1853 Christmas issue was finished and sent to press—and when the details of a moustache-growing contest with his travel companions, Wilkie Collins and Augustus Egg, were more exciting to Dickens than the Christmas number.[44] Dickens does not imagine his own stories, composed in Italy, specifically as framing pieces: "In making up the Christmas number, don't consider my paper or papers, with any reference saving to where they will fall best. I have no liking, in the case, for any particular place."[45] Consistent with the round metaphor, Dickens thinks that his stories will work equally well in any position, but Wills's placement of them in the first and last positions affords them extra prominence in published form and enhances their subsequent significance in the collection.

For the first time, Dickens's own stories stand as bookends for a Christmas number, but he is not the person who decided to place them there. This fact reinforces Wills's significance as a coeditor and leads one to envision the act of editing as a collaborative authorial endeavor.[46] The fact that Wills, not Dickens, was reviewing and ordering submissions doubles the layers of collaboration. Discussing the number-in-progress in a letter to Emile de la Rue, Dickens reports that he has not read several of the pieces Wills plans to include.[47] The same letter offers evidence that such confidence in Wills was not restricted to the Christmas numbers. Answering la Rue's question about a piece in the weekly issue from November 19, Dickens writes, "I diffuse myself with infinite pains through Household Words, and leave very few papers indeed, untouched. But Kensington Church is not mine, neither have I ever seen it."[48] Prevailing critical tendencies make it more likely for one to have seen Dickens's comment about self-diffusion cited as confirmation that he arrogantly controlled the journal rather than as an example showing that he was simultaneously ignorant of exactly what appeared in that journal. In this instance, travel presents itself as a logistical reason for such sharing of editorial authority, but as I demonstrate throughout the present volume, openness to other people's input and willingness to share power persist in varying degrees as Dickens produces fourteen more Christmas numbers. Beyond Wills, Dickens draws into the collaborative group another major figure, John Forster, as he anticipates the need to proofread "The School-boy's Story": "Let Forster have the MS. with the proof, and I know he will correct it to the minutest point."[49] The number of pens, and minds, at work on the collection does not seem to have worried Dickens in the slightest, as he accepts that he is not in complete control of his work.[50] Theories of collaboration in the periodical press must accommodate such an approach to authorship, as ceding control and allowing others to make decisions are crucial elements of Dickens's collaborative practices.

The success of the *Rounds'* structure is evident in its lasting appeal both to competitors and to Dickens. As *Household Words* attracted a growing audience, the Christmas numbers also increased in popularity throughout the 1850s and 1860s and spawned imitators. In 1856, Edwin Roberts published a collection titled *The Christmas Guests round the Sea-Coal Fire,* which an obituary for Dickens in *The Bookseller* lists as one of the most successful imitations.[51] Roberts is credited as sole author, and each story has two titles: "Phoebe Gray's Troth-Plight," for instance, is "The Niece's Story," and "The Lost Fiddler" is "The City Friend's Story." The double titling creates ambiguity, but the confusion feels unintentional, as if Roberts has patched together as many elements as possible from Dickens's previous Christmas numbers (snowed up people, telling tales around a fire, stories named for their tellers) without careful craft. Many of the stories begin by disclosing their plots, doing away with suspense and illustrating why Dickens's Christmas numbers, with their constantly evolving frame narratives, continue to grow in popularity over others.[52] Five years after the second *Round,* Dickens stated that if he and Wilkie Collins were unable to devise a satisfactory new frame idea, they could always fall back on yet another *Round*, but doing so was not Dickens's preference, as he wisely sensed that he had exhausted the *Round* structure by the end of 1853.[53] In the next Christmas numbers, Dickens moves to a much more fully developed and linear narrative frame and, perhaps inspired by Wills's placement of stories in the second *Round*, continues the practice of positioning his own work to start and finish the next two special issues.

3

Orderly Travels and Generic Developments
(1854–55)

Early in *The Holly-Tree Inn*, its narrator declares, "[W]hen I travel, I never arrive at a place but I immediately want to go away from it" (3). The speaker's back-and-forth desires could create an elliptical visual image, but in this case, a snowstorm prevents the traveller from being able to backtrack or skip to his next destination quickly. Instead, he must slow down and proceed through the space he currently inhabits in a direct, uncomplicated motion, which is a fitting way to visualize both the 1854 and 1855 Christmas numbers. For these years, in contrast to the preceding *Round*s, the numbers move from circularity to structures that are more linear, and the storytelling moves from one speaker to another with a clear sense of forward motion.[1] Dickens reins in the storytelling, limiting the mixing that characterizes the *Round*s and keeping his travellers under at least temporary control with his own narrator framing them.

The Seven Poor Travellers (1854) and *The Holly-Tree Inn* (1855) are Dickens's first forays into fully developed frame narratives for the Christmas numbers. The narrative lacing structures that emerge in each collection come to characterize the Christmas numbers for more than a decade. These heretofore-overlooked techniques enable the stories to cohere in contexts that feature group as well as individual storytelling, and Dickens's correspondence on the subject reveals intriguingly inconsistent stances toward the dynamics of collaboration: sometimes he embraces joint creative processes, and sometimes he complains about them. Even when contributors shared no apparent communication about their stories' emphases, the numbers for 1854 and 1855 evidence lively intertextual dynamics. Approaches that emphasize attribution blind critics to those dynamics and prevent appreciation of the symbiotic relationships that enhance both the interpolated stories and their respective frames. The frames enabling these collections to cohere are, for instance, important elements of the collaborative contexts from which detective fiction emerges. These collections also fold close male bonds into Christmas visions and exhibit the ways in which shifting representations of imperial projects continue to underpin celebrations of idyllic English holidays.

The Seven Poor Travellers

The first Christmas number in which a narrative frame completely encloses the other stories and is woven through them to enhance coherence, *The Seven Poor Travellers* succeeds in creating orderly storytelling. Each traveller speaks in numbered sequence, and the frame story gives good reason for possible variations in narrative style, theme, or idiom between the inset pieces. For its premise, the collection relies on Watts's Charity, an actual institution in Rochester, Kent (the same region featured in Chaucer's famous framed tales).[2] On May 11, 1854, Dickens visited the charity house with Mark Lemon, and although that visit may not have been Dickens's first, it would have been freshest in his mind during the composition of this issue.

Despite the very real place from which this Christmas number takes its name, its narrator immediately injects fiction into the reading experience with an opening disclaimer:

> Strictly speaking, there were only six Poor Travellers; but, being a Traveller myself, though an idle one, and being withal as poor as I hope to be, I brought the number up to seven. This word of explanation is due at once, for what says the inscription over the quaint old door?

> RICHARD WATTS, ESQ.
> BY HIS WILL, DATED 22 AUG. 1579,
> FOUNDED THIS CHARITY
> FOR SIX POOR TRAVELLERS,
> WHO NOT BEING ROGUES, OR PROCTORS,
> MAY RECEIVE GRATIS FOR ONE NIGHT,
> LODGING, ENTERTAINMENT,
> AND FOUR-PENCE EACH. (1)

Taking it upon himself to become the Christmas Eve benefactor of the six actually poor visitors at the charity, the narrator plays host by providing a sumptuous feast. The entire interaction relies on his difference from the travellers, yet his addition of himself to their number creates the illusion of comradeship. The only things linking the seven individuals in the title are their status as poor and their transience, but once the host asks each traveller to tell a story, the group shares another trait; they are joined in a project of speaking and listening. Each speaker's self-consciousness acts as a device to keep the seven figures connected to the frame, and in some cases, the content of the inset contributions further strengthens such cohesion.

The host/narrator's logic in requesting these stories may seem uncomplicated, but the moral reasoning behind his sudden benevolence questions the precepts of the type of charity often associated with Christmas. He is so moved by looking at Watts's tomb and the inscription on the house that he begins to regard the establishment possessively, thinking of it as "my property" (1) and calling the visitors "my travellers" as he imagines their destitution: "I made them footsore; I made them weary; I made them carry packs and bundles; I made them stop by fingerposts and milestones, leaning on their bent sticks and looking wistfully at what was written there; I made them lose their way, and filled their five wits with apprehensions of lying out all night, and being frozen to death" (3). The host somewhat sadistically enjoys envisioning the suffering of these people so that he can delight all the more in alleviating it. The exaggerated quality of the host's thought process reveals the self-serving rather than altruistic nature of this model of patronage as he revels even in another person's fear of being frozen to death, but the number avoids completely vilifying him by showing that he is aware of his self-aggrandizing wishes, then shifting to humor.

The host's Christmas Eve dinner preparations involve issuing orders at his inn for a grand meal that must be transported to the charity house, and the curious parade of hot dishes down the High Street draws readers into a cheering fantasy of a Christmas hastily done up for the comfort of others. Waiters sprinting with steaming puddings, the host bearing a pitcher of wassail (called his "brown beauty") as if it were an infant, and a "Man with Tray on his head, containing Vegetables and Sundries" join to form a "Comet-like" procession, while a servant boy waits for a whistle to dash down the street to "the sauce-female, who would be provided with brandy in a blue state of combustion" (3–4). The instant feast is just one aspect of the number's opening that recalls *A Christmas Carol* (1843). Although this host does not undergo a Scrooge-esque character transformation, the surprise turkey and his excessive joy in providing a meal call that character to mind. The host also echoes Scrooge in lamenting that Christmas is only a once-per-year event: "[F]or when it begins to stay with us the whole year round, we shall make this earth a very different place" (2).[3] The messages of the travellers' stories, however, turn out to be much more complicated than the vague notion that keeping Christmas in one's heart can solve the world's ills.

Before launching into the storytelling, the narrator provides a description of each traveller, which creates early interest in the interpolated tales to come and increases one's curiosity about what type of story each will tell. The group consists of the host; a man with an injured arm who smells like shipbuilding wood; a young sailor boy; a disheveled man with papers bulging out of his pockets and tape holding his clothes together; a Swiss watchmaker; a frightened, widowed young woman; and a book peddler (3). The transitions between stories are brief, but the frame is so strong that the pieces cohere despite radical differences in subject matter. Discussing Elizabeth Gaskell's use of a Dickens-inspired frame concept in 1859, Larry Uffelman notes that the reader progresses through such a text by "forming a series of loops that return at the end of each story to the setting and characters of the frame. Readers begin in the frame, read straight through a story, return to the frame, and then move into the next story in the sequence. . . . Furthermore, the 'metafictional frame' becomes a small drama in its own right, providing continuity, as readers move through the edition."[4] This process holds true for many of the Christmas numbers as the framing and looping form knots whose architecture relies on mental motion.

For *The Seven Poor Travellers*, the storytelling chain begins with the host sharing the story of Richard Doubledick, whom he identifies vaguely as a "relative."[5] The centrality of Dickens's Doubledick story to the number's intensely positive reception warrants a detailed examination of the piece, which celebrates intense bonds between men as part of Christmas.[6] Already "better known as Dick," Richard joins the army under a dubious, self-invented name so that he will be Dick Doubledick when killed (4). Full of shame, he hopes to die as penance for years of profligate behavior that have hurt himself and Mary Marshall, a fiancée he offends with an unnamed act of betrayal (5). Having failed to achieve his goal of being shot, Doubledick's severe insubordination puts him at risk of being flogged when Captain Taunton's looks and demeanor save him: "Now, the Captain of Richard Doubledick's company was a young gentleman not above five years his senior, whose eyes had an expression in them which affected Private Richard Doubledick in a very remarkable way. They were bright, handsome, dark eyes—what are called laughing eyes generally, and, when serious, rather steady than severe—but, they were the only eyes now left in his narrowed world that Private Richard Doubledick could not stand" (5). Given their closeness in age, the account-ability Doubledick feels in Taunton's presence is not paternal; rather, there is an attraction between the men that consistently prevents Doubledick from speaking or behaving in any way falsely to Taunton. Taunton's "bright, handsome, dark eyes" rivet Doubledick, inspiring his complete transforma-tion into a steadfast soldier and devotee.[7] Doubledick seals the pact of his own reformation "with a bursting heart" by kissing Taunton's hand, and the kiss remains significant enough for Doubledick to recount it decades later: "I have heard from Private Richard Doubledick's own lips, that he dropped down upon his knee, kissed that officer's hand, arose, and went out of the light of the dark bright eyes, an altered man" (6). The kneeling position equally resonates with oaths of fealty and oaths of marriage, and the story presents that ambiguity comfortably.[8]

This intensity of male emotion apart from a domestic heterosexual unit is as much a part of the Christmas tradition in this number as any-thing else. Doubledick and Taunton subsequently experience thirteen years of togetherness in which they travel to many sites of conflict, and although Doubledick saves Taunton's life repeatedly, the captain ultimately receives a fatal wound from a French officer at Badajoz. The description of his death mirrors the earlier account of the men's union:

> The bright dark eyes—so very, very dark now, in the pale face—smiled upon [Doubledick]; and the hand he had kissed thirteen years ago, laid itself fondly on his breast.
> "Write to my mother. You will see Home again. Tell her how we became friends. It will comfort her, as it comforts me."
> [Taunton] spoke no more, but faintly signed for a moment towards his hair as it fluttered in the wind. The Ensign understood him. He smiled again when he saw that, and gently turning his face over on the supporting arm as if for rest, died, with his hand upon the breast in which he had revived a soul. (6–7)

The fellow soldiers have lived in a professional and personal partnership that far surpasses the superior/subordinate relationship of rank. Their embrace at Taunton's moment of death is extended as Doubledick carries Taunton's lock of hair "near his heart" for over a year until he can deliver it to Taunton's mother (7). When Doubledick goes to France to visit Mrs.

Taunton, he discovers that her host is the officer who killed her son, but rather than vengefully murdering the man, Doubledick forgives. Reflecting the shift from English-French animosity to alliance that took place relatively quickly between the Napoleonic and Crimean conflicts, the children of the men grow up as friends who later unite to fight "in one cause . . . fast united" (10). Holly Furneaux's analysis of this story focuses on the Doubledick character and Dickens's treatment of "military men of feeling" while, refreshingly, including consideration of the resonances between Doubledick's plight and other pieces in the number: "Like Dickens's story Procter's poem considers the thorny question of allegiance in wartime. . . . Both contributions, too, are concerned with the appropriate gendering of military heroism and the personal characteristics of a hero."[9] Indeed, the heterosexual pairing of Doubledick with Mary, which the story barely mentions, takes place only because of the transformation he experiences in his relationship with another man. In a frame story that involves a man fantasizing about the succor he will provide to poor travellers, all but one of which are men, the relationship depicted in the first traveller's story suggests a path forward not just for individual travellers who might be in need of character reform but for the entire nation to overcome animosities that run through deeply violent episodes of its history.[10]

The direct, first-person voice of the next speaker keeps the second story anchored to the frame as the shipwright begins his portion by explaining that his arm sling results from an adze-wielding coworker having inflicted an "unlucky chop" at the shipyards. He then moves into the tale by saying, "I have nothing else in particular to tell of myself, so I'll tell a bit of a story of a seaport town" (10). Following the first traveller's references to an unspecified time in the future, the voice of the second traveller pulls readers right back into Christmas Eve at Watts's, which acts as a reminder that the storytellers are randomly assembled. Such a reminder is especially fitting to introduce George A. Sala's psychedelic story about Acon-Virlaz, a Jewish shopkeeper and jeweller whose characterization complicates critical understanding of ethnic "others" in Dickens's collaborative canon. In Acon-Virlaz's dream vision, he joins his friend Mr. Ben-Daoud on a shopping trip to Sky Fair, a bizarre place full of "live armadillos with their jewelled scales," diamonds the size of ostrich eggs, and jewels that are sold "by the gallon, like table beer" (14). Weighed down by treasures, Acon-Virlaz fails to leave the fair before the closing bell and offers the gatekeeper his daughter's hand in marriage to avoid being locked in for a hundred years. Although "women and children from every nation under the sun" (15) help block his way to the exit, the quick reference to other ethnicities does not lessen the story's excessive attention to Jewishness. Early in the tale, some attempt at moderation appears when, on the subject of Acon-Virlaz's name, the narrator says, "He went by a simpler, homelier, shorter appellation: Moses, Levy, Sheeny—what you will; for most of the Hebrew nation have an inner name as well as an inner and richer life" (11). Despite this defensive statement on behalf of "the Hebrew nation," the story's depiction of Ben-Daoud, who owes Acon-Virlaz money, is directly anti-Semitic. Ben-Daoud is "oily" with "a perceptible lisp" and pink eyes, and Acon-Virlaz casts him as the dream's villain because he lures Acon-Virlaz to Sky Fair only to abandon him (12). In actuality, Acon-Virlaz has returned home drunk, and falling out of his chair "into the fire-place" wakes him from the dream (16).[11]

One might be tempted to refer to the second traveller's story as an example of the inferior quality of the non-Dickens contributions to the Christmas numbers, but readers and scholars often struggle to distinguish Sala's writing from Dickens's. Harry Stone observes that Sala "had a Dickensian relish for picturesque oddities and trenchant details—all of which, plus Dickens' habit of editing and emending the work of his collaborators, sometimes makes it extremely difficult, in joint pieces, to disentangle [Sala's] writing from Dickens'."[12] In this case, a denial of collaboration in the Christmas number could seriously impact one's reading of Dickens's treatment of Jewish characters—a debate that regularly troubles critics of *Oliver Twist* (1837–39) and *Our Mutual Friend* (1864–65). Sala's portrayal of these Jewish characters clearly did not offend Dickens, who knew that the Conductor title put his stamp of approval on the story. This moment, which challenges one's ability to attribute the story entirely to Dickens or to Sala, benefits from consideration of Marjorie Stone and Judith Thompson's formulation of the author as an entity "woven of various strands of influence and agency, absorbing or incorporating differing subjectivities, and speaking in multiple voices."[13] This notion of a heterotext is not always fitting, particularly if dismissive of authorial agency, but in the case of a text that is invested in representing the multiple voices and subject positions of the narrators at Watts's, heterotextuality offers a path through the story of Acon-Virlaz that accommodates both Dickens's and Sala's involvement. The second traveller's tale also speaks to the collection's consistent concern with poverty versus wealth, bestowing on Acon-Virlaz's character a sentiment opposite to the one motivating the host.

Adelaide Anne Procter's "The Third Poor Traveller" then weaves its engaging connection to the frame into the verse's first lines:

You wait my story, next? Ah, well!
Such marvels as you two have told
You must not think that I can tell;
For I am only twelve years old.

(16)

Nothing in the poem's meter or the rhyme marks the opening lines as being written by Dickens, and because Dickens was, ironically, as unaware of Procter's authorship as were his original readers, it is impossible that they conferred about the transition into her story. Procter, having written a piece for a previous Christmas number, seems to have anticipated a frame like the *Rounds* that would accommodate a child speaker identifying himself as such. Another reason it seems unlikely that Dickens added the stanzas is that they appear only slightly altered in later collections of Procter's poetry with the reference to the speaker's age preserved.[14] Dickens admired Procter's poem, which he called "the little sailor's song," and even praised it in front of her while ignorant of the fact that she had submitted it using a pseudonym. Ensuring that Dickens's friendship with herself and her father did not affect his editorial decisions, Procter delighted in withholding her identity, and once Dickens learned the truth, he confessed embarrassment in a letter.[15] Gill Gregory claims that Dickens engages Procter directly in the framing sections, but Dickens's letter to Procter states that he discovered her identity only after the proofs of this number were printed. In part because of her pseudonymity, Procter's poem exemplifies how the lively dynamics of collaborative texts can occur even without direct author-to-author correspondence.

As *The Seven Poor Travellers* unfolds, following the order in which the first traveller describes the guests around the table, Procter's poem helps to prevent monotony, and the intertextual dynamics surrounding it develop the number's aesthetics. In addition to the change in genre, the freshness of Procter's child narrator lightens the number's tone and increases its pace after the weighty story of Acon-Virlaz. In the simple verse of the sailor boy, he dreams of going to sea so that he can save a princess from pirates or survive a shipwreck (16).[16] By referring to the "marvels" the others have recounted, the boy proves that he has been paying attention and fulfills the first traveller's hope that storytelling will interest the group. Sharing his life story of being raised by a "kinsman," the boy describes regular visits from a countess whom readers recognize as his widowed mother, a woman who has given up her son to please a vain earl.[17] Even in the poem's final line, the young boy does not realize that the countess is his mother when he says he is motivated by "what I will be for her sake!" (19). The dramatic irony resulting from the reader's awareness of the boy's parentage is shared by the other travellers listening to his verse at Watts's, and the next story intensifies the connectedness of those listeners.

Sympathetic commiseration turns to outright laughter as Wilkie Collins's "The Fourth Poor Traveller" begins with a challenge from the disheveled man: "Now, first of all, I should like to know what you mean by a story? You mean what other people do? And pray what is that? You know, but you can't exactly tell, I thought so!" (19). In repeating the group's responses to his interrogation, this lawyer includes the reader in the assembly while emphasizing the group's reaction: "To judge by your looks, I suspect you are amused at my talking of any such thing ever having belonged to me as a profession" (19). The listeners are obviously trading surprised or skeptical facial expressions, which again enhances the camaraderie between storytellers. The attorney then increases the metatextual playfulness of his remarks by declaring, "Now, I absolutely decline to tell you a story. But, though I won't tell a story, I am ready to make a statement. A statement is a matter of fact; therefore the exact opposite of a story, which is a matter of fiction. What I am now going to tell you really happened to me" (19). Casting doubt on the veracity of the previous and forthcoming stories, which according to this definition must be untrue, the fourth traveller points out that no one knows precisely what they are hearing from each person, just that the act of telling has met some unstated expectations. In a genre as multimodal as a Christmas number, these humorous comments point to the unanswerable questions of classification and method that underlie the form. This emphasis on a "statement" also anticipates Collins's later detective novels in which documents become narrators, and one could easily cite the paragraph as evidence of Collins teasing his readers as well as Dickens. This speaker plays with narrative expectations throughout the story, making regular references, for instance, to "my man in the corner," who he thinks will ask a question or contribute an unsanctioned remark (19, 20). Moving well beyond alignment with the framing concept, Collins contributes a story that strengthens the frame narrative.

At this point, identifying which sections can be classified as linking portions of the frame and how Dickens composed them might seem important, but exploring such questions surprisingly validates collaboration over individual attribution. As noted previously, Stone speculates that "Dickens probably wrote the introductory passages to the stories of the Second, Fourth, Sixth, and Seventh Poor Travellers."[18] Stone is more tentative about the fifth traveller and provides no explanation for a lack of comment on the bridging stanza at the start of Procter's "Third Poor Traveller" while assigning the prose opening of her second poem to Dickens. The impossibility of making attributions with certainty paradoxically reminds one that even if scholars thought they had reason to regard attributions as unquestionable, collaborative dynamics remain most pertinent. In the case of Collins's story, "The Fourth Traveller" has been identified as one of the first published British detective stories, but little attention has been paid to the role of collaboration in its literary life.[19] One of the strongest stories in the collection and Wilkie Collins's first contribution to a Christmas number, it takes extortion as its subject. Mr. Frank's unnamed fiancée, described in risqué terms as having "kiss-and-come-again sort of lips," is blackmailed by her father's former associate (20). Mr. Davager possesses letters in which the young woman's father, now dead after guilt drives him to suicide, confesses to forgery, and the letters' circulation would cause enough disgrace for Frank's family to cancel the wedding, which is why he hires a lawyer. Collins's story extends the anti-Semitism of Sala's story in stating that the lawyer has earned Frank's trust by saving him "from the Jews" with a low-interest loan (19). Using a hiccuping boy and a servant as spies, the lawyer tracks Davager, gains access to his room, cracks a written code, and finds the letters under a slit in the carpet (25).

Understanding "The Fourth Poor Traveller" as one of the first detective stories requires an understanding of coauthorship as part of the creative context that contributes to its unique achievement. Throughout, the speaker's repeated references to "my man in the corner" (19, 20) indicate that attributing the opening paragraphs, which include pert addresses to the audience, entirely to Dickens (as Stone does), may be a mistake. It seems much more likely that Collins and Dickens spoke or corresponded about the story's connection to the frame and that the opening portions—regardless of whose hand committed them to paper the first time—present the result of such discourse. Had Dickens been solely responsible for the tone of the story's opening, then when Collins reprinted the story, he most likely would have removed the references to "my man in the corner" and eliminated the conversational tone altogether, which he did not. Rather, in *After Dark* (1856), the references to "my man in the corner" become "Mr. Artist," which references that collection's frame narrative.[20] Several levels of metatextuality in *After Dark*'s frame lend the story a complex, playful tone, and Collins's construction of that frame concept may have been influenced by his work on the Christmas numbers. In the context of Collins's creative oeuvre, the two types of writing certainly cannot be sealed off from each other. The story's sparring with the listener/reader about detection and suspense is enabled by the collaborative frame. Reprintings, perhaps influenced by the similarities between the strongest aspects of both Collins's and Dickens's writing, appear with either one of them credited as author: *Harper's* publishes the story with Dickens listed as the author and calls it "The Lawyer's Story," while Collins reprints it as "The Lawyer's Story of a Stolen Letter" under his own name.[21] The same issue of *Harper's* also misattributes Eliza Lynn's Sixth Poor Traveller's story to Dickens, calling it "The Widow's Story." In Collins's case, the misidentification has further consequences because of the story's groundbreaking status in the detective genre. If we classify the piece as a key achievement in the history of the detective story, then we must include collaboration in that history. The story's ability to resonate within the collaborative frame as well as independently adds to its quality and importance, as does a view of it as the result of Collins's imagination working in conjunction and conversation with the minds of others.

Continuing the number's use of narrators who engage with the listeners at Watts's and of opening passages that blend smoothly into the interpolated pieces, George A. Sala and Eliza Lynn contribute tales from the fifth and sixth travellers. Sala's speaker builds rapport by posing three "do you know?" questions about the landscape in France to open a story in which a Swiss watchmaker, who dislikes France, meets two charming children there. The watchmaker encounters a curious eight-year-old who looks like a forty-year-old and takes noble care of his blind sister.[22] A drunken father has deserted the family, and the mother insists that the children always provide for hungry travellers while retaining their dignity by declining payment. Before moving on, the Swiss man insists on buying them gingerbread, displaying a generosity that recalls the first traveller and a penchant for the idyllic that joins Dickens's and Sala's styles. Lynn's story then cleverly folds its frame-linking title into its first sentence: "The Sixth Poor Traveller, was the little widow" (29). The opening paragraphs describe her pale color and nervous demeanor as "very near insanity" (29), and the ensuing story provides some explanation. The "widow's" husband is a counterfeiter who tries to seduce then murders her sister Ellen. The naïve wife misses Ellen's warnings and is saved from being killed herself only by a visit from Ellen's ghost. Mourning dress is now her disguise as she lives in constant fear of her husband's pursuit. Again, the resonance between the story's content and the frame is complex. The linking passages enhance Lynn's story by exaggerating the "widow's" shakiness and fragility, and Lynn's story benefits the frame as its open-ended conclusion contributes an unsettling feeling to the number. This woman's murderous husband could walk through the door of Watts's Charity at any moment.

The introductory prose paragraphs of the final interpolated piece are noteworthy in once more connecting previous storytellers. The group encourages the book peddler to share his legend, "except the Lawyer, who wanted a description of the murderer to send to the Police Hue and Cry, and who was with great difficulty nudged to silence by the united efforts of the company" (34). Singling out Collins's narrator from "The Fourth Poor Traveller" rekindles the humor of his story and heightens fellowship, as the shared endeavor now involves group policing. Once the peddler begins, Procter's "The Seventh Poor Traveller" tells of an Austrian maid who leaves home to support herself. Years later, she overhears townsmen planning to invade her home village so she charges across the country on horseback just in time to sound a warning. Such heroism results in a carving that honors the maid and a custom of the town guard calling out her name at midnight, which happens to be the time the crowd at Watts's breaks up.

The collection concludes with Dickens's "The Road," in which the first traveller places himself in a position similar to the number's readers. Unable to sleep, he muddles and mixes the stories: "Now, I was at Badajos with a fiddle; now, haunted by the widow's murdered sister. Now, I was riding on a little blind girl, to save my native town from sack and ruin. Now, I was expostulating with the dead mother of the unconscious little sailor-boy; now, dealing in diamonds in Sky Fair; now, for life or death, hiding mince pies under bedroom carpets" (36). Wassail inspired or not, this recollection acts as a tongue-in-cheek acknowledgment of the broad range of the stories. Reminding readers of the earlier pieces demonstrates that if one tries to force too many thematic connections between them, the stories will not oblige. Yet reading this collection through a collaborative lens enables one to see that the premise has established, justified, and executed a consistency within the inconsistency. Any awkwardness on the part of the speakers is excused by their having been put on the storytelling spot in front of a bunch of strangers who happen to be travelling on Christmas Eve. As the first traveller walks away from Rochester and "the mists began to rise" (36), the storytellers go their separate ways, but their tales stay yoked together.[23]

The Holly-Tree Inn

If *The Seven Poor Travellers* succeeds in imposing some order on the collaborative narrative, the following year's number goes further by filtering many voices through a single speaker. The idea of titling something after holly trees had been in Dickens's mind for at least five years. Writing to John Forster early in 1850, he considered naming his entire journal after the tree: "I really think if there be anything wanting in the other name, that this is very pretty, and just supplies it. THE HOUSEHOLD VOICE. I have thought of many others, as—THE HOUSEHOLD GUEST. THE HOUSE-HOLD FACE. THE COMRADE. THE MICROSCOPE. THE HIGHWAY OF LIFE. THE LEVER. THE ROLLING YEARS. THE HOLLY TREE (with two lines from Southey for a motto)."[24] *The Holly Tree* would certainly have been a better title than *The Household Face*, but *Household Words* and its nod to Shakespeare ultimately displaced Robert Southey's 1798 poem.[25] Modeled on Yorkshire's George and New Inn, the Holly-Tree Inn serves as an ideal location for a snowed-in traveller to collect stories.[26] The frame conceit for 1855 is that Charley, under the impression that his fiancée has abruptly run off with his cousin, becomes stranded on his way to Liverpool, whence he plans to emigrate to America. More harassed than charmed by elements associated with idyllic Christmases—a snowstorm, "Auld Lang Syne," refuge at a warm inn—Charley begins the number in a dejected tone that nevertheless piques readers' curiosity. After ruminating on wormlike drapery and recalling other inns, Charley surmounts his bashfulness and passes the time by interviewing others. The people telling stories do not gather haphazardly like the assortment of guests at Watts's but rather work or live at the inn on a permanent basis. Thus, the narrative framing draws upon an already existing community among speakers and commingles their voices by routing tales through a single traveller with a lacing structure that reinforces certain themes in alternate stories. Dickens's conducting for this number involves close collaboration, particularly with Wilkie Collins, that complicates even his own representation of the process.

In early October 1855, Dickens sent instructions to prospective contributors to try to communicate his narrative aims. As Jack Stillinger points out, such instructions, in conjunction with other factors such as length requirements for publication in certain venues, cannot be separated from the creative process: "[E]xternally exerted requests . . . in effect become intrinsic elements in the process of creation."[27] This creative atmosphere, then, is collaborative from the start, and Dickens's instruction letter is one of the lengthiest pieces of surviving evidence to describe his vision for a Christmas number:

> A traveller who finds himself the only person staying at an Inn
> on Christmas Day, is at his wits' end what to do with himself;
> the rather as he is of a timid and reserved character, and, being
> shut up in his solitary sitting-room, doesn't well know how
> to come out of it and speak to anybody. The general idea of

the Number is, that he overcomes this feeling—finds out the stories of the different people belonging to the Inn—or some curious experience that each has had—and writes down what he discovers.

Both for the sake of variety between this No. and the previous Christmas numbers, and also for the preservation of the idea, it is necessary that the stories should *not* be in the first person, but should be turned as if this traveller were recording them. Thus the Headings will not be The Waiter's Story, the Cook's Story, the Chambermaid's Story, &c, but simply The Waiter—The Cook—The Chambermaid— and under each head the traveller himself is supposed to tell whatever he heard from, or fancied about, or found out about, that particular person. Thus the person to whom the story belongs may be described, if necessary, as pretty or ugly—of such an age—of such a bringing up—and what is related about him or her may have happened at that Inn, or at another Inn, or at no Inn; and may belong to that person's present condition in life, or to some previous condition in life—and not only to himself or herself, but (if necessary) to other persons encountered in life.[28]

Several weeks later, Dickens casts himself as a victim of writers who fail to follow instructions whose vagueness he does not recognize:

I have received for the Xmas No.—with very blank feelings—besides my own paper and the Inn Pensioner, A question of mistaken identity, the Landlady, and the Actor—all running, by an extraordinary fatality, on criminal actions and criminal trials.

. . . I trust in our good starts that we shall get better matter than this, or by Heaven we shall come poorly off! The way in which they *don't* fit into that elaborately described plan, so simple in itself, amazes me.[29]

Dickens's idea of an "elaborately described plan" seems to include a fair amount of mind reading on the part of his collaborators, as his letter shares no thoughts on the topic or subject matter of the pieces to be contributed. The broadness of his explanation that the stories "may belong to that person's present condition in life, or to some previous condition in life—and not only to himself or herself, but (if necessary) to other persons encountered in life" escapes Dickens, who fails to realize that he could have assigned or excluded categories like criminality to each contributor.

Simultaneously, Dickens develops a much closer collaborative relationship with Wilkie Collins for the same collection, engaging him in conversations that share more detail about the number than other contributors receive and forecasting Collins's role as co-writer of frame stories to come. In the number's final form, Charley (the opening story's "guest") is the only visitor at the Holly-Tree Inn, and the other stories come from the ostler, the boots, the landlord, the barmaid, and a poor pensioner. Collins's "The Ostler" is titled accordingly but is told by the landlord, varying from Dickens's initial plan. Unlucky Isaac Scatchard is the mentally challenged ostler, and when the guest hears him mumbling, the landlord relates his story. Prior to his arrival at the inn, Isaac has a dream that foretells Rebecca Murdoch's seduction and attempted murder of him. After Isaac marries the fallen Rebecca to restore her character, her insulting misbehavior reaches a peak when she tries to attend his mother's funeral in a drunken state. Isaac admits to striking her for the first time on this day, and she later appears with a knife at his bedside. Rebecca flees before inflicting harm, but the police cannot locate her, and now Isaac lives in fear that she will reappear to kill him, which is why he cannot sleep.[30]

For unknown reasons, it seems to have mattered to Dickens that this story, or whatever Collins contributed, come from the ostler: "The Ostler shall be yours, and I think the Sketch involves an extremely good and startling idea. I am not, however, sure but that it trails off in the sudden disappearance of the woman without any result or explanation, and that some such thing may not be wanted for the purpose—unless her never being heard of any more, could be so very strikingly described as to supply the place of other culmination to the story. Will you consider that point again?"[31] This type of collaboration shows Collins and Dickens working together during multiple stages of the creative process, but scholarly attention has focused on Dickens's complaints about the stories that "*don't* fit" over such moments of genuine collaborative conversation and revision. Collins does not appear to have changed the story radically; the creepiness of Rebecca vanishing is what motivates the story to begin with and haunts the ostler. For the story to achieve its effect, she cannot be found, so at a basic plot level, the changes Collins made were probably not fundamental. Still, declarations such as "Whither had she gone? That no mortal tongue could tell him" and "[N]o man could say where the light found her," which exaggerate the drama of the woman's disappearance, may evidence Collins responding to Dickens's request for a more "strikingly described" absence (18).

Surviving letters do not resolve questions about the extent of Collins's revision but do showcase Dickens's representation of his collaborative work in different ways to different people. On December 12, 1855, he adds a post-script after his signature in a letter to E. F. Pigott: "I got Wilkie into the Xmas No. by Sledge Hammer force."[32] On the same day, he writes to Collins,

> I thought your Christmas Story *immensely improved* in the working out. The botheration of that No. has been prodigious. The general matter was so disappointing and so impossible to be fitted together or got into the frame, that after I had done the Guest and the Bill and thought myself free for Little Dorrit again, I had to go back once more (feeling the thing too weak), and do the Boots. Look at said Boots,—because I think its an odd idea, and gets something of the effect of a Fairy Story out of the most unlikely materials.[33]

Asking Collins to revise, then being pleased with the changes, hardly sounds like "Sledge Hammer force," but the dramatization of the process enhances Dickens's pride in his accomplishment. The way Dickens performs his dissatisfaction in the letters exemplifies how he writes and rewrites his editorial persona in a manner that repeats his crafting of an authorial persona. Robert L. Patten reminds us that Dickens uses public prefaces to reshape the stories he tells about his authorship earlier in his career as his level of control over texts and his public identity vacillates.[34] Such shifting performances, both privately and publicly, repeatedly take place throughout Dickens's collaborations as he navigates and depicts the experience. Dickens's letters to Pigott and Collins also highlight his own labor in the collaborative process, and that labor noticeably does not include a simplification of the narrative voices in the number. The mixing of the ostler and the landlord, and the lack of correspondence between the title and the speaker, appears not to have bothered Dickens, as he was in possession of Collins's story by October and did not change its framing.

In future editions of Collins's work, he publishes the story in a narrative frame that requires a character other than Isaac to relate it, indicating that an essential aspect of the story's technique is a lack of direct speech from the protagonist. In *Queen of Hearts* (1859), Collins rewrites the opening frame to make the story come from Brother Morgan, a medical man. The details about the ostler sleeping in the day and mumbling while gesturing in his sleep match the Christmas number. The new aspect Morgan contributes is that if he interviews the ostler, he thinks he might be able to offer a diagnosis, but the landlord remains the teller of the story, which undergoes only small editorial prose changes. A careful reading, then, would not view the framing sections of "The Ostler" in the Christmas number as solely Dickens's, as if there were a clear point where his words stop and Collins's begin. Rather, the passages stand as a combination of Collins's and Dickens's unique collaborative work. Collins's reworking of the framing also reveals a model of collaboration that is flexible enough for parts of a text to appear first under one writer's name and then under another's.[35]

The second interpolated piece, "The Boots," which Dickens wrote to fill space left by unprinted stories that he found unsatisfactory, is among the number's strongest, but Dickens deliberately did not place it first, and the ordering of stories is more complicated than it might seem.[36] In "The Boots," Charley presses Cobbs (the boots of the title, who used to be a gardener for the Walmers family) to share the "curiousest thing he had seen," and Cobbs explains how the eight-year-old Walmers boy suddenly appears at the Holly-Tree Inn in the midst of eloping with Norah, his seven-year-old paramour (18). Acting as a duplicitous confidant, Cobbs distracts the children while others fetch their parents. The elopement of lovers, albeit very young ones, and the finding of shelter at the Holly-Tree Inn link "The Boots" to Charley's experiences in the frame story, creating additional cohesion at the collection's midpoint. The opening frame lists the order of the people the guest will interview, emphasizing each story's placement. Dickens easily could have rearranged the original sequence but chose not to, which may mean that he thought Collins's piece a stronger lead than his own.

The number's careful ordering also creates a back-and-forth weaving pattern wherein every other story connects to a previous one. The collection avoids monotony because two stories in a row never treat the same subject, but thematic resonances between the stories enhance a sense of connectedness. Numbering the stories helps the patterns become traceable:

1. The Guest
2. The Ostler
3. The Boots
4. The Landlord
5. The Barmaid
6. The Poor Pensioner
7. The Bill

The themes of "The Boots" reappear in Procter's "The Barmaid," linking stories 3 and 5. A similar connection emerges between stories 4 and 6: William

Howitt's "The Landlord" and Harriet Parr's "The Poor Pensioner." Additionally, "The Ostler's" unresolved tension surrounding a possible murderess on the loose resurfaces in slightly different form in the ambiguity surrounding a murder in "The Poor Pensioner," drawing story 2 into connection with story 4. The threads between the stories are not the only factors complicating the number's progression. Although "The Ostler" is related by the landlord, "The Ostler" and "The Landlord" are written by two different authors—Collins and Howitt—and Dickens's editorial hand in addition to his prose possibly appearing in some bridging passages adds a third author to the mix of people who have created the landlord's voice. Distinguishing each authorial voice with precision is impossible, and all of those voices flow through Charley, the guest.

The landlord's story introduces a colonial theme to the number, recalling the emphasis of the first number in 1850. When the landlord launches into his second story (the ostler's having been his first), one anticipates hearing about the landlord himself, but his story is about his brother Uriah Tattenhall (22). Discontented with a comfortable life that requires too much labor to break even financially, Uriah moves his family to Australia in search of a "more proportionate result of a whole human existence" (24), and the children prepare for the journey by reading about other colonial travellers in South Africa.[37] Exhibiting the colonial mindset that disregarded the existence of indigenous people and cultures, Uriah sees Australia as an "open plain" and a "new country," but when the Tattenhalls arrive, they are surprised to find that the anticipated easy road to riches is a path of drudgery (24). A tribute to empire building, the rest of the story recounts the Tattenhalls' perseverance and rewards Uriah's risk taking when his land appreciates in value and he builds warehouses that support colonial trade (28).

Before the colonial theme briefly reappears in "The Poor Pensioner," "The Barmaid" returns us to the territory of childhood idylls that characterize "The Boots," and the beginning of the piece reintroduces questions of authorship. Charley, the narrator, maintains narrative consistency by describing the barmaid in his own first-person voice, and the lead-in prose sentences show Dickens using the fictional frame to acknowledge, somewhat awkwardly, that he did not compose the verse itself. The narrator explains, "She told me a tale of that country which went so pleasantly to the music of her voice, that I ought rather to say it turned itself into verse, than was turned into verse by me" (30). This qualification does not go so far as to credit Procter for the poem's aesthetic merit, but by saying that the tale "turned itself into verse," Charley aligns the rhythms and cadence of the piece with a talent not his own. The uncomplicated poem is about Maurice, a stable boy who admires a beautiful woman as she passes by the inn from girlhood to marriage, motherhood, and early death. He never speaks to the lady but pays "boyish, silent homage" and feels "honest sorrow" at her lavish funeral (31). Procter's Maurice shares the pure devotion of Harry Walmers in "The Boots,"[38] and the next story loops back to the ostler's concern with murder.

Parr's and Dickens's narrative voices blend seamlessly despite the confusing provenance of the story related in "The Poor Pensioner." The pensioner, Hester, runs into Charley in the hallway of the inn while muttering to herself as the ostler does. Her odd behavior includes walking outside to thrust snow "into her bosom," and her limited ability to communicate forces Charley to piece this story together from others' accounts; she only repeats, "I am more patient than death. I am more patient than injustice" (31). An impetuous girl, Hester marries at age sixteen then goes to India, where she leads "the life of camps." After returning as a widow to her parents' Yorkshire farm, Hester raises a spoiled and "wild" son, Wilfred, who is convicted of killing his rival in love (32). Hester, now the poor pensioner, loses the farm while paying Wilfred's legal expenses, and the story does not make clear whether he is actually guilty. Colonial adventure in this scenario leads to bad mothering and the opposite of riches, contrasting with the landlord's tale, but the stories share an emphasis on the way colonialism enhances existing strengths or weaknesses of character. Hester indulges inclinations toward wild behavior in India, which makes her an increasingly inept mother, and the story blames her more than Wilfred for his inability to accept rejection. If, however, her belief in his innocence is correct, then an actual murderer roams free in Yorkshire, just as one does at the end of the ostler's tale.

The number's final piece, "The Bill," continues to forge cross-story connections, with coaches speeding into the inn and dramatic shifts in Charley's romance plot that resonate with both "The Boots" and "The Barmaid." As Charley departs, he runs into his cousin Edwin climbing out of a coach on the way to Gretna Green, only Edwin is eloping with Charley's cousin Emmeline, not Charley's fiancée, Angela. The couple has been secretive because Angela's father disapproves of the match, but now Charley can rush back to London and marry Angela, which he does without ever telling anyone about the misunderstanding until the publication of this story. This conclusion also features Dickens blurring the boundary between his narrator and himself while drawing the stories together into a broader imperial project. "The Bill" begins, "I could scarcely believe, when I came to the last word of the foregoing recital and finished it off with a flourish, as I am apt to do when

I make an end of any writing, that I had been snowed up a whole week. The time had hung so lightly on my hands, and the Holly-Tree, so bare at first, had born so many berries for me, that I should have been in great doubt of the fact but for a piece of documentary evidence that lay upon my table" (35). Dickens's large flourish after his signature was well established by 1855, but he had not been trapped by a snowstorm in that or any other year when he visited Yorkshire. Wrapping the number up with his characteristic swoosh, the frame has successfully accounted for its multivocality, and Dickens is confident enough to crack jokes about his role in the collaborative process. The idea of the stories as "berries" brings them into an organically connected whole, growing naturally from a single source but not all on the same branches and not united for the long term in the number's final sentence: "And I say, May the green Holly-Tree flourish, striking its roots deep into our English ground, and having its germinating qualities carried by the birds of Heaven all over the world!" (36). Divinely aided colonialism perhaps loses some of its luster here as the stories become the feces of the heavenly birds that spread the tales. A lack of irony suggests that Dickens may have intended the metaphor as a compliment rather than a slight to the writers, including himself, whose stories become bird droppings.[39]

The thematic resonances between the frame and the inset stories have made the Holly-Tree Inn a place full of symbolic value in the narrator's individual family—whose existence comes about because of a miscommunication resolved there—but also in the broader national vision of mid-nineteenth-century Englishness, which insists on the goodness of English holly trees being spread "all over the world." Although free trade may be taken for granted to a greater extent than in previous issues, the range of characters' colonial experiences draws from the foundation of the first Christmas number while also working through the types of questions raised by "Christmas Day in the Bush" and "Christmas in India." Travel and lodging help organize both The Seven Poor Travellers and The Holly-Tree Inn, and even though the ventriloquizing of The Holly-Tree Inn's narrator is not always smooth, the stories cohere far more successfully than even Dickens thought. Immediately after the release of The Holly-Tree Inn, he writes in a celebratory tone: "Little Dorrit is still going amazingly, and the Xmas No. (published yesterday) seemed to have an enormous sale, thank God."[40] Seeming to sense that he could improve the framing for 1856, Dickens returns to an idea he had earlier put on hold and adjusts his tactics further.

Collaborative Survival and Voices Abroad
(1856–57)

In 1856, for the first time, Dickens asked someone else, Wilkie Collins, to collaborate on the Christmas number's frame story, which turned into a tradition for them. The two men collaborated frequently in the late 1850s as they travelled, enjoyed nights out in London, performed on stage, indulged Dickens's budding affair with Ellen Ternan, and created at least seven joint works in multiple genres. *The Wreck of the Golden Mary*, their first foray into shared narrative framing, takes the Christmas numbers into exciting territory both thematically and structurally. Studying *The Wreck* in its entirety reveals one of the most powerful examples of the polyvocal potential of the Christmas number form and illustrates how profoundly the form can complicate hierarchical models of collaboration. Restoring dialogue between the narrative parts of the original text shows that the interpolated pieces of the middle section are essential to the success of the frame story and exposes the text's exploration of relationships between trauma, memory, and storytelling—relationships that continue to emerge in future Christmas numbers.

After quickly considering the close and fruitful collaborative relationship that leads Collins and Dickens to write *The Lazy Tour of Two Idle Apprentices* and *The Frozen Deep* during the same period they were cowriting Christmas numbers, I argue that their voices in *The Perils of Certain English*

Prisoners (1857) are far more complementary than most scholars have been willing to acknowledge. The number's collaborative engagement with class- and gender-inflected questions of voice and storytelling accompanies a vituperative racism on the part of both authors. The 1856 and 1857 Christmas issues speak directly to questions of empire building and imperial fortune, and collaboration is crucial to the ways in which they engage the foundational ideologies laid out in the first two numbers.

The Wreck of the Golden Mary

The Wreck of the Golden Mary marks the first time that Dickens used the idea of a shared crisis to unite a number's storytellers.[1] The new framing idea had been on Dickens's mind for at least a year, but in September 1855, Dickens explained to Collins that the commencement of *Little Dorrit* did not leave him enough mental energy to develop the thought: "I have postponed the Shipwreck idea for a year, as it seemed to require more force from me than I could well give it with the weight of a new start upon me."[2] Once "the Shipwreck idea" did receive his attention, the tale of a diverse group of individuals left to endure cold, starvation, and each other's inescapable company in two lifeboats stands as one of the most complicated collaborative works Dickens published.

Most critical analyses of *The Wreck* discuss the frame tale of disaster and eventual rescue, written by Dickens and Collins, without remarking on the equally lengthy middle section of the narrative, "The Beguilement in the Boats." Strikingly powerful contributions from Percy Fitzgerald, Harriet Parr, Adelaide Anne Procter, and Reverend James White form "The Beguilement," in which suffering passengers share stories. The act of storytelling purportedly helps to sustain their spirits with the added benefit of warding off cannibalism. Only by paying attention to this section can we fully understand this Christmas number's thematic concerns and the complicated connections that exist between its narrative parts. The text itself resists critical approaches that privilege individual authorship and encourages exploration of plural authorship as multilayered yet cohesive.

The dominant editorial and critical trend has been to fragment *The Wreck*. Ruth F. Glancy's edition of Dickens's Christmas stories collects his stories from all eighteen Christmas numbers in one volume but includes only the frame of *The Wreck*: Dickens's portion, in which Captain Ravender tells of the shipwreck, and Collins's portion, in which the first mate, John Steadiman, describes the passengers suffering at sea then being rescued. To Glancy's credit, adjusting her editorial methodology to include Collins's portion avoids leaving the passengers foundering in the middle of the ocean in lifeboats, which many previous editions do.[3] Victorian critics expressed no more appreciation for "The Beguilement." The Examiner's review noted that, in comparison to the frame narrative (incorrectly attributed solely to Dickens), the interpolated stories "make a comparatively faint impression on the mind," and The Leader's positive review of the following year's Christmas number refers back to the "inferior workmanship" of The Wreck's interpolated tales.[4] That "faint impression," however, points to the lingering and unsettling ambiguities "The Beguilement" stories posit. Even while trying to identify precisely which sentences Dickens wrote, Harry Stone calls The Wreck of the Golden Mary "far and away the best conceived and most cunningly integrated of the Christmas stories written to this date [1856]" and claims, "For the first time, the storytelling interlude grew naturally out of what came before and what went after, and formed a subordinate and yet functional part of the whole."[5] The integration of the stories is indeed key to understanding this number; the subordination of "The Beguilement" section is what needs rethinking.

Viewing "The Beguilement" as expendable stems in part from critical appraisals of this number's narrative structure as a reflection of Dickens's relationship to his contributors. Yet too narrow a focus on Dickens's power as editor/ship captain, with Collins as first mate and the other contributors in the roles of powerless passengers, results in an inaccurate transference of that hierarchical vision to the narrative. Although Anthea Trodd and Lillian Nayder develop contrasting arguments about the level of complicity or resistance that Collins assumes in writing his portion, neither fully considers the significance of the interpolated narratives.[6] Deborah Thomas proposes that Collins's technique in "The Deliverance" elevates suspense over Dickens's concern with character, yet she does not consider the styles of any other contributors.[7]

One reason for this compartmentalization may be the sheer weirdness of "The Beguilement in the Boats": its emotional violence, physical distress, and unsanctioned interactions with the dead are ultimately far more unsettling than the frame story that critics prefer. Fully including "The Beguilement" demonstrates how the interpolated tales, rather than maintaining order in the lifeboats, call that order further into question and advance some of the collection's salient themes. A similar process occurs narratively; the narrative method of the text creates complex interactions between its parts that resist the kind of fragmentation much scholarship has encouraged. Trodd argues that the figure of the British Tar in The Wreck enables Dickens to impose discipline on the potentially threatening experience of collaboration. The Tar may well serve the purpose Trodd notes in that Dickens may have thought the Tar maintained a respected hierarchy through storytelling. Nevertheless, the thrust of the stories does not showcase the maintenance of order but rather illustrates the reverse: discipline will break down, often violently, in upsetting situations. Trodd also remarks that "the stories of the other contributors are presented as examples of how storytelling, the ultimate mark of civilization, enables those involved to resist the inhumanity of cannibalism."[8] Storytelling may sometimes represent the essence of civilization, but the telling of these particular stories points in a markedly divergent direction. Instead of drawing the passengers nearer to comforting institutions, the stories move them toward liminal and threatening spaces where taken-for-granted boundaries, including the ones between life and death, are transgressed.

In addition to Captain Ravender and the first mate, Steadiman, the *Golden Mary* carries an eclectic group. The ship's crew of at least twenty-five seamen includes a carpenter, a "black steward" by the name of Tom Snow who serves at the Captain's table, a young Scottish apprentice, and an armorer (4). The ship's gold rush–bound passengers are Mr. Rarx, an elderly miser figure; Mrs. Atherfield and her three-year-old daughter, Lucy; and Miss Coleshaw, Mrs. Atherfield's widowed friend. When "The Beguilement" begins, the only character positively identified as deceased is little Lucy, who dies quietly in a lifeboat on the eleventh day following the crash of the *Golden Mary* into an iceberg.

Fitzgerald's "The Armourer's Story" launches "The Beguilement" section with the violent tale of "Ding Dong" Will Whichelo, a blacksmith so named for the regularity and strength with which he swings his giant sledgehammer.[9] Whichelo leaves his reliable male companions for the seductive Mary Arthur, who appears to urge him to murder his rival, Mr. Temple. The armorer then discovers Ding Dong Will holding his hammer while standing over Temple's bloodied body.[10] Instead of detaining the blacksmith, the armorer walks away and roams the town all night before concluding, "What end Will Whichelo came to, it would not be hard to guess. But Mary Arthur—she who drove him to it, as everybody knew—she was let away, and went up to London, where she lived to do mischief enough" (18). Is Ding Dong Will lynched? Captured? Does he perish in the hills? All we know is that an angry mob pursues a murderous and strong man. Precisely what "mischief" Mary causes in London and whether she incites more men to murder is also unclear. Part of what makes this conclusion so unsettling is the abrupt appearance of extreme violence in the narrative. A run-of-the-mill love triangle morphs into premeditated, grisly murder in the space of a few paragraphs. Just as suddenly as the brutality appears, the tale ends with no apparent lesson for the desperate passengers apart from the knowledge that some people kill when their desires are frustrated.

Less physically violent than the saga of Ding Dong Will but no less disturbing in its emotional violence is Parr's "Poor Dick's Story," another tale of sexual frustration. Dick falls in love with his cousin Amy, who is engaged to a curate, and pleads so forcefully with Amy to change her mind that she faints repeatedly. After Amy dies of consumption, the family forbids Dick to visit, but he breaks through a window to spend the night with her corpse then disrupts the funeral. After this incident, the family finally "gave it out that he was mad. Perhaps he was" (21). Listeners may sympathize with Dick's broken heart but are also left with the image of a potentially mad, insistently menacing man in the lifeboat. In an attempt at resolution, the tale ends with Steadiman remembering a consoling tune about a patient and merciful God who may spare Dick from hell if he reforms. Dick, however, exhibits no signs of actual or potential change and, contradicting Steadiman's prediction that a fortune made in California will inspire rehabilitation, has hitherto indulged a reckless lifestyle. Furthermore, the fact that Dick has slept with a corpse in another instance is not exactly comforting to a boatload of passengers near death themselves.

A second contribution from Fitzgerald would seem to further agitate the vulnerable passengers, as "The Supercargo's Story" features a vicious pirate. Jan Fagel, supported by a crew that seems to question his murderous tendencies yet respects hierarchy too much to challenge him, kidnaps then drowns the wife and daughter of his nemesis. His ship haunts the seas each Christmas night, and the story ends with the long-dead Captain Fagel visiting the *Golden Mary's* supercargo in what may or may not have been a dream. For when the supercargo wakes, he hears the pirate's crew cry, "Yo, yo! Jan Fagel, yo!" (25). Such a tale increases the atmosphere of terror in the lifeboats as it emphasizes the fearsomeness of a pirate who preys on small boats just like their own: "[M]any a poor disabled craft that was struggling hard to keep herself afloat, would see the black hull of the *Maelstrom* coming down upon her in the storm, and so would perish miserably upon the rocks" (23). Further, the supercargo relates a dream in which he makes it to shore but all of the people he sees there look like corpses with "a curious dried look about their faces, and a sort of stony cast in their eyes" (25). The story's refraction of the passengers in a zombie-like state intensifies fear and worry, and the pervasiveness of the pirate's ghost haunts both the passengers and the narrative of *The Wreck*, implying that the appearance of a ship may portend a more perilous possibility than rescue. The loyalty of Fagel's crew, even when they feel sympathy for his murder victims, also serves as a reminder that nautical hierarchy does not always work for the best. A more pleasant seaman features in the next piece, but the plot of Procter's "The Old Sailor's Story" is no more uplifting. Thirty-six years prior to the wreck of the *Golden Mary*, another wreck results in this sailor's ten-year enslavement. Once liberated, he returns home to find that his wife has married and had a child with his best friend. In a moving tableau, the adults weep, "three broken hearts together," after which the sailor roams the ocean unconsoled for twenty-six years (27). This melancholy verse is unsettling in hinting that even if the *Golden Mary*'s passengers are rescued, their friends and families may be better off without them.

The old sailor's existence as a sort of living dead man brings us to perhaps the most radical way in which "The Beguilement" stories disrupt order in the boats. The passengers are not simply cast as potential victims of ghosts who will haunt them; like the old sailor, they occupy a more liminal space. White's "The Scotch Boy's Story" epitomizes this condition as its central figure and speaker, "delicate" Willy Lindsey, repeatedly moves between the realms of the living and the dead (27). Willy recounts the sad death of his sister, Jean, just before her marriage and her subsequent haunting of the family each year on her birthday. Losing strength quickly, Willy feels the presence of Jean's ghost in the lifeboat: "I felt a touch on my shoulder just now that made me creep as if the hand were ice; and I looked up and saw the same face we had noticed last year; and I feel the clammy fingers yet, and they go downward—downward, chilling me a' the way till my blood seems frozen, and I canna speak" (29). At this crucial juncture, an apparition presents itself to a person in the lifeboats. Willy narrates his own death; the moment at which he "canna speak" suggests that he can no longer breathe and has died. Yet he does continue to speak, explaining that he now haunts his parents with Jean: "Oh mither! Turn your face this way, for ye see I've kept my word; and we're both here. Jean's beside me, and very cold—and we darena come in" (29). That Willy convincingly narrates his haunting of his mother before Steadiman reports his death raises the question of where exactly the boundary between life and death lies. When Willy's mother turns around and sees him, he emits a "joyous scream" and narrates his death once more: "O mither, mither! tak' me to your arms, for I'm chilled wi' the salt water, and naething will make me warm again" (29). Steadiman fixes the time of Willy's physical expiration after this utterance, but something about the event unsettles the first mate.

Oddly, Steadiman feels the need to hide Willy's corpse but never shares his reasoning: "I tightened my hold of poor Willy as he spoke, for he gradually lost his power, and at last lay speechless with his head on my shoulder. I concealed from the rest the sad event that occurred in a few minutes, and kept the body hidden till the darkest part of the night, closely wrapped in my cloak" (29). On that bizarre note, "The Beguilement" stories come to a close. "Poor Dick" in Parr's contribution is called mad for sleeping with Amy's corpse, and Steadiman, while not infatuated with "delicate" Willy, adopts the same intimate posture. That Steadiman spends the night secretly embracing a corpse hardly purges cannibalism from the narrative. We do not know what exactly transpires under the "closely wrapped" cloak, but even absorbing Willy's dwindling body heat to help survive another night on the open sea would constitute a manner of using another's body for self-preservation. Earlier in the narrative, Captain Ravender explains that Lucy's corpse lies on her mother's lap for their thirteenth night in the lifeboats, which prompts Ravender to rewind his narrative abruptly to the fourth day in the boats when he ruminates upon "the instances in which human beings in the last distress have fed upon each other" (9). Ravender then decides to raise the subject directly with the passengers, offering storytelling as an effective antidote to cannibalism. Steadiman's secret overnight embrace of Willy's dead body so much later in the narrative at least raises questions about whether Ravender's antidote worked. Restoring order and championing "civilized" values may motivate the passengers to tell tales, but the act of storytelling leaves the section more alarming than beguiling.

Willy's unaccounted-for corpse troubles the number's resolution, especially because Willy is not unique in his occupation of a liminal space between life and death. Early in the account of the wreck, Captain Ravender calls attention to the already ghostlike state of the passengers as "spectres" with lively imaginations (9), a description echoed when the supercargo encounters "stiff" living-dead people in his dream (25). Later, in "The Deliverance," Steadiman recalls that "the waves and the wind hissed and howled about us, as if we were tossing in the midst of them, a boatload of corpses already!" (33). There may indeed be actual corpses bouncing around in the boat, in part because it is unclear whether Steadiman ever throws Willy overboard and exactly how long it takes him to disclose Willy's death. Furthermore, throughout the story, Captain Ravender lies beneath the other passengers "like a dead man" (30). The storytelling only lends further ambiguity to the question of exactly how dead the passengers, and their captain, are. As Ravender concludes his narrative, he relates his near death and haunting with language strikingly similar to Willy's. Ravender sees the ghost of the dead little girl, "the Golden Lucy," hovering above the boat, and his fiancée's apparition joins him inside the boat. Finally, he is too weak to write down his last words and loses consciousness: "When it had come to that, her hands—though she was dead so long—laid me down gently in the bottom of the boat, and she and the Golden Lucy swung me to sleep" (10). With this image of the Captain looming, the crossings between life and death in "The Beguilement" stories help to reveal and stress the uncertainty surrounding life and death in the frame. "The Deliverance" reports that the corpse-like Captain Ravender survives but is "the longest to linger between life and death" (35). In the complete number, then, the possibility that Willy and some of the other casualties might have been savable remains troubling. Considered together in relationship to *The Wreck* as a whole, "The Beguilement" stories heighten anxiety and tension at the very moments when starvation and desperation challenge the passengers most. The threats of violence and looming chaos radiate from the center of the number outward.

Given the thematic links between stories and their function in the plot of the shipwreck tale, it is somewhat surprising that critics have taken the existence of distinct narrative voices for granted. Stone states that the final paragraph of the first section "is probably by Dickens" even though it appears after a heading that states, "All that follows, was written by John Steadiman, Chief Mate," Collins's designated narrator.[11] Stone believes that Dickens wrote most of the connecting sections but checks even that claim: "Collins may have written some of the introductory paragraphs in 'Poor Dick's Story' and 'The Scotch Boy's Story,' linking the storytellers with the framework, but the rest of the material is almost certainly by Dickens."[12] Ultimately, determining exactly who wrote each linking word is impossible, and the narrative of *The Wreck* confuses notions of authorship and voice to such an extent that attempts to disentangle the collaborative threads push against the thrust of the text itself.

Consider the figure of John Steadiman. Usually regarded as a stable narrator that Dickens and Collins have well in hand as they share control of the boats as well as the narrative, Steadiman emerges as a conglomeration of each contributor's vision. One of the most surprising aspects of the narrative is that "The Beguilement" section casts Steadiman in a role so complicated that it succeeds in unsettling one of the strongest characters from the frame. The subtitle of *The Wreck*, "Being the Captain's Account of the Loss of the Ship, and the Mate's Account of the Great Deliverance of Her People in an Open Boat at Sea," indicates how constant Steadiman's presence will be. Although the full title initially seems to exclude the middle section, its terminology lays out the narrative sequence. Steadiman sometimes allows the voices of others to take center stage, but "The Beguilement" is narrated entirely by him. The voices of the passengers who tell the stories in the boats are recalled and edited by Steadiman;[13] he therefore narrates not only the "Deliverance" of the passengers but also their harrowing days in the lifeboats.

A sustained blending of several Steadimans recurs throughout the number, and that polyvocality is yoked to the collection's development of the thematic complexities discussed above. A few pages before the end of "The Wreck" section, Steadiman introduces "The Beguilement in the Boats": "I will stop a little here, for the purpose of adding some pages of writing to the present narrative, without which it would not be, in my humble estimation, complete" (13). Here, the text directly states that without the collaborative conversation of the interpolated pieces, the narrative is not "complete." A horizontal line next appears, followed by the start of the first story, "I come from Ashbrooke," which seems to mean that Steadiman is not speaking. Then follows, "(It was the Armourer who spun this yarn)," which suggests that Steadiman is indeed speaking (13). No quotation marks distinguish the armorer's voice from Steadiman's, and the parenthetical comment establishes that Steadiman continues to narrate. The armorer's "I," then, is spoken not by the armorer but by Steadiman, blending the voice of Collins's narrator with Fitzgerald's narrator. The absence of individual story titles in the text enhances this blending, and the bridging passages return us not to the voice of Dickens's narrator, who lies unconscious on the floor of one of the boats, but to Steadiman, who sometimes shares updates on the condition of the surviving passengers before launching into the next story.

The narrative voices of the stories do not always distinctly differ from Steadiman's voice in the frame, and this conflation again points to the futility of trying to separate each thread of collaboration as the narrative insists upon multilayered vocality. Steadiman, for instance, narrates Parr's "Poor Dick's Story" in the third person, marking off Dick's voice with quotations. He not only recounts Dick's backstory and his reasons for joining the voyage but also paraphrases the story of Dick's heartbreak. At this point, there are at least three Steadimans in *The Wreck*—Dickens's, Collins's, and Parr's—all merging fairly easily. Steadiman narrates the story's major events and passes judgment on the happenings, condemning the harassed Amy:

"I doubt very much myself whether Amy was worth such a sacrifice" (21). Because the "I" statement occurs in Parr's story, which is related by Collins's narrator, the question of who controls Steadiman's "I" is unanswered, and Dickens "conducts" the entire number. Determining whether the judgment of Parr's Steadiman differs from Collins's or anyone else's is impossible. A similar conflation occurs in Fitzgerald's "The Supercargo's Story," in which no quotation marks set off the supercargo's voice. The first-person narrator simply shifts from Collins's Steadiman to Fitzgerald's supercargo speaking via Steadiman, or, if one thinks that Dickens wrote the linking passage, the "I" voice shifts from Dickens's Steadiman to Fitzgerald's supercargo. Sometimes the rapid changes obscure how many narrative layers the text has traversed, and sometimes the jarring changes require one to reread a paragraph to determine who is speaking. Again, rather than functioning as a mark of narrative sloppiness, such a pause brings readers closer to the experience of the passengers in the lifeboats, who may also lose track of which voyager is speaking during the hours of traumatized storytelling. Alongside these shifts, one might expect to find aesthetically disruptive tonal changes, but the text is free from abrupt alterations in Steadiman's language that would put readers on edge: regardless of who controls Steadiman's voice, his character stays intact. In lieu of isolating Dickens's Steadiman, Collins's Steadiman, Parr's Steadiman, and so forth, exploring the notion of several overlapping Steadimans enhances one's reading of *The Wreck* as a whole. The collaborative narration works to emphasize the narrative's thematic point about the shared crisis of surviving in lifeboats with stories as a precious resource, and the interpolated tales enable the collaborative whole to function.[14]

The Wreck of the Golden Mary makes clear, perhaps more intensely than any other Christmas number, that the narrative and thematic particularities of each number need to be studied with respect for the integrity of the complete text in order to be understood most comprehensively. Having reevaluated Dickens's collaboration in this way, which his conducting metaphor encourages, one is able to approach the text under consideration on terms more closely resembling its own. For 1856, the metaphor is a wreck that nevertheless ends up looking, and sounding, remarkably whole. Moving into 1857, Dickens's collaborative work deepens as he works repeatedly with Wilkie Collins in a range of genres. A quick examination of that burst of collaborative production provides important context for the 1857 Christmas number, the first for which Dickens collaborates with only one other writer.

Pairing Voices: Charles and Wilkie

The intense collaborative relationship shared by Wilkie Collins and Charles Dickens was predominantly positive in nature and unique in each man's life. The friendship began in a collaborative context in 1851 when Augustus Egg proposed that Dickens cast Collins in one of his amateur theatrical productions, and in October 1856, Dickens invited Collins to become a regular staff writer for *Household Words*, which increased Collins's financial stability. When Collins accepted Dickens's request to join the staff, he added a special condition: that when his novel *The Dead Secret* appeared serially, it would include a byline. From January to June 1857, for the first time, a name other than Dickens appears as a credited author in *Household Words*. Although the lack of bylines for other writers is not always exploitative or demeaning, the Collins byline stands out as a distinction. It simultaneously separates and merges Collins's and Dickens's voices, signaling that they are at the same level and that Collins's name is partly representational of *Household Words'* voice.

In addition to their professional bond, Collins and Dickens found sustenance in their friendship throughout the 1850s as they faced domestic changes. Dickens had purchased Gad's Hill Place, a house in Kent he had admired since childhood, from Eliza Lynn, who wrote frequently for *Household Words*.[15] Just as domestic life might have begun to settle down following the house move in late May 1857, Charles's collaborative work led him to meet and fall in love with Ellen Ternan, which triggered the end of his twenty-year marriage.[16] During this same period, Wilkie was falling in love with the widowed Caroline Graves, acting as a father to her young daughter, and sharing a home with her by the end of 1858.[17] At many of the pivotal moments in these relationships, Collins and Dickens were writing together.

As *The Wreck of the Golden Mary* was coming together in 1856, Collins and Dickens produced a stage play, *The Frozen Deep*, which would unite them in personal and professional collaboration well into 1857. The men began conversing about the plot in the spring of 1856 and worked on it again in the autumn as they travelled in France. The collaboration was multifaceted as they formulated a scenario in which a vengeful lover encounters his rival in the Arctic only to save his life rather than kill him. After Dickens articulated the original concept, the two discussed it to develop a play that included Collins's thoughts. Collins wrote a script that Dickens helped to tweak, and the two corresponded regularly about revisions before splitting the leading roles in performance.[18] Dickens consistently respected Collins as a more experienced playwright and consulted him even about staging details. After receiving some feedback from John Forster, Dickens writes to Collins, "Stanfield wants to cancel the chair altogether, and to substitute a piece of rock on the ground, composing with the Cavern. That, I take it, is clearly an improvement. He has a happy idea of painting the ship which is to take them back ... Will you dine with us at 5 on Monday before Rehearsal. We can then talk over Forster's points?"[19] Dickens's tone demonstrates that he was reluctant to impose his own artistic vision upon Collins without discussion. Another letter requests: "I should like to shew [sic] you some cuts I have made in the second act (subject to Authorial sanction of course)."[20] And Dickens identifies Collins as the sole author in the playbill, which presents Tavistock House Theatre "Under the Management of Charles Dickens" and calls The Frozen Deep a "Romantic Drama, in Three Acts, by Mr Wilkie Collins." Here, then, Dickens's public advertisement of the men's joint work delineates individuated responsibilities, which one could read as a diminishment of the collaborative spirit that permeates the production or as insurance that Collins will receive ample credit for his portion of the creative process.

One spots creative cross-fertilization in Collins's and Dickens's individual publications before, during, and after this period. Various combinations of self-sacrifice (especially in the name of romantic love), doubled identities, and the French Revolution cycle through several of their works, including Collins's "The Lady of Glenwith Grange" and "Sister Rose" and Dickens's A Tale of Two Cities.[21] As their friendship matured, such interlinked imaginative productions persisted. The Frozen Deep was so successful that Queen Victoria commissioned a private performance after which she sent enthusiastic compliments, especially to Collins,[22] and in August, the men resumed their roles to stage benefit performances for the family of their deceased friend, playwright Douglass Jerrold. Those Manchester shows included the replacement of Dickens's female relatives by professional actresses and brought Ellen Ternan into Dickens's life, which led to yet another collaboration.

Just a month after producing the Frozen Deep in Manchester, Collins and Dickens took another trip northward, presumably for Dickens to see his recent inamorata, Ternan, who was in the area, and also to collect inspirations for their next collaboration: The Lazy Tour of Two Idle Apprentices. Appearing in five October issues of Household Words and inspired by William Hogarth's series of engravings Industry and Idleness (1747), The Lazy Tour is full of self-deprecation and good-humored jesting.[23] In it, Charles and Wilkie have created fictional alter egos who, as apprentices of Lady

Literature, attempt to enjoy a holiday. The men crack jokes about themselves as Francis Goodchild (the Dickens figure) struggles to be idle while Thomas Idle (the Collins figure) does not understand why they ever have to do anything. Idle declares, "Let us eat Bride-cake without the trouble of being married, or of knowing anybody in that ridiculous dilemma" while Dickens was in the midst of trying to figure out how to separate from his wife, and Goodchild helps a hobbled Idle down Carrock Fell, pointing to Collins's sprained ankle while at that site and regular pain from persistent gout.[24] Lightheartedly fictionalizing their relationship as they wove together a short collection of stories, the men were clearly in sync personally as well as creatively. Writing together was a core element of the friendship that carried them through domestic and personal upheaval.

Dickens's surviving letters to Collins from earlier in 1857 indicate that the friends were indulging in what sound like scandalous adventures together. Charles tells Wilkie as they plan a night out, "Any mad proposal you please, will find a wildly insane response."[25] Congratulating Wilkie on finishing The Dead Secret, Charles offers himself as a celebratory companion: "[O]n Wednesday, if the mind can devise any thing sufficiently in the style of Sybarite Rome in the days of its culminating voluptuousness, I am your man."[26] And after setting a time to meet, Charles casts himself as the gatekeeper of Wilkie's debauchery: "If you can think of any tremendous way of passing the night, in the meantime—do. I don't care what it is. I give (for that night only) restraint to the Winds!"[27] How Dickens may have imposed restraint on other nights remains a mystery, but given such a close personal bond and Collins's post as a paid staff writer, it is not surprising that the two would collaborate again on that year's Christmas collection, this time composing it without any other writers. Reading the number in light of Collins's and Dickens's frequent creative contact and tight friendship enables one to recognize the context from which it emerges as far more collegial than contentious.

The Perils of Certain English Prisoners

Similar to the way the exclusion of collaboration from a reading of The Wreck of the Golden Mary prevents understanding of how the atmosphere in the lifeboats affects the frame story, for The Perils of Certain English Prisoners, and Their Treasure in Women, Children, Silver and Jewels, a focus on attribution or authorial competition inhibits an integrated understanding of the number. The Perils is the most deeply collaborative of the numbers to date, and it is also the most unapologetically racist in its characterization of a villain. Exploring the relationship between discourses of race and collaboration opens up a view of how centrally this number is concerned with class and gender as they pertain to storytelling. *The Perils* contains three chapters: "The Island of Silver-Store," "The Prison in the Woods," and "The Rafts on the River." The first and third chapters are the ones for which Dickens identifies himself as primary author, attributing the second chapter mainly to Collins.[28] The English prisoners are marine private Gill Davis, some other soldiers, and the colonial residents of an island off the Mosquito Coast in Central America. The island houses silver mined from the mainland that Davis arrives to help protect. With the help of a mixed-race "Sambo" character who appears to be of African and Native American descent and whose allegiance to the English is temporary, pirates outsmart the colonizers, abscond with chests of silver, and take the survivors hostage (2). A grandiloquent, guitar-playing pirate captain (complete with lace ruffles) takes the captives to the mainland, marches them through a forest, and forces them to refurbish an ancient palace in ruins. While cutting down trees, the hostages devise a scheme to make rafts out of the lumber and escape in the dead of night after drugging the guards. Through these trials, Davis falls in love with Marion Maryon, a genteel woman he protects and who protects him when she reveals a surprising facility to wield broadswords and muskets. He weeps over the fact that social class disparity prevents him from trying to marry her, and when they part, she gives him a ring to honor his bravery; she later marries a captain who helps rescue them.

Davis narrates the story in his own first-person voice, but he cannot read or write, and the retrospective narrative is what Davis dictates decades later to Marion Maryon (now Lady Carton). Davis's stated intent "to express for my lady to write down, exactly what I felt then and there" acknowledges the filters through which his story passes, but he insists that the text will still capture his sentiments "exactly" (7). This framework creates intersections between textuality, gender, class, authorship, narrative, and voice that are predicated on Davis's and Maryon's subject positions as privileged white colonial actors. Critical attention to race and colonialism, however, has neglected the story's other dynamics, and a narrow focus on hierarchy in collaboration has blinded critics to the ways in which this jointly written story expresses deep anxiety about the ability of white subjects in violent colonial contexts to tell their own stories at all.

The Perils constituted a response to the Indian Rebellion, which began on May 10, 1857, after numerous factors led to violent agitation for independence. One trigger for this incident concerned the greasing of ammunition cartridges with pig and cow fats because an Indian soldier opening a cartridge with his teeth was forced to violate orthodox Muslim or Hindu beliefs. The British public was outraged to learn that some women and children were killed in the insurrection, and British military forces spent the next year reestablishing power at all costs, sometimes slaughtering entire villages.[29] Dickens's reaction, possibly fueled by concern for his son Walter, who had departed in July for military service in India, matched the hyperbolically fierce tones of much of the rest of the British citizenry. In a letter to Angela Burdett Coutts, after stating that the unfair promotion of commissioned officers over noncommissioned ones makes him feel "Demoniacal," Dickens continues,

> And I wish I were Commander in Chief in India. The first thing I would do to strike that Oriental race with amazement (not in the least regarding them as if they lived in the Strand, London, or at Camden Town), should be to proclaim to them, in their language, that I considered my holding that appointment by the leave of God, to mean that I should do my utmost to exterminate the Race upon whom the stain of the late cruelties rested; and that I begged them to do me the favor to observe that I was there for that purpose and no other, and was now proceeding, with all convenient dispatch and merciful swiftness of execution, to blot it out of mankind and raze it off the face of the Earth.[30]

Pondering the complexities of just this paragraph—including questions of translation, space, and religion—many admirers of Dickens have struggled to reconcile such sentiments with images of him as a benevolent reformer. Although Dickens fantasizes about commanding a sort of divinely sanctioned genocide in this letter, the story of The Perils does not enact retributive violence on a massive scale. Nor does it take place in India, as Dickens and Collins inserted several screens between themselves, their fiction, and events in India.

Those filters mandate that readers draw upon their own cultural experiences to fill interpretive gaps and identify social critique to a greater degree than a story set in India might require. Dickens is comfortable with some interpretive ambiguity, almost as if he creates the scaffold for a possible defense in advance of the number's publication should he need to plausibly deny its commentary on India. Indeed, one review immediately names multiple symbolic counterparts, calling the number "less a festive tribute to the season than a celebration of the great qualities displayed by our race in recent emergencies, Crimean and Indian."[31] Likening both the Crimea and India to Central America, the reviewer highlights the broad scope of the number's possible message. Still, Dickens valued accurate details and drew on Henry Morley's expertise to be sure that setting the story in what he calls South America will be historically precise enough to avoid censure.[32] Michael Hollington points out that Dickens had long indulged an interest in Latin America in the pages of Household Words and that its significance to the gold rush makes it a fitting locale for a story treating colonial themes. Hollington also shows that the description of the Mayan ruins echoes Wills's "A Mysterious City," published in Household Words in 1851.[33] This astute observation draws a line from the chapter that Collins primarily crafted to Wills, who always acted as coeditor but does not appear in the Office Book as a contributor to this number. Webs of periodical collaboration continue to encompass figures beyond Dickens and also stretch across years.

Confronting a text infused with racism, many critics have attempted to identify tensions or shifts in the story that might explain which collaborator is more responsible for offensive material. Lillian Nayder says of Dickens, "His two chapters are characterized by a series of displacements that enable the narrator, an illiterate private in the Royal Marines, to abandon his feelings of class hatred and to recognize his *real* enemies—his racial 'inferiors' rather than his social superiors." In contrast, she sees Collins "in his chapter of the story . . . associating the privates and sailors with native laborers, and criticizing imperial practices instead of defending them."[34] Laura Peters acknowledges coauthorship but examines only two chapters to consider "how Dickens narrativized the events of the [Indian] Rebellion in his section of the short story."[35] Patrick Brantlinger identifies The Perils as "the earliest work of fiction to deal with the Mutiny" but, despite mentioning Collins as coauthor, uses the text to discuss only Dickens's thoughts on the rebellion.[36] Grace Moore argues for a nuanced analysis of Dickens's attitudes in relation to imperial topics and references several pieces from the regular issues of Household Words that are attributed to others, seeming to accept the journal's assertion that the voices of contributors merge with the voice of its conductor. When addressing The Perils, however, Moore reverses course and isolates Collins's chapter as revisionary of Dickens's section while treating Dickens's portions as if they are solely his.[37] These (and many other) analyses differ on minor points but uniformly decline to treat the text as an integrated whole. Garrett Zeigler, for instance, persuasively illustrates that the effeminate pirate captain and his crew, marching the group through the forest in chapter

2, pose a threat of sodomy that parallels a rape threat to the Englishwomen in the first chapter. Then, because the argument presumes that Collins's and Dickens's sections of text must be in tension, Zeigler contends that in Collins's portion, "terror is ejected and peaceful and unifying emotions flow together as the captives and pirates enter the lost city of a past empire."[38] It is difficult to agree that peace and unity characterize the text when the hostages feel constantly threatened and plot escape ceaselessly; likewise, Ziegler's view that the sexual threat to women is "replaced and negated" by a fear of the homosexual that is made farcical does not account for the Englishmen's persistent anxiety and need to sleep in a protective position at the border of the women's space, using their bodies as barriers between the Englishwomen and racialized men.[39] To compound the heterosexual rape threat with a threat of homosexual rape makes the episode in the woods doubly, not less, terrifying.

I do not disagree that Collins's chapter slightly decreases the intensity of the number's rage at Christian George King (the "Sambo" villain) or that chapter 2 increases the number's comic tone. We cannot, however, take those differences to mean that the writers were necessarily opposing each other. The examples above point to the need for a deeper understanding of collaboration because they do not consider that Collins and Dickens might have conferred about the differences between sections and agreed that variations in emphasis could benefit the number as a whole. As Holly Laird notes, "Collaborative authorship has suffered from the skepticism of modern readers and scholars, who equate literary expression with single authorship . . . and who thus try to separate the contributions of one author from another even when collaboration is undeniable."[40] That Collins and Dickens may have strategically accommodated both of their visions into the story of *The Perils* to achieve the greatest combined effect is an interpretive option that most scholars have ignored along with the possibility that each writer may have provided cover for the other's racism. As Seth Whidden observes, one "great advantage is that of the protection in risk-taking; participation in a collective work minimizes each contributor's personal risk, offering each the possibility, if necessary, of blaming the other for anything that might be offensive or interpreted as such."[41] Both Collins and Dickens would be well aware of the potential to deflect critics by blaming the other, even if they chose not to do so. When one accepts collaboration as such rather than basing readings on its dismantling, and when one recognizes racism as part of this text's collaborative fabric, the Christmas number begins to resonate in new ways.

The racism of *The Perils* is fairly straightforward and unwavering in all of its chapters. Captain Carton repeats phrasing from two of Dickens's vituperative letters nearly verbatim when he says, "Believing that, I hold my commission by the allowance of God, and not that I have received it direct from the Devil, I shall certainly use it, with all avoidance of unnecessary suffering and with all merciful swiftness of execution, to exterminate these [pirates] from the face of the earth" (8).[42] We do not know if Collins objected to that bit of text, and Collins was no stranger to racist character portrayals himself. Those wishing to identify Collins as an opponent of Dickens's racism ignore the fact that the only appearances of the most offensive word, "nigger," appear in chapter 2, for which he is identified as the primary author. That section also includes an intensely racist image of the pirate captain not only using a black man's back for a writing table but also complaining that such a position places the man's sweating body too "close under my nose" (14). The fact that this episode is part of a comic portrait of the pirate with no consideration of the black man's subjectivity only adds to its offense. Collins's opinions about the rebellion do seem less extreme than Dickens's in that we do not have any record of Collins wishing to "exterminate" a people, and Collins's oeuvre includes sympathetic representations of mixed-race characters.[43] Nevertheless, a robust assertion of Englishness as a national and moral identity pervades this number, with "others" set in stark contrast to an exaggerated, emphatically white English purity.

There is no avoiding the hatred that is targeted specifically at dark bodies in this story, including the Portuguese Pirate Captain, whose "brown fingers" and other features make him a "man-monkey" (14). The number reiterates that threats to the most cherished English ideals are spearheaded by corrupt people of color who might not even be full people. Even the English-identified convicts under the command of the Pirate Captain seem to have been tainted more by "the West India Islands" than by their criminality, for they are singled out as the crew members who should have been murdering rather than obeying the Pirate Captain (12). Dickens and Collins conversed frequently enough for readers to conclude that the men concurred on the acceptability of these demeaning portraits as part of the agreed-upon tone and direction of the number. A Sotheby's catalog from 1890 for the sale of *The Perils* manuscript includes "the original sketch for the story, consisting of 4 pages, 8vo, by Wilkie Collins, and a long note by Dickens" and further describes "a long letter from Collins to Dickens . . . discussing the Title and also giving many particulars of the proposed plot."[44] These documents do not appear to have survived with the other Collins manuscripts sold in the auction lot, but the catalogue description, if accurate, further attests to both Collins and Dickens acting as engaged collaborators.

In the spectrum of creative possibilities that surround the genesis of *The Perils*, collaborative dynamics may also rest upon friendly competition. Hollington helpfully moves critical focus away from discourses that relentlessly cast Collins and Dickens as opponents by claiming that a "radical separation of the two authors cannot be sustained" and calling for critical "rereading in a manner that more carefully avoids the simplistic binarism of some post-colonial approaches to the story, and does greater justice to its complexities."[45] Persuasively attributing the racist moments in the story to its "comic first person narrative persona," Hollington sees the collaborative text as an amiable joust, with Davis evidencing "not two writers at odds with each other ideologically but vying with each other as satirists to make his expressions of prejudice as comically exaggerated as possible."[46] Hollington regards Davis as "a study of psychological edge and twitchiness issuing forth in racial prejudice to merit attention in terms of conscious artistic purpose, not just as an unconscious vehicle of Dickens's own ideological position."[47] Racism, then, is a built-in aspect of the collaboration and of the protagonist's character rather than an element that one can separate from the number's other traits. Davis's humility and interior frustration, along with his racism, are at the core of the number's success, and those character traits are co-drawn by both Collins and Dickens.[48]

The character of Gill Davis himself questions the feasibility of trying to narrate colonial violence through the screens created by class, gender, race, and desire. Told retrospectively, with Davis dictating to "my lady," his complete adoration of Marion Maryon throughout the story is as captivating as the adventure narrative (1). When Gill meets Marion (an officer's daughter) for the first time, he thinks, "Ah! *you* have got a lover, I'll be bound!" (3). Appreciating her beauty, Gill is cross with the imagined lover he assumes she has, ashamed of his own illiteracy, and continuously impressed with her kind treatment of the soldiers. Gill knows that Marion is out of his reach and feels the pain of romantic disappointment intensely after they walk arm in arm on a pleasant evening: "I laid myself down on my face on the beach, and cried, for the first time since I had frightened birds as a boy at Snorridge Bottom, to think what a poor, ignorant, low-placed, private soldier I was" (9). Marion asks Gill to kill her rather than allow the pirates to take her away alive, and Gill makes the promise only after declaring that he is more likely to die trying to defend her. Marion seals the deal by kissing his "rough, coarse hand," which gives him "the strength of half a dozen men" (10). Throughout the crisis, Gill and Marion are a team as she hands him bayonets, assists in keeping the children and other hostages in strong spirits, and eventually helps mastermind the escape plan. It is not only their unity against the racialized pirate crew that enables Gill and Marion to transcend the gulf of class difference but also their joint attempt to tell the tale.

References to the reunion of Gill and Marion and to the filtering of the story through her hand pervade the number. Gill declares his love in the present moment directly to Marion (now Lady Carton), and although Gill has resided in distant lands for years while in the marines, his love has still affected her: "It was my Lady Carton who herself sought me out, over a great many miles of the wide world, and found me in Hospital wounded, and brought me here" (36). The lasting nature of Marion's interest suggests that she returns Gill's love in some form. Whether she has been monitoring his movements over the decades and receives news that he is wounded or whether a spontaneous need to reunite motivates her, as a grandmother, Marion again faces physically harrowing travel "over a great many miles of the wide world" to retrieve him and his story. The number's first page depicts Marion's transcription, and the details of that description act as evidence of her faithfulness to Gill's speech: "My lady stops me again, before I go any further, by laughing exactly in her old way and waving the feather of her pen at me" (1). Such statements unite Gill's words and Marion's pen with the final text testifying to the success of their collaborative project, and the self-consciousness of the story's initial presentation serves to establish trust and credibility. Gill digresses as he stares at "her hand with the rings on it," plunging into a reverie of the time when they first meet (and when Marion gives Gill a ring). His request that she omit this digression allows him to relate their agreement: "She won't scratch it out, and quite honorable; because we have made an understanding that everything is to be taken down, and that nothing that is once taken down shall be scratched out. I have the great misfortune not to be able to read and write, and I am speaking my true and faithful account of those Adventures, and my lady is writing it, word for word" (1). At the halfway point, just before the escape, Gill reminds readers that he is not the story's actual writer by referencing a detail that he has "formerly given . . . out, for my Lady to take in writing" (26). Thus, the telling of the colonial adventure is also an exploration of the relationship between storyteller and writer, between man and woman, which merits further attention in light of collaboration.

Collins and Dickens simultaneously occupy the positions of male writers, the woman writer who is the story's scribe, and the illiterate elderly man who speaks the story. Inhabiting these roles, both Collins and Dickens comfortably leave the position of individual writer and agent, and the text asks quietly what turns a writer into an author and whether the storyteller who cannot write may also be regarded as an author.[49] Collins and Dickens are, of course, two highly literate men, but their desire is to voice an opinion about a set of events (the Indian Rebellion) in which they have no direct part. On top of not participating in the military action, they had no acquaintance with anyone who witnessed it firsthand. Although Dickens's son Walter went to India as a cadet while the British were continuing to try to reestablish control, for accounts of the violent events of the insurrection, both Dickens and Collins were forced to base their ideas on other people's accounts. The narrative device they create in *The Perils* routes their voices through someone who is unable to present his voice in print, who experiences a kind of narrative impotence that parallels his social inability to wed Marion Maryon. Wayne Koestenbaum views these types of collaborative productions from male pairs as metaphorically and inescapably sexual, positing that "the text they balance between them is alternately the child of their sexual union, and a shared woman."[50] In the case of *The Perils*, Collins and Dickens must rely on their narrator in the same way that he relies on Lady Carton, ironically unable to consummate a shared desire for a woman yet dependent on her writing. Perhaps there is an admission here, from both Collins and Dickens, that they are incapable themselves of creating a credible narrative voice for the Indian Rebellion.

The character acting as an illiterate proxy for Collins and Dickens is also full of emotional pain. Davis's blunt personality enables the humor of the number and its poignant conclusion, which Dickens describes as having affected him keenly. In a dramatic letter to Lady Duff Gordon, Dickens explains that overwhelming sentiment kept him from being able to face the proof pages until the very last moment: "It was only when the Steam Engine roared for the sheets, that I could find it in my heart to look at them with a pen in my hand dipped in any thing but tears!"[51] Davis accepts his fate as a person whose orphanhood keeps him from feeling firmly connected to England as a home place and whose lack of learning inhibits his military promotion, but he also stresses that his recognition of the class differences preventing him from marrying Marion does nothing to diminish his pain: "[T]he suffering to me was just as great as if I had been a gentleman. I suffered agony—agony. I suffered hard, and I suffered long" (36).[52] Collins and Dickens narrate the number through a series of defeats: Davis fights valiantly with Marion against the pirates, but they lose the battle; the forest escape involves passive poisoning in which Marion plays a larger role than Davis does; it is Captain Carton rather than Davis who finally shoots George Christian King; despite encouragement from officers, Davis is unable to educate himself enough to rise in rank; and the sting of heartbreak never diminishes. Davis's life after the adventure with Marion holds little joy, and recapturing some happiness is possible only through storytelling about white English people coming together to fight a racialized colonial threat. The number thus joins the racial ideologies of colonial adventure stories to the collaborative relationships that result in printed stories.

Without headings to designate primary authorship for each chapter, it is easy to hear a blended authorial voice in *The Perils*. The narrative voice does not shift radically for the middle section, nor does the tone or style vary so profoundly as to cause confusion. The pacing of the second chapter is rapid, consistent with many of Collins's novels, but the suspenseful events of that portion also coincide with the moments when readers would expect to find the plot's climax. The themes that one encounters—innocent children, cross-class romantic desire, imperial violence, heroic women, inventive escapes—arise in future works by both Collins and Dickens. Captain Carton's name famously reappears in Dickens's *A Tale of Two Cities* (1859), and the heroine of Collins's phenomenally popular *The Woman in White* (1859–60) is another Marian. Dickens's *Great Expectations* (1860–61) features a working-class man pining for a woman who has been raised to regard herself as his social superior, and in *The Moonstone* (1868), Collins questions the moral soundness of British imperial wealth acquired in India. Moore argues that Dickens returns to *The Perils* in *A Tale of Two Cities* to produce a novelistic "reworking of his initial narrative of the rebellion that seeks to revise his original stance."[53] His joint work with Collins on *The Perils* must remain a part of the reenvisioning Moore locates in the novel, and the conversation about race, violence, and power that courses through their individual works benefits from being understood as just that, a conversation, rather than a monolithic, single-authored set of views.

We will never know precisely how much, or in which ways, the social time Collins and Dickens shared, or the personal jokes they enjoyed as confidants, influenced each writer's individual publications, but their frequent collaborations and the apparent cross-pollination of themes in their works display persistent creative overlap. Surveying a later period of Dickens's journalistic career and noting the high level of creative exchange between major figures, John Sutherland makes a similar point: "It is certain that there was much more verbal give and take which we shall never know about."[54]

When Collins faced a health crisis, Dickens's representation of their relationship highlighted the frequent and thorough commingling of their voices over time. Collins's painful rheumatic gout worsened in 1862 and threatened his ability to complete the final volume of *No Name*, which was appearing in *All the Year Round* and *Harper's Weekly*. Collins had solicited feedback from Dickens on the *No Name* manuscript, variously taking and ignoring his advice, and when Collins worried that he would have to stop writing, Dickens volunteered to step in.

Writing to "My Dear Wilkie," Dickens first establishes common ground by recalling the anxiety he felt when illness interfered with his writing of *Bleak House*. Wishing to spare Collins such fear, Dickens offers to shorten his trip to Paris then states,

> I am quite confident that, with your notes, and a few words of explanation, I could take it up at any time and do it. Absurdly unnecessary to say that it would be a makeshift! But I could do it, at a pinch, so like you as that no one should find out the difference. Don't make much of this offer in your mind; it is nothing except to ease it. If you should want help, I am as safe as the bank. The trouble will be nothing to me, and the triumph of overcoming a difficulty great. Think it a Christmas Number, an Idle Apprentice, a Lighthouse, a Frozen Deep. I am as ready as in any of these cases to strike in and hammer the iron out.
>
> You won't want me. You will be well (and thankless) in no time. But there I am; and I hope that the knowledge may be a comfort to you. Call me and I come.[55]

I read the tone of this letter more generously than does Nayder, who regards Dickens's offer as a sign of "mastery over his junior collaborator," and my view diverges from Mary Poovey's sense that Dickens's gesture evidences a disrespectful attitude toward the serial fiction writer as "an interchangeable part subject to replacement."[56] As an editor, Dickens would have to be alarmed by the prospect of suddenly suspending the publication of a serialized novel, but his letter focuses more on reassuring Collins than on decreasing risk to the business. Pointing to the Christmas numbers, *The Lazy Tour*, and two stage dramas, Dickens's references to their collaborations in multiple genres is a potent reminder that their written voices have a long history of mixing, sometimes indistinguishably. That Dickens could write "so like" Collins that his own voice would be undetectable should not surprise us, given how regularly the two wrote together. His insistence that the quality of the final product would be safe yet "makeshift" and only necessary "in a pinch" also honors the fact that the men remain individuals who respect each other's independent work. Dickens, here, does not claim to be more talented than Collins or to be able to supplant him in a dismissive way. Rather, his offer "to strike in and hammer the iron out" reveals an understanding of their previous collaborations as a form of labor that has trained him to be able to help a friend in need.[57] Collins and Dickens continue to sustain each other in times of need in the years to come, although the frequency of their writing together diminishes as they each write long novels. The collaborations of 1857 coincide with the start of Dickens's marital separation, and as the personal drama attendant to that separation stretches into 1858, the Christmas numbers provide important space for Dickens to practice navigating the boundaries between his personal and professional personas with varying levels of success.

Moving Houses and Unsettling Stories
(1858–59)

Following two years of stories that revolve around dangerous travel, Dickens moves the setting of the Christmas numbers back to England for 1858 and 1859. The main characters in *A House to Let* and *The Haunted House* stay on decidedly English soil in solid structures. The numbers, however, do not provide an accompanying sense of stability. Instead, they are full of unsettled characters in frequent motion. Changing houses and renting lodgings, everyone seems on the move in these texts, whose publication coincided with a period of personal challenges in the lives of both Charles Dickens and Wilkie Collins, his chief collaborator. As Dickens negotiated an end to his marriage, he struggled to maintain an effective distinction between his professional and private personas. He was also managing two residences, using both Gad's Hill and Tavistock House when not on reading tours. Collins's concerns had mainly to do with his health and a professional failure. He spent nearly half of 1858 suffering from rheumatic gout, which may have been compounded by or acted as a veil for symptoms of venereal disease, then a production of *The Red Vial* (a play Dickens had read and commented on) was panned after its October debut.[1] In the midst of these challenges, Collins and Dickens worked together as co-framers for the 1858 number even more closely than they did for *The Wreck of the Golden Mary* but without as much success.

The blending of Collins's and Dickens's voices in *The Perils* does not hold when they return to a frame concept that includes interpolation, as the narrators in *A House to Let* trip over one another in a text whose polyvocality is often more confusing than entertaining. As interesting as it is to study the continued co-creation of story concepts and the appearance of the first woman frame narrator, it is equally helpful to the development of a complex view of collaboration in the Victorian periodical press to understand how the finished product comes close to collaborative failure. Studying the process that generates *A House to Let* is instructive in continuing to exhibit a flexible, nonauthoritative Dickens in the collaborative role, and the collection's weaknesses importantly exemplify Holly Laird's point that critics should not always privilege "full collaborations" over others.[2] Navigating personal mixed with professional upheaval at *Household Words*, which leads to its rebirth as *All the Year Round*, Dickens returns to more-effective narrative practices for the 1859 number, *The Haunted House*. The collection is concerned with domestic spaces and relationships as, in the midst of what nearly becomes a reputation crisis, Dickens regains a sense of how to playfully yet carefully blur the boundaries between his individual authorial persona and his collaborative one. The stories in *The Haunted House* ultimately comment on the core of the storytelling act: its ability to forge human connection as individuals process difficult or traumatic memories. Collaboration at the offices of *All the Year Round* and within the collection itself is crucial in enabling the text to develop and deliver that commentary.

A House to Let

The Wreck and *The Perils* prove that Collins and Dickens were more than capable of producing high-quality Christmas numbers together in varied structures, which serves as an important reminder that collaboration itself is not to blame for *A House to Let*'s deficiencies. Perhaps distracted by the melodrama Dickens created in his personal life, the two novelists did not manage to produce a compelling finished product, but the context from which this mediocre text emerged remains instructive, as the collaboration on *A House to Let* was especially tight. Collins and Dickens conversed throughout its composition and were, unusually, in the same location for the final stages of writing. For this number, several of Dickens's (but not Collins's) letters survive, and they provide deep glimpses into the collaborative Christmas writing process.

Showing that he is open to input while developing initial ideas, Dickens writes to Collins,

Do you see your way to our making a Xmas No. of this idea that I am going very briefly to hint? Some disappointed person, man or woman, prematurely disgusted with the world for some reason or no reason, (the person should be young, I think) retires to an old lonely house, or an old lonely mill, or any thing you like, with one attendant: resolved to shut out the world and hold no communion with it. The one attendant sees the absurdity of the idea—pretends to humour it—but really tries to slaughter it. Everything that happens—everybody that comes near—every breath of human interest that floats into the old place from the village, or the heath, or the four cross roads near which it stands, and from which belated travellers stray into it—shews beyond mistake that you can't shut out the world—that you are in it to be of it—that you get into a false position the moment you try to sever yourself from it—and that you must mingle with it, and make the best of it, and make the best of yourself into the bargain.

If we could plot out a way of doing this together, I would not be afraid to take my part. If we could not, could we plot out a way of doing it, and taking in stories by other hands? If we could not do either (but I think we could) should we fall back upon a Round of Stories again? That, I would rather not do, if possible. Will you think about it?[3]

The sudden reappearance of the *Round of Stories* concept five years after the second round indicates that Dickens feels he can always return to that successful structure in a pinch, and his preference for avoiding that idea treats the Christmas conceits as high priorities. Dickens's emphasis on the things he and Collins can do together—planning, dividing labor, organizing contributions from other writers—also exemplifies how thoroughly collaborative the genesis of the frame concepts could be. Dickens as editor in this instance is not pushy; he does not wish for Collins just to validate his own initial thoughts. Rather, he asks Collins to mull over the idea before they consult, and the two then choose not to pursue Dickens's idea at all. The hermit living as a recluse does not frame a Christmas number until *Tom Tiddler's Ground* three years later, although the premise resurfaces earlier in the character of Miss Havisham in *Great Expectations* (1860–61), which supports the idea that Dickens's collaborative work for the Christmas numbers informs the creative process for his novels.[4]

The joint work on this number continues in the compilation of the middle section through to the conclusion, and Collins may have been the primary selector of the interpolated stories, which places Dickens in the least controlling position since 1852, when Wills sequenced the stories (some of which Dickens had not seen). In October, Dickens engaged with potential contributors, having apparently discussed or corresponded about the most fitting points of view for the interpolated pieces, but by early November, Collins is the one tasked with sorting through submissions before he and Dickens finish the number together at Gad's Hill. Dickens asks, "How do you feel about having the big bedroom, and writing there through the week? I would go to work too, and we might do Heaven knows how much—with an escapade to town for a night, if we felt in the humour. . . . Wills arranged with me that you were presently to receive sacks of Christmas 'matter;'—not much 'mind' with it, I am afraid."[5] Dickens appears keen to keep sharing late-night debauchery as well as writing tasks with Collins. As the one vetting "sacks of Christmas 'matter,'" Collins shapes the number at least as much as Dickens and Wills do. Following the September visit to the "big bedroom," Dickens later tells Wills that he and Collins have worked out the timing for finishing the number together at Tavistock House: "Wilkie and I have arranged to pass the whole day here, on *Monday Week, the 29th.* to connect the various portions of the Xmas No. and get it finally together. If you arrange to have them ready at the Printers, for such cuts, and such short bits of copy as we shall send them from time to time in the course of that day, we can finally correct it before we leave here that night, and you can send your last revise for Press next day."[6] This description makes clear that Dickens's semiregular complaints about the burden of publishing a special issue in the midst of weekly issues do not exaggerate, as he, Wills, and Collins juggle the demands of several works in multiple genres simultaneously. Dickens's comment that he and Collins will work together to "connect the various portions" again reveals a collaborative approach to the number as a whole and supports my contention that bridging sections should not, by default, be regarded as exempt from the collaborative dynamics that characterize other sections of the numbers.

"Over the Way" holds a position of significance in the Christmas number oeuvre because it features the first woman character acting as a frame narrator, which has also made its authorship a point of interest, as the story may mark the first time someone other than Dickens acted as the primary writer for an opening frame section. The Office Book for *Household Words* is one of the most useful pieces of archival evidence in existence related to the journal, and no competing documents have emerged to contest its attributions. When Dickens's role in composing or editing a story reached the level of coauthorship, he or Wills added "+ C.D." to the ledger. For "Over the Way," no such amendment appears, and the only author listed is Collins. Harry Stone takes the rare step of contradicting the Office Book's attribution based on "characteristically Dickensian themes, images, tags and techniques"; even while calling the frame story "a thoroughly composite production," Stone claims, "Here, as elsewhere, Dickens' editorial decision was supreme, his right to add or modify virtually unquestioned."[7] Ruth Glancy follows Stone in acknowledging the Office Book attribution then opposing it, proposing that "Dickens probably wrote much of 'Over the Way' as well, especially the portions that concern the old lady [Sophonisba]. . . . The old lady is a Dickensian character."[8] Yet Harold Love cautions that even the most confident attributionist relying on stylistic evidence must admit that "it is also easy to be wrong."[9] In a context so saturated with collaboration, in which Collins and Dickens quickly traded ideas as they co-created characters, plots, and frames over several years, it seems impossible to identify Sophonisba as more typical of Dickens than Collins. That Collins is identified as the primary writer and that his and Dickens's stylistic tendencies blend in the story most accurately reflects the dynamics of collaboration. Furthermore, for the concluding frame story, "Let at Last," Dickens's name is clearly added after Collins's, which suggests an intentional decision against adding his name to the first story. The most likely reason for that choice is that the major figures involved in the collaboration (Collins, Dickens, and Wills) regarded Collins as the opening story's primary author and saw Collins's role in the creation of the final story as equaling Dickens's role. Dickens also did not include "Over the Way," any of the framing pieces, or "Going into Society" when he extracted some of his Christmas stories for the 1867 Diamond Edition. That choice may imply that Dickens regarded Collins as the primary author of the framing pieces but also paradoxically shows how deeply collaborative the final product was, as excluding the frame sections leaves portions of Dickens's stories almost incomprehensible.[10] As is the case for the other numbers, trying to trace a brilliant bit of writing or a unique character back to a single author ultimately leads away from a more interesting point: that two creative powerhouses, together, fail to develop or use Sophonisba as a storyteller whose investigations of the house across the street might engage readers.

The number's listing of the "contents of the house to let" positions the stories as objects within the house itself, but the ensuing exposition does not develop the ironies or thematic threads from object designations that future collections, such as *Somebody's Luggage*, exploit to great effect. To begin, the elderly Sophonisba explains that her doctor has sent her to London for healthful stimulation, or "Tone," and that she becomes obsessed with the vacant house across the street after her servant Trottle informs her that the neighborhood residents believe it will never be let (1–2). Trottle has worked in Sophonisba's household for thirty-two years, since she lived in India with her brother, but whether he identifies himself as Indian, English, or both is unclear. A high-spirited "Philanderer," Trottle maintains a competitive stance toward Jabez Jarber, Sophonisba's constant suitor, and once Sophonisba sees a "secret Eye" shining out then vanishing from the empty house, the men feel compelled to investigate (2). Although the Jarber-Trottle rivalry is amusing, one weakness of the frame story is that it does not produce readerly investment in the proposed mystery. The quest to determine why the house is empty is not suspenseful, nor has the frame generated as much entertainment as the first speaker does in *The Seven Poor Travellers*, for instance. The frame concept need not be as dramatic as 1857's abduction by pirates, but even the metatextual moments in *A House to Let* do not excite, and the number drags. Before the first interpolated story commences, Jarber discovers that Sophonisba's unkind first cousin, George Forley, owns the house to let. This news would seem to interject action into the number, but the transition between stories reinvigorates the Jarber-Trottle rivalry without heightening interest in the progression of the frame narrative's family drama. Uneven writing from both Collins and Dickens also plagues the number. Sophonisba, for instance, states that Trottle does not wish to listen to Jarber, who "tossed the words at him over his (Jabez Jarber's) own ear and shoulder" (6). The unnecessary parenthetical highlights the shift to Jarber's recitation awkwardly, and the inexpert feel of the writing is surprising given that Collins and Dickens pored over it at Gad's Hill. Despite a rough transition, the casting of the story's words as projectiles hurled at an adversary, and the vague nature of the document Jarber reads, Elizabeth Gaskell's story quickly lifts the quality of the collection.

Gaskell's "The Manchester Marriage" parallels Adelaide Procter's "The Old Sailor's Story" in *The Wreck of the Golden Mary*, linking Christmas numbers across years and raising the possibility that readers' (or editors') thematic expectations for the collections may have influenced contributors. Gaskell's piece shares the history of Mr. and Mrs. Openshaw, who come to London from Manchester to rent the house in question. Alice Openshaw's first husband, Frank, disappears at sea, leaving her to support herself and her disabled baby by letting rooms. Mr. Openshaw is a curmudgeonly tenant whose compassion for the chairbound little girl, Alisie, leads him to care for and then marry Alice. When Frank returns, having survived "for years a prisoner amongst savages" after the shipwreck, he presents himself only to Alisie and a servant, Norah (12). The domestic disruption in England is blamed on uncontrolled dark people, and Frank avoids traumatizing the happily remarried Alice by drowning himself (16). Mr. Openshaw eventually learns the full story of Frank's reappearance and is so affected by the heartbreak he imagines Frank to have endured that he grieves "as if [Frank] were [his] only brother" (17). Although Gaskell's story is emotionally moving, Trottle asks the obvious and practical question: what do the Openshaws have to do with why the house will not let? Jarber insists that, to understand, one must hear a second story from him, entrapping both Trottle and readers of *Household Words* in a fragmented narrative.

Dickens's "Going into Society" fails to improve the confusing storytelling situation. The story's opening adds to the number's uncoordinated dynamic as the tone of the speaker changes in jarring fashion and the document's writer remains unidentified. Because Jarber reads the first two documents, which he has not authored, no expectation for a uniform writing style exists, but one does anticipate that Jarber's speaking voice or his introductory comments would be consistent. Instead, when he begins with "At one period . . . ," no sense of chronology or of the document's genre establishes contextual grounding, and the story's setting in the reign of George IV causes further disorientation. "Going into Society" tells of a showman, Toby Magsman, who used to rent the now-vacant house and includes statements such as "Mr Magsman repeated" that draw attention to the moment of telling without specifying to whom Magsman speaks, leaving the story's provenance unnecessarily mysterious (19). The strange account tells of Magsman's relationship with "Major Tpschoffki, of the Imperial Bulgraderian Brigade," also known as Chopski or Chops, a performing dwarf who repeatedly declares that "the Public" keeps him from going "into Society" (18–19). Chopski irrationally expects to come into property then improbably wins the lottery, and when Magsman visits, he sees that false friends and servants abuse and exploit the dwarf, who returns to the performing caravan and dies peacefully. Sophonisba and Jarber speculate that this story accounts for the emptiness of the house because no one would let it after it had been turned into a caravan, but Trottle deflates that theory by pointing out that Magsman is not the most recent tenant. This debate does nothing to diminish the curiously random nature of the story; it fails to advance the frame, and the frame does not accommodate it effectively. Even Dickens sensed that his story was not good for the number, writing to Wills, "I want to prepare you for an H.W. disappointment, in case it should come off. My introduced paper for the Xmas No. involves such an odd idea—which appears to me so humourous, and so available at greater length—that I am debating whether or no I shall cancel the paper (it has gone to the Printer's to day), and make it the Pivot round which my next book shall revolve."[11] With the "sacks" of stories that Collins sorted available as replacements, Dickens's decision against pulling the piece seems to have been more concerned with last-minute stress it might have caused Wills and the printer than with the story's enhancement of *A House to Let.*

Fitting more neatly into the frame concept is Procter's "Three Evenings in the House," which illustrates that contributions from those more distanced from the close conversations of Collins and Dickens are not necessarily lower in quality. Jarber claims that while at the local circulating library, he comes across a poem written by a female relative of the last tenant (23). The library detail is a respectful yet coded nod to Procter, who had received letters at a circulating library when she communicated with *Household Words* using a pseudonym.[12] In the frame story, an anonymous woman has asked the library's proprietor to publish the poem, but he declines, and she leaves no address for its return. Although Jarber's explanation of how he finds the poem is implausible, it does justify the number's change in genre. In the verse's first evening, Bertha sacrifices her own love interest to devote herself to her brother, Herbert. In the second, Herbert is dying, and Bertha promises to care for his unkind wife, Dora. In the third, Bertha's former suitor returns but marries Dora instead of reuniting with Bertha, and Bertha leaves the house alone.[13] Sophonisba thinks the sad poem is nice, and it alters the rhythm of the number to avoid monotony as Procter's contributions to previous numbers have done, but the verse provides no information about why the house stands empty.

The return of Trottle in Collins's "Trottle's Report," particularly in the absence of Jarber (who falls ill), not only provides a new speaking voice but also picks up the number's pace, ironically highlighting the fact that the collection struggles to maintain interest. In contrast to Jarber's library excavations, Trottle investigates "by walking straight up to the House, and bringing himself face to face with the first person in it who opened the door" (27). His delightful boldness combined with improvisational performance lends the number a playful, unpredictable air that returns briefly to the type of brisk holiday storytelling that characterized the adventures of the previous two years, and Trottle's foray into the house leads to discoveries that finally pertain to the question of the house's vacancy. He learns that the house-keeper and her drunken adult son are awaiting a payment from the owner, Mr. Forley. Trottle immediately poses as Forley's agent then hears a mysterious scratching sound coming from the third floor and meets a five-year-old boy scrubbing the garret floor with imaginary water (29–30).[14] To keep tenants away from this unsavory household and to protect an inheritance stolen from the child, Forley advertises an outrageous rental rate forty pounds higher than any other property on the street, which solves the mystery (31). "Let at Last" resolves concerns about the neglected child and the status of the house in a convoluted conclusion worthy of sensation fiction: Sophonisba pays off the housekeeper, adopts the boy, and buys the house across the way to turn it into a children's hospital.

This Christmas number may not have been very good, but it was not the worst thing Dickens published in 1858, a year in which he made some spectacularly bad choices about what to put in print as he endangered his periodical by publicizing his personal affairs. Throughout the year, Charles was negotiating a separation from his wife, Catherine, and spinning a narrative of long-running marital discord that did not match the observances of their close friends. When Georgina Hogarth, Catherine's sister, persisted in sharing a residence with Charles and the children after Catherine moved out, some people speculated that their relationship had always been adulterous. Fueled by outrage at such rumors and against the advice of his friends, Charles published an uncharacteristic "Personal" statement in June 1858. After explaining, "[I am] presenting myself in my own Journal in my own private character," Charles seeks to discredit unspecified "misrepresentations, most grossly false, most monstrous, and most cruel." Calling his marital separation "sacredly private" in a document designed to reach the broadest public possible and proclaiming the innocence of "persons of whom I have no knowledge," Dickens's contradictions help to make this text one of the most bizarre printed performances of his career.[15] Republished in the *Times* (London) and the *New York Times*, the statement did more harm than good to his reputation, as what was envisioned as a defense drew increased attention to family affairs, which had not been as widely discussed as Charles presumed. Patrick Leary notes that many papers printed the "Personal" statement with head notes explaining that they had no idea what the fuss was about or what scandal Dickens was describing.[16] The ego-driven choice to publish the piece was a rare incident of Dickens completely mismanaging his celebrity and losing sight of crucial boundaries between his private activities and his public persona. Incensed that Bradbury and Evans refused to print the statement in *Punch*, where it would have been even more jarring, Dickens broke off relations with the publishers and managed to purchase the naming rights to *Household Words* so that he could shut it down.[17] *A House to Let* was composed in the midst of this quarrelling.

Dickens's poor choices were again in the news in the autumn of 1858 as he began to discuss the Christmas number with Collins. This time, Dickens tried to blame the press for his own mistakes. A letter he had written to Arthur Smith, manager of his public reading tour, with instructions stating that Smith should show it "to anyone who wishes to do me right, or to anyone who may have been misled into doing me wrong" was published in the *New York Tribune* on August 16 then reprinted in English periodicals.[18] With such directives, it is hard to believe Dickens's claims that he did not intend for the letter to become public. The text is shamelessly mean, calling Catherine a bad mother who has "thrown all the children on someone else" and accusing her of having a "mental disorder."[19] At a time when women with everything from migraine headaches to menstrual cramps to actual mental illness could be labeled mad on the testimony of one man, to make such accusations takes Dickens several steps toward occupying the villain role typical of the sensation novels he and his collaborators produced. The attack had a boomerang effect that damaged his reputation more than Catherine's. Months after the publication of the damning documents, Elizabeth Gaskell wrote privately that she was grateful for anonymous publication because it prevented her name from being associated with Dickens, "as Mr Dickens happens to be extremely unpopular just now,—(owing to the well-grounded feeling of dislike to the publicity he has given to his domestic affairs,) & I think they would be glad to announce my name on the list of their contributors. And I would *much* rather they did *not*."[20] Gaskell's comment makes clear that bylines were far from universally desirable and that Dickens's balancing of his personal and public personas affected his collaborative relationships.

In the same letter to Collins that shares initial thoughts for *A House to Let*, Dickens complains, "I have been greatly vexed by the wantonness of some of our English papers in printing what is evidently on the face of it a private document of mine, violated in America and sent home here. But it is one of the penalties and drawbacks of my position. Any man who wants to sell his paper, has but to lay hold of me for a fillip."[21] In casting himself as a victim of greedy newspapermen, Dickens appears in a particularly distasteful light, given that he had attempted to use those exact networks in the periodical press to condemn his wife. Relaunching a journal in the wake of this scandal probably made Dickens intensely aware that further public literary failure could seriously threaten his status as a literary superstar, and the strong association of Dickens's fame with the celebration of Christmas raised the stakes for the first Christmas issue of *All the Year Round*.

The Haunted House

In *The Haunted House*, Dickens probes some of the boundaries that separate reality from fiction and experiments with representing the relationships between his collaborators. Over the next few years of Christmas numbers, his confidence in blurring such boundaries builds, and *The Haunted House* is where he begins to test out daring references to his professional world. Dickens manages to do so without making the mistakes of his "Personal" statement and letter to Arthur Smith, bringing depictions of his private versus public selves back under control more successfully than he had in 1858 and building a number more solidly coherent than *A House to Let*. Mixing suspenseful and comic moments, *The Haunted House* pulls storytellers together tightly and returns to some of the effective techniques that characterize the numbers of 1856 and before. Strategically building individual characters and bonds between speakers in the frame sections, the sometimes-humorous collection also addresses serious questions about the relationship between storytelling and traumatic memory and, for the first time, uses the physical positioning of print on the page to complicate its presentation of authorial and narrative voices.

The premise for the 1859 number stems from a years-long debate Dickens waged with William Howitt over spiritualism. Late 1859 to early 1860 constituted one high period of tension as the men took their opposing views to press.[22] In this Christmas issue, Dickens—whose most famous piece of Christmas literature, *A Christmas Carol* (1843), revolves around a haunting in a house—set out to disprove the existence of haunted houses. He took direct aim at the spiritualist beliefs of Howitt, who had contributed to several regular issues of *Household Words* and to a previous Christmas number. Howitt shared details about a reputedly haunted house in Cheshunt, which Dickens and some friends went to investigate, but the party did not stay overnight or find any witnesses to support the theory that the building, which had been torn down, was haunted. Their trip took place on December 12, the day before the printing of the Christmas number, so the Cheshunt journey was not the direct inspiration for the number's events.[23] Unlike Dickens and his companions, who failed even to find a spooky building, the characters in *The Haunted House* take an extended holiday at a rented home. As the frame concept unfolds and the guests tell their stories, Dickens weaves together commentary not only on the psychological dynamics of perceiving a thing or place to be haunted but also on the interpersonal dynamics of collaboration.

The number's first sentence, kicking off Dickens's "The Mortals in the House," acknowledges and challenges ghost story conventions: "Under none of the accredited ghostly circumstances, and environed by none of the conventional ghostly surroundings, did I first make acquaintance with the house which is the subject of this Christmas piece" (1). Since the speaker immediately establishes the genre of this work as Christmas literature and uses a first-person "I" voice closely associated with Dickens as conductor, the idea that it is unconventionally approaching the topic of ghosts is immediately ironic because of the aforementioned popularity of Dickens's *Carol*. The blurring of the boundary between Dickens's fictional authorial persona and his real-life identity continues as he projects Howitt into the character of the man on the opposite side of a train carriage from the narrator, who is in search of a country house to rent.

The opening of *The Haunted House* is also noteworthy for demonstrating, particularly in light of the disappointing aspects of *A House to Let*, that moments of extraordinary writing consistently appear in the Christmas numbers. Dickens's narrator, for instance, shares a fascinating contemplation of why early morning hours are precious to witness:

> No period within the four-and-twenty hours of day and night, is so solemn to me, as the early morning. In the summer time, I often rise very early, and repair to my room to do a day's work before breakfast, and I am always on those occasions deeply impressed by the stillness and solitude around me. Besides that there is something awful in the being surrounded by familiar faces asleep—in the knowledge that those who are dearest to us and to whom we are dearest, are profoundly unconscious of us, in an impassive state anticipative of that mysterious condition to which we are all tending—the stopped life, the broken threads of yesterday, the deserted seat, the closed book, the unfinished but abandoned occupation, all are images of Death. The tranquillity of the hour is the tranquillity of Death. . . . Moreover, I once saw the apparition of my father, at this hour. (2)

The speaker moves from what one expects to be a tender appreciation of dawn's serenity to the declaration that being awake at such a time is the equivalent of residing in the stillness of death. Domestic objects—seats, books—simultaneously serve as reminders of one's companions in life and as harbingers of death. This morbid turn then moves into a confession that he, the denier of hauntings, has been visited by a ghost at such a time. Dickens skips lightly along the fiction/reality border here; his own work habits included early morning writing sessions, but he never claimed to have seen his father's (or any) ghost.

As the unnamed narrator builds the frame story, his multilayered introduction of the main characters and rich elucidation of the scenario they encounter is immediately engaging. After learning at a local inn that "a hooded woman with an owl" haunts "the Poplars," the narrator rents the property for six months (3). In October, he moves in with his sister, "a deaf stable-man, [his] bloodhound Turk, two woman servants, and a young person called an Odd Girl" (4).[24] Local residents help to amplify the fears of the servants, who are genuinely scared but also inventive. Out of frustration but not anger, the household dismisses several sets of servants, leading the narrator's unnamed sister to propose that they live without hired help except for the deaf and "speechless" stableman, Bottles (5). A sense of adventure linked to a willingness to forgo some manifestations of class privilege unites the participants in the experiment, which heightens the level of trust implicit in their storytelling. This setup dovetails with traditions of Christmas as a time for experiences that temporarily cross social boundaries, but it nonetheless happens in an atmosphere of condescension toward the spurned workers. Describing the incidents that lead to a servantless holiday, the narrator uses the language of disease: "As to our nightly life, the contagion of suspicion and fear was among us, and there is no such contagion under the sky.... We know [the servants] come here to be frightened and infect one another, and we know they are frightened and do infect one another" (5). The mind/body dichotomy blurs as the thrill of fearful sensations spreads like a virus but only to the weak-minded (yet strong-bodied) members of the working classes.

The higher-class guests who replace the servants are apparently impervious to such contamination of the psyche, and the brief descriptions of each guest include character-building details so that the introductory section immediately begins to construct narrative coherence. The narrator and his sister are joined by their cousin John Herschel and his pregnant wife; Alfred Starling, a twenty-eight-year-old bachelor in debt; the feminist Belinda Bates, "a fine genius for poetry"; Jack Governor, a handsome sailor and old

friend; Mr. "Nat" Beaver, an occasionally nervous sea captain and "old comrade" of Jack Governor's; and Mr. Undery, the narrator's whist-playing "friend
and solicitor" (6–7). The frame facilitates connections between the pieces
because, as is the case in *The Seven Poor Travellers*, readers anticipate that
each character will contribute a story. In this number, however, the bonds
between characters are even stronger because they are friends or relatives of
the narrator, not random people passing through a place. While delivering
these descriptions, the narrator pauses conspicuously to disagree with Belinda's feminism in a patronizing tone, mocking all causes that begin with
"Woman's" and irrelevantly proclaiming the existence of good men in the
world (7). The rant is a clear taunt of Adelaide Anne Procter, the contributor
who wrote Belinda's portion of the forthcoming narratives. As Gill Gregory
notes, Dickens's critique of the fictional Belinda's social activism is peculiar
given that he supported some of Procter's causes, such as the inclusion of
women at the Royal Academy.[25] Dickens even praises Procter's "endeavors
to do some good" in his introduction to her collected poetry, which serves
as an important reminder of the exaggeration and humor that accompany
fictionalized depictions of collaborative relationships.[26] Procter was such a
regular *Household Words* contributor and good friend that Dickens does not
seem to fear alienating her, but given his wrong instincts on the "Personal"
statement, he takes a risk in commenting publicly on his disagreement with
a woman. The narrator confesses to having digressed, but the antifeminist
tangent about Belinda is part of a narrative strategy in which playful ribbing
of narrators/collaborators resurfaces.

Even before the interpolated stories begin, the frame narrator deepens
the character development of narrators to come by sharing highlights from
their initial nights. The guests bond while preparing food under the guid-
ance of "Chief Cook" Jack Governor and the host's sister, "pastrycook and
confectioner" (7). Jack and Mr. Beaver revive their youthful, adventurous
selves by climbing on the roof in the middle of the night during a rainstorm
to take down a noisy weathercock and spend several other nights on similar
climbing expeditions to remove offending noisemakers. In this convivial atmosphere, the narrator boasts, "I never was happier in my life, and I believe it
was the universal feeling among us" (7). Thus, although the number is based
on a disagreement with one of Dickens's real-life acquaintances, his fictionalized rendering of sharing a house with his collaborators is full of joy and
amity. The guests agree to share truthful accounts of what they experience
in the house on Twelfth Night, positioning the reader as a Twelfth Night
listener alongside the other houseguests.

As the stories commence, the titles and linking passages run across both columns for the first time in a Christmas number (see figure 5.1). As Louis James points out, a "journal as a whole communicates through its layout, its selection, arrangement and general presentation, the use or absence of illustrations, the size of columns, paragraphs, the type itself. . . . A journal's format thus becomes a tone of voice, a way of conditioning our response."[27] Pausing the column breaks only to resume them risks confusing the reader, disorienting one's habitual manner of understanding the way *Household Words* communicates. That disruption in this case, however, succeeds in symbolically bridging not only the left and right columns but also the divisions between voices and authors. The spatial union of the two columns suggests that the stories in the number will continuously cross expected boundaries as they cohere. Fran Baker concurs in regarding the format of this number as Dickens's attempt to communicate that the text "should be read as a unified whole rather than dipped into and the isolated stories divorced from their overall framework."[28]

The first interpolated tale, "The Ghost in the Clock Room," written by Hesba Stretton (pseudonym of Sarah Smith), immediately compounds the collaborative dynamic. Neither Cousin Herschel nor his wife wants to tell the story of Stella, the "Spirit" who haunts their room, but Herschel finally agrees to take on the task of telling, "subject to her correction," as he asks the assembled group to "[s]uppose the Spirit . . . to be my wife here, sitting among us" (8). The supposition provides an air of realism, although Herschel's wife stays silent and does not embellish the story, which he speaks in the first-person "I" voice of Stella. An orphaned young woman, Stella quiets her sister's pressure to marry by attracting the notoriously isolated and unromantic Martin Fraser. "Worshipping" in the "temple" of Fraser's astronomical knowledge instead of carrying on in her coquette role, Stella falls in love but refuses Fraser's marriage offer in shame over her previous scheming (10). He then spots her longingly peeking through his window on Christmas Eve, she declares love, and they marry. The emotional story lacks comic elements or apparent connection to the clock of its title, and the Christmas setting at its conclusion connects it only loosely to the frame until Herschel reveals that he is Martin Fraser and that "the Spirit," Stella, is his actual wife. The woman speaker in the story, then, is the same woman who makes Herschel "promise to be the mouthpiece of the Spirit," which makes for a complicated self-silencing of her voice (8).

The ghost in the first story has turned out to be simply the younger self of one of the guests, and for the second story, the speaker of George A.

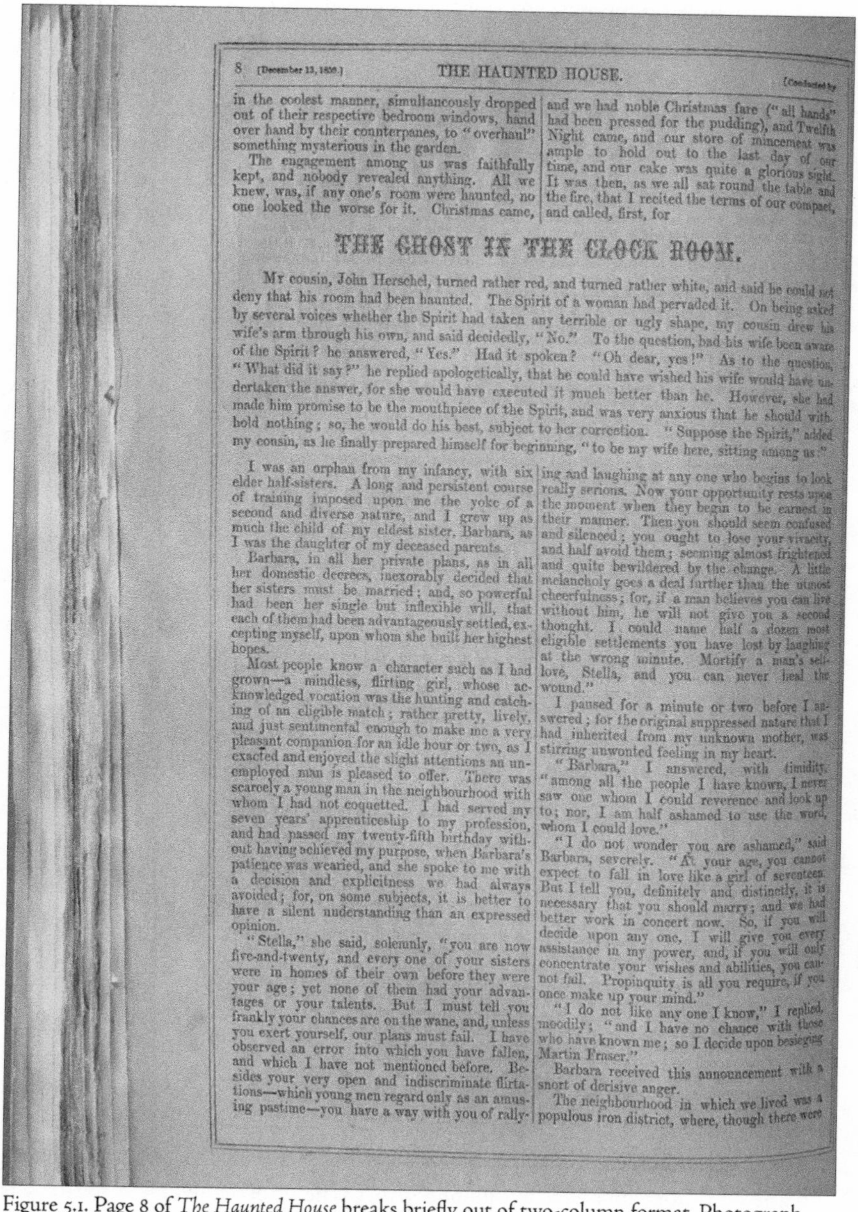

in the coolest manner, simultaneously dropped out of their respective bedroom windows, hand over hand by their counterpanes, to "overhaul" something mysterious in the garden.

The engagement among us was faithfully kept, and nobody revealed anything. All we knew, was, if any one's room were haunted, no one looked the worse for it. Christmas came, and we had noble Christmas fare ("all hands" had been pressed for the pudding), and Twelfth Night came, and our store of mincemeat was ample to hold out to the last day of our time, and our cake was quite a glorious sight. It was then, as we all sat round the table and the fire, that I recited the terms of our compact, and called, first, for

THE GHOST IN THE CLOCK ROOM.

MY cousin, John Herschel, turned rather red, and turned rather white, and said he could not deny that his room had been haunted. The Spirit of a woman had pervaded it. On being asked by several voices whether the Spirit had taken any terrible or ugly shape, my cousin drew his wife's arm through his own, and said decidedly, "No." To the question, had his wife been aware of the Spirit? he answered, "Yes." Had it spoken? "Oh dear, yes!" As to the question, "What did it say?" he replied apologetically, that he could have wished his wife would have undertaken the answer, for she would have executed it much better than he. However, she had made him promise to be the mouthpiece of the Spirit, and was very anxious that he should withhold nothing; so, he would do his best, subject to her correction. "Suppose the Spirit," added my cousin, as he finally prepared himself for beginning, "to be my wife here, sitting among us:"

I was an orphan from my infancy, with six elder half-sisters. A long and persistent course of training imposed upon me the yoke of a second and diverse nature, and I grew up as much the child of my eldest sister, Barbara, as I was the daughter of my deceased parents.

Barbara, in all her private plans, as in all her domestic decrees, inexorably decided that her sisters must be married; and, so powerful had been her single but inflexible will, that each of them had been advantageously settled, excepting myself, upon whom she built her highest hopes.

Most people know a character such as I had grown—a mindless, flirting girl, whose acknowledged vocation was the hunting and catching of an eligible match; rather pretty, lively, and just sentimental enough to make me a very pleasant companion for an idle hour or two, as I exacted and enjoyed the slight attentions an unemployed man is pleased to offer. There was scarcely a young man in the neighbourhood with whom I had not coquetted. I had served my seven years' apprenticeship to my profession, and had passed my twenty-fifth birthday without having achieved my purpose, when Barbara's patience was wearied, and she spoke to me with a decision and explicitness we had always avoided; for, on some subjects, it is better to have a silent understanding than an expressed opinion.

"Stella," she said, solemnly, "you are now five-and-twenty, and every one of your sisters were in homes of their own before they were your age; yet none of them had your advantages or your talents. But I must tell you frankly your chances are on the wane, and, unless you exert yourself, our plans must fail. I have observed an error into which you have fallen, and which I have not mentioned before. Besides your very open and indiscriminate flirtations—which young men regard only as an amusing pastime—you have a way with you of rallying and laughing at any one who begins to look really serious. Now your opportunity rests upon the moment when they begin to be earnest in their manner. Then you should seem confused and silenced; you ought to lose your vivacity, and half avoid them; seeming almost frightened and quite bewildered by the change. A little melancholy goes a deal farther than the utmost cheerfulness; for, if a man believes you can live without him, he will not give you a second thought. I could name half a dozen most eligible settlements you have lost by laughing at the wrong minute. Mortify a man's self-love, Stella, and you can never heal the wound."

I paused for a minute or two before I answered; for the original suppressed nature that I had inherited from my unknown mother, was stirring unwonted feeling in my heart.

"Barbara," I answered, with timidity, "among all the people I have known, I never saw one whom I could reverence and look up to; nor, I am half ashamed to use the word, whom I could love."

"I do not wonder you are ashamed," said Barbara, severely. "At your age, you cannot expect to fall in love like a girl of seventeen. But I tell you, definitely and distinctly, it is necessary that you should marry; and we had better work in concert now. So, if you will decide upon any one, I will give you every assistance in my power, and, if you will only concentrate your wishes and abilities, you cannot fail. Propinquity is all you require, if you once make up your mind."

"I do not like any one I know," I replied, moodily; "and I have no chance with those who have known me; so I decide upon besieging Martin Fraser."

Barbara received this announcement with a snort of derisive anger.

The neighbourhood in which we lived was a populous iron district, where, though there were

Figure 5.1. Page 8 of *The Haunted House* breaks briefly out of two-column format. Photograph courtesy of the Charles Dickens Museum, London.

Sala's "The Ghost in the Double Room" playfully identifies the ghost of the ague as a haunting force. In Alfred Starling's tale, he and Tilly are in a rush to marry when Alfred is struck by an ague attack. The people he knocks into while shaking think he is drunk, the marriage plans are cancelled, and he is disinherited. Alfred then joins the East India regiments, where further ague attacks result in his dishonorable discharge, and after surviving a shipwreck on his way home, he knocks over a rack of rings in a shop only to be sentenced to seven years' transportation on charges of shoplifting. Just as the story reaches this high level of absurdity, he wakes to find that it has all been a dream and that the tremors are the vibrations of a train; then he wakes again to find that marrying Tilly is also a dream (18). Starling dreaming that he is dreaming intensifies the story's farcical dynamic, and although Sala belabors some points, the story proceeds fairly swiftly, improving the number's pace. Once again, variation in writing style helps the number avoid monotony and demonstrates that multiple voices enhance overall quality.

Adelaide Anne Procter's "The Ghost in the Picture Room" maintains this paradoxical combination of continuity and differentiation as the story of the next room appears in verse form. A portrait of a nun in the room causes Belinda to think of a legend about a Mediterranean abbey. She tells of Sister Angela (the third orphan in the number), a devout girl raised in a convent. As Angela nurses a young soldier, trading stories leads to seduction as Angela flees with him, regrets it, becomes "reckless," then returns to the convent thinking that death is imminent (20).[29] Angela's return takes the number into supernatural territory when the Virgin Mary appears and explains that she has prevented anyone from noticing Angela's absence:

> I filled thy place. Thy flight is known to none,
> For all thy daily duties I have done;
> Gathered thy flowers, and prayed, and sang, and slept;
> Didst thou not know, poor child, *thy place was kept?*
>
> (21)

Here, the Virgin Mary is a shapeshifter, taking Angela's physical form to deceive the pious nuns in order to forgive and redeem the sinner. Angela resumes her place and, several years later, shares the full story on her deathbed. This legend does involve the tale of a ghost (the ghost of Mary functions as the unrecognized ghost of Angela within the walls of the convent), but the portrait in Belinda's room has no active role in the haunting. Neither the Virgin Mary nor Angela appears in the house, yet the legend's final message, that Christian redemption and forgiveness "[m]ay be the truer life, and this the dream," continues to blur the lines between worldly and ethereal realities that the number has set out to clarify (21).

In another tonal shift, Wilkie Collins's "The Ghost in the Cupboard Room" focuses on the comical before illustrating that, while not necessarily cathartic, storytelling can foster crucial camaraderie after trauma. Mr. Beaver's opening comments, which he delivers after leaping out of "an imaginary hammock" (21), appear lighthearted and seem to mock ghost stories yet lead to a terrifying account: "The fact of the matter is—and I give you leave, ladies and gentlemen, to laugh at it as much as you please—that the ghost which haunted *me* last night, which has haunted me off and on for many years past, and which will go on haunting me till I am a ghost myself (and consequently spirit-proof in all respects), is, nothing more or less than—a bedroom candlestick" (22). Rather than dismissing the power of an ordinary candlestick to haunt, Beaver speaks of personal torture. At age twenty-five, he works on a ship delivering gunpowder to South Americans fighting Spain for independence when he quarrels with and slaps "a coffee-coloured native pilot, who jabbered a little English" (23). Collins characterizes the pilot with racist terminology reminiscent of Christian George King from *The Perils*, and the character is similarly traitorous.[30] After the Spaniards overtake the ship and murder its crew, they spare Beaver's life to indulge the pilot's vengeance. Tied to the floor of the cargo hold, Beaver is bound, gagged, and within sight of a lit candle with a long wick that is rigged to blow up barrels of gunpowder (24). In the two hours it takes for the flame to reach the "slow-match" leading to the powder keg, Beaver marvels that he does not "die of the horror" (24). A sexual threat also infuses the scenario when Beaver wonders repeatedly what the pilot will do to him or with him. The story includes a prolonged, detailed description of the agony Beaver suffers as he cuts his hands on ropes trying to free himself, hallucinates, is unable to blow out the candle with his nostrils, and begins to laugh in hysterical fits that he has to control so that his breaths do not cause the tight gags to suffocate him. Beaver's riveting account concludes with his waking up in Trinidad eight months after an American vessel has rescued him (seconds before the wick ignites), but the trauma incapacitates him for nearly a year (26).

Building even more cohesion among the frame characters within *The Haunted House*, Beaver remarks not only on his storytelling style but also on the listeners' reaction to it: "That's another joke, if you please; and I'm much obliged to Miss Belinda in the corner for being good enough to laugh at it" (23). Collins's narrative technique here includes some of the successful quirks he exhibits in previous numbers, such as the moments in *The Seven Poor Travellers* when his narrator repeatedly addresses "my man in the corner" (19). Storytelling in this case has acted as an agitating activity that almost triggers another breakdown: "Bless your hearts, I'm all right now, as you may see. I'm a little shaken by telling the story, ladies and gentlemen—a little shaken, that's all." (26). The other guests now understand why Mr. Beaver never uses a candlestick in the dark; the haunting of his tale, rather than pointing to the supernatural, emphasizes the lasting effects of human violence on the psyche. By the end of the story, Mr. Beaver's assurances that he is just "a little shaken" reinforce the sense of fellow feeling among the guests, as does his willingness to have shared such a harrowing memory.

The reader's comfort with the collective dynamic of this group helps prevent the number from fragmenting at the point where Dickens contributes "The Ghost in Master B.'s Room," a strange tale that seems to work against the collection's mission. The host begins with a revealing comment on storytelling: "It being now my own turn, I 'took the word,' as the French say, and went on" (27). "Taking the word" might seem to treat stories as finished objects to be passed around, but in the context of guests sharing their experiences, "taking the word" from the previous teller places more emphasis on the collaborative nature of the project. Each teller is a custodian, not owner, of "the word," which is nurtured during the evening and then put to bed gently once the final teller has finished. In taking that "word" from Collins, Dickens also joins him in touching on some of the racist themes of *The Perils*. The host begins by thinking of all the things "B" could stand for, then sees a series of faces—a boy, a man in his mid-twenties, his own dead father, and the grandfather he never saw alive—in the room's looking glass (27).[31] Waking in the middle of the night, Master B. finds his own skeletal form sharing his bed and uses headless donkeys to take that visitor on a journey until the two are transformed into young boys at a school where the narrator startlingly proposes that they "should have a Seraglio" (28). The racialized fantasy that follows involves the narrator in boy form telling one of the girls "that she must be inveigled by a Merchant, brought to [him] veiled, and purchased as a slave" (28). Tabby, "the serving drudge of the house," occupies the role of "celebrated chief of the Blacks of the Hareem" because he is too dark and unattractive to pose a romantic threat, while the school's mistress, Miss Griffin, would be shocked to know that "she was walking with a stately step at the head of Polygamy and Mahomedanism" as the boys maintain a secret harem of eight beautiful little girls (29). The mildly pedophilic vision ends when the boy's father dies and he must leave the school, which leads the narrator to realize that the faces in the mirror are all his own:[32] "No other ghost has haunted the boy's room, my friends, since I have occupied it, than the ghost of my own childhood, the ghost of my own innocence, the ghost of my own airy belief" (30).

Although the disturbing, Orientalized sexual fantasy distinguishes this story from many of Dickens's others, its plot presents a version of the Spirits of Christmas Past, Present, and Future taking the form of shapes in a mirror. The narrator is generous from the start and does not undergo a Scrooge-like character transformation, but his journey through all stages of life in a single night is reminiscent of Scrooge's whirlwind Christmas Eve. Similar to Scrooge's presence at his own graveside, this man's vision of his grandfatherly self and the presence of a skeleton foreshadow his death. A dream of sleeping with one's own corpse, even when called "the ghost of my own airy belief," suggests the strong presence of otherworldly concerns. Despite his objective of disproving the supernatural phenomena, Dickens's weird story does the most to raise questions about the unusual circumstances in the house that would provoke such visions.[33]

"The Ghost in the Garden Room," Elizabeth Gaskell's contribution, then raises the stakes of the number's storytelling as a story itself becomes the haunting agent. Mr. Undery, the solicitor, says that the "Ghost of a Judge" and his accompanying story have haunted him in many places, and the saga of Nathan and Hester Huntroyd indeed proves deeply tragic (31). The rural couple sends their son, Benjamin, to school with the hope that he will become a gentleman before marrying Bessy, Hester's niece. Echoing depictions of ungrateful sons in previous Christmas numbers, Benjamin is a deceptive and pompous young man with no redeeming character traits.[34] Misunderstanding their son's absence and a returned epistle from the "dead letter office" as official notification that he has died, the family grieves. When thieves attack the house and beat the elderly couple, Bessy discovers Benjamin to be their leader and frees him once he promises to leave England, but the two detained criminals disclose his identity. Mr. Huntroyd is forced to testify that the couple has overheard their son telling his accomplice to strangle his own mother, the traumatized Mrs. Huntroyd retires to her deathbed, and even though Bessy marries a kind neighbor, the story's concluding platitude that "the broken-hearted go Home, to be comforted of God," does little to diminish its upsetting elements (48). Although the pacing of Gaskell's story is quite slow (even after Dickens trimmed its length) and the main characters' ignorance borders on implausibility, the piece remains haunting in its sadness.

In her edition of "The Ghost in the Garden Room," Fran Baker states that Gaskell was able to "rescue" her story from the Christmas number frame when she later published it independently, but the collaborative dynamic hardly signals a need for metaphorical rescue.[35] Dickens's explanation of his edits is almost apologetic in a letter to Gaskell, exposing his sensitivity to the delicate negotiations of collaboration: "In 'making up' the Christmas No. I was obliged—or I could not have managed it at all—to take a line here, and a line there, out of every paper in it. I hope I did this so tenderly and carefully in your case, as that you will hardly know where I touched it. My chief reason for mentioning the circumstance at all, is, that I may have an excuse for telling you that the force and beauty of your story impressed me more than I could easily find words to describe."[36] Dickens's admiration for Gaskell endures, and given his complaints about receiving too many stories with criminal plots,[37] the fact that he includes hers further attests to his regard. Gaskell's opinion of Dickens has also rebounded from 1858; she does not hesitate to advertise his support publicly in a collection of her stories published in 1859. Following Wilkie Collins's practice in *After Dark* (1856), Gaskell republishes pieces that first appeared in *Household Words* (and other pieces) with a framing device that draws upon more than one of Dickens's Christmas number strategies. Gaskell's *Round the Sofa* refers directly to Dickens's *Rounds* of 1852 and 1853, and its narrative method, in which a visitor to Edinburgh writes down stories told by others, recalls *The Holly Tree Inn*. The ways in which the Christmas number collections create conversation among stories from multiple contributors clearly leads some of those writers to imagine similar ways to create implicit dialogue among their own works.

The conversation of *The Haunted House* concludes in distinctive form with the full text of "The Ghost in the Corner Room" running across the page (see figure 5.2). This is the only time in all eighteen numbers that an entire story breaks out of the two-column format, illustrating visually that one cannot rely on the spatial arrangement of the pages to present a single, unchanging image of collaboration.[38] The passages between stories in this number cross the columns, but Dickens's opening story, related by the same narrator, stays in the two-column format. The conclusion of the number, then, is unique in bringing both the printed letters and the fictionalized versions of collaborators together in their own plot, crossing the vertical line between columns but not erasing the fiction/reality line.

The dialogue in this story also finally names the narrator and his sister (Joe and Patty), and that naming act decreases the autobiographical resonance between the narrator and Dickens at a moment when he is most playful

her noise, when hoo'd fain ha' cried for her niece to help. And now yo've truth, and a' th' truth, and I'll leave yo' to th' Judgment o' God for th' way yo've gotten at it."

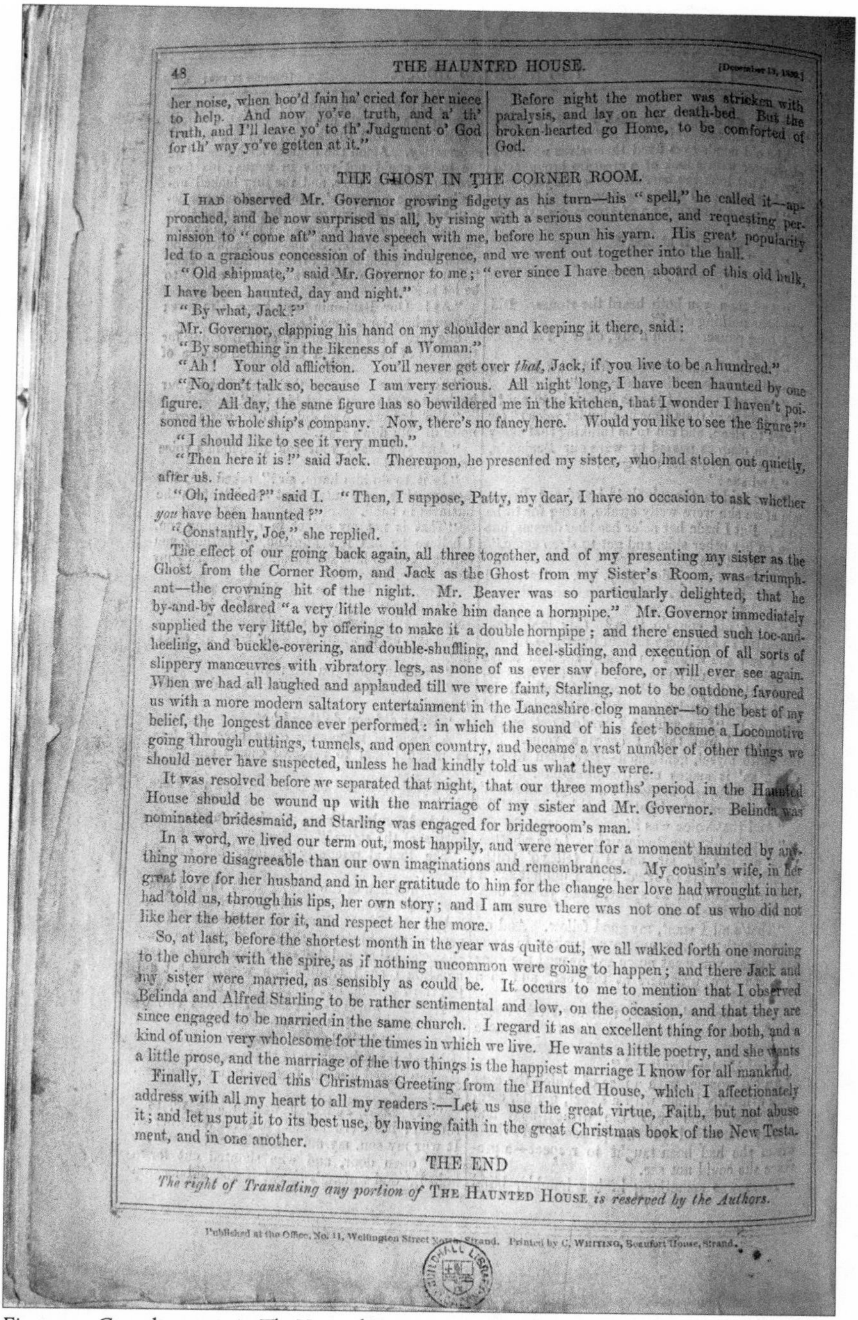

Before night the mother was stricken with paralysis, and lay on her death-bed. But the broken-hearted go Home, to be comforted of God.

THE GHOST IN THE CORNER ROOM.

I HAD observed Mr. Governor growing fidgety as his turn—his "spell," he called it—approached, and he now surprised us all, by rising with a serious countenance, and requesting permission to "come aft" and have speech with me, before he spun his yarn. His great popularity led to a gracious concession of this indulgence, and we went out together into the hall.

"Old shipmate," said Mr. Governor to me; "ever since I have been aboard of this old hulk, I have been haunted, day and night."

"By what, Jack?"

Mr. Governor, clapping his hand on my shoulder and keeping it there, said:

"By something in the likeness of a Woman."

"Ah! Your old affliction. You'll never get over *that*, Jack, if you live to be a hundred."

"No, don't talk so, because I am very serious. All night long, I have been haunted by one figure. All day, the same figure has so bewildered me in the kitchen, that I wonder I haven't poisoned the whole ship's company. Now, there's no fancy here. Would you like to see the figure?"

"I should like to see it very much."

"Then here it is!" said Jack. Thereupon, he presented my sister, who had stolen out quietly, after us.

"Oh, indeed?" said I. "Then, I suppose, Patty, my dear, I have no occasion to ask whether *you* have been haunted?"

"Constantly, Joe," she replied.

The effect of our going back again, all three together, and of my presenting my sister as the Ghost from the Corner Room, and Jack as the Ghost from my Sister's Room, was triumphant—the crowning hit of the night. Mr. Beaver was so particularly delighted, that he by-and-by declared "a very little would make him dance a hornpipe." Mr. Governor immediately supplied the very little, by offering to make it a double hornpipe; and there ensued such toe-and-heeling, and buckle-covering, and double-shuffling, and heel-sliding, and execution of all sorts of slippery manœuvres with vibratory legs, as none of us ever saw before, or will ever see again. When we had all laughed and applauded till we were faint, Starling, not to be outdone, favoured us with a more modern saltatory entertainment in the Lancashire clog manner—to the best of my belief, the longest dance ever performed: in which the sound of his feet became a Locomotive going through cuttings, tunnels, and open country, and became a vast number of other things we should never have suspected, unless he had kindly told us what they were.

It was resolved before we separated that night, that our three months' period in the Haunted House should be wound up with the marriage of my sister and Mr. Governor. Belinda was nominated bridesmaid, and Starling was engaged for bridegroom's man.

In a word, we lived our term out, most happily, and were never for a moment haunted by anything more disagreeable than our own imaginations and remembrances. My cousin's wife, in her great love for her husband and in her gratitude to him for the change her love had wrought in her, had told us, through his lips, her own story; and I am sure there was not one of us who did not like her the better for it, and respect her the more.

So, at last, before the shortest month in the year was quite out, we all walked forth one morning to the church with the spire, as if nothing uncommon were going to happen; and there Jack and my sister were married, as sensibly as could be. It occurs to me to mention that I observed Belinda and Alfred Starling to be rather sentimental and low, on the occasion, and that they are since engaged to be married in the same church. I regard it as an excellent thing for both, and a kind of union very wholesome for the times in which we live. He wants a little poetry, and she wants a little prose, and the marriage of the two things is the happiest marriage I know for all mankind.

Finally, I derived this Christmas Greeting from the Haunted House, which I affectionately address with all my heart to all my readers:—Let us use the great virtue, Faith, but not abuse it; and let us put it to its best use, by having faith in the great Christmas book of the New Testament, and in one another.

THE END

The right of Translating any portion of THE HAUNTED HOUSE *is reserved by the Authors.*

Published at the Office, No. 11, Wellington Street North, Strand. Printed by C. WHITING, Beaufort House, Strand.

Figure 5.2. Complete story in *The Haunted House*, page 48, running across full page. Photograph courtesy of the Charles Dickens Museum, London.

in representing his collaborators. Jack Governor takes Joe aside to say that "The Ghost in the Corner Room" is Patty and that "the Ghost from my Sister's Room" (unassociated with a full story) is Jack because they cannot stop thinking of each other. The two characters court in earlier days, but Jack marries another woman, who dies; now that Jack and Patty will marry, the whole group dances and celebrates. Glancy suggests that Jack Governor may be a tribute to Dickens's friend Clarkson Stanfield,[39] which would amplify the fiction/nonfiction crossing that takes place when another engagement occurs at Jack and Patty's wedding: "It occurs to me to mention that I observed Belinda and Alfred Starling to be rather sentimental and low, on the occasion, and that they are since engaged to be married in the same church. I regard it as an excellent thing for both, and a kind of union very wholesome for the times in which we live. He wants a little poetry, and she wants a little prose, and the marriage of the two things is the happiest marriage I know for all mankind" (48). The romantic pairing of Sala's and Procter's fictional counterparts acts as a risqué inside joke for those familiar with the world of journalism who knew that Sala wrote pornography and that Dickens valued Procter's work, but she may not have appreciated these fictional nuptials. Procter experienced at least one broken engagement to a man and may have maintained a lesbian relationship with Matilda Hays.[40] Dickens's skill at fictionalizing himself and others remains in flux in future numbers, but *The Haunted House* seems to have helped pull him out of the destructive tailspin of 1858. Camaraderie and ribbing, rather than mean-spirited characterization or mocking, lends a warm tone to the end of *The Haunted House* even if its antispiritualist statements are muddled in the telling.

Dickens again narrows the space between the fictional narrator and himself as he finishes the number with a broadly biblical Christmas message: "Finally, I derived this Christmas Greeting from the Haunted House, which I affectionately address with all my heart to all my readers" (48). The direct appeal brings the narrator back into close alignment with Dickens's editorial voice as he speaks to readers of *All the Year Round*, which adds to the challenge readers and critics face in attempting to distinguish Dickens's voice from the voices of others in this collection. Una Pope-Hennessey, for instance, attributes "six out of the eight chapters" of *The Haunted House* to Wilkie Collins, but she does not cite a source for the misattribution.[41] Early reviewers of *The Haunted House* also speculated that George Eliot, who declined Dickens's invitations to publish in his journal, had written Gaskell's "The Ghost in the Garden Room."[42] Contributors did not always object to these misattributions and sometimes even encouraged them. Earlier in 1859, for example, Gaskell was flattered when asked whether she was the person writing under the pseudonym George Eliot. Writing to Eliot via her publishers without fully knowing the writer's identity (Marian Evans), Gaskell volunteered to perpetuate the misidentifications: "[A]s you want to keep your real name a secret, it would be very pleasant for me to blush acquiescence. Will you give me leave?"[43] That Gaskell would write such a letter proves not that she was hoping to take public credit for Eliot's works but rather that, among Victorian authors, a confident willingness to play with notions of authorship and attribution permeated the literary atmosphere.

The stories in the Christmas numbers produced by Dickens existed in various forms and with different types of attribution simultaneously. Adelaide Anne Procter reprinted "The Ghost in the Picture Room" as "A Legend of Provence" in *Legends and Lyrics, Second Series* (1861). Gaskell included both "The Manchester Marriage" and "The Ghost in the Garden Room" (retitled "The Crooked Branch") in *Right at Last and Other Tales* (1860), drawing upon Dickens's notoriety in her preface as she thanked him for permission to republish.[44] In 1862, Tauchnitz, a well-respected German publisher, published three of Dickens's collaborative Christmas numbers (from 1859, 1860, and 1861) as part of the *Collection of British Authors* multivolume set and, unlike British publishers, identified the contributors.[45] The list of authors does not associate each writer with a specific story, but the title page makes clear who exactly participated in the joint effort of writing the number. Dickens maintained good relations with Tauchnitz over many years, calling him "a gentleman of great honor and integrity" as early as 1852, and the accuracy of Tauchnitz's information indicates that it came straight from the office of *All the Year Round*—if not from Dickens then from Wills.[46]

By Christmas of 1859, Dickens had finished ten of the special numbers. Whether one finds the quality of Dickens's conducting satisfactory or lacking, the metaphor was successful enough for one of Dickens's most renowned contemporaries to use. When William Makepeace Thackeray began his editorship of the new *Cornhill Magazine* in 1860, his opening letter directly addressed both readers and contributors, hoping they would "not be unwilling to try me as Conductor of a Concert, in which I trust many skillful performers will take part."[47] A professional competitiveness between Dickens and Thackeray had existed for decades, and Thackeray's lack of hesitation in casting himself as a conductor stokes the long-standing rivalry while also ascribing a high regard to editorship conceived in collaborative terms.[48] As a new decade begins, Dickens continues to develop the Christmas number as a unique collaborative form, sometimes using it as a venue for his most direct commentaries on conducting.

6

Disconnected Bodies and Troubled Textuality
(1860–62)

A sense of the collaborative project as unwieldy pervades Dickens's first three Christmas numbers of the 1860s, adding to the mystery that surrounded the compilation process. That process was common enough cause for speculation that it featured in the 1861 Christmas number of another widely circulated periodical, *The Queen*. Just before Christmas, Prince Albert died, and on December 21, *The Queen* released a black-bordered obituary supplement that allowed the journal to avoid "choosing to invade [the Christmas issue's] pages with anything sad-coloured."[1] *The Queen* thus advocates for different generic and tonal expectations than the ones governing Dickens's Christmas periodicals, which often featured "sad-coloured" tales, and its subsequent satire widens the scope of its commentary. Complete with a plate (see figure 6.1) depicting Dickens tied to a chair while three of his collaborators listen to Wilkie Collins read a story, "Tom Tiddler's Ground: Extraordinary Proceedings in Wellington-Street" takes aim at the process of devising a frame concept with Dickens suggesting dramatic titles like "The Flight of the Ladybird, in Seven Wings" before settling on the actual title of the 1861 number.[2] Ironically, no one identified in the illustration other than Dickens—Wilkie Collins, John Hollingshead, William Moy Thomas, and George Sala—is a contributor to *Tom Tiddler's Ground*, but those men had contributed to previous Christmas numbers and regular issues, enabling *The Queen's* publishers to satirize the dynamic between Dickens and his collaborators more broadly.

Figure 6.1. Page 313 of *The Queen*, December 21, 1861. © The British Library Board NEWS12537.

Trying to rein in the group's tangents by focusing their attention on the creative project, a fictionalized Wills in *The Queen's* story references the challenge of accommodating multiple storytellers: "True, his friend had mentioned the collective title under which seven stories by different authors were to look as much like one dramatic and homogenous production as the public would be good enough to fancy.... [H]e took for granted that each contributor had his preconceived idea of a tale which would fit in somehow, whatever title his friend the chairman would, in the most redundantly imaginative of moods, be likely to propose. Did any gentleman happen to have anything in his pocket?" (314). Aiming clearly at *The Seven Poor Travellers*, the piece does not neglect themes common to other previous frame concepts. Although having Wills call Dickens "redundantly imaginative" may portray the co-editorial relationship with excessive animosity, the essay also acknowledges that "the public," not Dickens, controls how much "homogeneity" to grant the stories. Relationships among collaborators are also a point of interest in the piece. Indulging the idea that contributions are prefabricated, Wilkie Collins pulls a story out of his pocket and begins to read it aloud. The tale satirizes the tropes of sensation novels and targets Collins's *The Woman in White* with a Fosco-like eccentric foreign villain who keeps "three tame oysters" for pets (314). The Hollingshead, Thomas, and Sala figures mock their respective originals' most known traits (such as Sala's writing about travel), then Dickens reiterates his frame concept, and they all agree to "help to work it out" (315). Overall, the essay speaks to those both inside and outside of the publishing world and shows how open Dickens and his collaborators were to ridicule in Christmas endeavors that no one pretended were works of individual genius.

The initial numbers of the 1860s are more self-conscious than ever about the piecing together of scripts and stories. *A Message from the Sea* (1860) introduces textual complexity right onto its pages with a nearly unreadable scrawled note, and questions of genre in the interpolated pieces interrogate the frame. *Tom Tiddler's Ground* (1861) admits the failure of its own storytelling project, and the next year's *Somebody's Luggage* is an entertaining reflection on the connectedness of crumpled-up manuscripts. As these three collections revel in the unruly aspects of collaborative storytelling, consistency arises in the chaotic dynamics between inset tales and their frames. A poem in *A Message from the Sea* depicts a shocking act of cannibalism antithetical to Dickens's usual aims, and reconnecting the frame to the interpolated sections reveals complicated generic developments in the realm of sensation fiction. This number benefits from generic tensions between pieces and demonstrates how a Christmas issue might take an ironic stance toward the storytelling its characters try to accomplish. *Tom Tiddler's Ground*, with a frame narrative that recalls *The Haunted House* in its blurring of the distinction between Dickens's real and fictional personas, also indulges irony by showing how storytelling can fail to have any positive effect on an audience. And *Somebody's Luggage*, the most playful number of all in its metatextuality, serves as a strong example of how collaborative texts themselves offer responses to the textual conundrums they raise.

A Message from the Sea

In November 1860, Wilkie Collins and Charles Dickens travelled together to Devon and Cornwall to brainstorm for that year's Christmas story.[3] The number's origins were thus collaborative from the very start, and the frame narrative mixes Collins's and Dickens's voices as well as their ideas. In 1860, Collins was helping Dickens out of a bind because the demanding weekly serial run of *Great Expectations* in *All the Year Round* did not leave much time for work on a Christmas number. As the collection came together, Dickens complained in a letter to Georgina Hogarth about Collins's narrative method: "Wilkie brought the beginning of his part of the Xmas No. to dinner yesterday. I hope it will be good. But is it not a most extraordinary thing that it began: 'I have undertaken to take pen in hand, to set down in writing—&c. &c—' like the W in W narratives? Of course, I at once pointed out the necessity of cancelling that, 'off,' as Carlyle would say."[4] Dickens associates the first-person narrator with *The Woman in White*, which had concluded in *All the Year Round* a few months earlier, and his annoyance forecasts (unfairly, considering the direction of Collins's future novels) *The Queen's* presumption that Collins would repeat the popular novel's style. Previous numbers, such as *The Holly Tree Inn*, also feature a frame narrator explaining the act of writing, and given the success of Collins's use of self-conscious narration, Dickens's opposition to the idea is perplexing. Even with the changes mentioned in Dickens's letter, the number's premise remains hinged on the reading and discovery of text, as the message from the sea itself is a note in a bottle. Ultimately, Dickens's complaint is so far out of line with the number's aesthetic and thematic concerns that his performance of dissatisfaction contradicts his actual editorial and authorial tendencies. Those tendencies result in a collection that includes sections with authorial voices melded together and sections in which individual narrators stick out awkwardly. The thematic complexities that arise from the stories exemplify how flexible Dickens's collaborative periodical voice had to be. In Harriet

Parr's and Henry Chorley's cases, a contributor's stance on the fictional representation of sensitive ethical questions—pertaining to madness and cannibalism, respectively—becomes part of Dickens's public voice in ways that force us to complicate our understanding of the fixity of his views and of his conducting persona.

Collins and Dickens collaborated thoroughly on the five chapters and linking sections of *A Message from the Sea*, and Dickens defended their joint work vigorously when Samuel Lane advertised an unauthorized stage version of the number at the Britannia Theatre that named Collins and Dickens as authors. In an attempt to thwart such piracies, Collins and Dickens had hastily published a description of their own plans for a theatrical adaptation, but their solicitors were not confident that a truncated synopsis of a play in place of a full script would hold up in Chancery.[5] After stopping the first production, Dickens and Collins deftly resolved the dispute by accepting a fee from Lane so that he could stage an adaptation, but before settling the suit, Dickens clarified the number's authorship to his solicitor in terms that both emphasize and dismiss collaboration:

> It occurred to us as we came back here from Council's chambers, that one point in the case is not explained to you. It may affect the clearing of the bill.
>
> Three introduced episodical stories and a poem—to be found in the Christmas No. are not by Wilkie Collins or by me. We invented, designed, and wrote, the whole of the No. with those exceptions. Therefore we are the authors of the story called the 'Message from The Sea,' and wrote the whole of that main story and plot. But the Episodes (which have nothing to do with it) are not ours.[6]

Dickens describes multiple models of collaboration operating simultaneously in a single number. The sections he and Collins coauthor are to be regarded as a complete fusion of their creative visions; the processes of invention, design, and writing mix together so thoroughly that no separation is possible. At the same time, Dickens positions the pieces from Henry Chorley, Charles Collins, Amelia B. Edwards, and Harriet Parr as discrete entities of their own. While the statement that those pieces have "nothing to do" with the "main story and plot" may initially seem to work against the project of integration Dickens and Collins advance in the bridging passages, in the context of the Chancery suit, the comment is protective. The main purpose of the letter to Frederic Ouvry, written on both Dickens's and Collins's behalf, is to ensure that they do not appear to be posing as the authors of the interpolated pieces. While advocating for their joint writing, Collins and Dickens maintain a concern for other collaborators, not wishing to take legal credit for others' work.

On the point of how much the interpolated stories have "to do" with the "main plot," there are far more connections between the pieces than even Dickens seems to have realized, but his description of the framing sections as being thoroughly collaborative matches the text. Some evidence beyond Dickens's letters, including reprinted collections of Christmas stories published in Dickens's lifetime, indicate that Dickens was the primary author of chapter 2, "The Money," and that Collins was the primary author for chapter 4, "The Seafaring Man," but further distinctions are difficult to support persuasively.[7] The main character in the frame story, Captain Silas Jonas Jorgan, is based on an acquaintance of Dickens's, Elisha Ely Morgan, to whom Dickens wrote, "Here and there, in the description of the sea-going Hero, I have given a touch or two of remembrance of Somebody you know."[8] Although Dickens's friend inspired his vision of the character, the "touch or two" metaphor leaves space for Collins to have added passages about Jorgan, particularly since the two worked on the frame together.[9]

A gregarious American, Jorgan begins the number by admiring the English seaside village of Steepways, and the narrator uses a jaunty tone to create a lighthearted atmosphere despite the seriousness of Jorgan's errand. Jorgan must share information related to the presumed death of Hugh Raybrock, Alfred's older brother, who left his wife and child at Steepways with his mother before disappearing in a shipwreck. Chapter 2 explains that Jorgan finds a bottle containing Hugh's message on the shore of an island where one of Jorgan's crewmen suddenly sinks into a pit and pleads for swift assistance because his "feet are among bones. . . . [T]hey were human bones; though whether the remains of one man, or of two or three men, what with calcination and ashes, and what with a poor practical knowledge of anatomy, I can't undertake to say" (5).[10] These grisly details raise the possibility of a communal grave close to the bottle bearing the following instructions: "Whoever finds this, is solemnly entreated by the dead, to convey it unread to Alfred Raybrock, Steepways, North Devon, England" (5).

The presentation of the message in the bottle—narratively and textually—is one of the number's most complex moments, and its layers set up the collection's engagement with multiple genres. Jorgan describes his and Alfred's reading process as they attempt to decipher the fragment, which prepares readers to share in the characters' detective work and to encounter a visual reproduction of the text: "The ragged paper, evidently creased and torn both before and after being written on, was much blotted and stained, and the ink had faded and run, and many words were wanting. What the captain and the young fisherman made out together, after much re-reading and much humouring of the folds of the paper, was this" (5). The handwritten script of the note, including marred spots and illegible words, then appears on the page (see figure 6.2). The details of the note are striking in the context of a Christmas number that follows the usual two-column format. The text fragment includes a torn corner and shadows for dimensionality, a fictional artifact that calls attention not only to the act of writing but also to the handwriting that establishes the provenance of the information motivating the number's plot. The only information one can glean from the note is that the five-hundred-pound legacy of Mr. Raybrock may have come from a disreputable source and that the mystery must be resolved before Alfred's finances are sound enough for marriage, but the invitation to decipher the note provides an air of realism that enhances generic elements of mystery and detection.

Notably, there are few changes in tone across the first three sections, which both Collins and Dickens wrote. It is impossible to tell without a substantial amount of speculation who wrote which passages, and the humor surrounding Captain Jorgan endures as the number's comic moments equal any passage from either Collins's or Dickens's novels. Regarding the Captain's relationship with the natural elements, for instance, chapter 3 follows Jorgan and Alfred across a dark Cornish moor on their way to investigate in Lanrean: "One might have supposed from his way, that there was even a kind of fraternal understanding between Captain Jorgan and the wind, as between two professed fighters often opposed to one another" (9). Despite the treacherous conditions, the Captain, "without any extra defence against the weather, walked coolly along with his hands in his pockets: as if he lived underground somewhere hard by, and had just come up to show his friend the road" (10). Once the pair arrives at the King Arthur's Arms hotel, the Captain's jolly disposition and presumption that they are welcome allow the men to join the meeting of the village's storytelling club. Only an hour previous to Jorgan and Raybrock's arrival, a sailor also arrived at the club, and the members testify that this individual astonished them by stopping abruptly midstory, refusing to share the conclusion of a shipwreck tale (11). Before we learn the fate of this seafaring man, the club's chairman chooses the next storyteller, and the interpolated tales of the number begin with Arson Parvis telling a brief yet rambling story about a famous waistcoat that befuddles the group.

bottle for a moment, that the young fisherman might direct a wondering glance at it; and then replaced his hand and went on:

"If ever you come—or even if ever you don't come—to a desert place, use you your eyes and your spy-glass well; for the smallest thing you see, may prove of use to you, and may have some information or some warning in it. That's the principle on which I came to see this bottle. I picked up the bottle and ran the boat alongside the Island and made fast and went ashore, armed, with a part of my boat's crew. We found that every scrap of vegetation on the Island (I give it you as my opinion, but scant and scrubby at the best of times) had been consumed by fire. As we were making our way, cautiously and toilsomely, over the pulverised embers, one of my people sank into the earth, breast high. He turned pale, and 'Haul me out smart, shipmates,' says he, 'for my feet are among bones.' We soon got him on his legs again, and then we dug up the spot, and we found that the man was right, and that his feet had been among bones. More than that, they were human bones; though whether the remains of one man, or of two or three men, what with calcination and ashes, and what with a poor practical knowledge of anatomy, I can't undertake to say. We examined the whole Island and made out nothing else, save and except that, from its opposite side, I sighted a considerable tract of land, which land

I was able to identify, and according to the bearings of which (not to trouble you with my log) I took a fresh departure. When I got aboard again, I opened the bottle, which was oilskin-covered as you see, and glass-stoppered as you see. Inside of it," pursued the captain, suiting his action to his words, "I found this little crumpled folded paper, just as you see. Outside of it was written, as you see, these words: '*Whoever finds this, is solemnly entreated by the dead, to convey it unread to Alfred Raybrock, Steepways, North Devon, England.*' A sacred charge," said the captain, concluding his narrative, "and, Alfred Raybrock, there it is!"

"This is my poor brother's writing!"

"I supposed so," said Captain Jorgan. "I'll take a look out of this little window while you read it."

"Pray no, sir! I should be hurt. We should all be hurt. My brother couldn't know it would fall into such hands as yours."

The captain sat down again on the foot of the bed, and the young man opened the folded paper with a trembling hand, and spread it on the table. The ragged paper, evidently creased and torn both before and after being written on, was much blotted and stained, and the ink had faded and run, and many words were wanting. What the captain and the young fisherman made out together, after much re-reading and much humouring of the folds of the paper, was this:

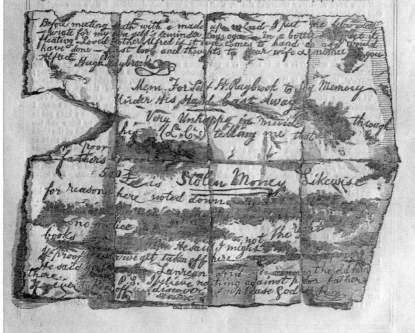

Figure 6.2. *A Message from the Sea*, page 5. *A Message from the Sea* is the only Christmas number to include such a drastic visual variation. Photograph courtesy of the Charles Dickens Museum, London.

A piece from Charles Collins, Wilkie Collins's younger brother (who had married Dickens's daughter Kate in July 1860), then ushers in more interpolated tales and enhances the metatextual reflection of the number. Dickens seems to ascribe pride of place to the position of the first interpolated story, writing to Georgina Hogarth, "Mrs. Gaskell being much too long for the purpose, I have put Charley Collins into the Christmas No. I have made his the first story too."[11] The speaker is John Tredgear, and the frame concept justifies changes in voice so completely that the shifts initially occur without abruptness. Tredgear's story pertains to a time when he was nearly murdered as a traveling businessman in France, and his ruminations on an inn are noteworthy: "The ceiling, as far as one could judge of anything at that altitude, appeared to be traversed by an enormous beam with rings fastened into it adapted for suicidal purposes, and splashed with the whitewash with which the ceiling itself and the walls had just been decorated" (14). This macabre setting contrasts sharply with the warmth of the inn Jorgan and Alfred have just entered. Whether the ceiling rings recently facilitated suicide (hence the whitewash) or portend self-inflicted violence to come is unclear. Tredgear suspects that the French landlord, who makes little effort to veil a desire to rob his visitor, has drugged the wine but then tries to talk himself out of the suspicion: "It was well to say 'Pooh!' it was well to remind myself that this was the nineteenth century, that I was not acting a part in a French melodrama, that such things as I was thinking of were only known in romances" (15). Bringing romance and melodrama into the mix of mystery and nautical adventure heightens the number's freewheeling movement through different storytelling modes as Collins pokes fun at the types of melodramatic plots both he and his collaborators manufacture.

Harriet Parr's "Passages from James Lawrence's Journal" multiplies the number of genres at play and makes a substantial portion of the Christmas number an exercise in document reading that is full of dramatic irony (20). Honor Livingstone, before killing herself, promises to haunt James Lawrence, the lover who jilts her, and Lawrence's surviving notebook supports the theory that her ghost leads him over a cliff. The fictional journal entries display a constant preoccupation with writing while enabling Parr to comment on genre. Lawrence claims only to keep the journal to record the possible haunting that Honor threatens: "I have never kept a diary of personal matters before, not being one who cares to see spectres of himself, at remote periods of his life, talking to him again of his adventures and misadventures out of yellow old pages that had better never have been written; but this is a marked event worth commemorating, and a well-authenticated ghost-story to me who never believed in ghosts before" (21). The genres invoked in the piece so far, then, are short story, diary, journal, and ghost story, but Lawrence's description makes a case for diaries always constituting a type of ghost story. And if first-person recollections turn such speakers into spectres, all of the storytellers in the frame's club are spectres of themselves, which blurs generic distinctions in the text as a whole.

The emergence of madness further complicates such questions as Parr's story participates in the contested discourses of sensation fiction. When Lawrence sees the ghost while in the presence of his wife, Anne, she calls a doctor who becomes so disturbed by Lawrence admitting to having seen an apparition that he starts evaluating Lawrence's sanity (21). Anne grows afraid of Lawrence, and when she tells him that he is too ill to travel, he strikes her (22). After calling him mad, Anne lives in "silent terror" while her husband keeps her isolated from her family and friends (22). This domestic imprisonment of a sane woman engages directly with contemporary narratives of madness and gender, flipping some of the usual conventions.[12] Wilkie Collins's *The Woman in White* features a villain who imprisons his completely sane wife in an asylum and at home. In Parr's story, the man's use of power to imprison a woman is a defense against a diagnosis of his own madness. The story, then, turns into a narrative questioning how definitions of sanity and madness operate, and that emphasis displaces the expected focus on supernatural hauntings. Firmly convinced of the conspiracy against him, Lawrence rants to his travelling partner: "Mad! All the world's mad, or on the way to it!" (23). Lawrence's insistence that everyone in the world occupies a position on the scale of madness is a striking predictor of Mary Elizabeth Braddon's *Lady Audley's Secret*, whose narrator's many thoughts on the subject of madness include the rumination, "Who has not been, or is not to be, mad in some lonely hour of life? Who is quite safe from the trembling of the balance?"[13] Parr's foray into these debates about sanity might appear to be disconnected from the frame narrative about shipwreck and family fortunes, but her tale converses with and sometimes challenges other pieces in the number.

As I discuss in more detail below, the jointly written narrative frame sections from Collins and Dickens also represent interactions with a madman. Parr's treatment of madness speaks to the contributions of both Dickens and Collins, forcing a reconceptualization of periodical textual collaboration as a multigendered and multidirectional set of relations. As Parr's narrator slowly moves toward lunacy and the story begins to interrogate the power relationships that result in the confinements of those deemed insane, it exhibits traits of both sensation and detective fiction. Lawrence's journal becomes the document that will prove or disprove the character's sanity, but readers lack any stability when searching for a point of view that will lead to a clear interpretation of it. Polreath concludes with the declaration, "I believe in the ghosts James Lawrence saw, as I believe in the haunting power of any great misdeed that has driven a fellow-creature into deadly sin" (24). Although Polreath's statement might seem to disavow belief in the supernatural, it actually does not. If Lawrence's perception was that an actual ghost haunted him, then Polreath validates that perception. If the haunting power of a misdeed, or a perception of haunting, is as strong as an actual visit from the dead, then no line separates a guilty conscience from an apparition. As frustrating as this story may be to Raybrock and Jorgan because it offers no information about the five-hundred-pound legacy, the suspense helps to achieve the frame narrative's goal of drawing out a quest. The generic complications of the inset stories continue to develop the number in productive fashion as a ballad from Henry F. Chorley follows Parr's piece with a less direct but more startling presentation of sanity questions.

At the exact center of this Christmas number lies one of the most shocking pieces to appear in any of the collections. Other than a few comments on attribution, Chorley's untitled poem has received no critical comment that I have been able to locate.[14] Given the frequent appearance of shipwrecks in the Christmas numbers, one might be excused for not paying particularly close attention to another tale of shivering passengers in lifeboats. Chorley's poem, however, deserves extended consideration given its treatment of cannibalism and race. Much critical discussion has surrounded Dickens's spirited remarks in *Household Words* about the demise of the Franklin expedition on its search for the Northwest Passage and accusations of cannibalism that surfaced in Dr. John Rae's report. Chorley's poem provides an entirely different view of the subject.[15]

As readers await the full explanation of Hugh's shipwreck, Chorley's ballad presents a short account of what happens to nine survivors of a different wreck. Without water or food, the men begin "To murmur, to curse, and to crave" before deciding to eat someone. The survivors do not recall exactly how they settle upon drawing numbered lots, and no one objects to the random method of determining "what their hideous morrow of meat must be." In the midst of lot drawing, the poem suddenly identifies a "rude black man," the most skilled sailor of the bunch, who volunteers his life to sustain the others (25). Given the general revulsion toward cannibalism and Dickens's much publicized opposition to the idea, the notion that the men in this boat accept the black man's offer, kill him, and eat him is astonishing. The poem is slow to disclose details, seeming to aim for the highest shock value, and the lines leading up to the man's declaration emphasize his racialized traits:

> And ugly and grim in the sunshine glare
>> Were his thick parched lips, and his dull small eyes,
> And the tangled fleece of his rusty hair—
>
>>>>> (25)

The enslaved man's explanation for his decision calls attention to his difference from them:

> "Let the play end, with your Number Four.
>> What need to draw? Live along, you few
> Who have hopes to save and have wives to cry
>> O'er the cradles of children free!
> What matter if folk without home should die,
>> And be eaten by land or sea?
>> I care for nobody; no, not I
>> Since nobody cares for me!"
>
> And with that, a knife—and a heart struck through—
>> And the warm red blood, and the cold black clay,
> And the famine withdrawn from among the few,
>> By their horrible meal for another day!

> So the eight, thus fed, came at last to land,
>> And the tale of their shipmate told,
> As of water found in the burning sand,
>> Which braves not the thirsty, cold.
> But the love of the listener, safe and free,
> Goes forth to that slave on that terrible sea.
>
> For, fancies from hearth and from home will stray,
>> Though within are the dance and the song;
> And a grave tale told, if the tune be gay,
>> Says little to scare the young.
> While they sing, with their voices clear as can be,
> Having called, once more, for the blithe old glee—
>> "I care for nobody, no, not I,
>> Since nobody cares for me."
>
>>>>> (25)

If one can bracket the physically revolting idea of drinking human blood in lieu of water, the primary factor making this episode so disturbing is not that a group of men decide one of them will die to ensure the survival of the others. Although tragic and upsetting to contemplate, cannibalism in a life-threatening situation can exist as a consensual arrangement promoting noble martyrdom. The poem goes to great pains to try to convince readers to take a merciful view of murder in these circumstances, but the instant the heroic, self-sacrificing figure is identified as a slave, the moral scenario changes. A captive person who chooses to die may possess an internal sense of autonomy that resists the mantle of victimhood, but one can never evaluate an act of suicide under such circumstances in a vacuum that erases the factors making an enslaved person's life unendurable. In this poem, the fact that the black man uses his enslavement as the reason for his willingness to be killed—in addition to the white men's swift consent—undercuts the notion that the killed man is making a free choice. The black man gestures toward his lack of freedom as the real reason for his death when he says that the other men's wives would weep "O'er the cradles of children free" because his own children would be unfree. He also points to his lack of citizenship when he says, "What matter if folk without home should die, / And be eaten by land or sea?" This man's perception of the conditions he would face once rescued are equivalent to being "eaten by land" because he does not enjoy personal liberty. If the enslaver died in the shipwreck, freedom or escape might be within reach once the survivors reach land, making the captive man's decision even more perplexing.

Furthermore, the white men's acceptance of the black man's proposed course of action flips typical cannibalism tropes and raises the question of whether race is the factor that sanctions this scenario. The ballad indirectly suggests that consuming the body of a degraded human is more acceptable because he is already classified as more of an animal than a person, making it less abhorrent to think about eating the black man than to imagine the consumption of white-identified English flesh. Although the speaker describes the black man in racist terms that accentuate his lips, hair, and ugliness, the story's events reverse the typical trope of savage people of color killing and eating innocent white travellers. Here, white men intentionally kill and eat a black man, but the poem's apparent lack of irony prevents those white men from being cast as savages.

The ballad is often a cautionary genre, but in this case, no clear picture emerges of what precisely it cautions against.[16] Its "gay tune" includes an intertextual refrain—"I care for nobody, no, not I, / Since nobody cares for me"—that the enslaved man offers as his final utterance and that comes from the popular folk song "The Miller of the Dee." Existing in various versions, the folk ballad is about a laborer whose mill fills the role of a family as it brings him wealth and steady, if not human, companionship. The miller's life, however, involves no acts of extreme self-sacrifice, so by putting the refrain in the enslaved man's voice, Chorley creates a conversation in which the comfort of a humble miller highlights the desperation of an owned human being. Furthermore, in this iteration, because children voice the "I" perspective, they occupy the enslaved man's vocal position. They are also watched by older generations that seem to include the survivors of the wreck, who recollect "a far midnight on the terrible sea, / Which comes back on the tune of their blithe old glee" (25). The slave history returns not just via the children's song; their very bodies carry the story. The children born after the wreck literally embody the dead man if his blood and flesh sustained their parents. In terms of mythologized racial purity, the ballad shows how the excavation of back-stories for idealized English songs reveals complicated racial relationships. In an era concerned with blood "purity" and possible contamination from servants like wet nurses, the idea that English parents have digested a black body profoundly unsettles dominant racial ideologies.[17] The final lines cast the man's sacrifice as the "good" that God showers on Earth, exempting the white men and their families from any culpability. The writer of this ballad labors intensely over the text then suffers from "indigestion" so severe as to require Captain Jorgan's nursing, which strongly implies that the writer is one of the survivors who eats a man (24). Jorgan has been preserving the fair copy on pipe-light paper since returning its writer home, and the fragile state in which the verses exist parallels the textual state of the message in a bottle that has spawned the plot of the number. As we shall see in a later story, the explanation of the circumstances surrounding that bottled message draw further upon the dynamics in Chorley's verse.

Neither the fictional characters nor Dickens expresses any negative opinion of the ballad. Captain Jorgan does not ask if there might be a connection to five hundred ill-gotten pounds, and in place of any remark on the poem, the narrator comments on Parvis's snoring (25). Dickens's harsh rejections of any contemplations of cannibalism involving the Franklin Expedition make it surprising for him to suddenly deem it an altruistic act, which places Chorley's presentation of the sailors' behavior in direct opposition to Dickens's contentions.[18] Yet Chorley is an author whom Dickens respects highly; earlier in 1860, Dickens praises Chorley's characterization of a heroine: "[T]here is a profound wise knowledge that I admire and respect with a heartiness not easily overstated in words."[19] The inclusion of Chorley's ballad under the "Conducted by Charles Dickens" mantle indicates that Dickens's stance on cannibalism may not have been as inflexible as he portrays it to be in other publications and that deep-seated racism influences his moral stance on the practice. Or, given Dickens's repeated opposition to the practice, this moment may require readers to redefine the voice of "Dickens" as one that can disagree with itself in the periodical press. Ultimately, this poem provides further evidence that the Christmas numbers are a place where voices of differing viewpoints mingle, and its placement at the center of the number makes clear that many messages from the sea trouble the number's characters.

Between Chorley's ballad and "The Seafaring Man," written chiefly by Wilkie Collins, the number's generic focus moves to a ghost story from Edwards in which Oswald Penrewen recounts his brother's encounter with the ghost of a fellow traveller on a trip through Switzerland. The traveller's haste to reach his fiancée because their wedding will take place in just one week leads to his demise, and his situation calls to mind Alfred Raybrock's marriage plans, which are set to take place one week from the time Jorgan arrives. The possibly bleak foreshadowing (on top of haunting) does little to calm the unease caused by Chorley's poem. As Alfred enters the bedroom where the seafaring man sleeps, an uncomfortable relationship between life and death permeates the number's atmosphere. For "The Seafaring Man," the narrator has said that Hugh will tell his story "in his own words," but we do not know to whom he speaks, and references to his audience fluctuate abruptly.[20] Six columns into the story, following an extra blank line, Hugh shifts from addressing a mysterious group of "sirs" to speaking directly to Alfred (whom he has discovered in the adjoining bed) (33). These jarring shifts are confusing, particularly in light of the fact that a single person, Collins, is identified as the lead writer for the section. Understood in light of the same flaw in A House to Let, which also emerged from a time of close joint work, the awkward transitions suggest that Collins and Dickens sometimes lose track of their own narrative layers.

Hugh's story also revisits questions of genre as he explains why he decides to overcome a considerable aversion to storytelling only to stop in the middle of the tale he begins to share with the club. Noting a long tradition that regards sailors as expert storytellers, Anthea Trodd observes, "Hugh's lack of narrative skills, his ordinariness, his difference from the fictional Tar, are offered as guarantees of the authenticity of his narrative."[21] In addition to establishing credibility, Hugh's explanation of his ineptitude identifies as its source his concern about the conventions of genre:"[H]aving all my life been a wretched bad hand at such matters—for the reason, as I take it, that a story is bound to be something which is not true. But when I found the company willing, on a sudden, to put up with nothing better than the account of my shipwreck (which is not a story at all), the unexpected luck of being let off with only telling the truth about myself, was too much of a temptation for me—so I up and told it" (32). Hugh's claim calls the veracity of other stories into question as it equates their narration with falsity, and he must categorize his own shipwreck experience as "not a story at all" because it is "the truth." That very story appears in this Christmas number under the mantle of fiction, placing Hugh in a narrative position that would be untenable if the number were not masterfully, as Trodd points out, using Hugh's performance of ineptitude to boost his integrity. As Alfred and Hugh walk the moors, Hugh shares the full context for the note in the bottle and includes all the parts of his story that he refused to tell the club, placing readers in a position of privilege alongside the unidentified "sirs" as they listen to a story whose teller refuses to call it one (34).

Throughout Hugh's recounting of his ordeals, the cannibalism that looms from Chorley's ballad resurfaces. When Hugh survives a shipwreck, he saves the life of Lawrence Clissold, a drunkard who constantly provokes Hugh by questioning the deceased Mr. Raybrock's integrity. Despite Clissold's taunts while the men are stranded on an island, Hugh behaves civilly, and they ultimately agree to split their provisions before retreating to separate territories. Clissold's belligerence does not cease, as he repeatedly attempts to kill Hugh and refers to the five hundred pounds Mr. Raybrock possesses at his death as "stolen money" (41). Clissold is obviously out of his mind, especially when he has no access to alcohol, and the irrationality of his ravings leads one to think that if he does kill Hugh, he may not hesitate to consume Hugh's body. Thus, the confusing messages of the ballad from Chorley are not limited to the context of the enslaved man in the lifeboat. Finally, the mad Clissold lights the whole island on fire using abundant dry brush. Hugh faints on the rocks after placing his message in a bottle and wakes up as "naked savages" tie him up and take him to a different island, again bringing fears of cannibalism to the surface. The story almost shifts in genre to a captivity narrative, but Hugh intentionally skips over his imprisoned time "among the savages," noting only that during the one to two years before his rescue, he is presented as a "curiosity" due to his whiteness. "When they were tired of showing me," he recollects, "they spared my life, finding my knowledge and general handiness as a civilised man useful to them in various ways" (44). The very tropes that Chorley's poem reverses reemerge here, showing that multivocality is crucial to the collection's inner workings and that ignoring the tales in the number's center excises the contextual richness that adds depth to Hugh's island narrative.

Once Hugh, Alfred, and Jorgan have shared information, clearing up the mystery of Clissold's accusations takes place with all the haste and improbability characteristic of sensation fiction. In "The Restitution," the men return to Steepways, and Jorgan quickly discerns that the deceased Mr. Raybrock had loaned five hundred pounds to Clissold, which Clissold repaid by stealing then framing Tregarthen for the theft (45). The five hundred pounds that was to purchase Alfred's share of the fishery goes to Tregarthen, who uses it to help Alfred and Kitty marry, and the number concludes by announcing that the couple dutifully names their son Jorgan.

The push and pull between the conventions of so many genres—sensation fiction, ghost story, madness narrative, journal, diary, ballad, and shipwreck tale—leaves no readerly expectation safe in this number and resembles the herky-jerky experience of Alfred Raybrock as he anxiously seeks a resolution to his own story. Overall, the collection is a strong example of how chaotic a Christmas number can feel without being completely incoherent, but that aesthetic has not garnered critical praise. Deborah Thomas blames Collins for the plot and complains, "A Message from the Sea illustrates the deleterious effect of a strong interest in plot on the emerging fictional form to which Dickens' monologues belong."[22] The possibility of Collins (or other contributors) ever improving Dickens's work is one that Thomas and others dismiss, which is not an uncommon problem. Considering the works of John Stuart Mill and Harriet Taylor Mill, Holly Laird notices that, distracted by questions of blame and competition, "critics have failed almost completely to attend to the knotty processes and effects of authorial collaboration."[23] A Message from the Sea exemplifies just such "knotty processes and effects," as it relies on voices that move in different directions while staying linked to a sturdy frame. Alfred Raybrock's constancy and Captain Jorgan's unshakeable confidence provide such framing stability even as the content of the number explores the most disordered possibilities for human behavior.

Tom Tiddler's Ground

In *Tom Tiddler's Ground* (1861), Dickens again transforms an actual person into the main character of a frame narrative: Mr. James Lucas, a recluse in Hertfordshire who accepted the visits of curious passersby and became something of a regional attraction, is the model for Mr. Mopes.[24] Dickens's unkind treatment of Mopes contrasts with his warm depiction of Jorgan as *Tom Tiddler's Ground* explores unusual human propensities in a failed attempt to insist on the fundamental goodness of companionship and storytelling. The first several pages of this number are downright unpleasant, not because of the hermit's filth but because his tense interaction with the traveller portends conflict, particularly once the hermit mentions his gun. The number opens unusually with a question: "'And why Tom Tiddler's ground?' asked the Traveller," as the traveller interrogates everything about the hermit, his surroundings, and his motives (1).[25] The narrator, called only "Mr. Traveller," walks five miles from a rural inn on a midsummer day to see Mopes, who resides on his own land and "scatters halfpence to Tramps and such-like," which has earned his home the name Tom Tiddler's ground (1).[26] On his way to discovering the hermit lying on a dirty floor, the traveller also finds a tinker lying on the ground outside the house. The number's contents list includes a final story called "Picking Up the Tinker," and knowing that this character from the opening frame section will return creates some early coherence. The Christmas numbers, by this point, have established their own traditions and tropes, including the introduction of narrators to come in the opening frame stories, which encourages readers to pay attention to newly introduced characters with the assurance of their reappearance.

The traveller's taunting of the hermit and the motives behind the storytelling he demands are worth examining in some depth because they articulate the lofty and ultimately unmet goals of this number as a whole. The traveller hurls insults, alleging that the hermit is motivated by "Vanity" and citing his "audience" as well as the beggars who collect coins as proof of serious offense: "[I]t is a general Nuisance to know that there *can be* such a Nuisance left in civilisation so very long after its time" (3–4). For the traveller, Mopes's existence threatens the social norms that enable people to imagine that they are civilized. That Mopes, a member of the noble class, has reduced himself to such filth also causes discomfort about his race, leading the traveller to contrast him to a "Hottentot" (2). The derogatory comparison to a South African suggests that Mopes's choices call his racial purity into question, and the traveller is so confused by the hermit's crossing of boundaries that he combines offensive places and people in his semicoherent description of Mopes as a "compound of Newgate, Bedlam, a Debtors' Prison in the worst time, a chimney-sweep, a mudlark, and the Noble Savage!" (3). Nevertheless, the traveller believes that storytelling might restore Mopes to his rightful, and whiter, identity.

In the setup for the interpolated section, "chance" excuses the potential randomness of the stories ahead; Mr. Traveller declares that they will spend the day listening to "every chance wayfarer who may come in at your gate" and claims it impossible for any person to appear at the hermit's residence who will "confute me and justify you" (5). The pompousness of Mr. Traveller's aim is apparent to the hermit, who responds, "You are an arrogant and boastful hero" (5). Although the traveller claims to be intent on using stories to prove that "every man must be up and doing, and that all mankind are made dependent on one another" (5), his animosity toward Mopes indicates that a deeper or less altruistic motive may lie behind his aggressive manner. The traveller insists that human existence is based on the understanding, "according to Eternal Providence, that we must arise and wash our faces and do our gregarious work and act and re-act on one another, leaving only the idiot and the palsied to sit blinking in the corner" (5). Ignoring the fact that, although not an "idiot," Mopes may be suffering from an illness that causes him to choose an unclean and semisequestered way of life, the traveller's essential objection seems to be that Mopes refuses to "act and re-act" in a way that he finds acceptable. One also wonders whether there is a defensive aspect to the narrator's offended feelings. If hermitude levies an implicit critique against those who crave constant social company and approbation—and against people (like Dickens) who glorify such socializing in their writing—Mr. Traveller's surprising level of anger may be the result of a wish to defend those with social dispositions. Rosemarie Bodenheimer's blistering critique of *Tom Tiddler's Ground* as an example of "Dickens in his most stupid frame of mind" certainly takes the traveller, as a projection of Dickens, to task, yet there remains more to learn about how the multifaceted conversation and storytelling of the number ultimately fails.[27]

Ironically, the traveller sets himself up for defeat, as his story titles engage him unselfconsciously in the same type of act as those whose attention to Mopes he finds so inappropriate. Each story's title begins with the phrase "Picking Up" because the traveller is collecting stories in place of the half crowns visitors usually retrieve. Charles Collins, both a painter and a writer, contributes the first story, "Picking Up Evening Shadows." Mr. Broadhead, who appears on Mopes's property with a sketchbook, prefaces his story by saying that it exemplifies the opposite argument from Mr. Traveller's: "I *do* remember one good thing which came, in some degree, of a man's leading a solitary life" (6). Charles Collins's story engages with questions about community relationships by turning Broadhead's act of spying on one's neighbors into an act of charity when he tries to send monetary aid to people whose silhouettes he observes from his small flat. The improbabilities in Collins's story point toward the absurdities embedded in sensation fiction. The couple Broadhead wants to help turns out to be his boss's estranged son and the son's wife, but he discovers that information only after intruding on a different couple, who receive his charity mistakenly. The story's happy ending brings the couple out of poverty, but the resolution is enabled by the artist's initial isolation, which makes a weak case for the necessity of constant social contact. The fact that financial rescue comes from a stranger who, instead of throwing half crowns on a lawn, throws pounds semimetaphorically across a mews rather contradicts the traveller's point.

Amelia B. Edwards's "Picking Up Terrible Company" also disappoints Mr. Traveller's hopes, illustrating the perils of certain types of togetherness. Francois Thierry, who has been branded as punishment for political opposition, tells a suspenseful story involving escape from a French prison then nearly being killed by a fellow escapee while illuminating a basilica in Rome (15). Edwards's fast-paced, intense tale skillfully depicts a dramatic prison escape, and the beauty of lighting St. Peter's dome at Easter resonates with the symbolic power of rituals associated with Christmastime. Still, the "terrible company" of the story's title does little to make Mr. Traveller's point and indeed may work against it. If some people will attempt murder in the midst of shared labor in service of a holy celebration, it is difficult to spot a message about the positive aspects of human community. The narrator's concluding remarks—"Since that time my fortunes have been various, and I have lived in many countries" (21)—provide no sense of how the story might support an argument that one should avoid living in isolation.

No transitions ease the shift from one story to another as Mr. Traveller persists in trying to make his case, with little success. Wilkie Collins's "Picking Up Waifs at Sea" is less touching than his brother's contribution but far funnier, building on the lively tone of Edwards's story. Mr. Jolly, a ship surgeon, does not—perhaps to the surprise of regular readers of the Christmas numbers who might expect another shipwreck—tell a tale of nautical disaster. Mrs. Smallchild, a wealthy woman with no children, and Mrs. Heavysides, a working-class woman with seven children, go into labor simultaneously while at sea, and Jolly's splitting of the main cabin into distinct birthing areas fails to prevent a mix-up of infants. The captain uses a three-ounce difference in weight to justify sending the heavier infant home with the larger woman. As they age, the baby raised as Heavysides (who tells the story) looks like the Smallchild family but has no recourse to change his situation or increase his income. The story puts the lie to class superiority based on "blood," as does much of Collins's fiction, and injects a rollicking sense of entertainment into the number but does nothing to make a case against living life as a hermit.

Nor does the next story, "Picking Up a Pocket-Book" by John Harwood, advance Mr. Traveller's goal; the story's consistent othering of non-English people participates in the kind of misanthropic attitudes that Mopes embraces more than it instructs against his lifestyle. The "sunburnt" Mr. George Walford tells of his time working as a clerk in San Francisco, where he courts his future wife, Emma (30). Emma's father needs George's help to help track down a thief who has colluded with Emma's brother to defraud the firm, which launches George on a dramatic journey spanning the North American continent. After attempting to rescue a rider from an Indian attack, George receives crucial assistance from the Pony Express (35). Once George locates the thief in New York, their hotel conveniently catches fire, enabling George to retrieve the fraudulent cheque from the "Russia-leather pocket-book" of the story's title (43). George derides the firm's junior partner, Mr. Housermann, calling him unproductive, mocking his accented English, and criticizing Germans in America for refusing to assimilate (31). He regards Native Americans—one of whom is a murderous and "muscular barbarian"—as "savages," and the story obsessively fears scalping, mentioning it three times on a single page (33). Exiting his train in New York, George also exaggerates the speech of an African American porter: "Massa get out? Dis New York, sare" (42). Collectively, the unnuanced disrespect of these references not only contributes to dominant racist ideologies but also aligns with Mr. Traveller's comments about "Hottentots" and "noble savages" in the opening section, showing that those claiming to be more gregarious and kind than Mopes are no more sensitive than he is when it comes to human difference.

One might expect a child narrator to more effectively spark a redemptive mood, as children in Dickens's oeuvre often do. Dickens's "Picking Up Miss Kimmeens," however, does no such thing. Miss Kimmeens has been left alone at school for a day while the mistress attends a wedding during summer holidays that have taken the other girls home. The girl's bitter rant as she sits alone showcases a Christmas number's ability to encapsulate characteristically Dickensian humor, concluding with her hope that the guests who "thought they were enjoying themselves" at the wedding "would all be dead in a few years, let them enjoy themselves ever so much. It was a religious comfort to know that" (47). Delightfully envisioning the deaths of others startles Miss Kimmeens into an awareness of her wickedness and pushes her out the door in search of human company, but she finds a scary hermit instead of a welcoming hearth. Charmingly precocious, even Miss Kimmeens fails to inspire Mopes, and none of the stories that the traveller collects persuade Mopes to change his ways.[28] The number documents something akin to a botched Scrooge conversion, and the concluding section, Dickens's "Picking Up the Tinker," reiterates the questioning of Mopes's racial purity when the traveller says that the "black" will not wear off of the hermit (48). The tinker does not do much more than repeat the traveller's dismay; his disgust stems from his opinion that a desire for attention motivates the hermit to live a deprived existence on a landed estate, while poverty compels unfortunate people to live without comforts.

Tom Tiddler's Ground stands as one of the weakest Christmas numbers in regard to the frame's success in yoking stories together. Although the frame accounts for why the stories are on random topics, the traveller's animosity, combined with a lack of depth in the character of Mr. Mopes, decreases readerly investment in what the stories relate. An "anything goes" attitude characterizes the number: babies switched at birth at sea; an Englishman racing across the American west on horseback, fighting Indians and dodging Mormons; a Frenchman dangling from a rope in Rome as another ex-convict tries to kill him. These stories hardly resemble ones that restore faith in human companionship and the benefits of sociability. Rather, they constitute a hodgepodge that, unlike most of the other numbers, does not help the frame advance a compelling project. The irony in having the traveller's storytelling fail is that it also leads to a weak storytelling performance on Dickens's part. The number sold well, but its quality is noticeably inferior to the numbers before and after. For the next year's number, the narrator begins with no illusions about successful storytelling. Instead, the discovery of manuscripts draws him toward the sharing of stories despite his own reservations. Although Dickens complained about Collins calling too much attention to documents in 1860's *A Message from the Sea*, the number for 1862 returns to a frame that emphasizes textuality even without any contribution from Wilkie.

Somebody's Luggage

Somebody's Luggage overflows with metatextual references. The number's premise revolves around textuality and writing, and its middle stories take up questions of authorship—attributed or unattributed—in relation to the valuation of labor. When a headwaiter discovers manuscripts in abandoned luggage at the coffeehouse rooms where he works, he publishes them in the Christmas number readers now hold. The form of his collection insists on textual divisions while simultaneously breaking them down, ultimately inviting readers to make the stories cohere despite formal obstacles. From the disorderly mess of *Tom Tiddler's Ground* emerges a narrator (and editor) confident and seasoned enough to use the disjointedness of collaboration to advantage.

One must note the similarity between *Somebody's Luggage* and *Master Humphrey's Clock*, a failed endeavor of Dickens's more than two decades prior. Begun in April 1840, Dickens's attempt at constructing a miscellany uses the framing device of an old man who has stashed papers in a clock and, from time to time, reads them to his friends. The story that turned into *The Old Curiosity Shop* was successful, but the awkward framing and lack of variety in the miscellany resulted in low sales that caused it to fold by the end of 1841.[29] In *Somebody's Luggage*, Dickens returns to the secreting of manuscripts in objects with much greater success. Writing to prospective contributors, he gives the authors free rein over most elements of the stories while emphasizing textuality:

> The slight leading notion of the No. being devised with a view to placing as little restriction as possible on the fancies of my fellow-writers in it, there is again no limitation as to scene, or first person, or third person; nor is any reference to the season of the year essential.
>
> It is to be observed that the Tales are not supposed to be narrated to any audience, but are supposed to be in writing. How they come to be in writing, *requires no accounting for, whatever*. Nothing to which they refer, can have happened within Seven Years.[30]

That Dickens does not simply share the full frame concept with the contributors is curious; the letter to Wills in which he encloses these instructions states that he has already written the opening and closing sections. Dickens is excited about having completed his work so early and is already looking forward to adding "His Boots": "You will be perhaps a little surprised (and not disagreeably) to learn that I have done the opening and end of the Xmas No. (!) and that I mean soon to be at work on a pretty story for it."[31] The exclamation mark not only expresses Dickens's enthusiasm more than three months in advance of the number's publication but also adds to the self-mocking irony that he uses to describe his own achievement in the rest of the letter. This enthusiasm, however, does not lead to an equal sense of openness with his fellow writers. In sharing instructions that only minimally aid each story's ability to fit into the frame he has finished and cryptically requiring that no actions take place within the previous seven years without explaining that the manuscripts have been abandoned in the luggage for that long, Dickens withholds information in a way that seems to purposely enhance the potential for variation in the contributions he will receive.

In "His Leaving It Till Called For," Dickens opens the collection with Christopher, a sixty-one-year-old waiter who embodies the profession and discovers the manuscripts that constitute the number. Christopher's amusing description of his entry into the world includes memories of having been born in a pantry then hidden there whilst his mother serves tables. The luggage Christopher finds has been abandoned for nearly six years under one of the room's beds after being left as excessive collateral for a bill of a little over two pounds. The set intrigues Christopher because each piece contains manuscripts stuffed into all available spaces: "There was writing in his dressing-case, writing in his boots, writing among his shaving-tackle, writing in his hat-box, writing folded away down among the very whale-bones of his umbrella" (5). The objects also include "a black portmanteau . . . a black bag, a desk, a dressing-case, a brown-paper parcel," and "a walking stick" to which the umbrella is fastened (5).

One expects to find paper in a writing desk, but the stuffing of manuscripts into boots suggests something rushed or unplanned about the owner's packing, and that tone pervades the number. Christopher imagines the actual writing of the manuscript in dramatic terms: "Utterly regardless of ink, he lavished it on every undeserving object—on his clothes, his desk, his hat, the handle of his toothbrush, his umbrella. Ink was found freely on the coffee room carpet by No. 4 table, and two blots was on his restless couch" (6). In addition to the introduction of some new objects (a toothbrush and clothing), Christopher's entertaining view of writing characterizes "Somebody" as a manic force. The presence of ink on all of his things unites them, and the flinging of the ink around the room makes clear that any object in its path might serve as the next piece of paper. The Somebody who leaves this luggage is a blank in the center of the set, the body around which the other items circulate. His form is drawn by their outlines, but the content of the writing also forms his body through items like his boots. It is as if Somebody has been torn apart and packed into the crevices of the luggage, and Christopher (the reader) puts him back together. Once the objects are sold, enabling Christopher to recoup his investment, the luggage and Somebody exist only in the writing.

Christopher's explanation of how he has arranged the manuscripts begins to establish the number's central concerns about the relationships among textual, human, and object bodies: "The writings are consequently called, here, by the names of the articles of Luggage to which they was found attached. In some cases, such as his Boots, he would appear to have hid the writings: thereby involving his style in greater obscurity. But his Boots was at least pairs—and no two of his writings can put in any claim to be so regarded" (6). In some respects, Christopher is wrong. The manuscripts in the boots indeed form a complete story, but so do others that are divided between multiple objects. Reading "His Boots," readers must connect the two luggage items because there is no break in the story to indicate when to move from one boot to the other. That practice sets a precedent for the other tales. Charles Collins's story begins in "His Black Bag," but its conclusion lies in "His Writing Desk." In the midst of the story, we are told abruptly that "the rest of this manuscript he had put into His Writing Desk" (24). Here, the text pointedly directs readers to carry authorial voice over from one story, and piece of luggage, to another. Similarly, Julia Cecilia Stretton's long tale is split between "His Portmanteau" and "His Hat Box." If readers are invited to see a necessary connection between two boots, between the black bag and the writing desk, and between the portmanteau and the hat box, then why not between the other pieces of luggage? The repeated joining of items, despite Christopher's denial, invites one to question whether the brown paper parcel might have something to do with the black bag or whether the umbrella is related to one or both boots. The narrative itself dismantles the textual divisions that it creates.

The story that fills "His Boots," by Dickens, appears as a coherent, singular tale with no demarcation of when the words switch from one boot to the other. A grumpy old Englishman, Langley, observes an attachment between Bebelle, a young orphaned girl in France, and Corporal Théophile, whom she has chosen to replace her inattentive adoptive parents. The story's charm stems primarily from Langley being exasperated by French sentimentalism while being sentimental himself, and its final emphasis on English-French comradeship recalls the resolution of Doubledick's story in *The Seven Poor Travellers*. Bebelle leads Langley to regret his unforgiving stance toward his own daughter, and after Théophile dies in a fire, Langley begins fathering Bebelle before taking her to England, where he intends to reunite with his daughter. Exemplifying "that blood is not the only means of forming a family," this series of events is one that Holly Furneaux notices as part of a trend throughout Dickens's oeuvre to validate non-biological family formations.[32] "His Boots" also joins many other Dickens narratives in depicting a hardened older man softening thanks to the influence of a child.[33] Fewer critics have noted a potentially disturbing element of the story: that the child functions as a commodified object. Mr. Langley pays the barber's

wife for Bebelle because his adoption of her will result in the loss of a sti-
pend. Notwithstanding such commodification, when Langley finds the child
on the Corporal's grave, the image of "a live child lying on the ground asleep"
above the recently buried corpse of her adoptive father is arresting (12).

The idealized conclusion of the story is startling when one recalls that
Christopher has referred to these pages in the boots as ones that the writer
might have been trying to conceal. The boots belong to the mysterious Somebody, not Langley or Théophile, but this strange hiding raises the question
of whether Somebody could be Langley and blurs the lines between the fictional characters of the inset stories and the frame characters. The hiding
also suggests that there may be an unsavory aspect underlying the story that
could cause trouble if discovered by readers acquainted with the mysterious
Somebody. Speculative biographical readings have proposed that Ellen Ternan was pregnant close to this time with a child fathered by Dickens that
did not survive, which would certainly qualify as a scandal-causing reason to
hide a story, but such readings do not tend to consider the story's relationship to the collection's frame.[34] The manuscript pages telling this girl's story
would take the rough shape of a man's foot. The unfurling of the pages both
dismantles and gives voice to an absent adult body, and how closely the story
of that body relates to the boots' owner remains unclear.

The metatextuality of John Oxenford's "His Umbrella" does not have to
do with authorship but rather stems from the umbrella's containing a story
about an umbrella. Such a coincidence would be unlikely if the manuscripts
had been placed accidentally into each object without forethought. Either
Somebody thought the umbrella story should reside in its inspirational
home or Christopher, without notifying the reader, has arranged the stories in the objects he thinks are most appropriate for their themes. Oxenford's story details Yorick Zachary Yorke's terrorization by his own umbrella,
which he acquires from a ghost woman outside of London on February 29 of
a leap year (14). Catherine Crackenbridge disappears in a field that she then
haunts, and when her umbrella is separated from her, the object moves on
its own, sometimes transporting other things with it. Four years must pass
for Yorke to rid himself of the cursed gingham umbrella because Crackenbridge's ghost can retrieve it only on the day it was taken; all other attempts
to destroy or pawn it fail in the interim. When Jack Slingsby, Yorke's friend,
witnesses the self-propelled movement of a hat with the umbrella, the story
blurs the line between the conventional and the supernatural so smoothly
that possible belief in the supernatural does not seem insane on Yorke's part.
Somebody's Luggage already revolves around items holding texts; by animating

one of the found things, "His Umbrella" enables objects to have an even more active presence in the number and foregrounds their role in forming one's impression of their missing owner.[35]

The next item containing text is not endowed with self-propulsion but does require that readers connect "His Black Bag" to "His Writing Desk." Charles Collins uses a narrator whose comments on writing point ironically both to Somebody and to Dickens. Collins's unidentified narrator tells of his trip to Creel, the estate of his friends the Duke and Duchess of Greta. Also visiting are Mary Crawcour and Jack Fortescue, whose nuptials are blocked by the duchess's wish for Mary to marry the wealthier, obnoxious Lord Sneyd. The story provides a humorous send-up of aristocratic dinner conversation when the narrator says that he wishes to craft a written voice that will capture "sound and thought and action" like a "camera obscura" or a photograph (19). Once again, the high quality of Charles Collins's contribution is notable, as his piece anticipates cinema (a frequently noticed aspect of Dickens's own work) and asks readers to recognize the visual elements of their imaginative practices. The speaker's candidness about his acts of composition resurfaces when he states, "The next day came, and I was again prevented, by certain literary labours to which I was obliged to devote myself, from going out in the early part of the day" (22). The story that has become "The Black Bag" is the labor to which he refers, creating a parallel between the speaker and Charles Collins; between the speaker and Charles Dickens; and between both of them and Somebody from the frame, who is the fictional composer of the text. Readers of the number might laugh at the "conductor" referencing the composition of his own number on a tight deadline, and Charles Collins masterfully riffs on the multiple layers of authorship that the number can conflate. Contributing to a Christmas number for the third year in a row, maintaining a close bond with his brother Wilkie, and having lived as Dickens's son-in-law for over two years, Charles Collins would have had ample opportunity to devise inside jokes about the collaborative numbers.

The act of splitting Charles Collins's story and others into two items could easily have been the result of conversations between these men, but even if it was the choice of Dickens alone, the bifurcation of stories complicates the number's pacing and structure. The first portion concludes with Lord Sneyd negligently leading Mary Crawcour to fall from her horse, at which point Sneyd's horse viciously kicks her in the face. The text then abruptly announces, "The rest of this manuscript he had put into His Writing-Desk," and the subsequent section begins "Some years after these things had happened" (24). No bridging passages act as a transition or explain the separation of the manuscript, but the "Some years after" clause requires one to have read the previous pages in the correct order. Christopher supplies a transition by placing the correct items next to each other even though the second part of the story is oddly short given that it is found in the writing desk, the item associated most obviously with the production of text (and that, as in Dickens's case, sometimes had secret compartments).[36] The story's conclusion clarifies that by fleeing Creel on the day of the riding accident after seeing Mary's disfigured face, the fickle Lord Sneyd enables her marriage to Jack Fortescue. Placing the story's resolution in its own piece of luggage could serve to heighten suspense, but the lack of bridging paragraphs and the speedy revelation of the protagonist's fate resolves any questions. Nor is it likely that separating the stories was a way to manage length, as any quantity of fictional pages could be crammed into a particular fictional item; it is not as if readers would have a sense of precisely how many words, for instance, would fit into a hat box. Rather, the primary outcome of splitting the story in two is to continue to develop strange relationships between the pieces and to enhance Christopher's role as compiler while constantly questioning whether each narrator might be the Somebody who has left the luggage.

Introducing no new metatextual elements, Arthur Locker's "His Dressing Case" instead features surprising reprisals of themes from other Christmas numbers. The narrator, Mr. Monkhouse, notices his ship is sinking and squeezes himself through a porthole to escape without waking his sleeping cabinmate, Schlafenwohl. Schlafenwohl survives, and Monkhouse's ability to pull his deserted fellow traveller out of the water begins to assuage his guilt, but Monkhouse's thoughts quickly turn more sinister as he contemplates cannibalism: "Two human beings floating at the caprice of the wind and the waves, on a frail deceptive mass of crystallised water, glaring at one another with famine-stricken eyes. At length it would become necessary to cast lots, and decide which should slay the other" (27). Luckily, the shipwreck survivors find assistance quickly, but the acceptance of cannibalism in a time of crisis again indicates that Dickens was open to multiple views of the subject. This ship's name, the *Golden Dream*, immediately echoes the *Golden Mary* of 1856, iceberg and all. The thematic concerns surrounding how the crew members and passengers will comport themselves mirror the predicament facing those in the *Golden Mary*'s lifeboats and converse with Chorley's poem in *A Message from the Sea* as well as Wilkie Collins's explanation of Hugh Raybrock's shipwreck in that same number. These links across years are important to acknowledge because, for so long, the restriction of scholarly attention to only the Dickens-authored stories has thwarted investigations of what it might mean for other contributors' stories to establish commonalities across the years while they also interact with the stories that Dickens wrote. In this case, connections exist between stories from Locker and Chorley; Locker and Collins; Locker and Dickens; and Locker, Chorley, Collins, and Dickens all together. The idea that Dickens's voice rings out most forcefully, or that the other voices are somehow hushed in comparison to his, does not match the unique collaborative cacophony issuing from the texts themselves.

Being able to see, for instance, that Tom White, the sailor in Locker's story who takes charge of the survivors on the iceberg before they discover the Captain in a different cave, may offer a humorous comment on John Steadiman from *The Wreck of the Golden Mary* is possible only if the numbers are read in their entirety. Tom White's enthusiasm in assuming the role of commander leads to his belief that with his trusty compass he is not simply reporting on the iceberg's speed and direction but actually steering it as if it were the ship. Correctly predicting that if the berg does not slow at exactly the right moment, it will hit the Falkland Islands and break up, Tom takes credit for averting that disaster when the berg slows and moves into a position that allows islanders to rescue the passengers (29). Tom's overinflated sense of his own importance in relation to his duties is similar to Christopher's investment in his status as headwaiter and can also deliver an ironic commentary on John Steadiman's professed humility when he takes over for Captain Ravender in *The Wreck*. Locker's story thus speaks to the frames for 1856, 1860, and 1862, drawing *Somebody's Luggage* further into ongoing collaborative Christmas conversations.

Returning to questions of textuality with "His Brown Paper Parcel," Dickens himself writes the most provocative story on the subject of attribution and collaboration. Tom, in "the Fine Art line," is a street painter who rents out his works because he dislikes begging in bad weather or performing for donations. Although Tom decides to allow another to take credit for his art, he begins to resent a lack of public acknowledgment. Tom's girlfriend Henerietta admires the street paintings without knowing that he is the actual artist, and his anger is so perplexing that she ultimately transfers her affections to the impostor. The irony of this plot, given that the contributors of the stories that constitute *Somebody's Luggage* are unacknowledged in *All the Year Round*, is so blatant that Dickens having been unaware of it seems implausible. Dickens may be laughing—perhaps in a nauseatingly arrogant fashion—at his ability to decide whether and when to identify authors. Dickens could also write the comic piece as a way to share a friendly laugh with his contributors because the comfort level among them was so high that matters of artistic attribution were regarded not as grave contemplations of exploitation but rather as small deals that were fair game for playful rendering.

The ironies of "His Brown Paper Parcel" also set up the number's conclusion, in which Christopher the waiter experiences great anxiety about publishing the discovered manuscripts, but before that resolution can happen, the number splits a final story between the two remaining pieces of luggage: "His Portmanteau" and "His Hat Box." Julia Cecilia Stretton is the only woman contributor to this collection, and her story constitutes nearly one-quarter (23 percent) of the number. It is the tale of Dick Blorage, a man who possesses the nicest possible human disposition. Jilted once, Blorage treats all women kindly but avoids marriage because he does not want to be hurt again. One evening, after drinking a few glasses of wine in advance of his housewarming, Blorage wishes that all people would tell the truth, which results in the arrival of a small fairy who enchants his stuffed chair so that anyone in it loses the ability to lie. The rest of the story charts people sitting in the magic "Chair of Truth" and exposing their actual natures to Blorage, who is horrified by the process but also falls in love with his future wife (42). As with Charles Collins's story, the middle of Stretton's abruptly announces, "The rest of this manuscript he had put into His Hat Box," and Blorage's saga proceeds without transition (40). Eventually, a set of bickering cousins have a row in the chair, precipitating a crescendo of anxiety for Blorage, at which point he knocks over the cursed piece of furniture and wakes up from what has been a drunken dream (42–43). Although the account of Blorage's night becomes a bit tedious, the accurate things he learns in the dream (about his brother's avarice, the scheming natures of his cousins, and his butler's disrespectful attitude) lend the story more depth as Blorage adjusts his behavior and becomes a more reasonable person. The story is not a complete reversal of the Scrooge narrative because Blorage does not become miserly,[37] but one does spot a sideways critique of the transformation tales that frequently appear in Dickens's Christmas works, and the story shares the Christmas numbers' frequent interest in the relationship between dreams and the supernatural.

Overall, the juxtaposition of humor and sorrow in this number is striking, and it does not occur because the contributors fail in consistency of subject matter. Within Dickens's "His Boots," the satirized depiction of "Mr The Englishman's" (6) hostility toward any and all things French alongside the repeated orphaning of little Bebelle leads to poignant scenes of compassion that are infused with lighthearted chuckles at the main characters. Charles Collins's contribution moves quickly from a ludicrous aristocratic dinner-table conversation to a horrifying horse-riding accident. Humor and tragedy are close neighbors throughout the number, sometimes sharing a single sentence. The act of reading *Somebody's Luggage*, of forming an idea of an individual based on a textual legacy, mimics the unpredictable, peaked rhythms of life that the number portrays.

Somebody's Luggage concludes with complete indulgence in the metatextuality it has practiced for forty-five pages. It is the only Christmas number to name Dickens's journal directly, simultaneously collapsing and complicating the relationships between Dickens, his colleagues, and the fictional characters they produce. Christopher the waiter returns to narrate Dickens's "His Wonderful End," taking up some of the tensions from the start of the number. In the opening story, an odd footnote appears when Christopher tries to share the name and address of his current employer, which are "editorially struck out" (3). The editing takes place against Christopher's wishes, and the identity of the editor is unclear: "If there should be any flaw in the writings, or anything missing in the writings, it is Him as is responsible—not me. With that observation in justice to myself, I for the present conclude" (6). At the start of the number, Somebody seems the most likely candidate for the pronoun "Him," but the interpretive ground shifts by the number's conclusion when Christopher attributes his low spirits to guilt for having published the manuscripts:

> It will have been, 'ere now, perceived that I sold the foregoing writings. From the fact of their being printed in these pages, the inference will, 'ere now, have been drawn by the reader (may I add the gentle reader?) that I sold them to One who never yet.*
>
> *The remainder of this complimentary sentence editorially struck out. (45)

We learn more about the publication and the editor's identity when the proof pages arrive and Christopher worries that the writings appearing in print will cause their true author to demand payment. The delivery messenger says that he is bringing "The Proofs. A. Y. R.," and Christopher thinks:

> A. Y. R.? And You Remember. Was that his meaning? At Your Risk. Were the letters short for *that* reminder? Anticipate Your Retribution. Did they stand for *that* warning? Outdacious Youth Repent? But no; for that, a O was happily wanting, and the vowel here was a A.

> I opened the packet and found that its contents were the
> foregoing writings printed, just as the reader (may I add the
> discerning reader?) peruses them. In vain was the reassuring
> whisper—A. Y. R., All the Year Round—it could not cancel the
> Proofs. Too appropriate name. The Proofs of my having sold
> the Writings. (46)

Once we know that Christopher is publishing the stories in *All the Year Round*, the "Him" faulted for any omissions or blunders refers more directly to Dickens or Wills than to Somebody.[38] The possibility of both identifications also unites Dickens and Somebody as potential authors of all the stories. The conflation is partial when we recall that many of the stories are not written by Dickens, which enhances the humor. Christopher's fear that the true author of the stories will accuse him of theft acts as a comic exaggeration of the collaborative relationships that Dickens maintains with his contributors. Dickens, of course, pays his staff and enjoys a far more peaceful process of collecting stories than does Christopher, who must pry things open, break seals, and pick locks to get to the pages (5). The fact that Christopher also refers regularly to his "unassuming pen" and "artless" narrative when his portions are written by Dickens furthers the number's self-reflexive humor (6).

The number's final lines simultaneously consign Somebody's words to flames and distribute them. In November, Somebody arrives at the coffee room, and when Christopher produces the proofs in what he thinks is a drunken act of confession, Somebody reacts with joy because he is ecstatic that his writing will be in print. The mysterious individual then scribbles unreadable corrections all over the proof pages, and the final collection is printed with Christopher's concluding explanation of the process:

> I noticed a message being brought round from Beaufort
> Printing House while I was a throwing this concluding
> statement on paper, that the ole resources of that establishment
> was unable to make out what they meant. Upon which a certain
> gentleman in company, as I will not more particularly name—
> but of whom it will be sufficient to remark, standing on the
> broad basis of a wave-girt isle, that whether we regard him in
> the light of—* laughed, and put the corrections in the fire.
>
> *The remainder of this complimentary parenthesis editorially
> struck out. (48)

The irony of the number ending with the fictionalized figure of Dickens burning text almost urges readers to throw the Christmas number into a fire. The reference to the Beaufort Printing House is a final veiled nod to *All the Year Round*, as its printer's offices were in Beaufort House on the Strand, and the footnote text ending the number points straight to Dickens as a powerful editor-in-chief.[39] The 1862 collection thus concludes with an emphatic focus on written text and laughter-filled negotiation of the power relationships behind publication.

The 1862 Christmas number also marks the first time in eight years that Wilkie Collins does not contribute. Two months before publication, Dickens writes to his friend, "[I]t seems very strange and bare to me not to have you in it," which shows that the nuance of each year's collaborative dynamic is something to which Dickens feels himself attuned.[40] Given the cacophony of voices in *Somebody's Luggage*, the thought of it as "bare" seems counterintuitive. Dickens's comment, however, reveals that his collaborative relationships are more than simply functional. His personal feelings for his contributors affect his sense of the voices that give each number as a whole its tonal flavor. The voice that feels most comfortable, most full, for Dickens is a voice that does not come from himself alone, and exactly who is in the mix influences his final experience of the complete text. Dickens is touched by the fact that Collins feels sorry that the writing of *No Name* keeps him too busy to write for the special issue, and as he responds to Collins's suggestions for the number, he continues to marry their endeavors: "I am bent upon making a good No. to go with No Name."[41]

After *A Message from the Sea*'s fusion of a textual fragment with a storytelling club in its frame and the mission of *Tom Tiddler's Ground* to use random acts of storytelling as a strategy for character reform, *Somebody's Luggage* reaches a peak of metatextual self-reflection with its presentation of discovered manuscripts that directly raise questions of authorship and attribution.[42] Dickens calms the frame concept down a bit in the years to come, as if the orchestrated chaos of the first three numbers for the 1860s have worn him out. With *Mrs. Lirriper's Lodgings*, one finds a steadier anchor in the frame narrative's main character. Collaborative dynamics are no less important to the number's success, but a strong sense of home for both Lirriper's lodgers and their listeners becomes the dominant sentiment for the upcoming years as first Mrs. Lirriper and then Doctor Marigold adopt children and share stories in their creation of snug domesticity.

7

Bundling Children and Binding Legacies
(1863–65)

The fragmented bodies and incomplete messages of the early 1860s Christmas collections are replaced by family themes and more orderly frames in *Mrs. Lirriper's Lodgings, Mrs. Lirriper's Legacy,* and *Doctor Marigold's Prescriptions* from 1863 to 1865. Mrs. Lirriper, an old woman who has run a lodging house for four decades, is only the second woman character in fourteen years to act as a frame story narrator.[1] Mrs. Lirriper is so engaging that Dickens spotlights her in the Christmas number for two years in a row, an honor granted to no other character. She collaborates with her partner, Major Jemmy Jackman, and is also the final woman to narrate a frame story, making her a truly distinctive character. In 1865, bringing Mrs. Lirriper and the Major back for a third year would have been difficult to justify, but Dickens is able to maintain the Christmas number's use of a benevolent grandparental narrator in Doctor Marigold. A traveling junk dealer, Marigold presides over a more itinerant but similarly secure domestic space. Jemmy and Sophy, the orphan children of these numbers, receive the collected tales as gifts from their father figures.

More than a decade after the two *Rounds* collections, which validate non–biological family relationships by including a charwoman and a widow alongside an uncle and a mother without specifying precise lineages, the *Lirriper* and *Marigold* collections make such bonds even more explicit by embedding families of choice into the frame plots and into the very project of storytelling.[2] Sharing, reading, listening to, and binding stories becomes an integral part of how to form such families. As Holly Furneaux notes, for both Doctor Marigold and the Major, "writing has a therapeutic element."[3] In the *Lirriper* numbers, collaborators become important components of a restorative and nurturing kinship network as their stories join the written record of a home that binds disparate individuals into a loving family, and the number's narrative strategies position readers within both the home space and the family. Collaboration and story gathering become crucial aspects of how all three of these collections validate non–biological family structures and advocate for working-class characters. In the case of *Doctor Marigold's Prescriptions*, the stitching together of stories also speaks to questions of agency for disabled, disempowered, or exploited individuals.

Mrs. Lirriper's Lodgings

For the 1863 number, two new contributors—Andrew Halliday and Edmund Yates—joined the more practiced Elizabeth Gaskell, Amelia B. Edwards, Charles Collins, and Charles Dickens to create a collection that became one of the most beloved. In "How Mrs. Lirriper Carried On the Business," Dickens launches the enterprise by introducing the title character in her own nearly breathless voice:

> Whoever would begin to be worried with letting Lodgings that wasn't a lone woman with a living to get is a thing inconceivable to me my dear, excuse the familiarity but it comes natural to me in my own little room when wishing to open my mind to those that I can trust and I should be truly thankful if they were all mankind but such is not so, for have but a Furnished bill in the window and your watch on the mantelpiece and farewell to it if you turn your back for but a second however gentlemanly the manners, nor is being of your own sex any safeguard as I have reason in the form of sugar-tongs to know, for that lady (and a fine woman she was) got me to run for a glass of water on the plea of going to be confined, which certainly turned out true but it was in the Station-House. (1)

Filling a number's entire first paragraph with a single sentence, Lirriper's opening pronouncement immediately unites the storytelling voice with the lodgings.[4] The reader shares Lirriper's "own little room," a private and cozy space in which she calls the reader "my dear," and the intimacy of the address increases when Lirriper makes clear that the recipients of her thoughts are "those that I can trust," which again places the reader in a privileged group.

The widowed Mrs. Lirriper emerges as a formidable maternal presence in the lodging house, where she employs various young women who need her corrective hand and whose shortcomings enable Lirriper to establish the racial parameters of the household in a manner that continues the Christmas numbers' linking of upright English customs to constructions of whiteness. Despite Lirriper's sage pieces of advice, such as "[D]o not brush your hair with the bottoms of the saucepans," one maid, Sophy, cannot keep herself clean. A lodger bothered by Sophy's dirty face declares, "Mrs. Lirriper I have arrived at the point of admitting that the Black is a man and a brother, but only in a natural form and when it can't be got off" (2). The connection between dirt and racial inferiority threatens the reputation of the house when Sophy answers the door, prompting Lirriper to suggest, "[W]hat do you seriously think of my helping you away to New South Wales where it might not be noticed?" (3). Indulging tropes that cast colonial territories as dirty and dark, the story takes care to emphasize Sophy's racialization when, after funding Sophy's travel, Lirriper boasts, "Nor did I ever repent the money which was well spent, for she married the ship's cook on the voyage (himself a Mulotter) and did well and lived happy" (3). Linking Sophy to her racially mixed husband, dirt moves from being an indication of possible blackness to signifying Sophy's comfort with racial mixture, and because the couple's darkness is not "noticed" in New South Wales, the colonial land acts as a space where racially suspect, or less than white, settlers can find comfort (3). In place of emigration, another unruly maid faces jail time for physically attacking annoying guests, but the sweet-natured Lirriper still meets her upon release and wishes her well (3–4). These incidents allow Lirriper to exhibit and discuss her maternal traits, which develops her as an effective frame narrator and builds confidence in her ability to occupy a parental role in advance of little Jemmy's birth.

Although Mrs. Lirriper envisions herself as an arbiter of moral conduct for younger women, she carries on an unconventional relationship with one of her lodgers that leads to the text's validation of non–biological families. Major Jemmy Jackman technically does not hold the rank of major, insisting only that he is "not a Minor," and the couple's constant use of the title—with an unspoken understanding that factual details matter less than feelings—characterizes the entire relationship (5). The two never marry, but their partnership is secure from the moment that the Major leaves the boardinghouse of Lirriper's competitor down the street (4). The Major acts as a protector for Lirriper and her possessions, she consults him before making decisions about tenants, and their vocal observance of etiquette rituals that preserve Mrs. Lirriper's respectability draws attention to the many ways in which their relationship crosses lodger/landlady boundaries. When Lirriper asks the Major whether he objects to the newly married Edsons taking rooms, his reaction is strangely suggestive of a sexual response. After the Major inquires about how direly Lirriper might need the income those rooms would provide, she says, "I was delicate of saying 'Yes' too out, for a little extra colour rose into the Major's cheeks and there was irregularity which I will not particularly specify in a quarter which I will not name" (5). Mentioning that the presence of a married couple causes blood to rush into parts of the Major's body that Mrs. Lirriper is embarrassed to specify urges listeners to imagine sexual tension in the relationship.

The Major's reaction to Lirriper's coded reference to the possibility that a couple could have sex in the house (and that the woman could potentially give birth there if they renew the lease) is doubly significant because of the relationship that ensues between the Major, Mrs. Lirriper, and the baby. Mr. Edson suddenly deserts Peggy, whom he has never actually married, and Mrs. Lirriper and the Major save Peggy from a suicide attempt (5–6). Nearing death after childbirth, Peggy is pleased that the elderly couple will raise the baby, and they subsequently give the boy a name that marks him as their own offspring: "[W]e called him Jemmy, being after the Major his own godfather with Lirriper for a surname being after myself" (8). Lirriper explains that, later, they nickname the boy "Jemmy Jackman for we had given him the Major's other name too," which makes his full name Jemmy Lirriper Jackman (10). The Major's flushed, aroused reaction to Lirriper's request that he approve of Peggy and Edson's stay functions symbolically as a moment of conception for Jemmy as the Major and Lirriper's child, and their adoption of him is embedded in the number's validation of storytelling.

This collection's comic depiction of familial intimacy creates sustained investment in the stories it comprises. The Major, for instance, teaches Jemmy his first mathematics lessons with household and kitchen objects, and Lirriper's account of the instruction draws the reader into the main characters' relationships: "But my dear to relate to you in detail the way in which they multiplied fourteen sticks of firewood by two bits of ginger and a larding-needle, or divided pretty well everything else there was on the table by the heater of the Italian iron and a chamber candlestick, and got a lemon over, would make my head spin round and round and round as it did at that time" (10). Understanding the charming way the older couple educates the young boy creates the mix of sentiment and seriousness that characterizes some of Dickens's best writing. When it is time for Jemmy to go to boarding school at age ten, Lirriper's soothing advice to the Major that "Life is made of partings and we must part with our Pet" (11) echoes Joe Gargery's comment that "life is made of ever so many partings welded together" in *Great Expectations*.[5] To combat the Major's ensuing depression, Lirriper gently manipulates him into writing what constitutes the Christmas number. She observes that Jemmy might enjoy knowing the history of the house and offers, "The walls of my Lodgings . . . might have something to tell, if they could tell it" (12). The Major agrees and says that the stories "shall be written for him" (12).

The frame device then puts readers in the place of Jemmy, the intended recipient of the written collection, and in the place of an unidentified individual whom Lirriper addresses when she describes the Major's intense writing efforts:

> [H]e wrote and wrote and wrote with his pen scratching like rats behind the wainscot, and whether he had many grounds to go upon or whether he did at all romance I cannot tell you, but what he has written is in the left-hand glass closet of the little bookcase close behind you, and if you'll put your hand in you'll find it come out heavy in lumps sewn together and being beautifully plain and unknown Greek and Hebrew to myself and me quite wakeful, I shall take it as a favour if you'll read out loud and read on. (12)

The reader, an intimate visitor trustworthy enough to join Mrs. Lirriper in her "own little room" (1), is cast as both listener and speaker, with the narrative layers imploring one to read out loud.[6] In so doing—speaking in the voices of Lirriper's lodgers—the reader's ventriloquism mirrors both the Major as the person recollecting the stories and Dickens in his conductor role. These multiple positionings place the reader firmly inside Lirriper's lodgings as a potential member of this family of choice while also involving the reader actively in the storytelling project.

For the interpolated stories of *Mrs. Lirriper's Lodgings*, the memories and experiences of the lodgers become part of the house, integrally linked to its rooms and titled after them, which makes the reader's positioning in that space all the more relevant to the number's success. The titles, such as "How the Second Floor Kept a Dog" and "How the Side-Room Was Attended by a Doctor," conflate each lodger with a room so that the space is formulated as having experienced the lodger's most significant life events. Because the first twelve pages develop the frame characters thoroughly and the family relationships existing among those characters result from the intimacy between the landlady and her lodgers, the frame story's solidity lends a sense of unity to the interpolated tales even before they appear.

Thematically, the tales from contributors all feature plots in which a working-class person, or a character with a social status lower than that of a rival, is the sympathetic protagonist or tragic victim. Gaskell's "How the First Floor Went to Crowley Castle" shares an eighteenth-century scandal in which Theresa, the proud daughter of an aristocrat whose misbehavior includes eloping with a French count, mistreats the humble daughter of the local vicar. Theresa, whose "mother had had some foreign blood in her" (13), lures Duke Brownlow's interest away from his wife, Bessy, and marries him after her vengeful maid poisons Bessy. Even though Theresa is not complicit in the murder, Duke subsequently banishes her, and she dies of heartbreak. The story adds to this number's focus on the righteousness of lower-class characters in contrast to the aristocracy, but the plot lacks suspense, and it ultimately stands as one of Gaskell's weaker Christmas contributions. Halliday's "How the Side-Room Was Attended by a Doctor" picks up the number's pace with a charming story of the Mutual Admiration Society. These humble friends form a club based simply on trading stories about their favorite writers and public figures. The group's addition of Doctor Goliath seems beneficial, but he slowly guides them in a negative direction. The members speculate on whether he may be a "Wandering Jew," and Tom guesses that he may be "the devil" since "he is diabolical in all his views and opinions," which lends an undercurrent of anti-Semitism to the story (28–29). The men grow sarcastic, and when Tom realizes what a terrible influence the newcomer exercises, a surprise visit to his home reveals that Goliath plays delicately with a kitten and a canary bird while enjoying a close friendship with a landlady who resembles Mrs. Lirriper (30). Condemning the feigned antisociability, Tom says more than once, "Doctor, you're a humbug," before the club forgives him, which recalls Ebenezer Scrooge's swift transformation (31). The amusing tale acts as a reminder that characters like Lirriper and the Major, who share the optimistic disposition of the friends who meet in the side-room, may sometimes need protection from the pitfalls of their own gullibility.

The close connection between Lirriper's physical space and the stories continues in Yates's "How the Second Floor Kept a Dog," a defense of Beppo, whose canine presence violates the usual house rules. Yates's story tells of Mr. John Mortiboy, a coarse Manchester man who joins a London firm and increases his wealth but not his social graces. On a visit to Wales, Mortiboy's lack of refinement offends the genteel household of Mrs. Barford, but he wins their admiration after he and an "old coast-guard-man" risk their lives to save Mr. Sandham, the drowning lover of Kate Barford. When Mortiboy's dog, Beppo, struggles to bring the man to shore, Mortiboy dramatically jumps in the water to save both the sinking man and the dog. After Sandham and Mortiboy marry the Bradford daughters, Beppo becomes Sandham's dog, and they all spend a Christmas at Lirriper's. The inclusion of the family, occupying an entire floor with the sisters sewing baby clothes and Beppo "stretched in front of the fire," adds to the themes of companionship in Halliday's story and to the number's overall idealization of Lirriper's domestic space (35). As host for the Mutual Admiration Society and now Beppo the dog's extended family, the lodging house unifies and protects families of all sorts while once again elevating a socially uncultivated hard worker as a heroic figure.

Moving up a level, the speaker of Edwards's "How the Third Floor Knew the Potteries" is an orphan, which parallels Jemmy in the frame story and possibly accounts for his trust in the Major. For the second time in the collection, a Frenchman (Louis Laroche) seduces a woman (Leah Payne) away from an Englishman with terrible consequences. Ben, the narrator, states that after his friend George Barnard spots Laroche exiting his lover's house, Barnard disappears in the middle of his shift as pottery yard foreman. Details at the scene point to murder or suicide even before the discovery of human remains in the hottest furnace. Ben repeatedly thinks that he sees Barnard's spectre and that Laroche has murdered him, but insufficient evidence exists to charge Laroche with a crime, and he flees (40). Ben does not know what happened to Payne, nor do we know why Ben is a guest at Lirriper's, which leaves the story centered on distrust of foreigners who wrong strong, laboring men.

Yet another young lover appears in Charles Collins's "How the Best Attic Was under a Cloud," a story full of comical blundering that evokes Yates's contribution. Oliver Cromwell Shrubsole, the story's speaker, loves Mary Nuttlebury, who prefers her wealthy cousin, Mr. Huffell. In despair, Oliver follows the dramatic advice of his friend Dewsnap (a Dickensian-sounding name in the story from his son-in-law) and insists on a duel, but just before the men are set to fire their pistols, Huffell relents and apologizes. As Huffell walks away to the chime of church bells, he chuckles, which Shrubsole later recognizes as a mark of the fact that Huffell is on his way to the church to marry Mary. Nursing his emotional wounds, Shrubsole finds a much-needed change of scenery at Lirriper's but cannot help telling the Major, "I regard Mrs. Lirriper as a most unexceptionable person, labouring indeed, as far as I can see, under only one defect. She is a WOMAN" (46). Collins's story again places one's sympathies with an earnest if presumptuous lover who is humiliated by a higher-class rival, and the story's final line laughs gently at Shrubsole while also reminding readers of how unusual it is for the frame protagonist to be a woman.

To conclude the number, Dickens's "How the Parlours Added a Few Words" accentuates collaborative relationships as the Major speaks and writes under Lirriper's direction. Jemmy is home for the Christmas holidays, and as they all visit, the Major's comments show writing and storytelling to be central to their reunion: "We talked of these jottings of mine, which Jemmy had read through and through by that time; and so it came about that my esteemed friend remarked, as she sat smoothing Jemmy's curls: 'And as you belong to the house too, Jemmy,—and so much more than the Lodgers, having been born in it—why, your story ought to be added to the rest, I think, one of these days'" (47). Lirriper once again connects the physical space of the house to the souls of the people inhabiting it, elevating Jemmy over the lodgers not because he has spent more time in the house but rather because its air provides his first breaths. Jemmy makes up a story that is a thinly veiled account of his crush on the schoolmaster's daughter in which all of his loved ones find wealth and happiness and "[n]obody ever died" (48). Jemmy's other story, the story of his orphaning, is what will also ultimately be "added to the rest," a textual complication the next year's collection takes up. Lirriper then asks the Major to conclude with Jemmy's declaration of everyone's immortality, which he does before ending the 1863 number with another validation of the collaborative project:

> In submission to which request on the part of the best of women, I have here noted it down as faithfully as my best abilities, coupled with my best intentions, would admit, subscribing it with my name,
>
> > J. Jackman.
> > The Parlours.
> > Mrs. Lirriper's Lodgings. (48)

Highlighting his "submission," the Major's signature and assumption of the storytelling pen is mitigated by Lirriper's authority and her embeddedness in the physical address, which helps to maintain her as a strong enough frame character to anchor a second number. Dickens felt confident in his writing of the Lirriper character but was nonetheless surprised at her tremendous impact on the journal's sales. Writing to Wilkie Collins in January 1864, Dickens reports, "The Xmas No. has been the greatest success of all; has shot ahead of last year; has sold about 220,000; and has made the name of Mrs. Lirriper so swiftly and domestic[ally] famous as never was."[7] In the face of such fame, far from exhausting the potentialities of her character, Dickens does not hesitate to return to Lirriper for the next year's collection.

Mrs. Lirriper's Legacy

In *Mrs. Lirriper's Legacy*, which Dickens began composing in October 1864, the interpolated stories advance the multiyear frame in several ways. Continuing to develop the thematic threads of *Mrs. Lirriper's Lodgings*, the 1864 number begins with an emphasis on the "otherness" of non-English characters and cultures that act as a threat to English-identified values then shifts to showing how that threat can surface through the presence of foreign customs in England or dangerous mixtures within the domestic sphere. To survive, one must embrace values identified as thoroughly English, and this number's depiction of those values joins the first *Lirriper* in elevating working-class figures as well as the Lirriper/Jackman family formation. In this process, families of choice become increasingly crucial to a vision of national character that sets England above its "others." Although the inset stories are thematically and stylistically varied, storytelling remains redemptive as the collaborative act draws one into the extended family of Mrs. Lirriper and the Major.

In "Mrs. Lirriper Relates How She Went On, and Went Over," Dickens begins the number by refreshing readers' memories (or bringing new readers up to speed) on the particulars of the family while also raising questions about the presumed structure of the collection. Mrs. Lirriper confesses that she and the Major have kept Jemmy's mother's story secret from him, encouraging him to believe that he is Mrs. Lirriper's biological grandchild. For the plot, this important information provides the rationale for how Lirriper handles the reappearance of Jemmy's father, but narratively, the information creates a complication. The story of Jemmy's mother's desertion is the first in *Mrs. Lirriper's Lodgings*, and because Jemmy has not heard that story but has read the others, the first narrative must be separated physically from the rest. Such a separation means that the collection exists in multiple forms. *Mrs. Lirriper's Legacy* continues to pull its stories from the same bundle of papers that includes the first collection, but Lirriper's comment indicates that she and the Major are arranging and sometimes hiding papers. Her statement also hints that they may have added the story of Jemmy's birth to a shared version of the text without having told Jemmy, demonstrating that the crafting of families is as challenging and delicate of a task as the compiling of texts. The story titles for *Mrs. Lirriper's Legacy* present regular acts of listening and telling, with the verb *relates* appearing in every one. After "A Past Lodger Relates a Wild Legend of a Doctor," the titles of four more tales repeat "Another Past Lodger Relates . . ." (1). The collection rekindles the intimacy of the first number by positioning the reader as "my dear" in the lodging house but also associates the stories more closely with the storytelling activities of the lodgers than with the house (1). This slight shift helps facilitate the progression of the family plot across the two years as the frame characters leave the house to travel abroad.

In the opening section, before detailing the circumstances that take them out of the country, Lirriper's musings firmly establish that London acts as a home place where the Major, Jemmy, and Mrs. Lirriper have bonds of friendship and home people, not just a house. The opening episodes stress how a sudden crisis can turn a foe into a friend. Mr. Buffle, the tax collector, for instance, is an adversary of the Major's until Buffle's house catches fire, causing the Major to sprint through the neighborhood, save the Buffle family, and bring them to comfort at Mrs. Lirriper's. When Miss Wozenham, Lirriper's long-time rival down the street, suddenly must sell her possessions, Lirriper loans her the substantial sum of forty pounds, and the story celebrates two businesswomen uniting to preserve their livelihoods. The Major's presence and protection might seem to lessen Lirriper's independence, but the number's repeated attention to Mrs. Lirriper's financial status undermines any potential threat, and the Major often appears as a man-child, as evidenced in the family's travel preparations.

Referring to the Major and Jemmy as unruly children neutralizes any challenge the Major might pose to Lirriper's independence while also reinforcing non–biological family bonds prior to what will prove to be an overseas trial. The plot is set in motion when Mrs. Lirriper learns that a dying man in Sens, France, has written a note stating that she should receive his possessions. Ignorant of the man's identity, the family decides to go to him, and in response to overly enthusiastic travel preparations (in addition to shared enthrallment with a model train), Mrs. Lirriper scolds, "'If you two children ain't more orderly I'll pack you both off to bed.' And then they fell to cleaning up the Major's telescope to see France with" (7). Once in Sens, Mrs. Lirriper realizes that the dying man is Mr. Edson, and before Edson dies, Jemmy prays over him without knowing the man is his father (9). Although Jemmy possesses a forgiving nature, the adults keep Edson's identity secret, and the rest of the Christmas number comprises the documents that dominate their evening rituals in France; Jemmy has brought a bundle of papers and reads to his parents "every evening," having promised to add his own piece at the end (10).

Lirriper's legacy is not only the small bit of money Edson leaves her but also the stories and the relationships that have resulted in their publication. The reader remains privileged as the mysterious "my dear" who is not Jemmy but shares his proximity to the family: "And so here is the rest of my Legacy my dear that I now hand over to you in this bundle of papers all in the Major's plain round writing. I wish I could hand you the church towers over too, and the pleasant air and the inn yard and the pigeons often coming and perching on the rail by Jemmy and seeming to be critical with their heads on one side, but you'll take as you find" (10–11). At the moment she parts with the stories, Lirriper emphasizes their collaborative genesis by mentioning the Major's handwriting. The legacy is no less hers for having been written down by another. This moment of the actual handing over of stories also conjures Dickens in his role as editor and publisher, which places the reader in the conductor's position. And Lirriper's humble yet instructive "you'll take as you find" again brings collaboration to the forefront of the narrative without diminishing her control.

As the interpolated stories begin, attention shifts to a doctor in France who deals more morbidly with the question of legacies. Charles Collins's unusual tale lives up to its title: "A Past Lodger Relates a Wild Legend of a Doctor." Dr. Bertrand kills by request, offering a dignified path for those who want to end their lives with poisoned dinners to which they subscribe. The charming doctor's most unnerving trait is that "[h]is eyes were dead. They never changed, and they rarely moved" (12).[8] Alfred de Clerval attends a dinner because he thinks that he has lost his beloved to her admiring cousin, Vicomte de Noel, only to realize that the man sitting next to him is the same Vicomte, heartbroken after his cousin rejected him. The doctor is able to administer an antidote in time to save de Clerval then faces prison time. This well-written story includes intriguing details about the poisoned dishes, and the suicide dinner scene contrasts starkly with idealized images of family Christmas dinners. Although the doctor's peers abhor his behavior, the story, as the first interpolated piece, focuses on fear of unknown customs in the country to which Mrs. Lirriper, the Major, and Jemmy are heading.

Rosa Mulholland's "Another Past Lodger Relates His Experience as a Poor Relation" also touches on themes of travel but moves away from

COLLABORATIVE DICKENS

criminal (if consensual) killing to more commonly recognized forms of familial mistreatment in its consideration of orphans. Guy Rutland returns from a fifteen-year trip and pretends to have no money as a test of his adoptive family's attitudes. His relations mistreat another adoptee: the teenaged, endlessly patient Teecie Ray, who uses crutches to walk (19). After the rest of the Rutland family accuses Teecie of attempting to seduce a flirty and wealthy gentleman (21), smashes her crutches (22), and excludes her from a local aristocrat's Christmas party, Rutland buys her a dress, replaces her crutches, takes her to the party, and marries her. Rutland indulges his fairy-tale fantasies by seeing her as "dear little Cinderella," and they marry on Christmas morning, when the family is doubly astonished to learn that Guy is a millionaire (23). Ultimately, "[t]ime and care cured [Teecie] of her lameness," enabling Guy to blame her disability on the Rutlands' negligence and keep them in villainous roles for the fairy-tale-esque ending (24). Readers never learn why Rutland stays at Lirriper's, but his story reinforces the collection's investment in happy outcomes for those who are not mercenary and in exposing the potential for abuse in orphan relationships (a frequent plot element, as Mulholland would have known, in Dickens's novels). Connecting not only to the frame characters in both *Lirriper* numbers but also to the questions of orphanhood and disability that worry *Doctor Marigold's Prescriptions* the next year, Mulholland's piece resonates internally and externally in the Christmas number canon.

Fairy-tale elements surface again in Henry Spicer's "Another Past Lodger Relates What Lot He Drew at Glumper House," which returns to the theme of navigating unfamiliar or foreign-feeling customs. Spicer's story features Charley Trelawny, a protagonist who temporarily orphans himself, and begins with an amusing account of the "beefsteak pie" at boarding school: "Into the composition of that dish beef entered as largely as the flesh of the unicorn into peas-porridge" (25). One student finds "a pair of snuffers" in his pie, and another "quietly and sternly removed to the side of his plate three fingers and a ligament of the thumb of an ancient dog-skin glove" (25). In the wake of such suffering and unsuccessful pleas for removal, the boys decide that someone must flee the school in protest, and Charley draws that lot. In his second week of destitution, Charley shares his last sixpence with an old man he thinks is starving, and later that night, the recovered man feeds, houses, and employs Charley. The man, Moses Jeremiah Abrahams, has a reputation as a miser and keeps his granddaughter Zell imprisoned in the house to discourage suitors. Zell—barefoot and clad in only white—appears as an exoticized goddess to Charley, striking awe into the boy even when she treats him unkindly (32).

The story indulges an anti-Semitic portrayal of the miserly Jew and follows through on the violence incited by such beliefs when Abrahams is robbed and beaten so badly that he dies from the injuries, but the moral message of its conclusion is sympathetic to cross-faith romance (33). Preparing to depart, Zell and Charley discover a fortune that Abrahams has hidden inside the rotting woodwork. Zell leaves for a new life without Charley, who rejoins his family; several years later, they reunite at a ball, where the much-courted Zell surprises her wealthy suitors by choosing Charley for her husband. The story ultimately advocates marriage between a Jew and a gentile, and while it traffics in stereotypes, it also shows how Charley's successful navigation of cultural difference leads to the realization that hard-working English boys will benefit from nurturing respectful relationships with those whose cultures vary. Enabled by a view of the complete Christmas numbers as a canon that has been developing over fourteen years, one can spot conversation between Spicer's Mr. Abrahams, Sala's Acon-Virlaz ten years earlier in *The Seven Poor Travellers*, and other stories that include Jewish characters. That Dickens composes *Our Mutual Friend* with attention to Mr. Riah while Spicer's story of Mr. Abrahams is making its way across Wills's and Dickens's desks for inclusion in the Christmas number also points toward the potential (as discussed in chapter 8) for critical consideration of conversation in the Christmas numbers to enhance appraisals of Dickens's novels.

Amelia B. Edwards's "Another Past Lodger Relates His Own Ghost Story" further illustrates how a contributor's style and thematic preferences can become integral parts of Dickens's Christmas canon, as the number's commentary on foreign people and places shifts to a chilling consideration of the homeland. Edwards writes a ghost story for each of the *Lirriper* numbers—the only pieces in these two collections that represent the supernatural. In this way, Edwards takes the mantle from Dickens in continuing the tradition of haunting stories at Christmastime that *A Christmas Carol* had made so widely famous and that persists in the Christmas numbers. Three of the four Christmas pieces that Edwards contributes up to 1864 are ghost stories, and she writes a final one for *Mugby Junction* in 1866. Edwards's style of ghost story, then, becomes difficult to distinguish from the style associated with Dickens and Christmas. To help deflect skepticism, her speaker inducts readers into a privileged group: "During those twenty years I have told the story to but one other person. I tell it now with a reluctance which I find difficult to overcome. All I entreat, meanwhile, is that you will abstain from forcing your own conclusions upon me. I want nothing explained away. I desire no arguments" (35). Like many of Dickens's narrators, Edwards's speaker combines a dictatorial approach to his audience with a complimentary one. Limiting "arguments" and explanations is at once conciliatory, as the speaker does not wish to limit anyone's formation of an opinion, and silencing, as he refuses to hear other perspectives.

In the unnamed man's tale, hazardous territory is located not in a different nation but rather in the north of England, where he gets stranded in a snowstorm after a day of shooting. A recluse and his servant, Jacob, save the man by providing shelter, supper, and fortification with fiery "usquebaugh," or whisky (37). Mindful of Jacob's warning about the dangerous place in the road where the night mail crashed nine years earlier, the man sets out on a five-mile walk to catch the train that will reunite him with his wife. Inside a reeking coach, separated from the coachman and one exterior passenger, three other men refuse to reply to his remarks, and the vehicle begins to fall apart. As the man comments on the coach's condition, he comes to a horrifying realization while looking at another passenger: "His eyes glowed with a fiery unnatural lustre. His face was livid as the face of a corpse. His bloodless lips were drawn back as if in the agony of death, and showed the gleaming teeth between. The words that I was about to utter died upon my lips, and a strange horror—a dreadful horror—came upon me. . . . I saw that he was no living man—that none of them were living men, like myself! . . . Only their eyes, their terrible eyes, were living; and those eyes were all turned menacingly upon me!" (40). When he wakes, recovering from a skull fracture, his wife explains that shepherds find him in the snow at the spot of the crash, and his caregivers blame fevered hallucinations for his memory of zombies. The man, however, believes firmly that he occupied the place of a dead person, declaring, "I *know* that twenty years ago I was the fourth passenger in that Phantom Coach" (40). This man's vision endorses the supernatural and raises the possibility that he actually died twenty years ago and exists in the present moment, speaking to the Major, as his own ghost. The threat posed by such a person would far exceed the imagined threats posed by "foreigners" in the other stories, as this man's very being—if his story's claims are true—defies all boundaries, worldly or otherwise.

The commonalities across Christmas numbers continue in Hesba Stretton's "Another Past Lodger Relates Certain Passages to Her Husband," which uses England as its setting and comments on the ability of impure individuals to threaten it. The story's narrative structure is similar to "The Ghost in the Clock Room," which Stretton wrote for *The Haunted House* five years earlier, in that the wife claims to be able to relate her engagement story only to her husband; the Major and Mrs. Lirriper, therefore, openly eaves-drop at dinner. The story's protagonists, Jane Meadows and Owen Scott, grow up together, but Owen's categorization of Jane as a sister leads him away from romance with her and into the arms of the flirty Adelaide. Niece of the aging rector, Mr. Vernon, Adelaide goes missing on the morning she is to wed Owen, and the presence of her bonnet in the nearby mountains con-vinces everyone that she has died in a fall (44). Owen eventually proposes marriage to Jane, but upon returning from their honeymoon, they discover that Adelaide did not die after all. In a Gothic twist, Mrs. Vernon tells Jane that she thwarted the marriage by locking the drugged girl in a soundproof wing of the house that had been set aside for Mrs. Vernon's secret fits of madness, which are implicitly linked to her "black browed and swarthy" ap-pearance (43).[9] Mrs. Vernon's motive is simply that Adelaide irritates her and she wants the girl to marry a wealthy nephew (46). The plot resolves itself when Adelaide recovers slowly from the laudanum addiction her incarcera-tion caused, Owen admits that he truly loves Jane, and Adelaide eventually marries another man (47). Stretton's story relies on the common trope that assigns dark, swarthy, or racialized traits to a Gothic villain. Its challenge to convention lies in its depiction of Jane as the heroine whose righteous love for Owen owes its fulfillment to the lunatic acts of Mrs. Vernon. Un-like many Victorian plots, the actions of this madwoman do not require the physical destruction of the racialized woman to affect the heroine's happi-ness,[10] but Mrs. Vernon's insanity does directly reward Jane, and the story exposes the existence of dangerous madwomen in England as well as abroad.

The two years of Lirriper stories conclude with Dickens's "Mrs. Lirriper Relates How Jemmy Topped Up," a final framing piece that wraps up the plot with domestic suspense as Jemmy takes over. One's final glimpse of the frame characters finds them making plans to go home as Mrs. Lirriper says, "Well my dear and so the evening readings of these jottings of the Major's brought us round at last to the evening when we were all packed and going away next day" (47). Jemmy declares that he is going to share "Mr. Edson's story," which freezes Lirriper and the Major, who have never disclosed the true story of Jemmy's birth or the identity of his father (47). In Jemmy's story, Edson falls in love with a penniless woman, stays true to her when disinherited, and appreciates the steadiness Mrs. Lirriper's house provides during their troubling time. Edson's wife then dies in childbirth, their son dies, and after a profligate life, the man faces death. Jemmy imagines Edson to have left his legacy to Lirriper in gratitude for her kindness and supposes that they ask Jemmy to pray over him because Jemmy is the age Edson's son would have been (48). Placing himself in the position of an imagined son strongly suggests that Jemmy at least suspects the truth and is teasing his adoptive parents. Because Jemmy is in possession of the paper bundle, and the very first story about his birth at some point resides in that bundle, the final story speaks to the first story in a manner that seems to bring Jemmy into the informational loop.

Mrs. Lirriper's Legacy concludes with her reaction to Jemmy's tale, which places him in the role of writer:

> "You little Conjuror" I says, "how did you ever make it all
> out? Go in and write it every word down, for it's a wonder."
> Which Jemmy did, and I have repeated it to you my dear
> from his writing.
> Then the Major took my hand and kissed it, and said
> "Dearest madam all has prospered with us."
> "Ah Major" I says drying my eyes, "we needn't have been
> afraid. We might have known it. Treachery don't come natural
> to beaming youth; but trust and pity, love and constancy—they
> do, thank God!" (48)

Jemmy is thus at once a creator of Mrs. Lirriper's Legacy and an embodiment of it. In repeating what Jemmy writes, Lirriper shares his position but also fuses herself with the reader who, in the first Lirriper collection, is positioned as the figure reading aloud to her. Circling back to the story of Jemmy's father further cements linkages between the two years, and the tableaux of Mrs. Lirriper and the Major at the second year's end makes clear that the non-biological family they have created—in, through, and with the help of storytelling—acts as a sustaining force for all three of them.

With the final Lirriper number published, Dickens had reached a pinnacle of Christmas number triumph. Reviewers glowed over the frame character, and critics still identify her as one of Dickens's best women characters.[11] If Lirriper indeed marks a distinctly positive achievement in Dickens's ability to develop a woman character, then collaboration needs to be factored in as an integral component of that success. Deborah Thomas regards Mrs. Lirriper as a unique comic old woman who is also a serious title character, "neither a mechanical object of laughter nor a serious heroine but a complex figure who is aware of the difficulties of the world, yet humorous despite them. . . . [S]he is not a haphazard manifestation or mutation, but the clear result of an evolutionary process in Dickens' art."[12] Yet Mrs. Lirriper does not emerge from or exist in a textual vacuum. Rather, part of what distinguishes her as a special character is her involvement in a storytelling project that includes many voices. She urges the Major to take up writing to cope with Jemmy's departure, directs the ordering of stories, and guides Jemmy's participation in the effort—conducting the whole affair while accommodating and bolstering other voices, which fill far more columns than does her own. The actions that form the core of her character are inescapably and inherently collaborative. Therefore, if we are to regard the *Lirriper* collections as "one of Dickens's most neglected masterpieces," as J. Isaacs encourages, the fact of collaboration in both the nonfictional realm of Dickens in the Victorian periodical press and the fictional realm of Mrs. Lirriper as a story gatherer must be a central element in the praise.[13]

Doctor Marigold's Prescriptions

The 1865 Christmas number advances many of the *Lirriper* themes as it explores the relationship between mobility, family, and cherished domestic spaces. Bundling stories as they bundle adopted children, parental characters enable these numbers to unite storytelling and family formation in a successful national project. *Doctor Marigold's Prescriptions* intrepidly moves deeper into the realms that complicate the making of such families than its predecessors. The "Doctor" is a softhearted Cheap Jack named in honor of the medical man who births him when his mother goes into labor on the road. With his characteristic mastery of mixing comic and serious elements in "To Be Taken Immediately," Dickens introduces the peddler, who lives in his cart. Insisting that his father's name was Willum, not William, Marigold wonders, "If a man is not allowed to know his own name in a free country, how much is he allowed to know in a land of slavery?" (1). The unanswered question forecasts the number's concerns with human agency and morality as Marigold shares the sad history of how he cobbles together a family.

With an emotionally moving opening scene drawing readers into the most wrenching of relationships, the number builds a connection between Doctor Marigold and his audience even stronger and more intimate than that between Mrs. Lirriper and the previous years' readers. Marigold's first marriage is plagued by tragic cycles of violence when his wife beats their daughter, Sophy, and Doctor Marigold's feelings of powerlessness over how to stop the mistreatment cause him to whip his horse while "sobbing and crying" in troubled solidarity with Sophy (4). When the girl falls ill with fever, Dickens's heartrending description of her final moments displays Marigold, having run out of money to feed her, feeling forced to hawk his wares while holding the dying child. He tells the crowd that Sophy "belongs to the

Fairies" then, while making sales pitches for items as varied as tools, a memo-
randum book, and a tea set, he also "touched little Sophy's face and asked her
if she felt faint or giddy," murmuring encouragement and kissing her (4–5).
She raises her head enough to request, "[L]ay me down to rest upon that
churchyard grass so soft and green," which he recognizes as her dying words
as he "staggered back into the cart with her head dropped on [his] shoulder"
(5). The irreplaceable bond between father and daughter is inseparable from
Marigold's livelihood at this moment, which torments him as he shouts at
his wife to close the door so that "those laughing people" cannot see that the
girl has died (5).

The trust Marigold earns—coupled with the emotional investment in
his affairs that the opening story creates—authorizes his presentation of the
interpolated stories, which the continuing saga of his parenthood also sets
up. After Sophy's death, Mrs. Marigold drowns herself in a river when she
sees another woman hurting a child. Within a few years, the lonely Marigold
hears that the proprietor of a traveling show mistreats his deaf and mute
stepdaughter, and when Marigold finds the neglected girl, he purchases her,
names her Sophy, and addresses her needs carefully.[14] He teaches her to read,
they develop a language of signs, and she decodes the minutiae of his facial
expressions so acutely that they communicate effectively without speech (6).
When Sophy is sixteen years old, despite the pain that separation causes
them both, Marigold nobly sends her to school for two years so that she can
learn to communicate even more effectively, and the stories in the collection
are anecdotes that he collects to present as a gift when she returns. Martha
Stoddard Holmes notes that, via Sophy's learning, the story "writes against
stereotypes of deaf people as uneducable, abject, or socially incapable, and it
specifically argues (through Sophy's teacher) against the exhibition of disabled people."[15] Jennifer Esmail contends further that the story's representation of signing "must be understood in the context of Oralism," which was "a
century-long campaign to eliminate signed languages and force deaf people
to lip-read and speak."[16] Recalling Marigold's opening question about how
much knowledge one expects a slave or a free person to be allowed to possess,
and remaining aware of the fact that Marigold purchases Sophy, I would add
that disability and impairment in this story are also crucial elements of the
number's preoccupation with the ethical implications of human ownership.
Although the story never questions Marigold's motives directly, the fact that
his wife's abuse of a previous child leads to that child's death validates one's
sense that Marigold's quest for redemption is vexed by guilt. The second
Sophy plot, as Holmes argues, does not screen the first but rather, in creating

a more functional family with the deaf-mute child, "keeps open the story's deepest wounds, extending that affective work to readers and audiences through the weeping narrator."[17] To complete this interpretive picture, however, we must also recognize that the inset stories from contributors keep anxieties about such relationships alive. Indeed, all but one of the interpolated stories take up issues of human subjectivity and ownership, conversing indirectly with the frame story in which an orphaned child is not only purchased but also manages serious physical disabilities in her quest to become an independent adult. The number's provocation to readers thus challenges them to identify the correct type of prescription for what ails Doctor Marigold during his separation from Sophy and to navigate textual confusion in order to discern ethical ways of treating people like her.

The collected writings are Marigold's "prescriptions" for Sophy, which lets the reader in on a family joke while also developing the number's commentary on the value of collaboratively compiled reading materials. Sophy misunderstands Marigold to be an actual medical doctor for several years, so the story's title adds to the father-daughter punning. Bringing readers into that laughter, the number also includes them in the reunion of a loving parent and child after a long separation. In constructing the book, Marigold places great importance on its provenance and progresses the number's integration of his work as a hawker, his family life, and storytelling: "Without being of an avaricious temper, I like to be the owner of things. . . . Well! A kind of jealousy began to creep into my mind when I reflected that all those books would have been read by other people long before they was read by her. It seemed to take away from her being the owner of 'em like. In this way, the question got into my head:—Couldn't I have a book new-made express for her, which she should be the first to read?" (8). Marigold's sophisticated view of how people perceive the act of reading speaks to the ways in which readers idealize the act, creating a fiction that there is a private relationship between each reader and widely disseminated, published words. Marigold clarifies that Sophy does indeed read the collection first, so readers are not impinging on her territory, and that he "added to and completed [the collection] . . . after her first reading of it" to prepare it for sale. The compilation, then, is both a public and a private text, as Marigold concludes the first story by selling the book itself.[18]

Describing the book in the same way he would catalogue one of his wares, Marigold builds the eclecticism of the collection into his formulation of its worth and points out that regarding the set as an article with a singular function would be an error. He details the number of columns and pages and mentions the "beautiful green wrapper, folded like clean linen come home from the clear-starcher's," which all costs only "Four Pence" (9). In a move that nods both to Christopher the Waiter in *Somebody's Luggage* and to *All the Year Round*, Marigold even specifies "Beaufort House" as the printer (9). Both Marigold and Dickens act as editors and sellers of the number, and the same section casts readers as Marigold's customers with a disclaimer that neutralizes potential criticisms of the forthcoming stories: "I hit on the plan that this same book should be a general miscellaneous lot—like the razors, flat-iron, chronometer watch, dinner plates, rolling-pin, and looking-glass—and shouldn't be offered as a single individual article like the spectacles or the gun" (8). Akin to the differences between a looking glass and a dinner plate, the stories' lack of thematic coherence does not indicate a low collective value. In fact, their range may enhance their value, reaching the needs of readers with various tastes. Still, Marigold sells the collection as an individual unit, a "book," and his framing narrative succeeds, as many of its predecessors have done, in creating a sense of unity in the midst of difference (9).

As we shall see, unexpected thematic commonalities emerge in the wittily titled assemblage of tales. Rosa Mulholland's "Not to Be Taken at Bedtime" appears as a warning and follows the Christmas numbers' pattern of racializing nonnormative behavior. The recluse Coll Dhu, or "Black Coll," so called "because of his sullen bearing and solitary habits," is a "big dark man" who obsessively loves his neighbor's daughter Evleen (9). An old woman conspires with Dhu in trying to force Evleen to return his love and places a charmed packet around the sleeping Evleen's neck, which subsequently causes her to wander around the hills in a drug-induced state. When Dhu tries to extricate her from a perilous position on the cliffs, his presence intensifies her madness instead of inspiring love. Unaware that she is in danger of falling, the struggling Evleen pulls Dhu backward and plunges them to their deaths (14–15). Dhu's wish to possess Evleen against her will—to create a family of choice through a love potion that comes wrapped in human skin stolen from a fresh corpse—adds a grisly element to the number's instructive messages about men's wishes to control people.

The abrupt change in tone of the next contribution fulfills Doctor Marigold's promise that the stories will vary from each other distinctly. Charles Collins's "To Be Taken at the Dinner Table" refers not to potions but rather to the place where the story's narrator, a riddler, deploys his art. Resonating with Dickens's story of the unacknowledged street painter in *Somebody's Luggage*, Collins's "epigrammatic artist" is a composer of conundrums who provides a detailed description of how he uses the dictionary to construct puzzles (17). The narrator does not complain about his anonymity but blames his downfall on an incident in which he sells the same riddle to two clients who attend the same dinner party. The riddler loses business, his puzzling powers decline, and his career plummets so swiftly that he is reduced to writing a rebus for which he cannot remember the answer. Collins's story does not connect to the themes of other contributions or seem to make much of a point, but the parallel between the puzzle writer and contributors to *All the Year Round* again raises the possibility that he uses the collaborative context of the Christmas number to tease his father-in-law. The story's more straightforward effect adds a lighthearted tone to the number and supports Marigold's claim that two stories indeed may have as little in common as a rolling pin and a chronometer.

Hesba Stretton returns the collection to the theme of women being purchased in "Not to Be Taken for Granted," which tells of a Moravian virgin who is nearly sold to two different men. Eunice Fielding abruptly encounters the threatening world of men when her mother dies, her father is imprisoned for debt, her stepsisters offer no assistance, and her maternal uncle offers to pay her family's debts, but only if Eunice vows to never see her father again. This unfamiliar uncle demands a kiss and "fondle[s]" her on his knee in the midst of making the repulsive offer, and the next man to make such an offer to Eunice is more blatantly sexual in his desires (22). Brother More, Eunice's stepsister's fiancé, claims that a vision from God demands that he change his choice to Eunice and swears to purchase her father's freedom on their marriage day. Mortified, Eunice feels obligated to marry More because, having written each scenario on paper lots stuck into her Bible and having randomly drawn the lot containing More's name, she regards that choice as divinely sanctioned. Ironically, Eunice has already likened herself to a slave when she writes in her journal, "I am sure I am willing to do anything, even to selling myself into slavery, as some of our first missionaries did in the slave-times in the West Indies. But in England one cannot sell one's self, though I would be a very faithful servant" (24). In England, however, women like Eunice are indeed bought and sold as wives in a marriage market. Eunice's salvation comes from a man outside her community but does little to assuage concerns about the selling of women that permeate the frame story; Gabriel arranges the payment of Eunice's father's debts and forces More to admit that his vision from God was a sham. The family then lives under the uncle's roof with Eunice acting as a daughter to both old men while implicitly betrothed to Gabriel. It is only luck that lands Eunice in the arms of a kind man, and the older men's sharing of her as an object is unsettling. Although Marigold's intentions are benevolent, Eunice's lack of agency reminds readers of questions first raised in the frame narrative.

One of the number's more exciting pieces, Walter Thornbury's "To Be Taken in Water," references the subjugation of women less literally. Herbert Blamyre accompanies a delivery of gold to Italy, and his journey is full of suspicious people, including a wily traveling salesman, Levison, who has a "Jewish nose," and the blustery Major Baxter (28). En route, Blamyre utters one of the letter-lock passwords in Levison's hearing then receives a message warning him that he is in imminent danger. He mistakenly suspects the disguised detective Major Baxter; thanks to Baxter's acumen, the two men interrupt Levison in the act of robbing one of the chests. Weighed down by the purloined coins, Levison drowns in the river, and Blamyre recovers all of the gold. The fast-paced story lends some much-needed suspense to the number and also touches lightly on the slavery motif. Blamyre dreams he is in Egypt, "where the camels jostle [him] and the black slaves threatened [him]" (31), and a woman inspector acting the part of the Major's wife says, "What slaves we poor women are!" when the major asks her to check on their hotel rooms at a stopping point in France (32). Through the figure of the woman inspector, the story turns the number's commentary from serious consideration of women being denied full personhood to more general jokes about sexism that refer to women's enslavement metaphorically. The number's tone then shifts to a now-familiar aspect of the canon with another Christmas ghost story.

Dickens undercuts the legitimacy of his own story with its title, "To Be Taken with a Grain of Salt," but its tone is not at all jesting, and its themes are ones that regularly preoccupy Dickens's Christmas stories. The narrator states that after reading a newspaper report of a murder, he sees two men walking through the streets, but nobody else sees the men. Later that day, a spectre beckons to him in his rooms, and the vision is transmitted to his servant via the narrator's touch (34–35). These incidents occur before the man is chosen to serve as the foreman at a murder trial, and when the accused appears in court, he is one of the men the narrator has previously spotted on the pavement outside his window. The ghost of the murdered man appears in various places, and each appearance causes bystanders to feel a shiver, dream about the dead man, or otherwise react to a presence that they cannot see. As soon as the accused is found guilty, the murdered man disappears, but the convicted man declares in the story's final lines that the foreman appears next to him one night and puts a rope around his neck, dooming him. The story implicitly asks whether the speaker who claims to see apparitions is a supernatural entity himself. One can regard the murderer's claim as the rantings of a madman, but they are so similar in content to the claims of the narrator, whose credibility is enhanced by his account of other people reacting to the spectre's presence, that dismissing the whole story as lunacy does not do it justice. Rather, the murderer's belief that the narrator has haunted him works to reinforce the narrator's visions. The confusion surrounding the narrator's mindset and possible supernatural existence forecasts Dickens's "The Signal-Man" in the next year's *Mugby Junction*, an often overlooked link between two Christmas numbers that helps to illuminate Dickens's crafting of ghost stories. Placing both narrators in uneasy positions that converge with what seem to be supernatural spectres, Dickens (in his authorial role) calls upon readers to question their beliefs even though Dickens (in his editorial role) has given the story a title that firmly places tongue in cheek.

Continuing to investigate murder, Gascoyne's "To Be Taken and Tried" depicts both murder and the ownership of women as forms of torture. In a pastoral village, Susan Archer and George Eade fall in love at a young age, but Susan's father wants her to wed the much wealthier Geoffrey Gibbs. Susan is true to George, but to escape the pressure of her mercenary brother and father, they agree that she should live with her aunt for the final weeks before their marriage. The week of the wedding, a letter of apology announces to George that Susan has married Gibbs, who beats her. Following an episode in which a stoic George saves Susan's son from a carriage accident caused by Gibbs's drunkenness, Gibbs turns up dead in the woods, and George is tried for the murder. He is acquitted, and one year later, a dying man appears at the clergyman's house to explain that he accidentally killed Gibbs in self-defense during a fight over money. The man also admits to acting as Gibbs's accomplice in kidnapping Susan during her previous separation from George, attesting to the fact that they threaten her with a loaded pistol until she agrees to marry Gibbs to save George's life (46). The story's conclusion places Susan and George together in a cozy cottage with a new baby but takes care to point out that the harrowing ordeal of an abusive marriage has taken a toll on Susan, who is "not as beautiful as of yore" but "still fair" (46). In contrast, George has regained his strength and wears a "bright cheery look on his honest English face," which maintains the alignment of strong morality with idealized English purity. Gascoyne's story joins the others in condemning men who restrict women's movements and choices, but the mitigated happy ending and the prolonged torture Susan has endured render women's suffering as part of accepted everyday life.

The final story, Dickens's "To Be Taken for Life," directly addresses questions of agency and choice for young women as it catches up with Sophy and Doctor Marigold once they reunite after her schooling. Their happy life is challenged when a deaf and mute student from Sophy's school secretly follows the cart and pleads with Sophy to marry him then travel to China, where his work as a merchant clerk awaits (47). A weeping Sophy says that she cannot bear to leave her father, but Marigold observes their conversation and understands that Sophy will be better off in the long term if she departs with her beloved. The scene featuring their subsequent communication exemplifies how deftly Dickens weaves together the frame concept of the prescription metaphor and the development of frame characters in the plot. The exchange (translated from signs)[19] takes place after Doctor Marigold asks Sophy why she has been crying:

> "A head-ache."
> "Not a heart-ache?"
> "I said a head-ache, father."
> "Doctor Marigold must prescribe for that head-ache."
> She took up the book of my Prescriptions, and held it up with a forced smile, but seeing me keep still and look earnest, she softly laid it down again, and her eyes were very attentive.
> "The Prescription is not there, Sophy."
> "Where is it?"
> "Here, my dear."
> I brought her young husband in, and I put her hand in his, and my only further words to both of them were these: "Doctor Marigold's last prescription. To be taken for life." After which I bolted. (48)

Here on its final page, the number perseveres in playing fast and loose with the treatment of people as objects when Marigold presents Sophy's husband-to-be as a prescription. Because he is a compassionate figure, Marigold's intent in uniting the young people seems unequivocally generous, but the way he places Sophy's hand into the other man's also treats her in a proprietary manner, mirroring his purchase of her when she was a child. In the context of Marigold having confessed in his compilation of the number that he likes to be the "owner of things," his depiction of his family relationships continues to exhibit a proprietary sentiment. When he confronts Sophy's lover, Marigold could easily come across as a shadow of Eunice Fielding's father or uncle, but the interpolated characters instead function as foils alongside Marigold's early, abuse-enabling self.

The conclusion of both the love story and the Christmas number move the collection toward its most comprehensive and positive responses to the questions it consistently raises. Sophy and her husband are away for five years, during which time Marigold and Sophy exchange letters, one of which announces the birth of Sophy's daughter. Marigold does not know whether the child has inherited her parents' deafness and muteness. On a Christmas Eve, Marigold dozes after a fine feast, dreams of Sophy and her child, then wakes as the actual granddaughter walks into the cart, saying "Grandfather!" (48). The tearful reunion reveals the girl's acumen, and Marigold concludes the number with an emphasis on multigenerational family bonds: "I saw the pretty child a talking, pleased and quick and eager and busy, to her mother, in the signs that I had first taught her mother" (48). Although Marigold's pity patronizes disability, his paternal role and his repeated sacrifice of Sophy's company to ensure her independence ultimately constitutes a more progressive approach to her challenges. Holmes points out that Sophy is an exceptional character because "when disabled women in Victorian narratives marry and become mothers, they almost always build their families through adoption rather than biology."[20] Sophy marrying by choice and giving birth to a child created by two disabled people makes the formation of biological family bonds, in this case, the most socially radical outcome. Because Marigold insists that Sophy is as intelligent as a person with hearing and speech then grants her young deaf and mute husband the same level of respect and responsibility for the family's welfare as any other man, Marigold's (and Sophy's) delight in her daughter's ability to speak does not dampen the story's final endorsement of self-determination for individuals facing profound communicative challenges. In the framing for this Christmas number, Dickens rounds out and develops those dynamics in a way that grants Sophy full personhood, a rare feat in nineteenth-century writing.[21]

Although Doctor Marigold and the previous year's Mrs. Lirriper may be equally humorous characters, when it comes to the poignancy of the bond between parent and adopted child, the 1865 collection surpasses its predecessors. The moments of separation and reunion for Marigold and Sophy are not simply infused with the feelings that characterize most idealized relationships between fathers and daughters; they are supercharged with the protective anxiety that accompanies one's care for a child who is unable to hear or speak. The appeal of Doctor Marigold is further evidenced in the popularity of Dickens's performance of the character in his public reading tours, which routinely packed venues in the months leading up to Christmas. Beginning in April 1866, Dickens embodied the Marigold character seventy-four times to rave reviews and enthusiastic audiences. He performed only one other piece adapted from the Christmas numbers, "Boots at the Holly-Tree Inn," more frequently than he did "Doctor Marigold," but his performances of "Boots" (totaling eighty-one) had been in progress for eight years before "Marigold" debuted.[22]

That *Doctor Marigold's Prescriptions* consistently discusses the selling of people alongside the sale of objects also makes for amusing reflection on the intertextual relationships between the prose of the Christmas number, its framing conceit, and the number's advertisements. For both this collection and the one to come, indirect conversation between the number and its advertisements extends the textual dynamics already at play. The advertisements appear on the inside and outside of the blue covers protecting the main text, not interspersed in it, and the metaphorical meanings of prescriptions in this collection are answered by advertisements for actual pills on the back covers. Re-creating the jumbling of disparate objects in one of Marigold's lots, the advertisements pitch everything from wasteless candles to crinolines to steel pens to perfume. In a single quadrant of the back cover, an advertisement for prayer books and Bibles (exemplifying Marigold's belief in text as prescription) appears immediately below an announcement for "Kaye's Worsdell's Pills, the best family medicine." Near another Bible advertisement describing "three hundred Bible stories" with pictures from John Field's Great Bible Warehouse is an announcement for Morson's Pepsine, an "invaluable medicine for weak and impaired digestion," available in powder or wine form.[23] Clearly, Dickens's tolerance for intertextual comedy and for laughter at his own story collections was high as he entered the final two years of producing them.

Coming to a Stop

(1866–67)

As Dickens finishes the Christmas numbers that span eighteen consecutive years of his career, he changes some of his approaches radically but keeps other collaborative practices intact. Identifying other authors in print for the first time and returning to a jointly conceived narrative with Wilkie Collins, the Christmas collections exhibit no more uniformity at the end of their run than at the start. The final numbers serve as reminders that the collaborative Dickens operates in two seemingly contradictory registers: one that attempts to separate Dickens's voice from others (with greater or lesser success) and one that blends his voice with others (intentionally or not). In the penultimate number, all contributing authors are listed on the title page for the first time (see figure 8.1). That naming is consistent with a shift toward bylines in many periodicals of the late 1860s, but the title page and the header on each page continue to state, "Conducted by Charles Dickens." The practice of including signatures does not obliterate the conducting dynamic, illustrating that the person labelled as the conductor does not inherently take all credit for the talent of contributing artists. Still, the shift to attribution does not necessarily happen smoothly. Dickens abandons the idea of his stories functioning as thematic bookends for the number in favor of dominating the first half of it, and that choice damages the narrative coherence of the whole.

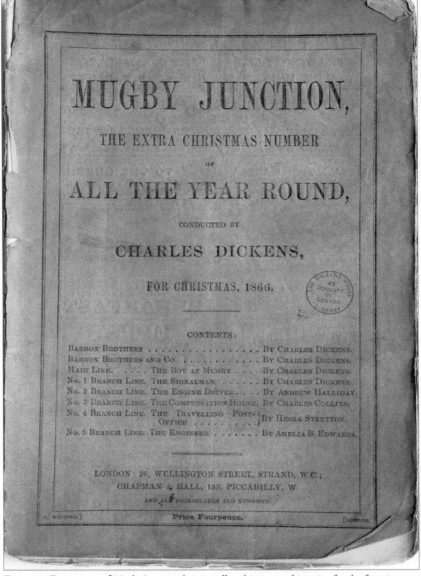

Figure 8.1. Front cover of *Mugby Junction*, showing all authors named in print for the first time. Photograph courtesy of the Charles Dickens Museum, London.

Mugby Junction is disjointed, with a seemingly misordered frame narrative, yet the complete text makes the point that when reconsidering or reshaping personal identity, the collaborative is crucial. Ironically, given its title, the collection's depiction of travel has more to do with memory making, metaphorical rebirth, and selfhood than with physical movement from one place to another, and none of those processes occur in isolation for the protagonist. In contrast, *No Thoroughfare* is full of physical motion as it mixes authorial voices seamlessly and returns to questions of race, purity, and English identity constructed in contrast to sometimes ambiguous others. The final Christmas number reveals that the collaborative conversations of Collins and Dickens persist through decades, referencing previous projects while also emerging in their novels of the late 1860s. Repositioning *No Thoroughfare* among *The Lazy Tour of Two Idle Apprentices*, Collins's *Black and White* and *The Moonstone*, and Dickens's *The Mystery of Edwin Drood* demonstrates the wide-ranging interpretive benefits of putting a conversational model of collaboration into practice.

Mugby Junction

Most critical attention to *Mugby Junction* has focused on the train station and its engines in the context of Dickens having survived a terrible railway accident at Staplehurst. On June 9, 1865, Dickens was returning to London from Boulogne when a failure in communication about construction work caused the train to derail. Dickens, Ellen Ternan, and her mother sat in the first first-class coach, which saved their lives, as several other carriages plunged off a bridge.[1] Lasting accounts of Dickens's actions during the accident omit the Ternans and describe him retrieving the manuscript of *Our Mutual Friend* then ministering kindly to the injured and dying in the ravine. Scholarly treatments that view Dickens's stories about railroads as representations of his reaction to Staplehurst have overindividualized both the experience and his response, particularly in relation to *Mugby Junction's* "The Signal-Man." Just as Dickens was not alone on the train that crashed, so too the story that many scholars include in his psychological processing of the event was not originally produced in a solitary context or published in an individual work. Dickens included "The Signal-Man" in later collections of his Christmas stories, but even then, it was accompanied by his own framing stories and did not stand completely alone. *Mugby Junction's* messages about storytelling—as a means of moving through trauma and as a way of processing memory in order to develop an improved identity—depend on collaboration.

Dickens opens the number with "Barbox Brothers," the professional identity of the middle-aged Mr. Jackson, who seeks a more individualized understanding of himself (1). Jackson has trouble escaping the legacy of the original Barboxes' dishonest business dealings and the pain of his girlfriend suddenly running off to marry his only friend. Tired of the bitter disposition these circumstances generate, Jackson dissolves the firm and sets out on a radical journey of self-reinvention (4). To prevent misreading the significance of the railway and the characters Jackson meets, one must realize that Jackson's personal transformation is already in progress when he arrives at Mugby Junction; the people he encounters and the trains he rides facilitate his change rather than cause it. Jackson meets Phoebe, a bedridden younger woman who runs a home school and spends many hours each day looking out of the window, and through Phoebe's explanation that, although her mobility is limited, she is not "an invalid," the story makes a strong point against patronizing those with physical challenges (6). Jackson must constantly put his reactions to her in check: "Even her busy hands, which of their own thinness alone might have besought compassion, plied their task with a gay courage that made mere compassion an unjustifiable assumption of superiority, and an impertinence" (7). Jackson surpasses even Doctor Marigold in his recognition that compassion can be misplaced but shows less sensitivity in regard to social class. Phoebe's father tends to the station's oil lamps, and Jackson diminishes his subjectivity by calling him only "Lamps." When "Lamps" begins to offer his name, Jackson interjects: "Stay! . . . What signifies your name! Lamps is name enough for me. I like it. It is bright and expressive. What do I want more!" (8). Lamps makes a distinction between his work identity "down at the Junction" and his home identity, but Jackson refuses to address the man outside of his service role (8). Despite Jackson's visit being motivated by his own attempt to shed the Barbox identity, he completely rejects the more equitable relationship, asserting that Lamps's actual name is meaningless in comparison to the brightness of the objectifying moniker.

The ensuing six weeks involve Phoebe in an investigative and collaborative project that provides the framing apparatus for the contributed stories. Jackson pleads for Phoebe's participation: "I want to bring you what I pick up at the heads of the seven roads that you lie here looking out at, and to compare notes with you about it. May I? They say that two heads are better than one. I should say myself that probably depends on the heads concerned. But I am quite sure, though we are so newly acquainted, that your head and your father's have found out better things, Phoebe, than ever mine of itself discovered" (10). Jackson's desire to "compare notes," coupled with his direct question, lays the foundation for an equitable endeavor. Humbling himself to Phoebe and acknowledging that Lamps's more simply expressed worldview may be superior to his own, Jackson also gives Phoebe an instrument he has acquired while exploring one line, and she consents to his plan for continued meetings.

Limiting his journeys to tracks that Phoebe can see from her window, Jackson's desire for her input as he chooses which line to take on the next step of his journey makes the endeavor a collaborative one from start to finish: "The results of his researches, as he and Phoebe afterwards set them down in fair writing, hold their due places in this veracious chronicle, from its seventeenth page, onward. But they occupied a much longer time in the getting together than they ever will in the perusal" (10). Working on the stories together, Jackson and Phoebe "set them down" over a long period of time to prepare the collection readers now hold. The reference to "fair writing" emphasizes Phoebe's and Jackson's hands, creating a double layer of authorship between Dickens's fictional characters and the writing hands of four different collaborators. The conducting metaphor, then, does seem appropriate to preserve alongside attribution, as Dickens's editorial persona attempts to coordinate the hands. Unfortunately, he fumbles that editorial task by positioning the second story prematurely and creating a confusing frame to explain the ordering of the stories.

Multiple awkward rewindings take place in "Barbox Brothers and Co.," the number's second story. Dickens begins by establishing that Jackson has already explored all of the railway lines Phoebe can see, and he cannot decide which one to take as he finally departs Mugby Junction for good. Phoebe suggests that Jackson should take the seventh road to Wales because she already associates it with the lovely instrument he has delivered. The story then follows Jackson as he takes that line and departs Mugby Junction with all of his belongings. That departure makes "Barbox Brothers and Co." sound like the end of the number because Jackson has already shared the results of his investigation of the other train lines with Phoebe, but readers have not heard those accounts yet. Even more oddly, Jackson has already learned lessons from those stories. When he arrives in Wales, "it began to be suspected by him that Mugby Junction was a Junction of many branches, invisible as well as visible, and had joined him to an endless number of byways. For, whereas he would, but a little while ago, have walked these streets blindly brooding, he now had eyes and thoughts for a new external world" (11). Not even a full quarter of the way into the number, the protagonist has experienced the growth he desires, and by the end of the story (just one-third of the way through the number), Jackson has returned to Mugby Junction permanently.

Dickens has placed the concluding frame story in the second position; readers see that Jackson's experiences at Mugby have changed him but are unable to comprehend why the stories, which they have not yet read, would have such an effect. The protagonist's completed character transformation is evident when, on his way to Wales, Jackson's newly calibrated attention to his surroundings cause him to react kindly to a lost little girl, Polly, who approaches him for help. The girl's mother is the woman who ran off decades earlier with Jackson's best friend, and she has sent Polly to him on purpose to request Jackson's forgiveness. Happening to see Jackson in a music store on the day he takes his first journey, the woman senses that he has softened in attitude and surveils the station until he appears again so that she can launch a scheme she believes will break the curse that has resulted from betraying him. He returns to Mugby Junction, where he can continue cheering Phoebe and "borrowing" Polly for visits, which concludes his moral journey (16). The narrative then awkwardly backtracks, announcing across both columns, "Here follows the substance of what was seen, heard, or otherwise picked up, by the Gentleman for Nowhere, in his careful study of the Junction" (17). This is only the second time that Dickens alters the two-column format in all eighteen years of Christmas numbers (*The Haunted House* being the first), and the temporal confusion heightens the strangeness of this unusual use of print space (see figure 8.2). As Jim Mussell argues, the consistent form of Victorian periodicals created "an interpretive structure" that enabled readers to distinguish new content and conditioned their ways of processing information.[2] To suddenly change the format of columns after hundreds of preceding issues signals emphatically that readers must not rely on preestablished generic or formal ways of knowing to understand the collection.

Although Jackson brings stories back and forth to Phoebe, by presenting them out of order, the number creates excessive layers of disassociation and disorientation. Moving backward in narrative time to retrace Jackson's steps does not match Jackson's movements over the course of the number, because the second story has already provided readers with the conclusion. The third story to appear in the collection, "Main Line. The Boy at Mugby," is actually the first story that Jackson collects. In a highly comical character portrait, Dickens describes the pride a boy takes in having not refreshed anyone while working in the refreshment room. The staff ignores customers, delivers

HERE FOLLOWS THE SUBSTANCE OF WHAT WAS SEEN, HEARD, OR OTHERWISE PICKED UP, BY THE GENTLEMAN FOR NOWHERE, IN HIS CAREFUL STUDY OF THE JUNCTION.

MAIN LINE.
THE BOY AT MUGBY.

I am The Boy at Mugby. That's about what *I* am.

You don't know what I mean? What a pity! But I think you do. I think you must. Look here. I am the Boy at what is called The Refreshment Room at Mugby Junction, and what's proudest boast is, that it never yet refreshed a mortal being.

Up in a corner of the Down Refreshment Room at Mugby Junction, in the height of twenty-seven cross draughts (I've often counted 'em while they brush the First Class hair twenty-seven ways), behind the bottles, among the glasses, bounded on the nor'-west by the beer, stood pretty far to the right of a metallic object that's at times the tea-urn and at times the soup-tureen, according to the nature of the last twang imparted to its contents which are the same groundwork, fended off from the traveller by a barrier of stale sponge-cakes erected atop of the counter, and lastly exposed sideways to the glare of Our Missis's eye — you ask a Boy so sitiwated, next time you stop in a hurry at Mugby, for anything to drink; you take particular notice that he'll try to seem not to hear you, that he'll appear in a absent manner to survey the Line through a transparent medium composed of your head and body, and that he won't serve you as long as you can possibly bear it. That's Me.

What a lark it is! We are the Model Establishment, we are, at Mugby. Other Refreshment Rooms send their imperfect young ladies up to be finished off by our Missis. For some of the young ladies, when they're new to the business, come into it mild! Ah! Our Missis, she soon takes that out of 'em. Why, I originally come into the business meek myself! But Our Missis she soon took that out of *me*.

What a delightful lark it is! I look upon us Refreshmenters as ockipying the only proudly independent footing on the Line. There's Papers for instance—my honourable friend if he will allow me to call him so—him as belongs to Smith's bookstall. Why he no more dares to be up to our Refreshmenting games, than he dares to jump atop of a locomotive with her steam at full pressure, and cut away upon her alone, driving himself, at limited-mail speed. Papers, he'd get his head punched at every compartment, first second and third, the whole length of a train, if he was to ventur to imitate my demeanour. It's the same with the porters, the same with the guards, the same with the ticket clerks, the same with the whole way up to the secretary, traffic manager, or very chairman. There ain't one among 'em on the nobly independent footing we are. Did you ever catch one of *them*, when you wanted anything of him, making a system of surveying the Line through a transparent medium composed of your head and body? I should hope not.

You should see our Bandolining Room at Mugby Junction. It's led to, by the door behind the counter which you'll notice usually stands ajar, and it's the room where Our Missis and our young ladies Bandolines their hair. You should see 'em at it, betwixt trains, Bandolining away, as if they was anointing themselves for the combat. When you're telegraphed, you should see their noses all a going up with scorn, as if it was a part of the working of the same Cooke and Wheatstone electrical machinery. You should hear Our Missis give the word "Here comes the Beast to be Fed!" and then you should see 'em indignantly skipping across the Line, from the Up to the Down, or Wicer Warsaw, and begin to pitch the stale pastry into the plates, and chuck the sawdust sangwiches under the glass covers, and get out the—ha ha ha!—the Sherry—O my eye, my eye!—for your Refreshment.

It's only in the Isle of the Brave and Land of the Free (by which of course I mean to say Britannia) that Refreshmenting is so effective, so 'olesome, so constitutional, a check *upon the public. There was a foreigner, which having politely, with his hat off, beseeched our young ladies and Our Missis for "a leetel gloss hoff prarndee," and having had the Line surveyed through him by all and no other acknowledgment, was a proceeding at last to help himself, as seems to be the custom in his own country, when Our Missis with her hair almost a coming un-Bandolined with rage, and her eyes omitting sparks, flew at him, cotched the decanter out of his hand, and said: "Put it down! I won't allow that!" The foreigner turned pale, stepped back with his arms stretched out in front of him, his hands clasped, and his shoulders riz, and exclaimed: "Ah! Is it possible this! That these disdaineous females and this ferocious old woman are placed here by the administration, not only to empoison the voyagers, but to affront them! Great Heaven! How arrives it? The English people. Or is he then a slave? Or idiot?" Another time, a merry widewawake American gent had tried the sawdust and spit it out, and had tried the Sherry and spit that out, and had tried in vain to sustain exhausted natur upon Butter-Scotch, and had been rather badly Bandolined and Line-surveyed through, when, as the bell was ringing and he paid Our Missis, he says, very loud and good-tempered: "I tell Yew what 'tis, ma'arm. I la'af. Theer! I la'af. I Dew. I oughter ha' seen most things, for I hail from the Onlimited side of the Atlantic Ocean, and I haive travelled right slick over the Limited, head on through Jee-rusalemm and the East, and likeways France and Italy, Europe Old World, and am now upon the track to the Chief Europian wrong things, and treats the travelling public as an enemy. Exemplifying that Jackson does not physically follow each track that leaves Mugby Junction but rather collects tales associated with them, the boy's story touches on the topic of travel without requiring the protagonist to move. I join Tamara S. Wagner in regarding *Mugby Junction* as a text that "displays a carefully crafted inner coherence" but remain troubled by the mounting problems the stories' ordering raises.[3] Anne Chapman reads the narrative chaos sympathetically, positing that the collection's structure "signals Dickens's interest in challenging the conventions of time and expectation," but Chapman's claims (especially those that reference "collaborative effort" among fictional characters in "The Boy at Mugby") are limited by a refusal to analyze the stories of contributors who are not Dickens.[4]

The shift in tone from "Main Line. The Boy at Mugby" to "No. 1 Branch Line. The Signal-Man" could not be more distinct, as the lighthearted humor of the boy who enjoys disappointing customers turns to chilling fear, and "The Signal-Man's" central mysteries require full consideration of its embeddedness in the collaborative collection. The story not only seems to endorse the existence of supernatural phenomena but also leaves abundant questions about which figure in the tale is the most otherworldly. Exploring a part of the station where the tracks are below ground level, Jackson descends into a trench to speak to a signal-man and immediately thinks that the man might be an apparition: "The monstrous thought came into my mind as I perused the fixed eyes and the saturnine face, that this was a spirit, not a man" (21). The space feels eerie, and the signal-man's strange behavior begins when he is startled by Jackson's greeting, "Halloa! Below there!" because he has heard those words recently from what appeared to be a foreboding spectre. Over a couple of visits, the signal-man explains to his skeptical visitor that he has seen a man by the red danger light gesturing with his left arm over his eyes and his right arm waving; when he tries to approach, the spectre disappears, but the next day, a terrible crash on that line results in dead and wounded people lying at the spectre's spot. Several months later, he sees the spectre in a posture of mourning, and the next day, a woman suddenly dies in a train on that track. Presently, he has witnessed the spectre making the waving gesture again but has no idea how to stop whatever calamity is about to happen. Jackson decides to take the signal-man to a doctor on the following day, but instead of finding his friend, he discovers men in the tunnel gathered around the signal-man's corpse. The engine driver pantomimes how he made exactly the same arm gesture that the signal-man had seen and called out the precise words Jackson associates with the gesture—"For God's sake clear the way!"—as his train approached and killed the signal-man, who was standing on one of the rails (23, 25).

The engine driver's gesture and words align him with the spectre, but Jackson says that he has associated the cautionary words with the gesture "only in my own mind," which also aligns Jackson himself with the supernatural. In addition to the signal-man seeming more (or less) than human, there are now three people in the story with supernatural traits, not counting the figure that may be one-hundred-percent ghost. Recall that the narrator of "To Be Taken with a Grain of Salt" in *Doctor Marigold's Prescriptions* is also suddenly ascribed supernatural status in the final lines of that story. Dickens practiced this maneuver a year in advance by having the jury foreman see spectres of both a living murderer and a dead man then being identified himself as the spectre who appears with a noose at the bedside of the accused. In that context, one observes Dickens fine-tuning and improving a ghost story technique, but because the first story has nothing to do with a railway accident and the Christmas numbers are so often read in fragments, "To Be Taken with a Grain of Salt" is rarely linked to "The Signal-Man." Although Jackson fails to help the signal-man decode the spectre's message, and indeed may contribute to the signal-man's death by dismissing belief in the ghost, his shock at the similarity between his own unspoken words and those of the engine driver validates the supernatural warning.

I have identified the narrator of "The Signal-Man" as Mr. Jackson, which is crucial to accurate evaluation of the story's treatment of the supernatural. When read in its original context, nothing in the story contradicts the logical presumption that the narrator is Jackson. We know that Jackson is staying at an inn for a prolonged period of time, which the townspeople identify as unusual behavior. Hence, when the narrator says in the middle of the story, "I got back to my inn without any adventure," readers naturally understand the comment to refer to Jackson's residence in the frame story (22). Also, stories communicating information about each line are prefaced with a heading identifying Jackson, "the Gentleman for Nowhere," as their collector; and he is the only character who meanders around the station on a daily basis in "careful study" (17). When one reads "The Signal-Man" on its own, as it appears in the 1867 Diamond Edition under the heading "Two Ghost Stories," questions about the narrator's identity invariably arise. Studying the story's original publication context helps respond to those questions and is especially necessary for analyses that make broad assertions about Dickens's oeuvre or psyche. David Ellison, for instance, offers an interesting reading of "The Signal-Man" as a post-Staplehurst reworking of Dickens's interactions with Elizabeth Gaskell over her portrayal of Captain Brown's death by train in *Cranford,* but Ellison's focus on anachronism and trauma, even while discussing Dickens's editorial relationship with Gaskell, ignores the relevance of the frame story to conclusions about authorship.[5] It is difficult to call Jackson "unconsciously creative," for instance, when we know that he purposely seeks out stories associated with each train line for Phoebe.[6] Without a rationale for excluding the frame context, one is left to wonder how notions of anachronism and trauma relate to the number's confusing sequencing and narrative rewindings. Ellison's point that "The Signal-Man" emerges from conversation is even more accurate than he proposes when one considers the frame, and because the production of the stories is a crucial element of Jackson's character growth, one must recognize that he fills speaking, writing, and listening roles dynamically. Jackson develops a new sense of himself as a result of both speaking and listening, and the number as a whole demonstrates that constant retelling is what leads to a healthy synthesis of the stories' contents. In this collaborative context, "The Signal-Man" remains haunting but not baffling.

The fact that the next story in the number continues to treat railway disasters is also relevant to discussions of Dickens's comfort level with various depictions of the violence accompanying a relatively new method of transport, but because "No. 2 Branch Line. The Engine-Driver" is written by Andrew Halliday, its relevance to such discussions has been overlooked. The number's final story addresses railway violence a third time. Again, foregrounding the impact of the other pieces on the significance of "The Signal-Man" is not the only way to analyze the story's significance, but ignoring the linking themes can result in problematic blind spots. The engine driver in Halliday's story is quite matter-of-fact about the inherent danger of the railway. Jim Martin boldly admits that he has killed "only" seven men and boys in twenty-five years on the job (25). He also states that passengers are oblivious to frequent near misses; one of his stokers dies because, as they brace for a head-on collision with another train, Martin tells him to jump to save his life. In another "half second," Martin would have jumped to his own death, but the other train suddenly veers off onto another track, and Martin's colleague has killed himself unnecessarily (27). Guiltless, the driver relates further gruesome details: "There are heaps of people run over that no one ever hears about. One dark night in the Black Country, me and my mate felt something wet and warm splash in our faces.... It was blood. That's what it was. We heard afterwards that a collier had been run over" (27). The seeming callousness of this engine driver contrasts starkly with the distress of the driver in "The Signal-Man." Halliday's driver creates an almost comical scene in relating the dialogue between himself and his assistant as they try to identify the blood, but such dialogue in "The Signal-Man" would offend the story's sensibility. The number accommodates both pieces comfortably, indicating that if one chooses to scan the collection for clues about Dickens's own psychological status, he was at ease working through memories of railway violence in diverse tones and with varying outcomes. Halliday's story also operates as a tale of warning, for if Jackson fails in his quest, he may make the poor choice of taking a train whose driver is quite comfortable with frequent railway deaths.

Halliday's and Dickens's stories converse and collide in a manner that, rather than compounding trauma, creates healthy conversation to dissipate it. Charles Collins's "No. 3 Branch Line. The Compensation House" continues the number's thematic interest in trauma but shifts to the effects of deliberate rather than accidental murder. At a house near the third line, Jackson meets an unusually free-speaking servant, Masey, who works for the dying Mister Oswald Strange. Strange has moved to Mugby to be near his doctor, who knows that when Strange sees his reflection, he either becomes enraged or enters a catatonic trance. Inexplicably, the doctor shares the history of Strange's case with Jackson and allows the stranger to be in the room with his patient. As he dies, Strange asks for a looking glass and confesses that while in Italy many years ago, he shoots his wife's lover in a rage rather than waiting to stage a duel (34). Since the killing, the face of the Italian seducer is all Strange can see in looking glasses, but owning his crime and sensing his own death puts a stop to Strange's disassociation with his image; his final gaze into a mirror reflects only his own face.

Again, Jackson's journey to various places associated with the rail lines at Mugby Junction brings him into contact with someone struggling to reconcile identities as Charles Collins's story simultaneously develops the number's interest in the effects of trauma, resonates with themes in other numbers, and communicates another warning to Jackson. In this case, Mr. Strange is shedding not a professional self but rather a guilty, jealous self. The story reminds one of James Lawrence in Parr's contribution to *A Message from the Sea*; Lawrence believes himself to be haunted by Honor's ghost because he is responsible for her death. Strange's experience, in addition to advising against that particular rail line, also warns against enraged vengeance when faced with infidelity, which relates directly to Jackson's previous reaction to the loss of his lover. The placement of Strange's tale after the story in which Jackson forgives those who wronged him reinforces my argument that these stories are poorly sequenced. Jackson has processed these stories with Phoebe, putting their "two heads" together prior to his encounter with his former lover (10). In placing the account of that reunion as the second story, Dickens prematurely presents the effect these interpolated stories have on Jackson, forcing readers to read backwards (if they can keep track of the confusing chronology) to sort through each story's consequence. Such a reading process may in some ways mimic the back and forth motion of trains at the junction, but the disrupted narrative sequencing breaks that rhythm when it separates the stories' messages from their order of appearance.

Although it does not depict murder, Hesba Stretton's "No. 4 Branch Line. The Travelling Post-Office" continues to associate the railway with intrigue and personal risk while injecting familiar colonial themes into the collection. Frank, a clerk in the travelling post office, develops a crush on the Clifton sisters based on their handwriting but is drawn into drama when a woman posing as one of them assists a man with "the swarthy aspect of a foreigner" in stealing an important correspondence box (35). A different clerk has perpetrated the conspiracy with the intention of fleeing to Egypt with the stolen money and marrying the impostor, who, once caught, is banished to a convent on the island of Malta, "where she would still be under British protection" (42). The role of colonial lands in this story is to produce the "foreigners" behind crime and subsequently provide the criminals with safe havens. Frank, the loyal English clerk who discovers the treachery, ultimately marries a legitimate Clifton sister (Mary), enabling the story to restore domestic order and associate line number four with optimistic potential for Jackson (39).

The final story returns to murderous love triangles, railway violence, distant locations, and hauntings as it gathers the collection's thematic threads. In "No. 5 Branch Line. The Engineer," Amelia B. Edwards begins the story with a straightforward declaration—"His name, sir, was Matthew Price; mine is Benjamin Hardy"—but ends it with serious questions about the boundaries separating the normal from the paranormal (42). Hardy, a successful iron engineer, offers work to his best friend Mat, and the men share an imperial attitude toward unfamiliar sites when delivering a train to Italy: "[T]he street of jewellers, like an Arabian Nights' bazaar; the street of palaces, with its Moorish court-yards, its fountains and orange-trees; the women veiled like brides; the galley-slaves chained two and two; the processions of priests and friars; the everlasting clangour of bells; the babble of a strange tongue" (43). Benjamin's idyllic objectification of all things un-English begins to subside when he and Mat fall in love with the beautiful Gianetta Coneglia (43).

When Benjamin realizes that their friendship is in serious peril, the homo-erotic charge in the friendship surfaces as he marvels, "I saw how the truest friendship that ever bound two lives together was drifting on to wreck and ruin, I asked myself whether any woman in the world was worth what Mat had been to me and I to him" (44).

A sudden eruption of violence then exposes another link back to "The Signal-Man." When Mat tells Benjamin that Gianetta has played them both false and plans to marry a Marchese for his money, Benjamin stabs his closest friend (45). Despite Benjamin's loving ministrations through a long convalescence, Mat dies (46). Without "all that made life life," a dev-astated Benjamin devotes his energy to hating Gianetta while claiming to attempt to deliver Mat's final message of forgiveness to her (46). Finally, his chance for vengeance materializes when someone bribes him to crash a train carrying Gianetta and her husband (48). As Benjamin commands the stoker to pile in as much coal as possible with the train speeding down the tracks on its way to destruction, a man suddenly materializes in the car and turns down the steam. Benjamin concludes, "All that I can say—all that I *know* is—that Matthew Price came back from the dead to save my soul and the lives of those whom I, in my guilty rage, would have hurried to destruction. I believe this as I believe in the mercy of Heaven and the forgiveness of repentant sinners" (48). Closing the number with references to heaven and "repentant sinners" resonates with Christianity at Christ-mastime, but more significantly, Benjamin equates his unequivocal belief in a supernatural haunting with Christian beliefs. The existence of heaven is as indisputable to him as Matthew's Jesus-like return "from the dead" to save him and others from his sinful act. Edwards's story, in which the appearance of a dead man positively averts a crash, enhances Dickens's treatment of the role spectres might play in averting train disasters in "The Signal-Man." That Edwards's narrator does not pause for even a second to wonder whether the ghost is real casts more blame onto the signal-man and Jackson for their inability to interpret a spectre's warning. Viewed through a biographical lens, Edwards's concluding piece also amplifies Halliday's story, revealing another example of Dickens's comfort with a literary reenactment that changes the conclusion of a crash like the one at Staplehurst.

To these fictional explorations of railway disaster, we may add an in-tertextual dialogue that suggests comfort with a macabre sense of humor about such misfortunes. The back cover of *Mugby Junction* features a full-page advertisement for railway insurance, complete with exclamations such as

"ACCIDENTS WILL HAPPEN!" (see figure 8.3). Offered by "The Railway Passengers Assurance Company" for "accidents of every description," and in an even larger font, "ACCIDENT OF ANY KIND," the plea for insurance does not stop at stoking fears of train crashes. Other hazardous behaviors include "riding, driving, hunting, shooting, fishing, &c.," but the locations of the offices for purchasing such insurance lie at "any of the Railway Stations," reminding readers that one may conveniently secure coverage just moments before taking a journey. For as little as three pounds per year, the advertisement promises "£1000 IN CASE OF DEATH, or £6 per Week while laid-up by Injury." To conclude the physical pages of a Christmas number whose title names a railway junction with such an advertisement makes humorous irony an appropriate response to life-threatening trauma.

Despite the Christian symbolism at the end of its final story, *Mugby Junction* seems to be missing its conclusion. Given that Jackson investigates each train line so that he and Phoebe can discuss them and then decide on his future path, the end of the story that comes from the branch line appears abruptly, and the relevance of each piece to Jackson's development ultimately remains unsynthesized. Although a simple reordering of the pieces to avoid the unusual clustering of Dickens's contributions at the beginning would have solved the problem, the structural weakness did not impact the number's popularity: "*Mugby Junction* sold out the entire printing of 265,000 within a month."[7] Nonetheless, Dickens may have sensed a need to pay closer attention to ordering the stories more effectively because, for the following year's number, he reverts to creating it with a single collaborator and works with Wilkie Collins to craft their chapters into a unified text.

No Thoroughfare

It seems fitting that for the final Christmas number Dickens worked closely with his only sole collaborator. Five years had passed since Wilkie Collins had contributed to a Christmas collection, but the lapse did not hinder the friends' ability to collaborate. Some scholars have speculated that there was a cooling in the Collins/Dickens friendship during in the late 1860s, but their collaborative process for *No Thoroughfare* was as close as ever.[8] The quantity and types of collaborations in this period point toward enduring artistic sympathy and solid trust between the writers. Dickens offered to use his relationships with publishers to help Collins negotiate copyright matters, and Collins (at Dickens's request) went to Liverpool to set Dickens asail for the United States in November 1867 then joined Wills as coeditor of *All*

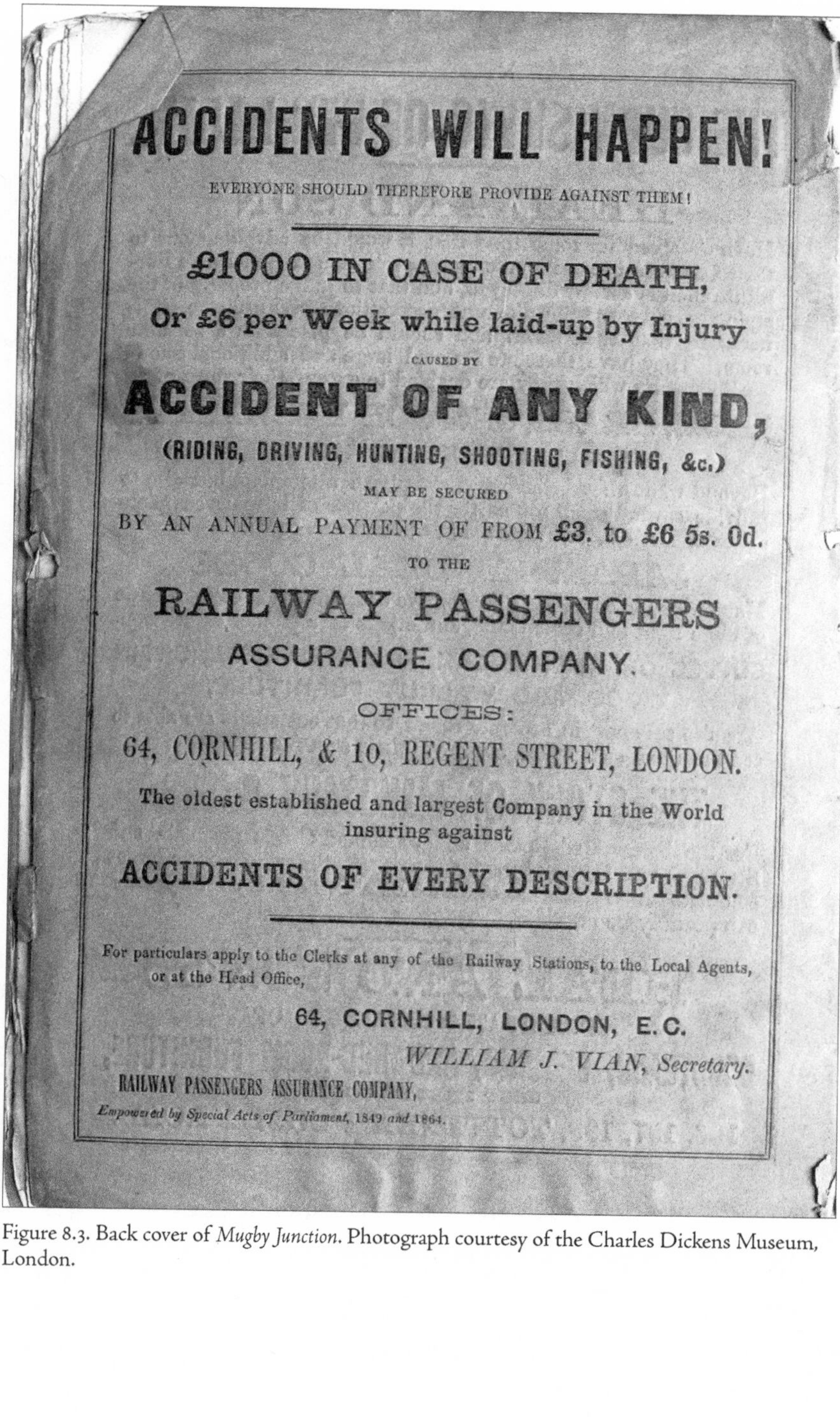

Figure 8.3. Back cover of *Mugby Junction*. Photograph courtesy of the Charles Dickens Museum, London.

the Year Round while Dickens travelled.[9] For *No Thoroughfare*, Collins and Dickens worked together in person and collaborated via letters for months, beginning in July 1867.

In response to Frederic Chapman's request for Collins to dissect the Christmas number and identify who wrote what, Collins writes, "It is impossible for me to indicate correctly my share in the Acts jointly written (I. and IV.),—we purposely wrote so as to make discoveries of this difficult, if not impossible. I inserted passages in his chapters and he inserted passages in mine. I can only tell you that we as nearly as possible *halved* the work. We put the story together in the Swiss chalet at Gad's Hill, and we finished the Fourth Act side by side at two desks in his bedroom at Gad's Hill."[10] Placing the collaborative act not merely in the chalet that Dickens's associates knew as his usual writing space but in "his bedroom," Collins's emphasis on the intimacy of the joint work calls to mind Wayne Koestenbaum's claim that "men who collaborate engage in a metaphorical sexual intercourse."[11] Rather than formulating the text as a shared woman through whom the men consummate a sublimated desire, however, Collins's description shows how the text alternately acts as each man's own body: "I inserted passages in his and he inserted passages in mine." "Passages" and "chapters" are the tools for this reciprocal insertion, which sometimes takes place "side by side" in a bedroom. In this case, the existence of Koestenbaum's "double talk" is evident. It bears repeating to say that my purpose is not to claim that Collins and Dickens engaged in sexual intercourse, nor to assign them anachronistic labels, but rather to consider "the relation between what we have tended to view as two distinct discourses: of sexuality and eroticism, and of writing and authorship."[12] In Collins's letter, separating intimacy from writing is impossible: intellectual closeness is experienced as appropriately in a study as in a bedroom, and placing written passages into the written work of another can take place in as many different styles as a physical act.

Despite Collins's description—which may be infused with nostalgia a few years after Dickens's death—some critics continue to persist in pulling apart the text of *No Thoroughfare* while insisting on a divide between the two friends.[13] Lillian Nayder, for example, is dismissive of Collins's letter, claiming that his characterization of the joint work presents "an image of equity and partnership that was rarely, if ever, achieved in his working relationship with Dickens."[14] To resist Collins's statement betrays an insistence on simplifying collaborative dynamics and ignores Collins's emphasis on the men's effort to mix their voices "purposely." Chapman's goal was to exclude sections written solely by Collins from a forthcoming edition of Dickens's collected works, which may have led Collins to react defensively, but Collins does not claim full collaboration for all of their works. His insistence on the mixture of their voices in the Christmas number is followed by an explanation in which he identifies himself as the primary writer of the stage drama, sketching out a vision of differing degrees of collaboration that he and Dickens enact. Collins's description also reminds critics to avoid overreliance on handwriting. As Holly Laird notes, "Partners in successful collaborations often describe their contributions as ultimately inseparable, merging in complex ways at every stage of composition, so that handwriting itself becomes an unreliable indicator of authorship."[15] Trading sections of text and collaborating *in praesentia*,[16] Collins and Dickens produce works in 1867 that clearly call for a conversational model of analysis.

In questioning the relationship between complexion and character, for instance, Collins and Dickens continue an exchange that has been running through their works for years. *No Thoroughfare*'s unsettling of biological determinants and questioning of the relationship between complexion, blood, and character emerges from a collaborative literary context that profoundly destabilizes the relationship of those factors to definitions of family. Arbitrary assignation of racial identifications and varied ways of understanding racial mixture continue to surface regularly in Collins's and Dickens's works, becoming particularly salient in two novels published after *No Thoroughfare*: Collins's *The Moonstone* and Dickens's *The Mystery of Edwin Drood*. My examination of the final Christmas number thus points to the broad interpretive impact of a respect for conversational collaboration.

Written with stage adaptation in mind, *No Thoroughfare* consists of an overture, four acts, and a convoluted plot. Twelve years after a woman leaves her baby at the Foundling Hospital, she returns to adopt him, having learned that he is named Walter Wilding. After her death, Wilding discovers that the Foundling Hospital recycles names and that he is not her biological son after all. Wilding is so upset by feeling that he has benefited fraudulently from his mother's love that he dies prematurely at the age of twenty-five and makes his business partner, George Vendale, promise to give his fortune to the first Walter Wilding, should he be found within two years. The rest of the story tracks Vendale through his courtship of Marguerite Obenreizer and his quest to identify a thief who recently defrauded his wine trading firm. Marguerite's swarthy uncle, Mr. Jules Obenreizer, is the thief Vendale seeks, and in a dramatic journey through Switzerland, Obenreizer repeatedly tries to murder Vendale to avoid capture. After a final attempt in which Obenreizer admits his treachery and a heavily drugged Vendale rolls himself off a cliff to protect evidence, the astoundingly strong Marguerite material-izes in the middle of a blizzard to rescue Vendale.[17] To charge Obenreizer, who has announced that Vendale is in fact the first Walter Wilding, with attempted murder and fraud would threaten George and Marguerite's mar-riage plans, so they let the criminal walk free, but justice prevails when an avalanche conveniently crushes him.

No Thoroughfare, through Walter Wilding's misplaced feelings of guilt, agrees with many of Collins's and Dickens's novels and several previous Christmas numbers in advocating for non–biological family relationships. Although Wilding's mother does not consciously adopt another woman's child, as Doctor Marigold and Mrs. Lirriper do, and although the text vali-dates the mother's desperate desire to reconnect with her biological son, the loving bond that she and Wilding enjoy connects them as tightly as shared blood. When Wilding hastens his own death and insists on trying to return his fortune, other characters' reactions make clear that his torment dishonors the genuine feelings of the mother who has raised him.

In the midst of the number's melodramatic plot, notions of complexion further enable the text to probe definitions of individual identity. Walter Wild-ing has "a remarkably pink and white complexion" even for an Englishman, while George Vendale's "brown-cheeked" face has seen more sun (4, 12). The Swiss Obenreizer has an even darker complexion, and his coloring provokes suspicion (13). To grasp how these representations operate in No Thoroughfare, we must first consider what the term *complexion* signifies and how it communi-cates meaning. Reading the *Oxford English Dictionary*, one recognizes a conver-sation already in progress between multiple definitions of the word:

complexion

1. In the physiology and natural philosophy of the Middle Ages: The com-bination of supposed qualities (*cold* or *hot* and *moist* or *dry*) in a certain proportion, determining the nature of a body, plant, etc.; the combination of the four 'humours' of the body in a certain proportion, or the bodily habit attributed to such combination; 'temperament.' *Obs. exc. His.*

2. Bodily habit or constitution (*orig.* supposed to be constituted by the 'hu-mours'). *Obs.*

3. Constitution or habit of mind, disposition, temperament; 'nature.' *Obs.* (exc. as *fig.* of 4).

4. The natural colour, texture, and appearance of the skin, *esp.* of the face; orig. as showing the 'temperament' or bodily constitution. [Now, without any such notion, the ordinary sense.]

5. *Transf.* Of other things: Colour, visible aspect, look, appearance.

6. A colouring preparation applied (by women) to 'give a complexion' to the face. *Obs.*

7. a. *fig* (from senses 1–3). Quality, character, condition; in modern use, often with some notion of 'tinge, colour, aspect' from senses 4–5.

complexionless

Devoid of complexion, i.e. of colour in the cheeks; pale, colourless.

1860 Dickens *Uncomm Trav.* xxv (D.), Four male personages. . complexionless and eyebrowless.[18]

Although the first three definitions are marked as obscure, the seventh draws upon them. The first three definitions provide a sense of complexion as the inner makeup or composition of a person, and the fourth connects that inner character with outward appearance. Definitions four through six focus on skin and external display, but the seventh must rely on the earlier sense of complexion as one's inner constitution to correlate "quality" with "tinge" or "colour." Number seven also seems to contradict the square brackets in number four, as the "modern use" of the term does not necessarily separate quality or "some notion of tinge, colour, aspect" from associations with "bodily constitution." Indeed, the relationships between discourses of quality and discourses of color remain highly problematic, particularly when it comes to formulations of race and physical bodies. Determining what these definitions fail to explain is difficult until one reads the definition for complexionless, which happens to also reference Dickens.

If one's complexion is one's natural, inner composition as manifested in the outward appearance of one's skin, then there can be no such thing as a complexionless person unless one, impossibly, has no skin. Every skin has a describable tone or appearance; therefore, one can be complexionless only if a single tone or color is identified as the base. That is how the definition for *complexionless* lays bare the presumption of whiteness that permeates the concept. If *pale* is equivalent to *colorless*, then what has come to be called white becomes the base color, which inscribes and embeds into standardized language the notion of whiteness as a neutral norm against which all other color is measured. Finally, definition seven, in its allusion to no fewer than five other usages and definitions, demonstrates that the word *complexion* has negotiated but not stabilized shifting senses of whether skin, and its color, expresses interior character.

Even this brief analysis reveals *complexion* to be a term that forces one to question concepts of appearance and identity, which are matters of great concern in *No Thoroughfare*. Obenreizer curiously exhibits features both dark and pale: "Mr. Obenreizer was a black-haired young man of a dark complexion, through whose swarthy skin no red glow ever shone" (13). To be swarthy, that is, "of a dark hue; black or blackish" (OED), infuses Obenreizer's skin with color, but the narrator also is disturbed by his lack of color: "When colour would have come into another cheek, a hardly discernible beat would come into his, as if the machinery for bringing up the ardent blood were there, but the machinery were dry" (13). This description avoids the fallacy that dark-skinned people cannot blush but runs into a different problem. In stating that the "internal machinery" that would flush Obenreizer's skin is faulty, the text strongly connects outward appearance to internal character. Obenreizer's heart both literally and figuratively functions improperly, as evidenced by his unglowing skin. That lack of flushing is the main indicator of his villainy, and his dusky, "swarthy" skin compounds the association in a basic stereotyping of dark as negative and light as positive.

The dark/light dichotomy attaches moral judgment to the marked contrast between Mr. Obenreizer's darkness and Marguerite's fairness despite the fact that they are both Swiss. In Obenreizer's case, maliciousness accompanies a foreign, un-English character, but Marguerite is more complicated. She has a "white forehead" (13), "a wonderful purity and freshness of colour in her dimpled face" (14), and a "fair brow" (22). Her appearance is so light that wearing the color black sets off the "dazzling fairness of her hair and her complexion" (22). As Vendale praises her beauty, he describes all of her features as being "rounder" than English ones (13–14). She is decidedly Swiss, fair, and pure in contrast to Obenreizer, whose Swiss identity is linked to his swarthiness. In Obenreizer's opinion, he and Marguerite are "poor peasants who have risen from ditches," and they come from "the obscurest and poorest peasantry" or "peasant stock," which Obenreizer classifies as mysterious but Marguerite insists is solidly Swiss (14–15). Beyond his own childhood mistreatment, Obenreizer's main emphasis is on the lack of purity in their heritage, which he combines with indeterminate but distinctly laboring-class elements to "darken" their origins (13). Obenreizer addresses the issue of racial purity directly: "Out of England there was no such institution as a home, no such thing as a fireside, no such object as a beautiful woman. His dear Miss Marguerite would excuse him, if he accounted for *her* attractiveness on the theory that English blood must have mixed at some former time with their obscure and unknown ancestry" (22). As the villain, Obenreizer's exaltation of English institutions is obviously feigned to keep Vendale unaware of his hatred. Vendale's account notes that Marguerite's outward appearance differs from an Englishwoman's, but to value it, Obenreizer says it must have an internal component (blood) that is English. Because his character is so discredited, a belief in English blood as the carrier of all good traits as evidenced in one's complexion becomes a notion at which this Christmas number scoffs even as its plot questions whether anyone can really be sure of an identity.

No Thoroughfare's central point is that one's identity (familial, national, and racial) depends on the declarations of other people, usually parents but sometimes nurses at foundling hospitals. The insecurity created by the unreliability of these sources is what sends Wilding to his deathbed, and the narrative continues to take up the question in a later exchange. Obenreizer remembers his mother then says, "[I]f she was my mother" (32). The "if" troubles Vendale, who reassures himself by saying, "At least you are Swiss" (33). Obenreizer replies, "How do I know? . . . I say to you, at least you are English. How do you know?" Vendale relies on "what [he has] been told from infancy" and early "recollections." Obenreizer continues to point out that this reasoning is satisfactory only because it "must" be, not because there is any reassuring logic in it (33). Obenreizer makes Vendale aware of the fact that his identity is based entirely on verbal statements, not something constitutional that can be verified in his blood. Vendale thinks he is from an aristocratic English family, an implicitly white Englishman who happened to spend his infancy in Switzerland, but Obenreizer ultimately proves that Vendale has no clue who he really is.

Regarding *No Thoroughfare* as truly collaborative requires that we view these depictions of identity and complexion as the jointly developed work of both Collins and Dickens. As Koestenbaum claims, "A double signature confers enormous interpretive freedom: it permits the reader to see the act of collaboration shadowing every word in the text."[19] In this case, the double signature moves well past allowing "interpretive freedom" when combined with archival sources that encourage one to see the type of collaborative "shadowing" Koestenbaum describes. The section in which the above descriptions of Obenreizer appear, for instance, is subtitled "New Characters on the Scene," which most scholars, even when trying to isolate a single author for each act, identify as being by both Collins and Dickens. A surviving manuscript contains some chapters of act 1 written in Dickens's hand and others written in Collins's hand,[20] but remaining mindful that one individual putting pen to paper does not nullify the fact of collaboration, the fact that Dickens wrote the manuscript pages for "New Characters on the Scene" does not mean that we should disregard Collins as an equally generative coauthor. Furthermore, on September 10, 1867, Dickens writes to Collins,

> Let us meet at the office at 1/2 past 12 on *Friday*. I don't think I shall have done Wilding's death by that time (I have been steadily at work but slowly, laying ground); but the Obenreizer-introduction-Chapter will be ready to run over. All the points you dwell upon, are already in it.
>
> It will be an immense point, if we can arrange *to start you for a long run, beginning immediately after Wilding's death,* and if I can at the same time be told off to come in, while you are at work, with the alpine ascent and adventures. *Then,* in two or three days of writing together, we could finish. I am very anxious to finish, my mind being so distracted by America, and the interval so short.
>
> . . . Have you done—or are you doing—the beginning of the chapter "Exit Wilding." I shall very soon want it.[21]

Collins's letters confirm that the plans Dickens mentions take place, and Collins tells his mother that they "created some sweet things, for the forth-coming number."[22] Even for portions Dickens initially drafts, he describes himself "laying ground," using a metaphor that makes Collins's thoughts necessary for creative completion.[23] The men coordinate who will start which section and trade chapters. Sections that one person begins need to be "run over" jointly, and "writing together" will enable them to finish. Assuring Collins "the points you dwell upon, are already in it," Dickens's approach makes clear that the unrecorded conversations of collaborators form and inform a text regardless of whose hand writes the manuscript. *No Thoroughfare,* then, may be the Christmas number that most completely synthesizes conversation, presenting a document that records creative exchange between two writers who were open to each other's ideas.

Working through *No Thoroughfare's* positions on complexion, race, and character also provides an excellent example of how attention to collaborative conversations across space, time, and genre can enhance one's understanding of their long-lasting effects. Reaching back to a co-written piece from 1857 before considering the novels that Collins and Dickens were writing in this period helps to uncover the ongoing conversation. As noted in chapter 4, *The Lazy Tour of Two Idle Apprentices* features the men poking fun at their fictionalized selves ten years prior to *No Thoroughfare.* Idle and Goodchild do their best to enjoy being unproductive while hiking, eating shrimps, and complaining. Collins and Dickens collaborated throughout the writing of *The Lazy Tour*, from the travel that inspired the piece to its publication. The first installment appeared within a fortnight of the end of the trip, which indicates that the pair were writing and editing at a brisk pace. It is difficult to know how frequently they passed drafts back and forth or cross-corrected, especially with the passages that introduce a "set piece" story. For certain sections, one can identify Collins or Dickens as the primary author, but I use that term with an insistence that the presence and input of the nonprimary author remains strong in the set pieces. For the second chapter, Dickens is the primary author of the opening portion, which leads into a set piece written primarily by Collins, and the collaborative dynamics of this portion of text demonstrate how impossible it is to extricate individualized ideas from the final products.[24]

When Goodchild accompanies Doctor Speddie to his home to retrieve a lotion for Idle's sprained ankle, Goodchild's account of the doctor's assistant, Mr. Lorn, resonates strikingly with future characters in both Collins's and Dickens's works: "What was startling in him was his remarkable paleness. His large black eyes, his sunken cheeks, his long and heavy iron-grey hair, his wasted hands, and even the attenuation of his figure, were at first forgotten in his extraordinary pallor. There was no vestige of colour in the man. When he turned his face, Francis Goodchild started as if a stone figure had looked round at him."[25] Although he is pale rather than swarthy, the intense focus on complexion links Lorn to Obenreizer, and Goodchild's discomfort with Lorn's colorlessness (his lack of whiteness prevents him from being able to reach even the base color for an acceptable complexion) prefigures Vendale's discomfort with a seeming lack of blood flowing behind Obenreizer's skin. This story's presentation of Lorn also parallels Collins's introduction of Ezra Jennings in *The Moonstone*, in which Franklin Blake says, "The door opened, and there entered to us, quietly, the most remarkable-looking man that I had ever seen.... His complexion was of a gipsy darkness; his fleshless cheeks had fallen into deep hollows, over which the bone projected like a pent-house."[26] The outsider status of both Jennings and Lorn thus depends heavily, though not solely, on complexion.

In subsequent passages, just as Blake stares at Jennings, so too Goodchild "cannot withdraw his gaze from" Lorn, and the narrative chain here requires clarifying (340). The description of Lorn appears in a portion of *The Lazy Tour* written primarily by Dickens: an opening paragraph in chapter 2. Dr. Speddie tells the story of Lorn to Goodchild, and he gives that fictional version of Dickens permission to use the story in fictional form with fake names. Collins, however, writes the rest of Lorn's story. One can imagine Collins and Dickens laughing over this convolution, winking as they combine their voices in a way that will frustrate those trying to make separations. Identifying Lorn as a decade-earlier forerunner to Jennings illustrates that collaborative conversations have lengthy imaginative afterlives and that the question of complexion is something these two writers pondered at least semiregularly.

Using attribution and influence as a guiding critical approach, one might feel the need to try to determine whether Collins took Dickens's idea for Jennings or whether the description of Lorn requires a moving back of the starting point for Collins's part of *The Lazy Tour*. Using conversation as a model, one is more able to comprehend Lorn as part of a collaborative discourse that includes the discussion of complexion in *No Thoroughfare*. The writing of *No Thoroughfare* overlapped not only with Collins preparing to step in as coeditor of *All the Year Round* while Dickens travelled but also with Collins's composition of the first sections of *The Moonstone*, which began to appear in the journal on January 4, 1868, and was advertised on the cover of *No Thoroughfare* (see figure 8.4).[27] This trio of texts—*The Moonstone*, *The Mystery of Edwin Drood*, and *No Thoroughfare*—has attracted consistent critical attention, usually with an emphasis on rivalry and influence. Discussing questions of attributions in such contexts, Harold Love offers precursory authorship as an apt model in which "a precursory author . . . makes a substantial contribution to the shape and substance of the work." Love notes that "precursory authorship may be multiple or collective," which establishes parameters flexible enough to accommodate the range of collaborative influences at play in the Victorian periodical press.[28] Regarding collaborative conversation as a component of precursory authorship, Collins revisiting the figure of Lorn in his novel does not have to be read as resistance to the previous characterization. The rekindling of an old exchange is just as likely to act as a resurrected joke or as a tribute to earlier joint work, and a conversational approach to analysis enables us to view such rethinkings most comprehensively.

Consistently, *The Moonstone* questions race and its relationship to complexion, recalling issues that Collins and Dickens jointly raise in *No Thoroughfare*. Character formation's connection to coloring is a central if comical aspect of how *The Moonstone* presents its protagonist, Franklin Blake. He comes "of good blood" with aristocratic connections but has grown up outside of

NO THOROUGHFARE

BY

CHARLES DICKENS AND WILKIE COLLINS.

BEING

THE EXTRA CHRISTMAS NUMBER

OF

ALL THE YEAR ROUND,

CONDUCTED BY

CHARLES DICKENS,

FOR CHRISTMAS, 1867.

CONTENTS:

THE OVERTURE.

ACT I.

THE CURTAIN RISES.
ENTER THE HOUSEKEEPER.
THE HOUSEKEEPER SPEAKS.
NEW CHARACTERS ON THE SCENE.
EXIT WILDING.

ACT II.

VENDALE MAKES LOVE.
VENDALE MAKES MISCHIEF.

ACT III.

IN THE VALLEY.
ON THE MOUNTAIN.

ACT IV.

THE CLOCK-LOCK.
OBENREIZER'S VICTORY.
THE CURTAIN FALLS.

LONDON: 26, WELLINGTON STREET, STRAND, W.C.;
CHAPMAN & HALL, 193, PICCADILLY, W.
AND ALL BOOKSELLERS AND NEWSMEN.

C. WHITING.]   **Price Fourpence.**   [LONDON.

ADAMS & FRANCIS, 59, Fleet Street, E.C., General Advertising Agents, and by special contract for
"ALL THE YEAR ROUND."

Figure 8.4. Cover of *No Thoroughfare*, showing Wilkie Collins as named coauthor, with an advertisement for his novel. Photograph courtesy of the Charles Dickens Museum, London.

England (68). Uncertainty about whether "foreign training" and influences have compromised the core of Blake's character manifests itself in the language of complexion: "At the age when we are all of us most apt to take our colouring, in the form of a reflection from the colouring of other people, he had been sent abroad, and had been passed on from one nation to another, before there was time for any one colouring more than another to settle itself on him firmly" (98). These comments are not strictly metaphorical, as they express concern not only about Blake's Englishness but also about his whiteness. The novel's anxiety about whether the hero of its romance plot might actually have turned less white lingers, as does confusion about the cause/effect relationship between coloring, individual constitution, and character. Perhaps ineffectively, the novel displaces that anxiety onto Godfrey Ablewhite, who dies in brown face paint. Ablewhite's natural skin tone and Englishness mask his villainy; he exists as a brown Indian sailor, a white Englishman, and a thief all at once. The three Indians are brown, reasonably try to retrieve the diamond from the Verinders, and murder someone. The novel excuses one white Englishman's taking of the Moonstone while condemning two others' taking of it. Essentialist understandings of race are further challenged in Mr. Murthwaite, a suntanned Englishman passing easily for Indian whose racial ambiguity dismantles most Victorian ideas about what race even is. Jennings, multiracial mystery solver, sends more complicated messages. His piebald black and white hair signals a lack of mixture as boldly as his skin displays hybridity, but his hair's imperviousness to mixing also makes people scream. The suspicions of Jennings based on his racial mixture turn out to be as erroneous as the trust in Ablewhite based on his supposed purity. Altogether, *The Moonstone* makes farcical the idea of complexion having an unambiguous, consistent connection to morality (or to the "character" referenced in the OED's seventh definition).

The conversation continues in *Black and White,* a play that Collins wrote with Charles Fechter in early 1869 and that appeared between *The Moonstone* and Dickens's *The Mystery of Edwin Drood.*[29] Dickens was not just aware of his friend's play as he began writing *Drood*—he read it "with great attention," predicted that it would be "A GREAT SUCCESS," and even offered suggestions.[30] Set in Trinidad in 1830, the play revolves around Miss Emily Milburn and her rival lovers. Milburn has fallen in love with Count Maurice de Leyrac on a trip to Paris, so she refuses to marry a local planter, Stephen Westcraft. When Leyrac (having been adopted by a count and countess who conceal his origins) comes to Trinidad to court Milburn, a dying "quadroon" identifies herself as his biological mother, which means that Leyrac has the

legal standing of a slave on Trinidadian soil, and the spurned Westcraft purchases him. Through this melodramatic plot, the play challenges the tenets
of race-based chattel slavery and race itself. *Black and White* is not radical in
opposing slavery by showing how people understood to be "white" may be
affected by the institution rather than focusing on the horrors experienced
by black-identified people, the vast majority of those who were brutalized.
Rather, the speed with which the central characters radically change their
impassioned feelings about race is what evidences the play's more radical
critiques. Miss Milburn rapidly shifts from being horrified by Leyrac's newly
conceived blackness to avowing love and touching him publicly, which violates a strict taboo.[31] Because someone has to see contact between black
and white skin for contamination to take place but no one can see Leyrac's
blackness, the fallacies behind the whole ideology emerge undeniably.[32] The
play, however, does not shun biological essentialism completely. When Leyrac thinks that he must leave Miss Milburn, he refers to the "slave's blood in
[his] veins—the slave's nature in [his] heart" that will enable him to submit
to the pain of leaving her.[33] The character ultimately reworks the significance
of "black blood" to empower himself. Furthermore, Collins and Fechter
characterize black Trinidadians and their speech as comically and offensively
simple, yet the leader of an opposition group, Mr. Plato, accounts for his
name by contending that white men should not get all the "good names,"
such as Milton and Shakespeare.[34] The play caricatures Plato while also acknowledging his clever critique of the linguistic ways in which white culture
(and its literary canon) continues to perpetuate its supremacy.

    Black and White engages deeply with questions about the relationship be-
tween racial heritage (or blood) and character, what it means to be European,
and how racial identity is constituted—Dickens thought it was all fabulous.
He told Wills that the play had "real merit" and that the debut went "brilliantly."[35] Less than a year later, Dickens writes *The Mystery of Edwin Drood*,
which picks up conversational threads related to race and complexion in the
characters of Helena and Neville Landless. Especially in regard to Neville, the
novel's remarks about "dark blood" in his ancestry and strength in the face of
persecution suggest that he may be moving toward a similar reworking of race
as the Leyrac character.[36] As John Sutherland observes, Dickens "influenced
the novels he published and was himself influenced by his fellow authors."[37]
Neville's outbursts certainly include the melodramatic kind of staging we see
both in Collins's *Black and White* and in *No Thoroughfare*.

    The Mystery of Edwin Drood's contributions to conversations about how
to view and understand race are quite nuanced even when causing offense.

The basic plot of the novel, left unfinished at Dickens's death, is that John Jasper, his nephew Edwin Drood, and Neville Landless all seek to marry Rosa Bud. Edwin disappears, and although Neville is apprehended for the possible murder, Jasper's suspicious behavior makes him equally likely to have killed his nephew; the novel stops in the middle of the suspense. The novel depicts Neville sympathetically when his coloring affects his treatment. An "insulting allusion to his dark skin" is what causes Neville to become violent (79). Drood says, "You may know a black common fellow, or a black common boaster, when you see him (and no doubt you have a large acquaintance that way); but you are no judge of white men" (79). It is not the class insult of Neville as "common" that sets him off but rather the racial insult. Neville's explanation for his flinging a glass at his tormentor is that Drood "had heated that tigerish blood," and Jasper asserts, "There is something of the tiger in his dark blood" (80–81). Both Neville and Jasper blame non-English stock for Neville's impulsive temperament. Still, the novel plainly contradicts Drood's point that men with lighter complexions are superior and that darker men can hold no accurate view of them when, for instance, Neville accurately assesses Edwin's lack of love for Rosa. Mr. Sapsea plunges the book deeper into an uneasy questioning of whether complexion and heritage share causal links with morality. Coming from "the purest jackass" in town, Sapsea's pronouncement that Neville's "un-English complexion" proves him to be Drood's murderer joins a long list of his ridiculous thoughts (35; 162). Neville's own opinion expresses comfort with racism that attributes violence and unpredictability to un-English "others," but Sapsea makes the idea that skin tone would reflect those propensities absurd. Each time Sapsea uses the term "un-English complexion," the novel mocks him (171–72). That method of critical characterization parallels the moments in *No Thoroughfare* when a distasteful and discredited character (Obenreizer) connects complexion to biological superiority. Even when racialized stereotypes remain in place—as Neville Landless indeed is unpredictable and prone to outbursts of anger—the novel questions their underpinning assumptions.

An increased awareness of collaborative conversations also provides some assistance in parsing one of the strangest moments in *Drood*. Referencing vicious rumors about Neville, the narrator states,

> Neville was detained, and the wildest frenzy and fatuity of
> evil report arose against him. He was of [a] vindictive and
> violent nature. . . . Before coming to England he had caused
> to be whipped to death sundry "Natives"—nomadic persons,
> encamping now in Asia, now in Africa, now in the West Indies,

and now at the North Pole—vaguely supposed in Cloisterham to be always black, always of great virtue, always calling themselves Me, and everybody else Massa or Missie (according to sex), and always reading tracts of the obscurest meaning, in broken English, but always accurately understanding them in the purest mother tongue. (183)

This passage's most direct allusion is to the controversy over Governor Eyre's brutal behavior following a rebellion against British rule in Jamaica,[38] but in the context of Dickens's ongoing textual conversation with Collins over these issues, the reference to Neville's being responsible for the whipping of black people is even more intriguing. The black people's language pointedly echoes the character of Plato in Black and White. The passage criticizes the mob mentality that condemns Neville for irrational reasons, and one such reason is the unjust whipping of black people, which makes this an extremely troubling and racist piece of text. The passage mocks the mob's persecution of a figure like Governor Eyre or Neville for murdering black people or any "Natives" whom the mob identifies as virtuous. At the same time, the passage criticizes the mob for condemning Neville on account of his dark skin. The mob is discredited, but the racism underlying their hounding of Neville based on his complexion is exactly the type of racism the passage approves of in a figure like Governor Eyre.

The way in which this reasoning stops making sense reveals the illogic into which such racial ideologies descend, and a conversational model of textual analysis enables one to find coherence without oversimplifying the evidence. There is a kind of chaos in this passage about the mob that gets tripped up in its inability to navigate race, and that chaotic thinking is similar to The Moonstone's inability to make a singular point about the correspondence of its characters' skin tones to their moral standing. Because conversation is an interaction that involves looping thoughts, questioning, revisiting, then rethinking without necessarily settling on a single conclusion, it is an ideal approach for a scenario in which exploring and exposing the contradictions embedded in notions of race and character take a text to the point of ideological absurdity. Thus, a moment like the final representation of the diamond in the shrine in The Moonstone is part of a conversation in which the three Indians who retrieve the diamond are both morally righteous and racially othered murderers. The Landless twins in Drood are sympathetic while also generating fear. And No Thoroughfare's Marguerite can be a quintessentially Swiss English heroine. Victorian texts are often cited as pinnacles of a culture that took blood-based racial purity and white superiority for granted as unassailable foundational beliefs, and there are moments in which these texts indeed showcase Victorian racism in all of its hideousness. By putting *No Thoroughfare* back into conversation with *The Moonstone, Black and White,* and *The Mystery of Edwin Drood,* we can hear and honor the contradictions and complexities that also fundamentally question race.

As we have seen, such questioning runs through the Christmas numbers consistently. Confusion about idealized Englishness and racial superiority continues to saturate the final two numbers, perhaps less explicitly than the Genius of the Nutmeg or "Christmas Day in the Bush" in the first two numbers but no less recognizably. The opening Christmas number in 1850 presents visions of Christmas, people, and places from around the world in a manner that intertwines whiteness, Englishness, and proper Christmas, but even in Oldknow's 1851 Christmas pudding vision, the troubling negotiation of such a world—where the brutality of slavery enables the consumption of sweet sugar—appears distinctly. "The Mother's Story" (1852) worries about mistreatment based on racial mixture, while the characterization of Christian George King in *The Perils of Certain English Prisoners* (1857) relies on racist stereotyping. The ballad in *A Message from the Sea* (1860) seems to valorize the cannibalization of a black man when the consequences of that same act undermine myths of racial purity. The final Christmas issue places its protagonist in another country and weaves ambiguity about purity and knowledge of one's own birth into a tenuous assertion of English superiority.

Over an eighteen-year period, these complex formulations depend on exchanges between Dickens's voice and the voices of others. Each piece resonates with one or more of the others as Dickens's (and Wills's and Collins's) "conducting" facilitates conversation within and across years. For *Mugby Junction,* the conducting metaphor persists in the page headers even though all contributor names appear on the title page (see figures 8.1–8.2). For *No Thoroughfare,* the conducting metaphor disappears as its title page lists Collins and Dickens as authors (see figure 8.4). The running titles then repeat "by Charles Dickens and Wilkie Collins" with Dickens's name appearing to the left of the issue's crease and Collins's name to the right, creating a new way of acknowledging collaboration consistently.

The final two numbers also show that up to the end, whether in public readings from "The Boy at Mugby" or in dramatical performances of *No Thoroughfare,* Dickens envisioned his collaborative writing as being flexible enough for multiple genres and performative modes. On December 26, the stage version of *No Thoroughfare* debuted at London's Adelphi Theatre. Starring Charles Fechter and Carlotta Leclercq, the well-received production ran for two hundred nights with notices congratulating both Collins and Dickens.[39] Bintrey immediately dislikes Obenreizer and calls him "tigerish," which, in light of the language to come in Dickens's *Drood*, marks a shift in emphasis in the racialization of Obenreizer's character in the stage version.[40] Discussing the play's humor, Jerome Bump recognizes that the dramatized version parodies many melodramatic conventions and that, sometimes in tribute to a genre they admire, the "self-parody and mutual parody" comes from both authors.[41]

Theatrical productions are, by definition, more collaborative in performance than written texts can be on the page, but even before a show reaches the stage, playwriting is immersed in collaborative dynamics, especially when two writers work together closely on the ideas for a script. As Will Sharpe says of collaborators in the early modern period, "In any instance, a writer could be modifying their style to accommodate the abilities or limitations of their co-author, or closely working together with them to make the play feel more of a piece, . . . [and] we need to consider that both writers may be present within a single scene, or even a single speech."[42] Dickens includes actors in the composition process when he agrees with Benjamin Webster that Obenreizer should die on stage, which leads Bump to conclude, "The Dickens-Collins play thus amply demonstrates the limitations of the dominant myth of creativity theory, namely, that real creativity is almost exclusively the product of the individual in isolation."[43] In addition to discussing the play and detailing that the number was structured as a play from the start, Collins's diary documents his sending every act, either in manuscript or in print form, to Dickens in the United States between November 3 and December 28; some chapters he sent multiple times, illustrating how much effort the men put into collaborating across great distances.[44]

The 1867 Christmas number and its coauthors were so fascinating that before reviewing the Adelphi production, *The Mask* published a parody that takes aim not only at the plot and genre of *No Thoroughfare* but also at the dynamics of collaboration.[45] Actors portraying both Collins and Dickens appear on stage, confronting their characters and ridiculing their own creative process. The levels of parody are not restricted to the 1867 Christmas number, as Sally Goldstraw uses Dickens's fictional character Mrs. Gamp (a drunken nurse from *Martin Chuzzlewit*) and her imaginary friend Mrs. Harris as employment references (16). Some moments are especially bizarre, such as Dickens's appearance at Walter Wilding's bedside to proclaim, "I am the author of your being!" before fatally impaling him with a "gigantic pen" (16–17). The parodied Dickens posits that while he is in America, Collins would be unable to "manage" Wilding because the character is "neither comic nor sentimental," a dig that exploits popular critiques of the sensation fiction for which Collins was famous (17). In a concluding "tag," the parodied Collins mounts something of a defense when he encounters his own characters at an inn and resolves the plot. Having assigned marriage partners and declared that Obenreizer shall die in an avalanche, he then comments on collaboration: "But you must admit it is a difficult business for two authors, so completely opposed in style and imagination as Dickens and myself, to write a story together. He, poor fellow, had to take my plot and galvanize my characters. However, I think we have got through it pretty well, and, if you doubt it, go and take your places at the Adelphi Theatre directly you get back" (18). Part of the humor here relies on the irony that the works of Collins and Dickens are not, in fact, "so completely opposed in style and imagination" as the parodied Collins argues. In the context of the Christmas numbers, their voices have sometimes sparred and conversed while also blending, particularly in years like 1857 and 1867 when they were the only two writers, and *The Mask* draws on that history. Highlighting the "difficult business" of collaborating and the already popular production at the Adelphi, the parody congratulates the authors on overcoming the hurdles that complicate collaborative work. Clearly, the Victorian periodical press was comfortable with the idea that collaborators would tease and accommodate each other, assuming that Collins and Dickens would laugh at such renderings of their respective and joint styles. *The Mask's* response displays an attunement to at least one type of collaborative dynamic that runs through the numbers and reminds one of how easily the seriousness of much scholarship on this topic can lose sight of the lightheartedness that often accompanies joint work.

Without complaining specifically about parodies, Dickens's public statement on the halting of the Christmas numbers paradoxically blames their popularity for their demise (see figure 8.5): "As it is better that every kind of work, honestly undertaken and discharged, should speak for itself than be spoken for, I will only remark further on one intended omission in the New Series. The Extra Christmas Number has now been so extensively, and regularly, and often imitated, that it is in very great danger of becoming tiresome. I have therefore resolved (though I cannot add, willingly) to abolish it, at the highest tide of its success."[46] In portraying him as a victim who unwillingly ceases creation of the Christmas numbers because of the plague of imitations, Dickens's statement does not exhibit sound reasoning. Imitations were hardly a new occurrence, and the quality of Dickens's collections surpassed them solidly, as indicated by high sales figures and positive reviews

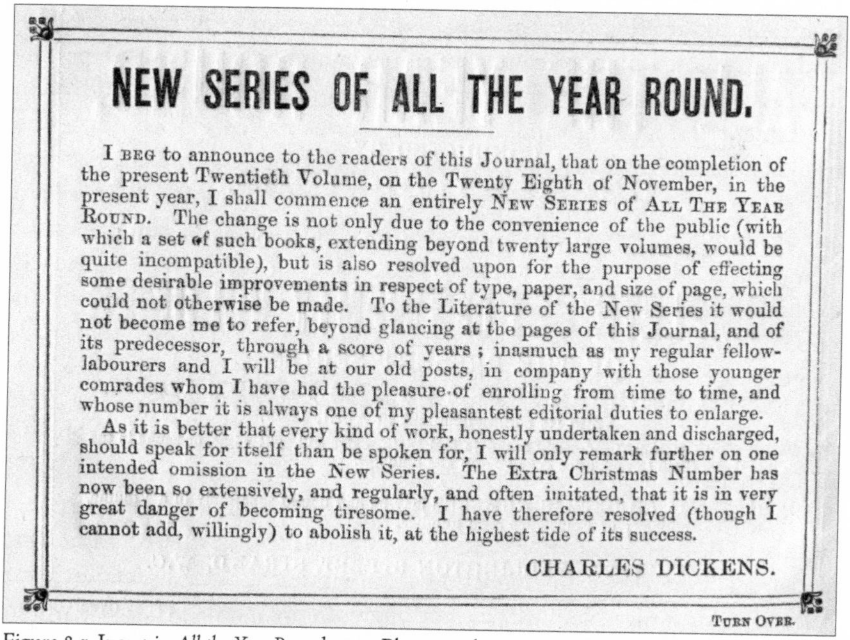

NEW SERIES OF ALL THE YEAR ROUND.

I BEG to announce to the readers of this Journal, that on the completion of the present Twentieth Volume, on the Twenty Eighth of November, in the present year, I shall commence an entirely NEW SERIES of ALL THE YEAR ROUND. The change is not only due to the convenience of the public (with which a set of such books, extending beyond twenty large volumes, would be quite incompatible), but is also resolved upon for the purpose of effecting some desirable improvements in respect of type, paper, and size of page, which could not otherwise be made. To the Literature of the New Series it would not become me to refer, beyond glancing at the pages of this Journal, and of its predecessor, through a score of years ; inasmuch as my regular fellow-labourers and I will be at our old posts, in company with those younger comrades whom I have had the pleasure of enrolling from time to time, and whose number it is always one of my pleasantest editorial duties to enlarge.

As it is better that every kind of work, honestly undertaken and discharged, should speak for itself than be spoken for, I will only remark further on one intended omission in the New Series. The Extra Christmas Number has now been so extensively, and regularly, and often imitated, that it is in very great danger of becoming tiresome. I have therefore resolved (though I cannot add, willingly) to abolish it, at the highest tide of its success.

CHARLES DICKENS.

TURN OVER.

Figure 8.5. Insert in *All the Year Round*, 1868. Photograph courtesy of the Charles Dickens Museum, London.

for at least the previous five years.[47] "To abolish" the Christmas number also implies that failing to produce a new one would somehow obliterate the previous ones, a troubling approach to their legacy. The decision to forgo their production was not one that Dickens took lightly, and his surviving correspondence identifies an entirely different cause for their disappearance: his own lack of ideas.

Dramatic as ever, Dickens writes to Wills several months before the deadline,

> I have been, and still am—which is worse—in a positive
> state of despair about the Xmas No. I cannot get an idea for
> it which is in the least satisfactory to me, and yet I have been
> steadily trying all this month. I have invented so many of these
> Christmas Nos. and they are so profoundly unsatisfactory
> after all with the introduced Stories and their want of cohesion
> or originality, that I fear I am sick of the thing. I have had
> serious thoughts of abandoning the Xmas No.! There remain
> but August and September to give to it (as I begin to read in
> October), and I CAN NOT see it.[48]

Ironically, the reading tour that began in October and shortened the time Dickens could dedicate to composing a new number would feature performances of characters from the very Christmas numbers that he belittles. In the same letter, Dickens's mood remains sour as he reports the death of a friend and criticizes *The Moonstone*'s narrative techniques, which he had previously appreciated. Less than a week later, he complains to Wills of "a hard day at the office" then writes, "I am very unwilling to abandon the Xmas No. though even in the case of my little Xmas Books (which were immensely profitable) I let the idea go, when I thought it was wearing out."[49] He rejects one "very droll" idea because it "could not in the least admit of even that shadowy approach to a congruous whole on the part of other contributors which they have ever achieved at best" and another "because the stories must come limping in after the old fashion." From Charles Collins, he hears an idea "in which there is *something* though not much"; given the high quality of Charles Collins's consistent contributions to the Christmas collections, one wonders whether Dickens's estimation of the idea might have been skewed.[50] His final decision is even closer on August 9 when he reports, "I am exactly in statu quo, as to the Xmas No. I can see nothing with my mind's eye which would do otherwise than reproduce the old string of old stories in the old inappropriate bungling way, which every other publication imitates to death."[51] To another correspondent, he claims, "My reason for abandoning the Christmas No. was, that I became weary of having my own writing swamped by that of other people."[52] The surviving letters describing the composition process for *No Thoroughfare* as well as the end product expose no such swamping, and Dickens's own works clustered at the front of *Mugby Junction* create the very type of overshadowing about which he complains.

In all of these letters, one notices a derisive attitude toward the previous collections. It is as if to justify stopping them, which pains him, Dickens must denigrate the frame stories for the previous years as "bungling." As we have seen, the stories for some years certainly do "come limping in," but even then, the intertextual dynamics and surprising collaborative energies keep most of the collections entertaining and lively. That Dickens is sometimes unaware of thematic connections, loud stylistic echoes, or narrative choices that enable the numbers to cohere does nothing to diminish those traits. Rather, over eighteen years, the Christmas collaborations exhibit the rich possibilities that emerge when one's creations must converse with those of others.

Conclusion

The influences and legacies of the collaborative Christmas numbers are sometimes as strange as the collections themselves and are not limited to Dickens's lifetime. Nor is their legacy restricted to imitation. Ten years after Dickens's death, his son Charley was continuing to publish *All the Year Round* when *The Pearl: A Journal of Facetia Voluptuous Reading* released a pornographic issue titled *The Haunted House, or the Revelations of Theresa Terence, Being the Christmas Number of The Pearl.* The text is surprising for many reasons, including its detailed depictions of women's sexual pleasure alongside problematic rape tropes, captivity plots, and direct references to Dickens. On a monthly basis, William Lazenby published 150 illustrated copies of *The Pearl,* "the most well-known periodical of Victorian pornography."[1] The premise of the 1880 issue is that Dick Fenn, mourning his aunt, has inherited a "considerable source of revenue" in the form of an estate that includes a sex palace called "the haunted house."[2] Dick Fenn sets out with two of his friends to find his beloved, Nellie, who has disappeared near a pretty inn called the "Hollytree" (8). Before departing, the men's verbal foreplay with a maid includes a test of the girl's sexual slang: "'Bravo, Val,' said Dick, 'it is like the bit in Nicholas Nickleby—W.I.N.DOW, window; go and clean it,'" which comment helps launch the group into an orgy (11). Referencing multiple Christmas collections and a novel, *The Pearl* speaks directly to an audience versed in Dickens's oeuvre. On their way to the haunted house, the men stay at the aforementioned Hollytree Inn, where they "were much amused by the comical ostler, who would certainly have made a character for Dickens," and whose appearance leads to interpolated stories (35). *The Pearl* uses the formal qualities of Dickens's Christmas numbers, recasts their characters, and even mimics their collaborative dynamics. The ostler character in Dickens's collection is actually a character crucial to Wilkie Collins's story, and the group of Dick Fenn and his friends parallels groups of Dickens's contributors.

Published twenty-six years after *The Holly-Tree Inn* and twenty-one years after *The Haunted House*, this special issue of *The Pearl* demonstrates the longevity of the Christmas numbers and their firm association with Dickens. Privately printed pornography of this nature would not have been marketed to or available to a mass audience; with a price tag as high as two guineas for an issue and twenty-five pounds for a multivolume set, such a literary indulgence would have been affordable to only the wealthiest of patrons.[3] The abundance of Dickensian allusions and jokes is likely to have reached such an audience, and the distance in time from the original publication of the referenced texts displays confidence in the enduring familiarity of multiple Christmas collections. The Christmas number form and its conventions were so strongly associated with Dickens that a pornographic riff could effectively draw upon their collaborative relationships—literary, sexual, and otherwise—for its thrill.

Reconsidering salacious aspects of Dickens's legacy or conventional adaptations of his works can be unnerving, potentially dislodging the idea of Dickens as an individual genius. Doing so can threaten one's sense of Dickens as unique, masterful, and talented in a truly unusual way. Yet understanding how Dickens's voice interacts with the voices of others can also enhance our sense of his brilliance. It may come as a surprise, for instance, to find that Dickens's prose did not dominate most of his collections (see appendix B). He wrote less than a full third of their columns, and women wrote 26.5 percent of their content: more inclusive statistics than many would expect. Although one-upsmanship (or upswomanship) occurs, competitive dynamics are no more common than helpful cowriting, ignoring of another's prose, textual teasing, or straightforward desire for an editor or coauthor to change one's words.

My hope is that *Collaborative Dickens* makes it difficult for readers to responsibly discuss the intricacies of the Christmas number stories, or theorize authorship in them, without taking collaboration into account. Important interpretations might stem from focusing exclusively on a single story from one of the numbers, but such an approach must not be premised on denial or erasure of the collaborative. Pointing to the great need for "a theory of the periodical as a genre," Margaret Beetham explains that the periodical functions as both open and closed text and, in that seeming paradox, "both offers and withholds the possibility of what we may call 'polymorphously diverse' readings."[4] The case I build in the foregoing chapters illustrates the numerous ways in which texts like the collaborative Christmas numbers Dickens compiled, which may be viewed as a periodical subgenre, can simultaneously facilitate and restrict collaborative polyvocality. In this way, a consideration of form always weaves itself into analyses of authorship and narrative conversation. Yet even striving to clarify part of a "theory of the periodical as a genre" risks regarding "the periodical" as too stable of a notion. Reflecting on such questions, Jim Mussell observes, "We want an object of study, not a kaleidoscopic range of forms. We want a single originary source, not plural accounts of writers, editors, illustrators, engravers, publishers, printers, and readers. We want a neat set of objects, accessible and delimited, not the fragmented remains of a publishing process."[5] I would add that we also want a single, clearly identified authorial voice embodied in a person, not an ambiguous identification, and not a mix of authorial voices that result in a sort of aural kaleidoscope. The Christmas numbers, however, give us precisely that type of overlapping narrative landscape and soundscape. Their variability demands a methodological flexibility that can accommodate inconsistency, ambiguity, and above all, conversation.

Both the form and the content of these annual holiday collections require one to abandon some entrenched expectations. Having viewed all eighteen numbers in their complete forms, one is able to appreciate, for instance, that linking sections are not simply functional as bridges between stories. The connective portions cannot be emotionally moving, formally effective, or humorous without interpolated talents, and that synergy is uniquely collaborative. One can imagine an editor's delight at receiving a good story to riff on in a narrative frame or the pleasure of a contributor in seeing how a submitted piece has been incorporated into a broader collection. The Christmas number canon shows these relationships to be mutually beneficial. In some numbers, linking paragraphs synthesize what others have written to move an entire collection forward. In others, framing sections rely on the middle stories for effect. Far from exhibiting Dickens as a genius who always outshines others, the complete collections reveal a blending of voices that marks the quality and talent of the contributors as much as Dickens. The intertextuality and ongoing conversations of the Christmas numbers also bring attention to myriad ways in which they rehearse, develop, or continue narrative and interpretive structures central to genres like detective and sensation fiction. Detective fiction often relies on intertextuality and collaboration as people try to solve a crime or work together to respond to a crime and tell its story. The reader assumes a collaborative role in stitching together connections between documents and narrators, and similar dynamics hold true for sensation fiction. Restoring an understanding of the collaborative to the development of those genres deepens one's comprehension of the literary landscape from which they arise. We may also add ghost stories to the generic mix, as a homesick Dickens did in 1868 when he anticipated trying to come up with ideas for another Christmas number (which he never did) and wrote to Charles Fechter from New York in the midst of a grueling reading tour: "I feel as if I had murdered a Christmas number years ago (perhaps I did!) and its ghost perpetually haunted me."[6] Fascinating as the idea of textual murder is, even more intriguing is to realize that murdering a Christmas number would involve violence toward collaborators whose contributions would also be destroyed and whose voices remained active in Dickens's authorial mind.

My view of Dickens as a collaborator—and the Dickens that emerges from the chapters above—requires serious reconceptualization of him as a solitary icon. Discussing *All the Year Round*, Hyungji Park almost proposes a collaborative blending of voices in Dickens's journalistic work but then harnesses the creative multiplicity when remarking, "Dickens's pool of writers thus became extensions of his own pen, writing for him rather than for their own fame."[7] If we put more pressure on this image, Dickens's pen also becomes his collaborators'. The dynamic moves in two directions, which profoundly destabilizes the idea of an individual "Dickens." John Sutherland includes Wilkie Collins, John Forster, and William H. Wills in his elucidation of the collaboration that took place at *All the Year Round*, noting astutely, "In many ways *All the Year Round* enjoyed the atmosphere of what we might call a writing workshop. It is wonderful to think of the ferment of ideas about fiction that were current there at this period."[8] The Christmas collections arose from that same fertile "atmosphere" that informed Victorian serial novel writing, and examining the numbers in their complete forms helps to permeate the already unstable boundaries between periodical content and novel content.[9] Given Dickens's offer to finish *No Name* for Wilkie Collins, if the collaborative voice of the Christmas numbers and plays could be channeled into the narrative voice of Collins's novel without anyone knowing and without sacrificing artistic quality, why could not that same collaborative voice inform, seep into, or directly speak in Dickens's novels?

In *Bleak House* (1852), for example, Dickens experiments with multiple narrators whose chapters do not always follow a straight chronological timeline, while the Christmas number for that year explores the idea of voices in a round. Robert Newsom points out that throughout *Bleak House* "we are both moving in circles and having them described to us."[10] To revisit a novel many regard as Dickens's masterpiece with new respect for his contemporaneous collaborative collections enables us to restore dialogue between his artistic development and the work he did with others. Or consider scholarly treatments of *Great Expectations* (1860–61), which seem unaware of the fact that the 1856 Christmas number includes Fitzgerald's story of an angry blacksmith in a love triangle. The novel's exploration of jealousy and the centrality of Orlick's hammer to the narrative's treatment of his assaults on Pip and his sister may signify differently in light of Fitzgerald's earlier story in which a blacksmith uses his giant hammer to smash his rival's head.[11] We might also reconsider the much-debated changes to the end of *Great Expectations* and what seems like Dickens's unusual willingness to do what Edward Bulwer-Lytton wanted. Perhaps knowing that Dickens gave the last word of the 1852 Christmas collection to a relatively unknown poetess or that he desperately pleaded with Elizabeth Gaskell to change the ending of "The Old Nurse's Story" then printed it as she wished (with his name on it) might lessen our surprise that someone else's idea for an ending displaced Dickens's original thought. Just as consideration of installment timing, periodical discourse, accompanying advertisements, and other important contextual matters brings new insight to our readings of Dickens's corpus, we should include the non-Dickens voices that spoke alongside, or as, his voice in our analyses.

A single metaphor or theoretical model cannot accommodate the range of collaborations one finds in periodicals or even in the eighteen Christmas numbers Dickens produced. A round, a wreck, a web, a messy matrix, a looping bundle: these unwieldy metaphors work best for certain years but will not do for all, and that conclusion is one of the most instructive we can draw. For each author and each contribution to a periodical or to a collection, we must remain willing to see how context-specific textual dynamics encapsulate a collaborative moment. With that important qualification, I remain convinced that a conversational interpretive paradigm can accommodate the most varied shapes and dynamics. The nuances of conversation—written or verbal, across years or at precise moments—help to move us toward what Holly Laird calls "a model of coauthorship as distinct from both solitary genius and an authorless textuality. In this model, a large range of different kinds of coauthorship includes, surrounds, and renders anomalous the idea of the autonomous, original author."[12] In Laird's suggestion of a conversational model that achieves these aims, the poles between "solitary genius and authorless textuality" leave a space that does not diminish or erase agency. Rather, we discover the possibility for agency to be less strictly individualistic. Harold Love posits that attribution studies "requires a model of authorship, not as a single essence or non-essence but as a repertoire of practices, techniques and functions—forms of work—whose nature has varied considerably across the centuries and which may well in any given case have been performed by separate individuals."[13] A repertoire does not stagnate, and part of its vitality includes conversations, limiting the extent to which "separate individuals" operate as discrete creative entities. Acknowledging the work involved in author functions allows us to respect the labor each contributing individual performs without limiting the scope of the effects of that labor.

Brainstorming, drafting, editing, collecting, revising, arranging, and writing afresh are all phases of the creative process that conversations shape within and across the eighteen years of Christmas numbers in *Household Words* and *All the Year Round*. Defaulting to a conversational rather than a hierarchical model will continue to stretch our notions of what is possible in Victorian storytelling and publishing while challenging our ongoing construction of Dickens's legacy. Hearing Dickens's voice, for instance, as a woman's voice demands a reconsideration of gender in the context of periodical publishing and also (particularly if one finds this exercise difficult) of the ways in which gendered binaries continue to permeate reading practices. In valuing each contribution, we are more able to account for the ways in which anonymous women's voices, even when "conducted" by powerful men like Dickens, can simultaneously question the primacy of a male voice. Marital relationships that include literary and creative interactions also need reassessment in this context. Writing the libretto for the 1836 operetta *The Village Coquettes*, Dickens used some ideas from his then-fiancée Catherine Hogarth.[14] When Charles was unable to write because of ongoing pain and the need to lie on his stomach following an anesthesia-free operation to repair an anal fistula in 1841, Catherine acted as his amanuensis.[15] Lillian Nayder identifies Catherine as Charles's first reader early in his career but limits the potential significance of that role by ruling out collaboration: "But generally Catherine was his first reader—not an author or collaborator but a proud witness and auditor whose reactions gave Dickens his first sense of a work's success. . . . These acts of reading on Catherine's part, like her writing from dictation, were forms of wifely service."[16] Catherine's contributions to Charles's career do not launch their marriage out of patriarchal constraints, but dismissing Catherine's acts as "forms of wifely service" uses too limited of a scale to measure her contributions, which deserve further consideration in a collaborative context.[17]

That Dickens himself did not promote a flexible view of his conducting and authorial activities as a highlighted part of his celebrity persona makes our task all the more difficult. Laurel Brake notes the worth and the difficulty of "seeing around, behind, beyond 'Dickens.'"[18] I propose (in a mixing of visual and aural metaphors) that a conversational model also enables us to see through "Dickens"—to nurture a through-line of sight that makes him variously translucent so that the other voices constituting "Dickens" can surface without his presence, or theirs, obliterating the other. Robert L. Patten's consideration of Dickens's early career is again helpful regarding paratextual apparatus in which Dickens tries to explain an inconsistent narrative voice in *The Old Curiosity Shop:* "The 'author' for whom Dickens speaks in the Preface is a rationalization of an outcome the actual writer, editor, and proprietor neither anticipated nor intended. This preface is one of the most blatant instances of Dickens writing himself into being as a professional, not only after the fact but also after the facts."[19] Dickens's professional identity is much more securely established by the time he launches the Christmas collections, but his desire to manage and re-narrate the unpredictable, overlapping effects of his authorial, editorial, and proprietary work persists. That Dickens did not always plan for the Christmas numbers to blend his voice with others and that the journal's conducting achieved effects he did not always control was a fluctuating process to which his responses varied. His identifications commingle, morph, and rub against each another, as in *Mugby Junction* where Dickens appears as both named conductor and named author. The process of Dickens writing himself into being while playing fast and loose with "facts" never ceases. It is incumbent upon us, then, to remain ever mindful of the ways in which we participate in the ongoing reshaping of "Dickens." Some of those reshapings may contradict one another; some may engage in shouting matches; and some may agree with aspects of Dickens's versions of himself and his relationships. That vibrancy testifies to the richness of Dickens's oeuvre, which includes the complete Christmas numbers and the voices of thirty-nine other people.

Appendix A
The Complete Christmas Numbers
Contents and Contributors

Household Words

The Christmas Number (1850)

A Christmas Tree	Charles Dickens
Christmas in Lodgings	William Blanchard Jerrold and William Henry (W. H.) Wills
Christmas in the Navy	James Hannay
A Christmas Pudding	Charles Knight
Christmas among the London Poor and Sick	Frederick Knight Hunt
Christmas in India	Joachim Heyward Siddons ("J. Stocqueler")
Christmas in the Frozen Regions	Dr. Robert McCormick and Charles Dickens
Christmas Day in the Bush	Samuel Sidney
Household Christmas Carols	Richard H. Horne

Extra Number for Christmas (1851)

What Christmas Is as We Grow Older	Charles Dickens
What Christmas Is to a Bunch of People	Richard H. Horne
An Idyll for Christmas Indoors	Edmund Ollier
What Christmas Is in Country Places	Harriet Martineau
What Christmas Is in the Company of John Doe	George Augustus Sala

The Orphan's Dream of Christmas	Eliza Griffiths
What Christmas Is after a Long Absence	Samuel Sidney
What Christmas Is if You Outgrow It	Theodore Buckley
The Round Game of the Christmas Bowl	Richard H. Horne

A Round of Stories by the Christmas Fire (1852)

The Poor Relation's Story	Charles Dickens
The Child's Story	Charles Dickens
Somebody's Story	William Moy Thomas
The Old Nurse's Story	Elizabeth Gaskell
The Host's Story	Edmund Ollier
The Grandfather's Story	Rev. James White
The Charwoman's Story	Edmund Saul Dixon
The Deaf Playmate's Story	Harriet Martineau
The Guest's Story	Samuel Sidney
The Mother's Story	Eliza Griffiths

Another Round of Stories by the Christmas Fire (1853)

The Schoolboy's Story	Charles Dickens
The Old Lady's Story	Eliza Lynn (later E. Lynn Linton)
Over the Way's Story	George Augustus Sala
The Angel's Story	Adelaide Anne Procter
The Squire's Story	Elizabeth Gaskell
Uncle George's Story	Edmund Saul Dixon and W. H. Wills
The Colonel's Story	Samuel Sidney
The Scholar's Story	Elizabeth Gaskell and William Gaskell
Nobody's Story	Charles Dickens

The Seven Poor Travellers (1854)

The First	Charles Dickens
The Second Poor Traveller	George Augustus Sala
The Third Poor Traveller	Adelaide Anne Procter
The Fourth Poor Traveller	Wilkie Collins
The Fifth Poor Traveller	George Augustus Sala
The Sixth Poor Traveller	Eliza Lynn (later E. Lynn Linton)

The Seventh Poor Traveller	Adelaide Anne Procter
The Road	Charles Dickens

The Holly-Tree Inn (1855)

The Guest	Charles Dickens
The Ostler	Wilkie Collins
The Boots	Charles Dickens
The Landlord	William Howitt
The Barmaid	Adelaide Anne Procter
The Poor Pensioner	Harriet Parr
The Bill	Charles Dickens

The Wreck of the Golden Mary (1856)

The Wreck	Charles Dickens
"The Beguilement in the Boats"	
The Armourer's Story	Percy Fitzgerald
Poor Dick's Story	Harriet Parr
The Supercargo's Story	Percy Fitzgerald
The Old Sailor's Story	Adelaide Anne Procter
The Scotch Boy's Story	Rev. James White
The Deliverance	Wilkie Collins

The Perils of Certain English Prisoners (1857)

The Island of Silver-Store	Charles Dickens
The Prison in the Woods	Wilkie Collins
The Rafts on the River	Charles Dickens

A House to Let (1858)

Over the Way	Wilkie Collins
The Manchester Marriage	Elizabeth Gaskell
Going into Society	Charles Dickens
Three Evenings in the House	Adelaide Anne Procter
Trottle's Report	Wilkie Collins
Let at Last	Wilkie Collins and Charles Dickens

All the Year Round

The Haunted House (1859)

The Mortals in the House	Charles Dickens
The Ghost in the Clock Room	Hesba Stretton
The Ghost in the Double Room	George Augustus Sala
The Ghost in the Picture Room	Adelaide Anne Procter
The Ghost in the Cupboard Room	Wilkie Collins
The Ghost in Master B.'s Room	Charles Dickens
The Ghost in the Garden Room	Elizabeth Gaskell
The Ghost in the Corner Room	Charles Dickens

A Message from the Sea (1860)

The Village (Chapter I)	Charles Dickens (with Wilkie Collins?)
The Money (Chapter II)	Charles Dickens and Wilkie Collins
Club Night (Chapter III) framing	Charles Dickens and Wilkie Collins

Included in Chapter III without titles:	
Story of Tredgear in France	Charles Allston Collins
Story of James Lawrence	Harriet Parr
Poem about cannibalism	Henry Fothergill (H. F.) Chorley
Story about Penrewen's brother	Amelia B. Edwards
The Seafaring Man (Chapter IV)	Wilkie Collins ("chiefly")
The Restitution (Chapter V)	Charles Dickens and Wilkie Collins

Tom Tiddler's Ground (1861)

Picking Up Soot and Cinders	Charles Dickens
Picking Up Evening Shadows	Charles Allston Collins
Picking Up Terrible Company	Amelia B. Edwards
Picking Up Waifs at Sea	Wilkie Collins
Picking Up a Pocket-Book	John Harwood
Picking Up Miss Kimmeens	Charles Dickens
Picking Up the Tinker	Charles Dickens

Somebody's Luggage (1862)

His Leaving It Till Called For	Charles Dickens
His Boots	Charles Dickens

His Umbrella	John Oxenford
His Black Bag	Charles Allston Collins
His Writing Desk	Charles Allston Collins
His Dressing Case	Arthur Locker
His Brown Paper Parcel	Charles Dickens
His Portmanteau	Julia Cecilia Stretton
His Hat Box	Julia Cecilia Stretton
His Wonderful End	Charles Dickens

Mrs. Lirriper's Lodgings (1863)

How Mrs. Lirriper Carried On the Business	Charles Dickens
How the First Floor Went to Crowley Castle	Elizabeth Gaskell
How the Side-Room Was Attended by a Doctor	Andrew Halliday
How the Second Floor Kept a Dog	Edmund Yates
How the Third Floor Knew the Potteries	Amelia B. Edwards
How the Best Attic Was under a Cloud	Charles Allston Collins
How the Parlours Added a Few Words	Charles Dickens

Mrs. Lirriper's Legacy (1864)

Mrs. Lirriper Relates How She Went On, and Went Over	Charles Dickens
A Past Lodger Relates a Wild Legend of a Doctor	Charles Allston Collins
Another Past Lodger Relates His Experience as a Poor Relation	Rosa Mulholland
Another Past Lodger Relates What Lot He Drew at Glumper House	Henry Spicer
Another Past Lodger Relates His Own Ghost Story	Amelia B. Edwards
Another Past Lodger Relates Certain Passages to Her Husband	Hesba Stretton
Mrs. Lirriper Relates How Jemmy Topped Up	Charles Dickens

Doctor Marigold's Prescriptions (1865)

To Be Taken Immediately	Charles Dickens
Not to Be Taken at Bedtime	Rosa Mulholland

To Be Taken at the Dinner Table	Charles Allston Collins
Not to Be Taken for Granted	Hesba Stretton
To Be Taken in Water	Walter Thornbury
To Be Taken with a Grain of Salt	Charles Dickens
To Be Taken and Tried	Mrs. Gascoyne
To Be Taken for Life	Charles Dickens

Mugby Junction (1866)

Barbox Brothers	Charles Dickens
Barbox Brothers and Co.	Charles Dickens
Main Line. The Boy at Mugby	Charles Dickens
No. 1 Branch Line. The Signal-Man	Charles Dickens
No. 2 Branch Line. The Engine-Driver	Andrew Halliday
No. 3 Branch Line. The Compensation House	Charles Allston Collins
No. 4 Branch Line. The Travelling Post-Office	Hesba Stretton
No. 5 Branch Line. The Engineer	Amelia B. Edwards

No Thoroughfare (1867)

The Overture	Charles Dickens
Act I	Charles Dickens and Wilkie Collins
Act II	Wilkie Collins
Act III	Charles Dickens
Act IV	Charles Dickens and Wilkie Collins

Appendix B
Authorship Percentage Charts

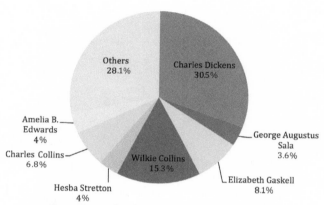

Figure B.1. Authorship in the Christmas numbers

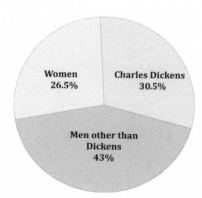

Figure B.2. Authorship by gender in the Christmas numbers

Percentages based on the number of text lines for stories in the first published edition of each collection. Thanks to Erin Mercurio and Benjamin Gardner for design assistance.

Notes

Introduction

1. John M. L. Drew, *Dickens the Journalist* (New York: Palgrave Macmillan, 2003), 147–48. See also Robert L. Patten, *Charles Dickens and His Publishers* (Oxford: Oxford University Press, 1978), 301.

2. Jerrold's remark appears uncorroborated in Frederic Beecher Perkins's *Charles Dickens: A Sketch of His Life and Works* (New York: Putnam and Sons, 1870), 88. Edgar Johnson's citation of Perkins has been regarded as authoritative in several subsequent studies; see Johnson, *Charles Dickens: His Tragedy and Triumph*, 2 vols. (New York: Simon and Schuster, 1952), 2:704.

3. Kelly J. Mays, "The Disease of Reading and Victorian Periodicals," in *Literature in the Marketplace: Nineteenth-Century British Publishing and Reading Practices*, ed. John O. Jordan and Robert L. Patten (Cambridge: Cambridge University Press, 1995), 167. Laurel Brake and Julie F. Codell also note that "a journal title promises a false unity, appearing to present, despite its many articles, topics, and illustrations, a unified policy, or set of beliefs, as if the journal itself were a single author." Brake and Codell, introduction to *Encounters in the Victorian Press: Editors, Authors, Readers*, ed. Laurel Brake and Julie F. Codell (Houndmills, UK: Palgrave Macmillan, 2005), 1.

4. Alexis Easley, *First Person Anonymous* (Aldershot, UK: Ashgate, 2004), 5. Also see Hilary Fraser, Stephanie Green, and Judith Johnston, *Gender and the Victorian Periodical* (Cambridge: Cambridge University Press, 2003); Barbara Onslow, *Women of the Press in Nineteenth-Century Britain* (Basingstoke, UK: Macmillan, 2000), 61–62; and Graham Law, *Serializing Fiction in the Victorian Press* (New York: Palgrave, 2000).

5. Joanne Shattock, "*Household Words* and the 'Community of Print' in the 1850s," in *Charles Dickens and the Mid-Victorian Press, 1850–1870*, ed. Hazel Mackenzie and Ben Winyard (Buckingham: University of Buckingham Press, 2013), 6. For a more pessimistic view that focuses on nonfiction, see Jasper Schelstraete, "'Literary Adventurers': Editorship, Non-fiction Authorship and Anonymity," in Mackenzie and Winyard, *Charles Dickens*, 147–56.

6. Johnson, *Charles Dickens*, 2:707; Ruth F. Glancy, introduction to *The Christmas Stories*, ed. Ruth F. Glancy (London: Everyman, 1996), xxiii.

7. Lillian Nayder, *Unequal Partners: Charles Dickens, Wilkie Collins, and Victorian Authorship* (Ithaca, NY: Cornell University Press, 2002), 21, 2.

8. Melissa Valiska Gregory, "Dickens's Collaborative Genres," *Dickens Studies Annual* 41 (2010): 216.

9. John M. L. Drew, introduction to Mackenzie and Winyard, *Charles Dickens*, x.

10. Catherine Waters, *Commodity Culture in Dickens's* Household Words: *The Social Life of Goods* (Aldershot, UK: Ashgate, 2008), 6–7. Revivals of interest in M. M. Bakhtin's *The Dialogic Imagination* (ed. Michael Holquist, trans. Caryl Emerson and Michael Holquist [Austin: University of Texas Press, 1981]) led to surprisingly little attention falling on more literal examples of dialogism outside the novel.

11. For more on the emergence of the editor in the nineteenth century, see Joel H. Wiener, ed., *Innovators and Preachers: The Role of the Editor in Victorian England* (Westport, CT: Greenwood, 1985), and on editing as authorship, see Jack Stillinger, *Multiple Authorship and the Myth of Solitary Genius* (Oxford: Oxford University Press, 1991), 139–62.

12. Letter dated August 26, 1855, from Dickens to Robert Lytton in *The Pilgrim Edition of the Letters of Charles Dickens*, ed. Madeline House, Graham Storey, Kathleen Tillotson, K. J. Fielding, and Angus Easson, 12 vols. (Oxford: Clarendon, 1965–2002), 7:694. Hereafter, citations of the letters of Charles Dickens (abbreviated CD) reference the correspondent and letter date followed by the *Pilgrim* volume number and page(s).

13. Deborah Thomas, *Dickens and the Short Story* (Philadelphia: University of Pennsylvania Press, 1982), 158n1.

14. Harry Stone, ed., *Charles Dickens's Uncollected Writings from* Household Words, *1850–1859*, 2 vols. (Bloomington: Indiana University Press, 1968), 2:409.

15. Stone, *Charles Dickens's Uncollected Writings*, 2:524.

16. Stone, *Charles Dickens's Uncollected Writings*, 1:ix–x. For thorough treatment of the use of stylistic evidence, see Harold Love, *Attributing Authorship: An Introduction* (Cambridge: Cambridge University Press, 2002), 98–118.

17. Fran Baker also takes issue with Stone's premise that there is value in "enshrining the 'lost' passages of Charles Dickens," although she continues to value presumed authorial intent. Of the linking passages between stories, Baker argues that Dickens "clearly saw these as ephemeral, in that they formed an inseparable part of the unique collective and collaborative nature of each Christmas number." Baker, introduction to "The Ghost in the Garden Room," by Elizabeth Gaskell, ed. Fran Baker, *Bulletin of the John Rylands University Library of Manchester* 86, no. 1 (Spring 2004): lxvii, lxviii.

18. See Dickens Journals Online, www.djo.org.uk; *The Dent Uniform Edition of Dickens' Journalism*, ed. Michael Slater and John Drew (Columbus: Ohio State University Press, 1994–2000); and "Victorian Networks and the Periodical Press," ed. Alexis Easley, special issue of *Victorian Periodicals Review* 44, no. 2 (Summer 2011): 111–213.

19. Quoted in Ruth F. Glancy, introduction to *The Christmas Stories*, ed. Ruth F. Glancy (London: Everyman, 1996), xxxviii.

20. Robert L. Patten, *Charles Dickens and "Boz": The Birth of the Industrial-Age Author* (Cambridge: Cambridge University Press, 2012), 20.

21. Harold Neville Davies, "The Tauchnitz Extra Christmas Numbers of *All the Year Round*," *Library* 33, no. 3 (September 1978): 216.

22. Stillinger, *Multiple Authorship*, 155.

23. Baker, introduction to "Ghost in the Garden Room," iii.

24. Margaret Oliphant, *Women Novelists of Queen Victoria's Reign* (1897; Folcroft, PA: Folcroft Press, 1969), 204–10.

25. Edmund Saul Dixon, *Treatise on the History and Management of Ornamental and Domestic Poultry* (London, 1848).

26. Rosemarie Bodenheimer, *Knowing Dickens* (Ithaca, NY: Cornell University Press, 2007), 16.

27. CD to Collins, October 14, 1862, *Pilgrim*, 10:142.

28. CD to Collins, October 14, 1862, *Pilgrim*, 10:142.

29. Stillinger, *Multiple Authorship*, v, 3. See Roland Barthes, "The Death of the Author," in *Image, Music, Text: Essays*, trans. Stephen Heath (London: Fontana, 1977), 142–48 and Michel Foucault, "What Is an Author?" trans. Josué Harari, in *The Critical Tradition: Classic Texts and Contemporary Trends*, ed. David H. Richter (New York: Bedford St. Martin's Press, 1989), 978–88. Harold Love points to a relevant irony in the practice of poststructuralist theory: "There was never any doubt as to where royalty cheques for Barthes, Foucault, Lacan, Kristeva and Derrida ought to be sent: they reasserted heroic authorship even in their questioning of it" (*Attributing Authorship*, 7).

30. Rachel Sagner Buurma, "Anonymity, Corporate Authority, and the Archive: The Production of Authorship in Late-Victorian England," *Victorian Studies* 50, no. 1 (2007): 29–30.

31. Bette Lynne London, *Writing Double: Women's Literary Partnerships* (Ithaca, NY: Cornell University Press, 1999); Holly Laird, *Women Coauthors* (Urbana: University of Illinois Press, 2000), 3; Jill Ehnenn, *Women's Literary Collaboration, Queerness, and Late-Victorian Culture* (Aldershot, UK: Ashgate, 2008), 9. On creative movements with a shared purpose, such as impressionism, see Michael P. Farrell, *Collaborative Circles: Friendship Dynamics and Creative Work* (Chicago: University of Chicago Press, 2001); for a recent study of creative pairs, see Joshua Wolf Shenk, *Powers of Two: How Relationships Drive Creativity* (New York: Mariner Books, 2015).

32. Laird, *Women Coauthors*, 10.

33. Wayne Koestenbaum, *Double Talk: The Erotics of Male Literary Collaboration* (New York: Routledge, 1989), 2. As Laird and others have noted, even foundational theorists of collaboration such as Koestenbaum and Stillinger remain invested in attribution and power dynamics (Laird, *Women Coauthors*, 3–4).

34. Studying biographical connections between the forty contributors to the Christmas numbers may further complicate the collaborative dynamics this book begins to explore.

35. Jeffrey Masten, *Textual Intercourse: Collaboration, Authorship, and Sexualities in Renaissance Drama* (Cambridge: Cambridge University Press, 1997). Further examples include Whitney Chadwick and Isabelle de Courtivron, *Significant Others: Creativity and Intimate Partnership* (London: Thames and Hudson, 1993); Yopie Prins, "Sappho Doubled," *Yale Journal of Criticism* 8, no. 1 (1995): 165–86.

36. Seth Whidden, introduction to *Models of Collaboration in Nineteenth-Century French Literature*, ed. Seth Whidden (Burlington, VT: Ashgate, 2009), 7.

37. Whidden, introduction, 5.

38. Laird, *Women Coauthors*, 12.

39. Laird, *Women Coauthors*, 2, 7.

40. Marjorie Stone and Judith Thompson, "Contexts and Heterotexts: A Theoretical and Historical Introduction," in *Literary Couplings: Writing Couples, Collaborators, and the Construction of Authorship*, ed. Marjorie Stone and Judith Thompson (Madison: University of Wisconsin Press, 2006), 19. This collection focuses primarily on pairs of writers whose texts and publishing histories differ significantly from Victorian Christmas numbers.

41. *Oxford English Dictionary* (1974 ed.), *s.v. converse*, definition 4.

42. For a strong argument that views Dickens's relationship with illustrator Hablot K. Browne as collaborative, see Michael Steig, *Dickens and Phiz* (Bloomington: Indiana University Press, 1978).

43. Jerome McGann, *A Critique of Modern Textual Criticism* (Chicago: University of Chicago Press, 1983), 81.

44. Mary Shannon, *Dickens, Reynolds, and Mayhew on Wellington Street: The Print Culture of a Victorian Street* (Farnham, UK: Ashgate, 2015).

45. Joanne Shattock and Michael Wolff, introduction to *The Victorian Periodical Press: Samplings and Soundings*, ed. Joanne Shattock and Michael Wolff (Leicester: Leicester University Press, 1982), xiii.

46. John Plunkett and Andrew King, *Victorian Print Media: A Reader* (Oxford: Oxford University Press, 2005), 291.

47. Drew, *Dickens the Journalist*, 156.

Chapter 1: Writing Christmas with "a Bunch of People" (1850–51)

1. Patrick Leary and Andrew Nash, "Authorship," in *The Cambridge History of the Book in Britain*, vol. 6, *1830–1914*, ed. David McKitterick (Cambridge: Cambridge University Press, 2014), 185. On corporate identity, see Mays, "Disease of Reading," 164–94; on the move toward signature in the 1860s, see Dallas Liddle, "Salesmen, Sportsmen, Mentors: Anonymity and Mid-Victorian Theories of Journalism," *Victorian Studies* 41, no. 1 (1997): 31–69.

2. See Patten, *Charles Dickens and "Boz,"* 34–35.

3. Waters, *Commodity Culture*, 107–9.

4. Lohrli, *Household Words: Table of Contents, List of Contributors, and Their Contributions* (Toronto: University of Toronto Press, 1973), 21. See also Hilary Schor, *Scheherezade in the Marketplace: Elizabeth Gaskell and the Victorian Novel* (Oxford: Oxford University Press, 1992), 89.

5. Drew, introduction to Mackenzie and Winyard, *Charles Dickens*, xvii.

6. Shu Fang Lai, "Fact or Fancy: What Can We Learn about Dickens from His Periodicals *Household Words* and *All the Year Round?*" *Victorian Periodicals Review* 34, no. 1 (2001): 41–53.

7. CD to Wills, November 5, 1852, *Pilgrim*, 6:799.

8. CD to Wills, July 12, 1850, *Pilgrim*, 6:130.

9. Wills to CD, July 12, 1850, in R. C. Lehmann, *Charles Dickens as Editor: Being Letters Written to Him by William Henry Wills, His Sub-editor* (1912; New York: Kraus, 1971), 30–32.

10. Wills to CD, July 12, 1850, in Lehmann, *Charles Dickens*, 32. For more on Wills's coeditorial role, see Drew, *Dickens the Journalist*, 120–22.

11. On literary annuals—popular Christmas gift books that remained in fashion through at least the 1850s—see Katherine D. Harris, *Forget Me Not: The Rise of the British Literary Annual, 1823–1835* (Athens: Ohio University Press, 2015). On other genres, see Tara Moore, *Victorian Christmas in Print* (New York: Palgrave Macmillan, 2009).

12. *Household Words* 1, no. 39 (December 21, 1850): 289–312, 303.

13. Christmas supplement to the December 23, 1848, issue of *Illustrated London News*.

14. Waters, *Commodity Culture*, 109.

15. John Forster, *The Life of Charles Dickens*, 2 vols. (1872–74; London: Dent/ Everyman's Library, 1966), 1:13; Michael Slater, *Charles Dickens* (New Haven, CT: Yale University Press, 2009), 11, 17.

16. The *Oxford English Dictionary* cites Dickens in its definition of *genius*: "1843 Dickens *Christmas Carol* i. 19 It seemed as if the Genius of the Weather sat in mournful meditation on the threshold."

17. Paul Young, "Economy, Empire, Extermination: The Christmas Pudding, the Crystal Palace, and the Narrative of Capitalist Progress," *Literature and History* 14 (2005): 15.

18. The Genius of the Nutmeg appears in the Banda Islands, where the Dutch ruled with slave labor and fiercely defended a monopoly over the profitable sale of nutmeg.

19. Young, "Economy, Empire, Extermination," 24.

20. For more on racialization of the Irish as savage "white apes," see Patrick Brantlinger, *Taming Cannibals: Race and the Victorians* (Ithaca, NY: Cornell University Press, 2011), 136–56; on depictions of Ireland in *Household Words*, see Sabine Clemm, *Dickens, Journalism, and Nationhood: Mapping the World in Household Words* (New York: Routledge, 2009).

21. Contact with the Franklin Expedition ceased in 1845, but Dr. John Rae's report alleging cannibalism was not published in the *Times* until October 22, 1854. Dickens published his heated response, "The Lost Arctic Voyagers," in *Household Words* on December 2 and 9, 1854.

22. Waters, *Commodity Culture*, 108.

23. Clemm, *Dickens, Journalism, and Nationhood*, 14.

24. The advertisement appears in *Household Words* on December 20, 1851.

25. Regarding Martineau's contributions to *Household Words*, Iain Crawford observes that "even with the veil of anonymous publication, she brought to the new magazine her prestige and authority as one of the leading social commentators of the day. For Martineau, meanwhile, the decision to write for Dickens gave her a lucrative opportunity to reach a large reading public on contemporary social issues and to work with an author for whom she had a great deal of admiration." Crawford, "'Hunted and Harried by Pseudo-philanthropists': Dickens, Martineau and *Household Words*,"

in Mackenzie and Winyard, *Charles Dickens*, 160. See also Drew, *Dickens the Journalist*, 123–25.

26. *Harper's New Monthly Magazine*, December 1851; *New York Times*, December 25, 1971, 17; Lohrli, *Household Words*, 423.

Chapter 2: Reading in Circles

1. Laurel Brake, *Subjugated Knowledges: Journalism, Gender, and Literature in the Nineteenth Century* (New York: New York University Press, 1994), xiv. Brake's pathbreaking work on nonfiction periodical writing, anonymity, and the gendered dynamics of the press remains pertinent in the context of fiction.

2. CD to White, October 19, 1852, *Pilgrim*, 6:780–81.

3. For volumes 8 and 9 of the 1859 Chapman and Hall Library Edition of his works, Dickens isolated "A Christmas Tree," "The Poor Relation's Story," "The Child's Story," "The Schoolboy's Story," and "Nobody's Story" from the first four Christmas numbers for publication in *The Old Curiosity Shop and Reprinted Pieces*.

4. Dickens was in the thick of writing *Bleak House* (published from March 1852 to September 1853) when he put together *A Round of Stories by the Christmas Fire* and had just concluded the novel when contemplating *Another Round*. The *Rounds'* techniques present intriguing points of comparison to shifts between first- and third-person narrators, gaps between chapters, and moments of narrative overlap in *Bleak House*. For more on circularity, see chapter 2 of Robert Newsom, *Dickens on the Romantic Side of Familiar Things: Bleak House and the Novel Tradition* (New York: Columbia University Press, 1977).

5. Elizabeth Gaskell, clearly influenced by Dickens's framing concepts, used a similar structure for a later collection of her stories, *Round the Sofa* (London: Sampson and Low, 1859). Larry K. Uffelman views Gaskell's frame, in which an ailing woman hears and tells stories from the sofa to which she is confined, as "imposing a circular, not a linear movement on the reading of her collection." Uffelman, "From Serial to 'Novel': Elizabeth Gaskell Assembles *Round the Sofa*," *Gaskell Society Journal* 15 (2001): 30.

6. See act 2, scene 7, lines 139–66 in William Shakespeare, *As You Like It*, in *The Riverside Shakespeare* (Boston: Houghton Mifflin, 1974), 381–82.

7. Dickens sensed the weakness in "Somebody's Story," writing to Wills, "I don't think there's enough in Thomas's story," yet it remains in the number ([? November 4–5, 1852, *Pilgrim*, 6:798).

8. The eighth edition of the *Norton Anthology of English Literature*, for instance, states in a footnote that the story was originally published anonymously in the 1852 Christmas number but omits the collection's title and information about possible connections between Gaskell's story and the others.

9. CD to Gaskell, April 13, 1853, *Pilgrim*, 7:62.

10. Linda K. Hughes and Michael Lund, *Victorian Publishing and Mrs. Gaskell's Work* (Charlottesville: University Press of Virginia, 1999), 98; Margaret Homans, *Bearing the Word: Language and Female Experience in Nineteenth-Century Women's Writing* (Chicago: University of Chicago Press, 1986), 229. Hughes and Lund's superb volume does not comment specifically on the editorial and authorial dynamics surrounding the pieces

Gaskell wrote for the collaborative Christmas numbers other than (uncharacteristically) misidentifying "The Poor Clare" as a Gaskell piece for the 1856 Christmas issue. "The Poor Clare" appeared in *Household Words* on December 12, 1856, but not in *The Wreck of the Golden Mary*, which includes no writing from Gaskell.

11. See Thomas Recchio, *Elizabeth Gaskell's* Cranford: *A Publishing History* (Aldershot, UK: Ashgate, 2009). On the Dickens/Gaskell relationship, see Schor, *Scheherezade in the Marketplace*.

12. CD to Gaskell, November 6, 1852, *Pilgrim*, 6:800.

13. CD to Gaskell, November 9, 1852, *Pilgrim*, 6:800–801.

14. Harry Stone, "Dickens Rediscovered: Some Lost Writings Retrieved," *Nineteenth-Century Fiction* 24, no. 4 (March 1970): 528.

15. Sending Gaskell the proofs, Dickens writes, "I shall be glad to know whether you approve of it. . . . Of course if you wish to enlarge, explain, or re-alter, you will do it" (December 1, 1852, *Pilgrim*, 6:812). On the Gaskell/Dickens editorial relationship, see Hughes and Lund, *Victorian Publishing*, esp. chap. 4.

16. Dickens replied to multiple inquiries about authorship, informing Mrs. Cowden Clarke, for instance, that Ollier wrote "The Host's Story" (December 28, 1852, *Pilgrim*, 6:839).

17. CD to Gaskell, December 4, 1852, *Pilgrim*, 6:815. "Nous verrons" translates to "we will see."

18. CD to Gaskell, December 6, 1852, *Pilgrim*, 6:817.

19. CD to Gaskell, December 17, 1852, *Pilgrim*, 6:822–23.

20. Buurma, "Anonymity, Corporate Authority," 29–30.

21. CD to White, October 19, 1852, *Pilgrim*, 6:780–81.

22. CD to White, November 22, 1852, *Pilgrim*, 6:809.

23. Dickens, while working on *The Cricket on the Hearth*, uses the phrase "*Carol* Philosophy" in an 1845 letter to Forster. The phrase appears in his aspirations for the journal he hopes to found, which he envisions as including "notices of books, notices of theatres, notices of all good things, notices of all bad ones; *Carol* philosophy, cheerful views, sharp anatomization of humbug, jolly good temper" ([early July 1845?], *Pilgrim*, 4:327-28). Dickens articulates a similar vision of Christmas in his earliest piece on the topic, "Christmas Festivities," which appears in *Bell's Life in London* on December 27, 1835, and, later, as "A Christmas Dinner" in *Sketches by Boz* (1836).

24. See Jennifer Esmail, *Reading Victorian Deafness: Signs and Sounds in Victorian Literature and Culture* (Athens: Ohio University Press, 2013); Lennard Davis, *Enforcing Normalcy: Disability, Deafness and the Body* (London: Verso, 1995); Martha Stoddard Holmes, *Fictions of Affliction: Physical Disability in Victorian Culture* (Ann Arbor: University of Michigan Press, 2004).

25. Master Humphrey describes his relationship with "the deaf gentleman," who is never otherwise named, in the April 18, 1840, issue; see Charles Dickens, *Master Humphrey's Clock and Other Stories*, ed. Peter Mudford (London: Everyman, 1997), 57–66. For more on the Martineau/Dickens relationship, including an excellent discussion of Dickens's and Wills's rejection of the contribution they solicited from Martineau for the 1854 Christmas number, see Crawford, "'Hunted and Harried.'"

26. Eliza Griffiths, whose identity remains untraced, wrote twelve verse pieces for *Household Words* between 1850 and 1853 (Lohrli, *Household Words*, 289).

27. In this period, the plantation would presumably be in the Indian Ocean on an island like Mauritius.

28. CD to Wills, [? November 4–5, 1852], *Pilgrim*, 6:798.

29. I discuss Dickens's depictions of race in more depth in chapter 4. Also see Grace Moore, *Dickens and Empire: Discourses of Class, Race and Colonialism in the Works of Charles Dickens* (Aldershot, UK: Ashgate, 2004); and Laura Peters, *Dickens and Race* (Manchester: Manchester University Press, 2013).

30. CD to Gaskell, April 13, 1853, *Pilgrim*, 7:62.

31. See Buurma, "Anonymity, Corporate Authority."

32. Eliza Lynn changed her name to Eliza Lynn Linton after her 1858 marriage.

33. For more on non–biological family formations in Victorian literature, see Holly Furneaux, *Queer Dickens* (Oxford: Oxford University Press, 2009); and Melisa Klimaszewski, "The Contested Site of Maternity in Charles Dickens's *Dombey and Son*," in *The Literary Mother: Essays on Representations of Maternity and Child Care*, ed. Susan Staub (Jefferson, NC: McFarland, 2007), 138–58.

34. Philip Collins, "Sala, George Augustus Henry," in *Oxford Reader's Companion to Dickens*, ed. Paul Schlicke (Oxford: Oxford University Press, 2000), 515. Harry Stone likewise notes that Sala was able to "brilliantly imitate—at times parody—certain of Dickens' stylistic mannerisms and literary strategies." Stone, *Charles Dickens's Uncollected Writings*, 2:409.

35. Gill Gregory makes a similar point in *The Life and Work of Adelaide Procter: Poetry, Feminism and Fathers* (Aldershot, UK: Ashgate, 1998), 205–6. In *Legends and Lyrics* and other collections, the poem has an additional final stanza suggesting that the boys are buried together: the rich boy's "tomb of marble rare" and the poor boy's unmarked "humble grave beside it." See Procter, *The Poems of Adelaide A. Procter* (New York: Lovell, 1881), 28.

36. Gregory, *Life and Work*, 206.

37. CD to Gaskell, September 19, 1853, *Pilgrim*, 7:151.

38. CD to William Allingham, September [9], 1853, *Pilgrim*, 7:140.

39. Lohrli, *Household Words*, 282–83.

40. CD to Gaskell, April 13, 1853, *Pilgrim*, 7:62.41. See Helena Michie, *Outside the Pale: Cultural Exclusion, Gender Difference, and the Victorian Woman Writer* (Ithaca, NY: Cornell University Press, 1993), 85.

42. On the history of attribution in regard to this collaborative piece, see Lohrli, *Household Words*, 282–83.

43. The verse is translated from "The Clerk of Rohan" in Théodore Hersart de La Villemarqué's 1845 edition of *Barzaz-Breiz* (*Ballads of Brittany*), which he claimed was a collection of ancient Breton folk ballads. The extent to which Villemarqué included newer material or supplemented the ancient oral tradition he purported to document remains in dispute.

44. CD to Georgina Hogarth, October 25, 1853, *Pilgrim*, 7:175–76.

45. CD to Wills, November 17, 1853, *Pilgrim*, 7:200.

46. On editing as authorship, see Stillinger, *Multiple Authorship*, 139–62. On Wills as coeditor, see Drew, *Dickens the Journalist*, 120–22.

47. CD to la Rue, December 4, 1853, *Pilgrim*, 7:221.

48. CD to la Rue, December 4, 1853, *Pilgrim*, 7:220.

49. CD to Wills, November 17, 1853, *Pilgrim*, 7:200.

50. For further consideration of Dickens's male friendships in relation to his composite journalism and a slightly different discussion of narrative hierarchies, see Gregory, "Dickens's Collaborative Genres."

51. Edwin F. Roberts, *The Christmas Guests round the Sea-Coal Fire* (London: G. Vickers, 1856); "Charles Dickens," *Bookseller*, no. 150 (July 1, 1870): 577.

52. Drew, *Dickens the Journalist*, 156. For more on publication history and circulation numbers, see Patten, *Dickens and His Publishers*, 301. On Christmas literature in other genres and Christmas books, see Moore, *Victorian Christmas in Print*.

53. CD to Collins, September 6, 1858, *Pilgrim*, 8:650.

Chapter 3: Orderly Travels and Generic Developments (1854–55)

1. At the story's beginning, the narrator is already on the road, so although he returns home to London in the number's final paragraph, the bulk of the number is more linear than circular.

2. The Poor Travellers House, now part of the larger Richard Watts Charities, remains an almshouse on its upper floors at 97 High Street in Rochester, Kent. Visitors may tour the lower rooms, many of which are architecturally unchanged since the time of Dickens's visit. For more on pilgrimage, storytelling, and "Chaucerian resonances" in Dickens, see Jeremy Tambling, "Dickens and Chaucer," *English* 64, no. 244 (2015): 53.

3. Scrooge says to the Spirit of Christmas Yet to Come, "I will honour Christmas in my heart, and try to keep it all the year." Charles Dickens, *A Christmas Carol* (Peterborough, ON: Broadview, 2003), 117.

4. Uffelman, "From Serial to 'Novel,'" 31.

5. In one of the multiple stage adaptations that were licensed for performance in London, the traveller reveals himself at the end of the performance to be Richard Doubledick. See *The Seven Poor Travellers: Drama in Three Acts, Taken from Mr. C. Dickens' Popular Tale in* Household Words, licensed for performance at the Victoria Theatre, February 5, 1855, British Library Manuscripts. This play acknowledges Dickens and *Household Words* without mentioning other contributors, but its content adheres fairly closely to the original Christmas number and includes scenes from each story.

6. On January 3, 1855, Dickens wrote that 80,000 copies of the number had been sold and attributes at least part of the number's success to "the first ten pages or so," which contain the Doubledick story (CD to W.W. F. de Cerjat, *Pilgrim* 7:495). Seven different theatrical stagings (six in London) of the Christmas number took place in 1855, and productions continued intermittently until at least 1870. See H. Philip Bolton, *Dickens Dramatized* (Boston: G. K. Hall, 1987), 375.

7. The story's emphasis on transformation is clear even in reprints. When published in the United States, Doubledick's story is titled "The Redeemed Profligate" in *Harper's*

New Monthly Magazine (vol. 10, no. 57 [February 1855]: 371–77), which includes other reprints from *The Seven Poor Travellers*.

8. Homoerotic dynamics are enhanced by the fact that Doubledick weds Mary, the lover he mistreated, while only semiconscious. Mary appears at the hospital in Brussels to help nurse Doubledick, and he does not remember marrying her when he wakes up. The rest of the story focuses on the legacy of Doubledick's relationship with Taunton, not Mary.

9. Holly Furneaux, "*Household Words* and the Crimean War: Journalism, Fiction, and Forms of Recuperation in Wartime," in Mackenzie and Winyard, *Charles Dickens*, 248.

10. Despite this thematic of reconciliation, Furneaux aptly notes, "Dickens's expansive definition of a military masculinity, which can encompass deep feeling and tenderness, works not to critique a militarised society per se, but to critique the inefficiencies of the current system" ("*Household Words*," 259).

11. The technique of using a drunken man's dream as a story reappears in *Somebody's Luggage* (1862) with Julia Cecilia Stretton's contributions. In both cases, the dream terminates when the sleeping man falls out of a chair.

12. Stone, *Charles Dickens' Uncollected Writings*, 2:409.

13. Stone and Thompson, "Contexts and Heterotexts," 19.

14. See, for instance, "The Sailor Boy" in Procter, *Poems*, 131–44.

15. CD to Procter, December 17, 1854, *Pilgrim*, 7:486–87. Dickens also explains how he learned of Procter's identity in his introduction to her poetry (*Poems of Adelaide A. Procter*, 3–12). Alexis Easley makes a similar point about Harriet Martineau, who briefly enjoyed withholding her authorial identity from her brother and consistently kept her authorship secret from male friends who admired her work. See Easley, "Authorship, Gender, and Power in Victorian Culture: Harriet Martineau and the Periodical Press," in *Nineteenth-Century Media and the Construction of Identities*, ed. Laurel Brake, Bill Bell, and David Finkelstein (New York: Palgrave, 2000), 157–58.

16. This detail partly illustrates why Gill Gregory's reading of the sailor boy as "like a stillborn child who lacks animation" (*Life and Work*, 220) is not persuasive, particularly in light of the vigor that causes the boy to wish to go to sea for years. Gregory claims that in the Christmas numbers, "Procter's poetry challenges implicitly [Dickens's] authoritative voice through her choice of themes and tropes and in her resistance to the narrative frameworks devised by Dickens" (192).

17. The boy fears the earl, and the countess tells him not to envy the son she bears with the earl, but no acrimonious encounters take place. Stage adaptations of the story add more violence to the scenario, with the earl attempting to kill his wife's first son, for instance. See *The Seven Poor Travellers; or, Life's Faults and Follies: Domestic Dramatic Sketch in Two Acts* by G. D. Pitt, licensed February 9, 1855, for performance at the Pavilion, February 10, 1855, British Library Manuscripts.

18. Stone, *Charles Dickens's Uncollected Writings*, 2:524.

19. Collins's story shares similarities with Edgar Allan Poe's "The Purloined Letter" (1845), and Poe influenced Collins as he began to write novel-length mysteries.

20. Wilkie Collins, "The Lawyer's Story of a Stolen Letter," in *After Dark*, 2 vols (London: Smith Elder, 1856), 1:87–90.

21. Attributed to Charles Dickens [Wilkie Collins], "The Lawyer's Story," *Harper's* 10, no. 57 (February 1855): 385–91. There are also similarities between characters in this story and future characters that both Collins and Dickens create in individually authored novels. Tom, the lawyer's servant and errand boy, is a talented spy who forecasts both Gooseberry in Collins's *The Moonstone* (1868; Peterborough, ON: Broadview, 1999) and Deputy in Dickens's *The Mystery of Edwin Drood* (1870; London: Penguin, 2002).

22. Gregory links these child figures, "arrested in time," to the sailor boy in Procter's verse and to the boy figures in "The Angel's Story" from the previous year's Christmas number (*Life and Work*, 218–19).

23. The rising of the mists and the traveller's intense experience of the landscape surrounding Rochester on Christmas morning clearly prefigure Dickens's *Great Expectations* (1860–61; Boston: Bedford St. Martin's, 1996). Again, Dickens's collaborative work functions as a place to begin, test, or repeat ideas that his longer fiction showcases.

24. CD to Forster, [February 1 (?), 1850], *Pilgrim*, 6:26.

25. Robert Southey, "The Holly Tree," in *The Poetical Works of Robert Southey in Ten Volumes* (Boston: Little Brown, 1863), 2:193.

26. Nicolas Bentley, Michael Slater, and Nina Burgis, *The Dickens Index* (Oxford: Oxford University Press, 1988), 122.

27. Stillinger, *Multiple Authorship*, 182.

28. Dickens, letter draft "To Prospective Contributors," [Early October 1855], *Pilgrim*, 7:713–14.

29. CD to Wills, November 24 and 25, 1855, *Pilgrim*, 7:753.

30. The dramatic final words of the story, "Who can tell!," match the concluding words of Collins's later pathbreaking detective novel, *The Moonstone*.

31. CD to Collins, October 14 [and 19], 1855, *Pilgrim*, 7:721.

32. CD to Pigott, December 12, 1855, *Pilgrim*, 7:763.

33. CD to Collins, December 12, 1855, *Pilgrim*, 7:762.

34. Patten, *Charles Dickens and "Boz,"* 94, 275.

35. When Collins later performed public readings, he lightly revised "The Ostler" and performed it as "The Dream Woman." See Catherine Peters, *The King of Inventors* (Princeton: Princeton University Press, 1991), 361.

36. Dickens performed "Boots at the Holly-Tree Inn," one of his favorite stories, eighty times during his popular public reading tours, and the story was adapted for the stage as a stand-alone piece. See Philip Collins, introduction to *Charles Dickens: The Public Readings* (Oxford, UK: Clarendon, 1975), xxvii. For more on the public readings, see Malcolm Andrews, *Charles Dickens and His Performing Selves: Dickens and the Public Readings* (Oxford: Oxford University Press, 2006).

37. Howitt's piece later appears as "The Melbourne Merchant" in his *Tallangetta, the Squatters Home: A Story of Australian Life* (London: Longman, Brown, Green, Longmans, and Roberts, 1857).

38. Procter's speaker also recalls the innocence of her child narrator in *The Seven Poor Travellers*, who has not realized that the lady he admires is his mother.

39. Dickens later republished his three stories as "Three Branches" of the tree in the Diamond Edition of his works, leaving silent space for other branches to exist and

jettisoning the notion of stories as "berries." In the reprinted collection, however, Dickens fails to revise linking passages successfully. The guest has not spent enough time at the inn for his concluding comments to make sense, and without the buildup of colonial themes in the other stories, the narrator's final comments seem sudden and irrelevant.

40. CD to Catherine Dickens, December 6, 1855, *Pilgrim,* 7:764.

Chapter 4: Collaborative Survival and Voices Abroad (1856–57)

1. For more on Dickens's development and use of the frame narrative in other works, such as *Master Humphrey's Clock,* see Ruth F. Glancy, "Dickens and Christmas: His Framed-Tale Themes," *Nineteenth-Century Fiction* 35, no. 1 (1980): 53–72.

2. CD to Collins, September 30, 1855, *Pilgrim,* 7:712.

3. See, for instance, *The Charles Dickens Edition of the Works of Charles Dickens* (London: Chapman and Hall, 1871) and *The Centenary Edition of the Works of Charles Dickens,* 36 vols. (London: Chapman and Hall, 1911). Hesperus Press restores "The Beguilement" section in its 2006 edition.

4. See "The Wreck of the *Golden Mary,*" *Examiner* (December 20, 1856): 804; and "Literature," *Leader* 402 (December 5, 1857): 1168.

5. Stone, *Charles Dickens's Uncollected Writings,* 1:563.

6. Anthea Trodd, "Collaborating in Open Boats: Dickens, Collins, Franklin, and Bligh," *Victorian Studies* 42, no. 2 (2000): 201–25; Nayder, *Unequal Partners,* 41n11, 48.

7. Thomas, *Dickens and the Short Story,* 87. Thomas views *The Wreck* stories as "self-contained" (64).

8. Trodd, "Collaborating in Open Boats," 205. For more on Dickens and cannibalism, see Harry Stone, *The Night Side of Dickens: Cannibalism, Passion, Necessity* (Columbus: Ohio State University Press, 1994), esp. 546.

9. Titles of "The Beguilement" stories do not appear in *Household Words* but were recorded in the Office Book (Lohrli, *Household Words,* 161). Percy Fitzgerald wrote several pieces for *Household Words* and published *Memories of Charles Dickens* (Bristol, UK: J. W. Arrowsmith, 1913) as a glowing remembrance of what it was like to be included in Dickens's collaborations.

10. Four years later, Dickens begins publishing *Great Expectations,* which features a lovestruck blacksmith-in-training in the figure of Pip. Orlick's jealous attacks on Pip and his sister resonate with the violence in Fitzgerald's story.

11. Stone, *Charles Dickens's Uncollected Writings,* 1:564.

12. Stone, *Charles Dickens's Uncollected Writings,* 1:564.

13. For an analysis of narrative temporality and its relationship to nation space in *The Wreck,* see Jude Piesse, "Dreaming across Oceans: Emigration and Nation in the Mid-Victorian Christmas Issue," *Victorian Periodicals Review* 46, no. 1 (Spring 2013): 37–60.

14. Dickens's comments in a letter to Wills suggest that the stories flow together smoothly, "I find the Narrative too strong (speaking as a reader of it; not as its writer) to be broken by the stories. I have therefore devised with Collins for getting the stories in between his Narrative and mine, and breaking neither. I never wrote anything more easily, or I think with greater interest and stronger belief" (November 13, 1856, *Pilgrim,* 8:222). Although Dickens speaks of each "Narrative" as belonging exclusively

to himself or to Collins, he ultimately feels that "The Beguilement" section does no "breaking."

15. For more on the sale and price negotiations, see CD to Wills, November 18, 1855, *Pilgrim*, 7:747–48. As the *Pilgrim* editors note, later accounts of the sale from Eliza Lynn's perspective (published after she added Linton to her name) vary, as described in *My Literary Life* (London: Hodder and Stoughton, 1899), 58–59 and W. R. Hughes, *A Week's Tramp in Dickens-land* (London: Chapman and Hall, 1891), 193–94.

16. For an authoritative account of the Dickens/Ternan relationship, see Claire Tomalin, *The Invisible Woman* (New York: Knopf, 1990). Michael Slater's *The Great Charles Dickens Scandal* (New Haven, CT: Yale University Press, 2012) succinctly charts public discussion of the relationship from its beginnings to the early twenty-first century and tracks the resistance of Dickens scholars to the importance of Ternan in narratives of Dickens's life.

17. The precise date of Collins's and Graves's meeting is unknown. For a time, Wilkie Collins lived in the neighborhood where she kept a shop, which suggests that they met between 1854 and 1856.

18. See Robert Louis Brannan, ed., *Under the Management of Mr. Charles Dickens: His Production of* The Frozen Deep (Ithaca, NY: Cornell University Press, 1966), 1–3.

19. CD to Collins, November 1, 1856, *Pilgrim*, 8:217–18. Clarkson Stanfield was a scenery painter for the production and the person to whom Dickens dedicated *Little Dorrit* (1857).

20. CD to Collins, October 9, 1856, *Pilgrim*, 7:203.

21. "The Lady of Glenwith Grange" appears in Collins's 1856 collection *After Dark*, and "Sister Rose" appears in four consecutive issues of *Household Words* beginning April 7, 1955. Dickens's *A Tale of Two Cities* was published in *All the Year Round* from April 30 to November 26, 1859. For more on mutual influence, see Sue Lonoff, "Charles Dickens and Wilkie Collins," *Nineteenth-Century Fiction* 35, no. 2 (1980): 150–70; and John Sutherland, *Victorian Novelists and Publishers* (Chicago: University of Chicago Press, 1976), 186.

22. CD to John Forster, July [5–6], 1857, *Pilgrim*, 8:366n1.

23. Robert L. Patten reports that in a different collaborative context more than twenty years earlier, George Cruikshank had suggested an illustrated retelling of Hogarth's *Industry and Idleness* that Dickens did not pursue (*Charles Dickens and "Boz,"* 139).

24. "The Lazy Tour of Two Idle Apprentices," *Household Words*, October 17, 1857, 367. Also see Melisa Klimaszewski, *Brief Lives: Wilkie Collins* (London: Hesperus Press, 2011), 61.

25. CD to Collins, May 11, 1857, *Pilgrim*, 8:323.

26. CD to Collins, May 22, 1857, *Pilgrim*, 8:330.

27. CD to Collins, May 22, 1857, *Pilgrim*, 8:330.

28. CD to Lady Duff Gordon, January 23, 1858, *Pilgrim*, 8:507–8.

29. Among the many scholarly treatments of literary reactions to the Indian Rebellion, see Patrick Brantlinger, *Rule of Darkness: British Literature and Imperialism, 1830–1914* (Ithaca, NY: Cornell University Press, 1988); David Finkelstein and Douglas M. Peers, *Negotiating India in Nineteenth-Century Media* (Basingstoke: Macmillan, 2000); and Grace Moore's *Dickens and Empire*.

30. CD to Coutts, October 4, 1857 *Pilgrim*, 8:459.

31. Samuel Lucas, "Charles Dickens's Christmas Story," *Times*, December 24, 1857, 4.

32. CD to Henry Morley, October 18, 1857, *Pilgrim*, 8:468–69.

33. Michael Hollington, "The Perils of Certain English Prisoners: Dickens, Collins, Morley, and Central America," *Dickensian* 101, no. 3 (Winter 2005): 198, 201.

34. Nayder, *Unequal Partners*, 117, 121.

35. Laura Peters, "'Double-Dyed Traitors and Infernal Villains': *Illustrated London News*, *Household Words*, Charles Dickens, and the Indian Rebellion," in *Negotiating India in Nineteenth-Century Media*, ed. David Finkelstein and Douglas M. Peers (New York: Macmillan, 2000), 111. Problematically, Peters uses as her source text the *Oxford Illustrated Christmas Stories* (mistitled *Christmas Books* in the essay's bibliography), which omits chapter 2 of *The Perils*.

36. Brantlinger, *Rule of Darkness*, 206. Brantlinger views the story, along with selected letters and journalism, as evidence of Dickens's view of "genocide as a solution to the Mutiny" (208). Also see William Oddie, "Dickens and the Indian Mutiny," *Dickensian* 68 (January 1972): 3–15.

37. Moore, *Dickens and Empire*, esp. chapter 6.

38. Garrett Zeigler, "The Perils of Empire: Dickens, Collins and the Indian Mutiny," in *Pirates and Mutineers in the Nineteenth Century: Swashbucklers and Swindlers*, ed. Grace Moore (Farnham, UK: Ashgate, 2011), 163.

39. Zeigler, "Perils of Empire," 162.

40. Laird, *Women Coauthors*, 87.

41. Seth Whidden, "Poetry in Collaboration in the 1870s: The Cercle Zutique, 'Le Fleuve' and 'The Raven,'" in *Models of Collaboration in Nineteenth-Century French Literature*, ed. Seth Whidden (Burlington, VT: Ashgate, 2009), 81.

42. Carton's statement is prompted by Commissioner Pordage's direction to "treat the enemy with delicacy, consideration, clemency, and forbearance" (8), which is a satiric representation of Lord Canning's policy of discriminating between sepoys involved directly in the Indian Rebellion and sepoys in other regiments, whom he exempted from violent retribution. Carton's speech nearly matches Dickens's articulation of his own feelings in the above-quoted letter to Coutts and in a letter to Emile de la Rue from October 23, 1857: "I wish I were Commander in Chief over there! I would address that Oriental character which must be powerfully spoken to, in something like the following placard, which should be vigorously translated into all native dialects, 'I, the Inimitable, holding this office of mine, and firmly believing that I Hold it by the permission of Heaven and not by the appointment of Satan, have the honor to inform you Hindoo gentry that it is my intention, with all possible avoidance of unnecessary cruelty and with all merciful swiftness of execution, to exterminate the Race from the face of the earth, which disfigured the earth with the late abominable atrocities'" (*Pilgrim*, 8:473).

43. Collins also published "Sermon for Sepoys" in *Household Words* on February 27, 1858; Collins's piece reminds readers of the long, respectable history of non-Christian religious beliefs and opposes mainstream depictions of Indians as ruthless savages. Dickens clearly did not find Collins's views too repugnant to publish.

44. Sotheby, Wilkinson and Hodge, *Catalogue of the Original Manuscripts, by Charles Dickens and Wilkie Collins, of* The Frozen Deep, *and* The Perils of Certain English Prisoners, *by Dickens and Collins . . .* (London: J. Davy, 1890).

45. Hollington, "Perils," 204.

46. Hollington, "Perils," 205.

47. Hollington, "Perils," 208.

48. My reading here is in disagreement with Deborah Thomas, who claims, "The relationship between Davis and Lady Carton seems peripheral to the actions that Davis relates, and the comparative unimportance of Davis's personality in this Christmas number as a whole indicates the result of Dickens' increased reliance on Collins' style of writing" (*Dickens and the Short Story*, 89).

49. For a different reading of this dynamic that acknowledges the importance of collaboration in *The Perils* but suggests that Marion Maryon is a parallel for Dickens and Gill Davis reflects Collins, see Laura Callanan, *Deciphering Race: White Anxiety, Racial Conflict, and the Turn to Fiction in Mid-Victorian English Prose* (Columbus: Ohio State University Press, 2006), 83.

50. Koestenbaum, *Double Talk*, 3.

51. CD to Lady Duff Gordon, January 23, 1858, *Pilgrim*, 8:507–8.

52. For more on Davis's identity as an orphan (but with consideration of only two of *The Perils'* chapters), see Laura Peters, "Perilous Adventures: Dickens and Popular Orphan Adventure Narratives," *Dickensian* 94, no. 3 (Winter 1998): 172–83.

53. Moore, *Dickens and Empire*, 129.

54. Sutherland, *Victorian Novelists and Publishers*, 186.

55. CD to Collins, October 14, 1862, *Pilgrim*, 10:142.

56. Nayder, *Unequal Partners*, 200; Poovey, *Uneven Developments: The Ideological Work of Gender in Mid-Victorian England* (Chicago: University of Chicago Press, 1988), 104, 230n19.

57. Writing to Wills on October 15, 1862, Dickens shows concern for Collins's anxiety: "He [Collins] is rather knocked up by the bye. Don't seem to know it, for he is nervous. I have told him to have no fear of failure, for if he should break down, I would go on with his story so that nobody should be any the wiser" (*Pilgrim*, 10:145–46).

Chapter 5: Moving Houses and zUnsettling Stories (1858–59)

1. William Baker, *A Wilkie Collins Chronology* (Houndmills, UK: Palgrave, 2007), 97–102. For more on the possibility that some of Collins's ill spells may have resulted from venereal disease, see Klimaszewski, *Brief Lives: Wilkie Collins*, 48, 68–69. For discussion of *The Red Vial*, see Catherine Peters, *The King of Inventors*, 183.

2. Laird, *Women Coauthors*, 7.

3. CD to Collins, September 6, 1858, *Pilgrim*, 8:650.

4. Collins and Dickens discussed the idea of the recluse in detail as they worked out the frame concept. Sophonisba may be an example of Collins taking the idea in one direction while Dickens continued to think about the recluse differently. Notably, the two Christmas numbers that work with this idea are among the worst in terms of coherence and overall story quality. In this case, an individually authored novel (*Great Expectations*) drawing upon the collaborative conversation emerges as the best outlet for the concept.

5. CD to Collins, November 9, 1858, *Pilgrim*, 8:701.

6. CD to Wills, November 20, 1858, *Pilgrim*, 8:705–6.

7. Stone, *Charles Dickens's Uncollected Writings*, 2:597.

8. Ruth Glancy, ed., *The Christmas Stories*, by Charles Dickens, 257–58.

9. Love, *Attributing Authorship*, 100.

10. See Thomas, *Dickens and the Short Story*, 89–90. Ruth Glancy contradicts herself when describing her edition: "The whole number is reprinted here, with the exception of Elizabeth Gaskell's story and Adelaide Anne Procter's poem, because the framework is clearly collaborative and does not make sense when not published in its entirety" (Glancy, ed., *The Christmas Stories*, by Charles Dickens, 257). The "whole number," of course, would have to include Gaskell's and Procter's pieces, but Glancy is correct that "Trottle's Report" is crucial to the coherence of the framing sections.

11. CD to Wills, November 25, 1858, *Pilgrim*, 8:709–10.

12. Dickens explains in an introduction first published with the *Legends and Lyrics* collection of Procter's poetry that "she was to be addressed by letter, if addressed at all, at a circulating library in the western district of London." Charles Dickens, introduction to *The Poems of Adelaide A. Procter*, 3–12 (London: Bell and Daldy, 1861).

13. Gill Gregory views this piece as a "bitter poem" that seeks to "convey despair"; Gregory claims that "Procter's narrative voice is in direct opposition to the solutions which Dickens provides for the single woman depicted in his frame narrative." Gregory, *The Life and Work of Adelaide Procter: Poetry, Feminism and Fathers* (Aldershot, UK: Ashgate, 1998), 230.

14. Exploring the topics of philosophy, ethics, and metafiction in *A House to Let*, Brian Sabey reads "the spectre of this child's presence" as "the central haunting" of a frame story not explicitly concerned with haunting. Sabey acknowledges the collection's collaborative context yet disregards the metafictional elements and ethics of the tales written by Dickens's collaborators. See Sabey, "Ethical Metafiction in Dickens's Christmas Hauntings," *Dickens Studies Annual* 46 (2015): 123–46.

15. Charles Dickens, "Personal," in *Selected Journalism, 1850–1870*, ed. David Pascoe (London: Penguin, 1997), 51–52.

16. Patrick Leary, "How the Dickens Scandal Went Viral," in Mackenzie and Winyard, *Charles Dickens*, 309. Leary's chapter also provides a helpful discussion of the differences between periodical coverage of the scandal in the United States versus Britain.

17. When Dickens split from Bradbury and Evans and replaced *Household Words* with *All the Year Round*, he became the publisher, eliminating a powerful middle figure. For more on Dickens's status and achievements as publisher, see Sutherland, *Victorian Novelists and Publishers*, 166–87. On the contractual details of *All the Year Round's* founding, see Drew, *Dickens the Journalist*, 137–39; Patten, *Charles Dickens and His Publishers*; and Johnson, *Charles Dickens*, 2:943–47.

18. CD to Arthur Smith, May 25, 1858, *Pilgrim*, 8:568.

19. *Pilgrim*, 8:740.

20. Elizabeth Gaskell to Charles Eliot Norton, March 9, 1859, in *The Letters of Mrs Gaskell*, ed. J. A. V. Chapple and Arthur Pollard, 2nd ed. (Manchester, UK: Mandolin, 1997), 535.

21. CD to Collins, September 6, 1858, *Pilgrim*, 8:650.

22. For a comprehensive overview of the Dickens/Howitt debate, including a careful chronology of their correspondence and publications on the matter, see Stone, "Unknown Dickens."

23. See *The Public Face of Wilkie Collins: The Collected Letters*, ed. William Baker, Andrew Gasson, Graham Law, and Paul Lewis, 4 vols. (London: Pickering and Chatto, 2005), 1:184–85; and CD to Howitt, December 17, 1859, *Pilgrim*, 9:178–79. Howitt and his ally, Thomas Shorter, misunderstood or misrepresented the timeline of the Cheshunt visit in relation to the composition of the Christmas number. See Shorter, "Mr Howitt and Mr Dickens," *Spiritual Magazine* 1, no. 2 (February 1860): 58–62. Shorter refers to a "set of jovial and quizzical authors and artists" who "laugh at the ghosts they professed to seek, that they might figure in a funny Christmas number" (61).

24. Dickens owned a mastiff named Turk. See Slater, *Charles Dickens*, 540; and Forster, *Life of Charles Dickens*, 2:214.

25. Gregory, *Life and Work*, 197–98.

26. Dickens, introduction to *Poems of Adelaide A. Procter*, 11.

27. Louis James, "The Trouble with Betsy: Periodicals and the Common Reader in Mid-Nineteenth-Century England," in *The Victorian Periodical Press: Samplings and Soundings*, ed. Joanne Shattock and Michael Wolff (Leicester: Leicester University Press, 1982), 351. Also see Jim Mussell, "Cohering Knowledge in the Nineteenth Century: Form, Genre and Periodical Studies," *Victorian Periodicals Review* 2, no. 1 (Spring 2009): 93–103.

28. Baker, introduction to Gaskell's "Ghost in the Garden Room," lvii.

29. For more on Procter's depiction of the fallen woman, particularly in relation to the poetry of her father, Bryan Procter, see Gregory, *Life and Work*, 169–91.

30. Retrospective narration from a noncommissioned soldier also parallels Gill Davis in *The Perils of Certain English Prisoners*.

31. Michael Slater notes that Dickens's "framing narrative and 'Master B's Room' story for *The Haunted House* anticipate these 'Uncommercial' essays [*The Uncommercial Traveller*] both in style and tone" (*Charles Dickens*, 481).

32. Wesley Stace, introducing one of the rare complete print editions of *The Haunted House*, calls this story a "bizarre and unsettling tale of a child's imagined harem." Stace, introduction to *The Haunted House*, by Charles Dickens (New York: Modern Library, 2004), xviii. Even Peter Ackroyd, nearly always reverential of Dickens, deems the story to be "all in the worst possible taste." Ackroyd, foreword to *The Haunted House*, by Charles Dickens (London: Hesperus Press, 2002), viii.

33. Deborah Thomas takes a different view of this story, overlooking the sexual oddities and viewing it as anticipatory of James Joyce's modernism and as a reflection on "the imaginative process itself" (*Dickens and the Short Story*, 79).

34. See, for instance, Buckley's "What Christmas Is if You Outgrow It" in the 1851 Christmas issue and Parr's "The Poor Pensioner" in *The Holly-Tree Inn*. This plot, especially the ruining influence of London, is reminiscent of William Wordsworth's "Michael," although Gaskell does not emphasize the pastoral.

35. Baker, introduction to "Ghost in the Garden Room," lxxxviii.

36. CD to Gaskell, December 8, 1859, *Pilgrim*, 9:176.

37. See CD to Forster, November 25, 1859, *Pilgrim*, 9:169–70. Dickens also complained dramatically to G. H. Lewes in a letter of November 20, 1859, declaring himself to be "in a state of temporary insanity (Annual) with the Xmas No." (*Pilgrim*, 9:168).

38. See James, "Trouble with Betsy," 351.

39. Ruth Glancy, ed., *The Christmas Stories*, by Charles Dickens, 815n29.

40. See Gregory, *Life and Work*, 24–25.

41. Una Pope-Hennessey, *Charles Dickens* (London: Chatto and Windus, 1968), 398.

42. See Baker, introduction to "Ghost in the Garden Room," xxi and *Letters of Mrs. Gaskell*, ed. Chapple and Pollard, 596. For Dickens's solicitation of George Eliot, to whom he refers as "Mrs Lewes" (referencing her life partner), see letter to G. H. Lewes, November 20, 1859, *Pilgrim*, 9:168.

43. J. A. V. Chapple and John Geoffrey Sharps, *Elizabeth Gaskell: A Portrait in Letters* (Manchester: Manchester University Press, 1980), 135.

44. Elizabeth Gaskell, *Right at Last and Other Tales* (London: Sampson and Low, 1860).

45. *Collection of British Authors*, vol. 609 (Leipzig: Bernhard Tauchnitz, 1862).

46. CD to Angela Burdett-Coutts, December 9, 1852, *Pilgrim*, 817. Harold Neville Davies claims persuasively, "That Tauchnitz published the attributions with Dickens's consent can hardly be doubted" ("Tauchnitz Extra Christmas Numbers," 219–20).

47. William Thackeray, "A Letter from the Editor to a Friend and Contributor," *Cornhill Magazine* (January 1860), inside front cover.

48. This rivalry surfaced, for instance, during the overlapping serialization of Dickens's *Dombey and Son* (1846–48) and Thackeray's *Vanity Fair* (1847–48).

Chapter 6: Disconnected Bodies and Troubled Textuality (1860–62)

1. "Death of His Royal Highness the Prince Consort," *The Queen* 1, no. 16 (December 21, 1861): 285.

2. "Tom Tiddler's Ground," *The Queen* 1, no. 16 (December 21, 1861): 313–14.

3. Norman Page, *A Dickens Chronology* (Boston: G. K. Hall, 1988), 107; Baker, *Wilkie Collins Chronology*, 110–11. See also CD to Georgina Hogarth, November 1, 1860, and CD to Wills, November 3, 1860, *Pilgrim*, 9:335–36.

4. CD to Georgina Hogarth, November 14, 1860, *Pilgrim*, 9:339.

5. The summary of the first act is almost four pages long and the second act almost two pages, both including a fair amount of detail and quoting dialogue. The description of the third act is only seven lines long. Charles Dickens and Wilkie Collins, *A Message from the Sea: A Drama in Three Acts by Charles Dickens and Wilkie Collins* (London: Holsworth, 1861). For more on the synopsis and the Chancery suit, see CD to Charles Reade, January 9, 1861, *Pilgrim*, 9:366–67.

6. CD to Frederic Ouvry, January 7, 1861, *Pilgrim*, 9:363.

7. Harry Stone reviews various sources that attribute portions of the text to Collins or Dickens and makes his own attributions in "Dickens Rediscovered." Jeremy Parrott of the University of Szeged, Hungary, recently discovered a complete set of *All the Year Round* volumes annotated in a hand that may be Dickens's with notes identifying authors for nearly every published piece. In that set, which may have been an office copy,

the notations for *A Message from the Sea* confirm previous attributions. Jeremy Parrott, pers. comm., February 15, 2015.

8. CD to Elisha Ely Morgan, January 3, 1861, *Pilgrim*, 9:360–61.

9. CD to Morgan, January 3, 1861.

10. The detail about bones was significant enough for Collins and Dickens to include it in their registered synopsis.

11. CD to Georgina Hogarth, November 28, 1860, *Pilgrim*, 9:343.

12. For more on Victorian depictions of madness, see Sandra Gilbert and Susan Gubar, *The Madwoman in the Attic: The Woman Writer and the Nineteenth-Century Literary Imagination* (New Haven, CT: Yale University Press, 1979); Jenny Bourne Taylor, *In the Secret Theatre of Home: Wilkie Collins, Sensation Narrative, and Nineteenth-Century Psychology* (London: Routledge, 1988); Andrew Maunder and Grace Moore, eds., *Victorian Crime, Madness and Sensation* (Aldershot, UK: Ashgate, 2016); and Rick Rylance, *Victorian Psychology and British Culture* (Oxford: Oxford University Press, 2000).

13. Mary Elizabeth Braddon, *Lady Audley's Secret* (Peterborough, ON: Broadview, 2003), 408.

14. In *The Minor Writings of Charles Dickens* (London: Elliot Stock, 1900), Frederic Kitton suggests that Robert Buchanan may have been the author of this poem (163), but he provides no reasoning for the attribution to Buchanan over Chorley. Jeremy Parrott confirms that the annotated volumes appearing to be an office copy identify Chorley as the poem's author. Parrott to Klimaszewski, pers. comm., February 15, 2015.

15. As noted in chapter 1, Rae's report alleging cannibalism was published in the *Times* on October 22, 1854; Dickens published his heated response, "The Lost Arctic Voyagers," in *Household Words* on December 2 and 9, 1854. For an extensive study of Dickens and cannibalism, see Stone, *Night Side of Dickens*.

16. For more on nineteenth-century ballads, see Meredith L. McGill, "What Is a Ballad? Reading for Genre, Format, and Medium," *Nineteenth-Century Literature* 71, no. 2 (2016): 156–75.

17. See Melisa Klimaszewski, "Examining the Wet Nurse: Breasts, Power, and Penetration in Victorian England," *Women's Studies: An Interdisciplinary Journal* 35, no. 4 (2006): 323–46; and Jennifer DeVere Brody, *Impossible Purities: Blackness, Femininity, and Victorian Culture* (Durham, NC: Duke University Press, 1998).

18. In an essay that brings important attention to collaborative dynamics between Collins and Dickens in this number yet also exemplifies the danger of ignoring other contributors, Anthea Trodd mentions the importance of a message in a bottle in the debate about whether Franklin resorted to cannibalism but says nothing about the cannibalism in Chorley's poem. See Trodd, "Messages in Bottles and Collins's Seafaring Man," *Studies in English Literature, 1500–1900* 41, no. 4 (Autumn 2001): 751–64.

19. CD to Chorley, February 3, 1860, *Pilgrim*, 9:206.

20. This story's setup shares traits with Collins's story for chapter 2 of *The Lazy Tour of Two Idle Apprentices* (1857), later republished as "Brother Morgan's Story of the Dead Hand," in which a stranger sharing an inn bedroom with what he thinks is a corpse sees the body move then discovers that the man is alive and is his brother. This is the third Christmas number story (see *The Wreck of the Golden Mary* and *A House to*

Let) featuring a shipwreck victim who is not really dead. Winona Ruth Howe notes the common return of presumed-dead shipwrecked sailors on the Victorian stage and in Tennyson's "Enoch Arden." See Howe, "Writing a Book in Company: The Collaborative Works of Charles Dickens and Wilkie Collins," PhD thesis, University of California–Riverside, 1991, 241n3.

21. Trodd, "Messages in Bottles," 753.

22. Thomas, *Dickens and the Short Story*, 90.

23. Laird, *Women Coauthors*, 44.

24. On the similarities between Mr. Mopes and Miss Havisham in *Great Expectations*, see Susan Shatto's two-part "Miss Havisham and Mr. Mopes the Hermit: Dickens and the Mentally Ill," *Dickens Quarterly* 2, nos. 2 and 3 (June and September 1985): 43–50 and 79–84.

25. The only other number to present an opening question is *Mugby Junction* (1866), which begins with, "Guard! What place is this?" (1).

26. See Richard Whitmore, *Mad Lucas: The Strange Story of Victorian England's Most Famous Hermit* (Hertfordshire, UK: North Hertfordshire District Council, 1983), 40. "Tom Tiddler" references a children's game, played in many forms, that involves one child protecting turf against the invasion of others; in one Victorian version, "youngsters would dash over a line and pick up imaginary pieces of gold and silver without being caught by Tom Tiddler, the one who was 'it'" (Whitmore, 40).

27. Bodenheimer, *Knowing Dickens*, 202.

28. Miss Kimmeens's fictional visit resonates with Mopes's preference for young girl visitors. Although Dickens is unlikely to have known about Lucas's possible pedophilic tendencies, Lucas's heartbreak was well-known, and Richard Whitmore has determined that the neighboring young woman with whom Lucas became infatuated was no more than twelve years old during the years when Lucas stalked her (*Mad Lucas*, 22).

29. For more on *Master Humphrey's Clock*, see Patten, *Charles Dickens and "Boz,"* esp. 253–59.

30. Draft of letter to Contributors to *All the Year Round*, September 18, 1862, *Pilgrim*, 10:126–27.

31. CD to Wills, September 14, 1862, *Pilgrim*, 10:125.

32. Furneaux, *Queer Dickens* (Oxford: Oxford University Press, 2009), 61.

33. The presence of a granddaughter, for instance, solidifies Mr. Dombey's transformation in *Dombey and Son*. John Bowen, pointing out similarities between Langley and Scrooge, views "His Boots" as more characteristic of *A Christmas Carol* and Dickens's 1840s books than his Christmas stories of the 1850s and early '60s. Bowen, "Bebelle and 'His Boots': Dickens, Ellen Ternan and the *Christmas Stories*," pt. 3, *The Dickensian* 96 (2000): 200. The Langley-Scrooge similarities are strong, but elements of the story outside of Langley's transformation, such as its resonance with "The First" in *The Seven Poor Travellers* noted above and the innocent child figure that recalls both "The Boots" and "The Barmaid" in *The Holly-Tree Inn*, also align it with contributions to the Christmas numbers from Dickens and others during this period.

34. See, for example, Bowen, "Bebelle and 'His Boots,'" 200. Langley's landlord, Monsieur Mutuel, nods to Ferdinand Beaucourt-Mutuel, Dickens's landlord in

Boulogne for intermittent periods between 1853 and 1856 when Dickens used false names to hide his relationship with Ternan; see Slater, *Charles Dickens*, 499.

35. John Bowen uses umbrellas as an entry point for approaching the daunting task of defining and delimiting Dickens's style, arguing that they "have a close affinity with the question of style. . . . Umbrellas in Dickens's work, then, are both an instance or set of instances of style and an analogy for it, neither a concept nor simply an occasional metaphor but a term that can be used both to illustrate and to exemplify my argument about his style and, when necessary, to waylay and distress it." Bowen, "Dickens's Umbrellas," in *Dickens's Style*, ed. Daniel Tyler (Cambridge: Cambridge University Press, 2013), 27. Bowen does not mention Oxenford's piece in *Somebody's Luggage*, missing an opportunity to comment on how Dickens's collaborative or conducting voice may factor into his distinctive style (and on how this haunted umbrella converses with other such apparatus in Dickens's oeuvre).

36. Although it is not clear whether Charles Collins knew about the secret compartment in Dickens's travel desk, Dickens and/or Collins may be indulging an inside joke here. Thanks to the generosity of Isaac Gewirtz and Lyndsi Barnes at the Berg Collection of the New York Public Library, who allowed me to view Dickens's travel desk, I can confirm that the manuscript pages of a story this length would indeed have fit into the secret compartment.

37. Stretton's story forecasts a later spoof of Scrooge that turns him from a generous man into a miser: *Blackadder's Christmas Carol*, dir. Richard Boden (BBC, 1988).

38. February 1856 is the date of Somebody's neglected bill, and the luggage is left for over six years, which confirms that Christopher publishes the collection in 1862, when Dickens and Wills are the editors of *All the Year Round*.

39. Nicolas Bentley, Michael Slater, and Nina Burgis, *The Dickens Index* (Oxford: Oxford University Press, 1988), 17.

40. CD to Collins, October 8, 1862, *Pilgrim*, 10:137.

41. CD to Collins, October 8, 1862.

42. As discussed in chapter 5, the Tauchnitz editions published in Germany identified contributors in print before British publications did. *Somebody's Luggage* appeared in volume 888 in 1867 with each contributor named and linked to his or her specific story. See Davies, "Tauchnitz Extra Christmas Numbers" (218–19), which includes a convincing case for 1867 as an accurate year of publication notwithstanding dating challenges that surround many Tauchnitz editions. Some advertisements may have listed authors even earlier; see Stone, "Dickens Rediscovered," 530n5.

Chapter 7: Bundling Children and Binding Legacies (1863–65)

1. *A House to Let* (1858) is the only previous number to have a woman character narrating the frame. As discussed in chapter 5, Dickens and Wilkie Collins conversed about the 1858 frame concept, but the Office Book identifies Collins as the primary author of that issue's opening frame story, making Mrs. Lirriper the first woman frame narrator for which Dickens can be identified confidently as the primary writer.

2. Furneaux, *Queer Dickens*, 60.

3. Furneaux, *Queer Dickens*, 63.

4. Some scholars cite Lirriper's speech pattern as an example of Dickens forecasting modernist narrative techniques. J. Isaacs identifies Mrs. Lirriper and Mrs. Nickleby as sources for James Joyce's Mrs. Bloom in *Ulysses*; see Isaacs, *An Assessment of Twentieth-Century Literature: Six Lectures Delivered in the B.B.C. Third Programme* (Port Washington, NY: Kennikat Press, 1968), 96–100. Also see Harry Stone, "Dickens and Interior Monologue," *Philological Quarterly* 38 (1959): 52–65; and Randall Quirk, "Some Observations on the Language of Dickens," *Review of English Literature* 2 (1961): 25. For a different view of Mrs. Lirriper's speech as "eccentrically structured discourse" that lacks enough interior qualities to forecast stream of consciousness, see Norman Page, *Speech in the English Novel* (Atlantic Highlands, NJ: Humanities Press International, 1988), 41–42.

5. Dickens, *Great Expectations*, 215 (chapter 27).

6. Other moments in the text clarify that Mrs. Lirriper is indeed able to read.

7. CD to Collins, January 25, 1864, *Pilgrim*, 10:346.

8. This detail in Charles Collins's story forecasts a significant description in Wilkie Collins's and Dickens's 1867 Christmas number, *No Thoroughfare*; the villain in *No Thoroughfare*, Jules Obenreizer, has filmy eyes that mask his interior thoughts.

9. In creating a home asylum, Mr. Vernon echoes Mr. Rochester in *Jane Eyre* (1848), although Stretton's story lacks evidence suggesting that Mrs. Vernon may actually be sane, whereas in *Jane Eyre*, multiple passages question Mr. Rochester's diagnosis of Bertha Mason as mad.

10. See Gayatri Chakravorty Spivak, "Three Women's Texts and a Critique of Imperialism," *Critical Inquiry* 12, no. 1 (Autumn 1985): 235–61.

11. See Philip Collins, ed., *Dickens: The Critical Heritage* (New York: Barnes Noble, 1971), 413–14.

12. Deborah Thomas, "Dickens' Mrs. Lirriper and the Evolution of a Feminine Stereotype," *Dickens Studies Annual* 6 (1977): 164, 156.

13. Isaacs, *Assessment*, 98.

14. Holly Furneaux views Collins's *Hide and Seek* (1854), which he dedicated to Dickens eleven years earlier and which Dickens admired, as "the direct inspiration for elements of *Doctor Marigold's Prescriptions*" because the plot of Collins's novel also features a deaf and mute young girl whose parents adopt her from a traveling circus (*Queer Dickens*, 60). The men appear to have conversed about this topic over several years, and Dickens may have given Collins a source text: John Kitto's *The Lost Senses* (1845). See Catherine Peters, introduction to *Hide and Seek*, by Wilkie Collins (Oxford: Oxford University Press, 1993); and Jennifer Esmail, "I Listened with My Eyes: Writing Speech and Reading Deafness in the Fiction of Charles Dickens and Wilkie Collins," *ELH* 78, no. 4 (2011): 997.

15. Martha Stoddard Holmes, "'Happy and Yet Pitying Tears': Deafness and Affective Disjuncture in Dickens's 'Doctor Marigold,'" *Victorian Review* 35, no. 2 (Fall 2009): 57.

16. Esmail, "I Listened," 998–99. Also see Christine Ferguson, "Sensational Dependence: Prosthesis and Affect in Dickens and Braddon," *Literature Interpretation Theory* 19 (2008): 1–25. For a full treatment of nineteenth-century literary depictions of deafness, see Esmail, *Reading Victorian Deafness*.

17. Holmes also astutely notes that "deafness, otherwise unneeded in the story, works as both a metaphor and realist plot trope to code, conceal, and soothe the story's more authentic zones of pathos, which are first catalyzed by a disturbed mother's chronic beating of her non-disabled daughter" ("'Happy and Yet Pitying,'" 54).

18. Melissa Valiska Gregory views this moment as an instance in which "Dickens portrays himself in the title role as a Cheap Jack hawking junk from the back of his cart" ("Dickens's Collaborative Genres," 222).

19. Jennifer Esmail rightly notes that although Dickens attempts to capture the father-daughter communication, "Sophy's thoughts and feelings are filtered through Doctor Marigold's first-person narration"—but the conversation I quote above contradicts Esmail's claim that "Marigold simply describes Sophy's body language and emotions in his own Cheap Jack patter instead of actually translating her linguistic communications" ("I Listened," 1003).

20. Martha Stoddard Holmes, "The Twin Structure: Disabled Women in Victorian Courtship Plots," in *Disability Studies: Enabling the Humanities*, ed. Sharon L. Snyder, Branda Jo Brueggemann, and Rosemarie Garland-Thomson (New York: Modern Language Association, 2002), 231. Holmes also notes that the granddaughter's speech dispels Marigold's former muteness during the years his first daughter was abused ("'Happy and Yet Pitying,'" 59).

21. See Holmes, *Fictions of Affliction*; and Davis, *Enforcing Normalcy*.

22. P. Collins, introduction to *Public Readings*, xxvii. On the public readings, also see Andrews, *Charles Dickens*.

23. *Mugby Junction* first edition with covers, National Art Library, Victoria and Albert Museum, London.

Chapter 8: Coming to a Stop (1866–67)

1. See Slater, *Charles Dickens*, 534–37.

2. Jim Mussell, "Moving Things: Circulation and Repetition in Victorian Print Culture," pt. 2, December 19, 2013, jimmussell.com/2013/12/19/moving-things -circulation-and-repetition-in-victorian-print-culture-25/.

3. Tamara S. Wagner, "Dickens's 'Gentleman for Nowhere': Reversing Technological Gothic in the Linkages of *Mugby Junction*," *Dickens Quarterly* 28, no. 1 (2011): 52. Wagner astutely analyzes Dickens's representation of the Gothic and the railway, noting that "the resulting interplay between divergence and coupling generates the narrative's shaping force" (52).

4. Anne Chapman, "'I Am Not Going On': Negotiating Christmas Publishing Rhythms with Dickens's *Mugby Junction*," *Victorian Periodicals Review* 51, no. 1 (2018): 74, 78.

5. David Ellison, "The Ghost of Injuries Present in Dickens's *The Signalman*," *Textual Practice* 26, no. 4 (2012): 659.

6. Ellison, "Ghost of Injuries Present," 662–63.

7. Patten, *Dickens and His Publishers*, 301.

8. John Forster's biography (*The Life of Charles Dickens*) is unhelpful in this regard; motivated by personal dislike, Forster excluded Collins from his account of Dickens's

life and major relationships. For more discussion of the Collins/Dickens friendship, see Peters, *King of Inventors*, 311–13.

9. Wilkie Collins to Harriet Collins, September 12 and October 26, 1867, *The Letters of Wilkie Collins*, vol. 2, *1866–1899*, ed. William Baker and William M. Clarke (Houndmills, UK: Macmillan, 1999), 293, 296–97.

10. Collins to Frederic Chapman, May 11, 1873, *Public Face of Wilkie Collins*, 2:398. The rest of this letter states, "As everything connected with *his* writing is part of the literary history of England, I may add that the Scenes and Acts of the dramatic version of this story were arranged by Dickens and Fechter, while I was engaged in completing a work of my own. The 'scenario' was then placed in my hands, and the Drama was entirely written by me."

11. Koestenbaum, *Double Talk*, 3.

12. Masten, *Textual Intercourse*, 6. Future investigations of potentially queer dynamics in this period of Collins's and Dickens's careers may build fruitfully on Eve Kosofsky Sedgwick's pathbreaking discussion of *Drood* in *Between Men: English Literature and Male Homosocial Desire* (New York: Columbia University Press, 1985).

13. Lillian Nayder's summation of manuscripts in Collins's hand, including "preliminary drafts and sketches for the Christmas Number," at the Pierpont Morgan Library, makes further determinations of primary penmanship (*Unequal Partners*, 141).

14. Nayder, *Unequal Partners*, 202.

15. Laird, *Women Coauthors*, 86.

16. Whidden, introduction, 5.

17. For a reading of Marguerite's strength as evidence of Collins's influence on Dickens, see Lonoff, "Charles Dickens and Wilkie Collins," 160.

18. All parentheses and square brackets appear in the 1974 OED. As of March 2015, the OED online edition has made no changes to this definition. In *The Fireside Dickens*, the quotation from *The Uncommercial Traveller* appears in chapter 27, "In the French-Flemish Country."

19. Koestenbaum, *Double Talk*, 2.

20. Nayder, *Unequal Partners*, 141.

21. CD to Collins, September 10, 1867, *Pilgrim*, 11:423–24.

22. Collins to Harriet Collins, September 12, 1867, *The Letters of Wilkie Collins*, 2:293.

23. In contrast, Nayder concludes that Collins and Dickens are "writing at cross-purposes" in this number and that various partnerships in the story act as fictionalized reflections of "working relationships characterized by subordination and resentment" (*Unequal Partners*, 143).

24. Collins later republished the story in the second chapter as "Brother Morgan's Story of the Dead Hand" in *Queen of Hearts* (1859).

25. [Wilkie Collins and Charles Dickens], *The Lazy Tour of Two Idle Apprentices. In Five Chapters, Household Words*, October 10, 1857, 339.

26. Collins, *Moonstone*, 390. Lorn's sad disposition and isolation in the small town as Dr. Speddie's assistant also parallel Jennings.

27. See Lonoff, "Charles Dickens and Wilkie Collins"; Michael Hollington, "'To the Droodstone'; or, From *The Moonstone* to *Edwin Drood* via *No Thoroughfare*," QWERTY 5 (1995): 141–49; and Nayder, *Unequal Partners*.

28. Love, *Attributing Authorship*, 40–42.

29. Collins and Fechter, *Black and White: A Love Story in Three Acts. As First Performed at the Adelphi Theatre, London, Under the Management of Benjamin Webster, Esq. on Monday, March 29, 1869*, DeWitt's Acting Plays no. 296 (New York: DeWitt, n.d.).

30. CD to Wilkie Collins, February [15], 1869, *Pilgrim*, 12:289.

31. *Black and White*, act 2, scene 1, page 20; act 3, scene 2, page 30; and act 3, scene 3, pages 26–27.

32. As Nayder notes, Collins's characterization of Leyrac works "to suggest that the grounds of racial difference are arbitrary and shifting" (*Unequal Partners*, 162).

33. *Black and White*, act 2, scene 1, page 20.

34. *Black and White*, act 1, scene 2, page 13.

35. CD to Wills, March 30, 1869, *Pilgrim*, 12:321.

36. Dickens, *Mystery of Edwin Drood*, 80, 64. I limit my remarks to Neville here, but Helena Landless's character also merits further analysis in the context of collaborative conversations about race and identity.

37. Sutherland, *Victorian Novelists and Publishers*, 186.

38. See Grace Moore, "Swarmery and Bloodbaths: A Reconsideration of Dickens on Class and Race in the 1860s," *Dickens Studies Annual* 31 (2002): 175–202. On the rebellion, see Callanan, *Deciphering Race*, 96–121.

39. Andrew Gasson, *Wilkie Collins: An Illustrated Guide* (Oxford: Oxford University Press, 1998), 116–17; see "The Adelphi Thoroughfare," *The Mask: A Humorous and Fantastic Review of the Month*, ed. Alfred Thompson and Leopold Lewis, vol. 1 (London: February–December 1868): 34. Notwithstanding positive reviews, Dickens did not like the London stage production, but his own attempt to stage a version in France failed. See Page, *Dickens Chronology*, 131; and Gasson, *Wilkie Collins*, 116–17.

40. Charles Dickens and Wilkie Collins, "No Thoroughfare: A Drama in Five Acts (Altered from the Christmas Story for Performance on the Stage)" (London: Office of *All the Year Round*, 1867), act 2, scene 1, page 20.

41. Jerome Bump, "Parody and the Dickens-Collins Collaboration in *No Thoroughfare*," *Library Chronicle of the University of Texas at Austin* (1986): 46.

42. Will Sharpe, "Authorship and Attribution," in *William Shakespeare and Others: Collaborative Plays*, ed. Jonathan Bate and Eric Rasmussen, with Jan Sewell and Will Sharpe (Houndmills, UK: Palgrave, 2013), 648.

43. Bump, "Parody," 40, 43.

44. Collins, Diary, 1867 (New York Public Library). Because of the conception process described above and the frequent communication between Collins and Dickens, I regard the stage adaptation as a continuation of their collaboration even though Collins was the one who composed the script once Dickens went to the United States. For a different view, see Nayder, *Unequal Partners*, 140n32.

45. "No Thoroughfare," *The Mask: A Humorous and Fantastic Review of the Month*, ed. Alfred Thompson and Leopold Lewis, vol. 1 (London: March 1868): 14.

46. Yellow slip bound with *No Thoroughfare* first edition (Dickens House Museum, London).

47. John Drew presents the following figures: "References in Christmas-time letters of the 1860s rejoice in steadily-growing UK sales reports of 191 000 (*Somebody's Luggage*), 220 000 (*Mrs Lirriper's Lodgings*), 250 000 (*Dr Marigold's Prescriptions*), 265 000

(*Mugby Junction*), and ultimately reaching, Forster records, 'before he died, to nearly three hundred thousand' (*No Thoroughfare*)" (*Dickens the Journalist*, 148). Also see Ella Ann Oppenlander, *Dickens' All the Year Round: Descriptive Index and Contributor List* (New York: Whitston Publishing, 1984), 49.

48. CD to Wills, July 26, 1868, *Pilgrim*, 12:159.

49. CD to Wills, July 31, 1868, *Pilgrim*, 12:161–62.

50. CD to Wills, July 31, 1868, *Pilgrim*, 12:162.

51. CD to Wills, August 9, 1868, *Pilgrim*, 12:167.

52. CD to Mr and Mrs J. T. Fields, October 30, 1868, *Pilgrim*, 12:212.

Conclusion

1. Laurel Brake and Marysa Demoor, eds., *A Dictionary of Nineteenth Century Journalism* (Ghent: Academia Press; London: British Library, 2009), 484.

2. *The Haunted House, or the Revelations of Theresa Terence. Being the Christmas Number of The Pearl* (London: Privately printed [William Lazenby], 1880), 4.

3. Brake and Demoor, *Nineteenth Century Journalism*, 484.

4. Margaret Beetham, "Towards a Theory of the Periodical as a Publishing Genre," in *Investigating Victorian Journalism*, ed. Laurel Brake, Aled Jones, and Lionel Madden (New York: St. Martin's Press, 1990), 30.

5. Jim Mussell, "Repetition; or, 'In Our Last,'" *Victorian Periodicals Review* 48, no. 3 (Fall 2015): 344.

6. CD to Fechter, March 8, 1868, *Pilgrim*, 12:67.

7. Hyungji Park, "'The Story of Our Lives': *The Moonstone* and the Indian Mutiny in *All the Year Round*," in *Negotiating India in Nineteenth-Century Media*, ed. David Finkelstein and Douglas M. Peers (New York: Macmillan, 2000), 103.

8. Sutherland, *Victorian Novelists and Publishers*, 186.

9. Although this project's scope precludes placing all eighteen Christmas numbers in conversation with the nonfiction these authors wrote (sometimes collaboratively) for Dickens's journals and others, I hope *Collaborative Dickens* helps to facilitate such inquiry.

10. Newsom, *Dickens*, 26.

11. Deborah Thomas, although maintaining that Dickens's contributions can be separated from those of his collaborators, views the Christmas frame stories as testing grounds that "perhaps helped to prepare for Dickens's sophisticated handling of the technique of first-person narrative in *Great Expectations*" (*Dickens and the Short Story*, 82).

12. Laird, *Women Coauthors*, 12.

13. Love, *Attributing Authorship*, 33.

14. CD to Catherine Hogarth, January 21, 1836, *Pilgrim*, 1:119. Also see Slater, *Charles Dickens*, 62.

15. See, among other letters documenting the surgery, Dickens to Thomas Beard, October 12, 1841, and to Macvey Napier, October 21, 1841, *Pilgrim*, 2:401, 405–6.

16. Lillian Nayder, *The Other Dickens* (Ithaca, NY: Cornell University Press, 2011), 67.

17. The prospect of collaboration also strengthens the possibility that the spouses' nicknames for each other—"Bully" for Charles and "Meek" for Catherine—were ironic in nature; see Dickens to David C. Colden, July 31, 1842, *Pilgrim*, 3:291.

18. Laurel Brake, "Second Life: *All the Year Round* and the New Generation of British Periodicals in the 1860s," in Mackenzie and Winyard, *Charles Dickens*, 11.

19. Patten, *Charles Dickens and "Boz,"* 275. For more on prefaces, see chapters 9–10 of Gerard Genette, *Paratexts: Thresholds of Interpretation* (Cambridge: Cambridge University Press, 1997).

Bibliography

The Christmas Numbers

Another Round of Stories by the Christmas Fire. Being the Extra Christmas Number of *Household Words*. Conducted by Charles Dickens. London: Bradbury and Evans, 1853.

The Christmas Number. Household Words. Conducted by Charles Dickens. London: Bradbury and Evans, 1850.

Doctor Marigold's Prescriptions. The Extra Christmas Number of *All the Year Round*. Conducted by Charles Dickens. London: 1865.

Extra Number for Christmas. Household Words. Conducted by Charles Dickens. London: Bradbury and Evans, 1851.

The Haunted House. The Extra Christmas Number of *All the Year Round*. Conducted by Charles Dickens. London: 1859.

The Holly-Tree Inn. Being the Extra Christmas Number of *Household Words*. Conducted by Charles Dickens. London: Bradbury and Evans, 1855.

A House to Let. Being the Extra Christmas Number of *Household Words*. Conducted by Charles Dickens. London: Bradbury and Evans, 1858.

A Message from the Sea. The Extra Christmas Number of *All the Year Round*. Conducted by Charles Dickens. London: 1860.

Mrs. Lirriper's Legacy. The Extra Christmas Number of *All the Year Round*. Conducted by Charles Dickens. London: 1864.

Mrs. Lirriper's Lodgings. The Extra Christmas Number of *All the Year Round*. Conducted by Charles Dickens. London: 1863.

Mugby Junction. The Extra Christmas Number of *All the Year Round*. Conducted by Charles Dickens. London: 1866.

No Thoroughfare. Being the Extra Christmas Number of *All the Year Round*. By Charles Dickens and Wilkie Collins. London: 1867.

The Perils of Certain English Prisoners, and Their Treasure in Women, Children, Silver, and Jewels. The Extra Christmas Number of *Household Words*. Conducted by Charles Dickens. London: Bradbury and Evans, 1857.

A Round of Stories by the Christmas Fire. Being the Extra Christmas Number of *Household Words.* Conducted by Charles Dickens. London: Bradbury and Evans, 1852.

The Seven Poor Travellers. Being the Extra Christmas Number of *Household Words.* Conducted by Charles Dickens. London: Bradbury and Evans, 1854.

Somebody's Luggage. The Extra Christmas Number of *All the Year Round.* Conducted by Charles Dickens. London: 1862.

Tom Tiddler's Ground. The Extra Christmas Number of *All the Year Round.* Conducted by Charles Dickens. London: 1861.

The Wreck of the Golden Mary. The Extra Christmas Number of *Household Words.* Conducted by Charles Dickens. London: Bradbury and Evans, 1856.

Primary Sources

"The Adelphi Thoroughfare." *The Mask: A Humorous and Fantastic Review of the Month* 1 (March 1868): 33–34. Edited by Alfred Thompson and Leopold Lewis. London.

Blackadder's Christmas Carol. Dir. Richard Boden. BBC, 1988.

Braddon, Mary Elizabeth. *Lady Audley's Secret.* Peterborough, ON: Broadview, 2003.

"Charles Dickens." *The Bookseller* 150 (July 1, 1870): 573–78. London.

"Christmas with John Doe." *New York Times,* December 25, 1971, 17.

Collection of British Authors. Vols. 609 and 894. Leipzig: Bernhard Tauchnitz, 1862 and 1867. Available in Forster Collection, National Art Library, Victoria and Albert Museum, London.

Collins, Wilkie. *After Dark.* 2 vols. London: Smith Elder, 1856.

———. Diary, 1867. Holograph. [Kept on the blank leaves of John Goldsmith's *An Almanack for the Year of Our Lord 1867.*] Available in Charles Dickens Collection of Papers, Berg Collection, New York Public Library.

———. *The Letters of Wilkie Collins.* Vol. 2, *1866–1889.* Edited by William Baker and William M. Clarke. Houndmills, UK: Macmillan, 1999.

———. *The Moonstone.* Peterborough, ON: Broadview, 1999.

———. *The Public Face of Wilkie Collins: The Collected Letters.* Vols. 1–4. Edited by William Baker, Andrew Gasson, Graham Law, and Paul Lewis. London: Pickering and Chatto, 2005.

———. *Queen of Hearts.* London: Hurst and Blackett, 1859.

[Collins, Wilkie, and Charles Dickens.] *The Lazy Tour of Two Idle Apprentices: In Five Chapters. Household Words,* October 3, 10, 17, 24, and 31, 1857. London.

Collins, Wilkie, and Charles Fechter. *Black and White: A Love Story in Three Acts. As First Performed at the Adelphi Theatre, London, Under the Management of Benjamin Webster, Esq. on Monday, March 29, 1869.* DeWitt's Acting Plays no. 296. New York: DeWitt, n.d.

"Death of His Royal Highness the Prince Consort." *The Queen* 1, no. 16 (December 21, 1861): 285–88.

Dickens, Charles. *The Centenary Edition of the Works of Charles Dickens.* 36 vols. London: Chapman and Hall, 1911.

———. *The Charles Dickens Edition of the Works of Charles Dickens.* London: Chapman and Hall, 1871.

———. *A Christmas Carol*. Edited by Richard Kelly. Peterborough, ON: Broadview, 2003.

———. *The Christmas Stories*. Edited by Ruth Glancy. London: Everyman, 1996.

———. *The Dent Uniform Edition of Dickens' Journalism*. Edited by Michael Slater and John Drew. 4 vols. Columbus: Ohio State University Press, 1994–2000.

———. *Great Expectations*. Edited by Janice Carlisle. Boston: Bedford St. Martin's, 1996.

———. Introduction to *The Poems of Adelaide A. Procter*, 3–12. London: Bell and Daldy, 1861.

———. "The Lost Arctic Voyagers." *Household Words*, December 2 and 9, 1854. London.

———. *Master Humphrey's Clock, and Other Stories*. Edited by Peter Mudford. London: Everyman, 1997.

———. *The Mystery of Edwin Drood*. Edited by David Paroissien. London: Penguin, 2002.

———. "Personal." In *Selected Journalism, 1850–1870*, 51–52. Edited by David Pascoe. London: Penguin, 1997.

———. *The Pilgrim Edition of the Letters of Charles Dickens*. Edited by Madeline House, Graham Storey, Kathleen Tillotson, K. J. Fielding, and Angus Easson. 12 vols. Oxford, UK: Clarendon, 1965–2002.

———. *Sketches by Boz*. Edited by Dennis Walder. London: Penguin, 1995.

———. *The Wreck of the Golden Mary*. Edited by Melissa Valiska Gregory and Melisa Klimaszewski. London: Hesperus Press, 2006.

Dickens, Charles, and Wilkie Collins. *A Message from the Sea: A Drama in Three Acts*. London: Holsworth, 1861. Available in Berg Collection, New York Public Library.

———. "No Thoroughfare: A Drama in Five Acts (Altered from the Christmas Story for Performance on the Stage)." London: Office of *All the Year Round*, 1867. Available in Berg Collection (copy 1), New York Public Library.

Dickens Journals Online. www.djo.org.uk. Hosted by the University of Buckingham.

Dixon, Edmund Saul. *Treatise on the History and Management of Ornamental and Domestic Poultry*. London, 1848.

Gaskell, Elizabeth. *The Letters of Mrs Gaskell*. Edited by J. A. V. Chapple and Arthur Pollard. 2nd ed. Manchester: Mandolin, 1997.

———. *Right at Last, and Other Tales*. London: Sampson and Low, 1860.

———. *Round the Sofa*. 2 vols. London: Sampson and Low, 1859.

The Haunted House, or the Revelations of Theresa Terence. Being the Christmas Number of *The Pearl*. Illustrated with six colored plates. London: Privately printed [William Lazenby], 1880. Available in British Library Rare Books.

Howitt, William. *Tallangetta, the Squatters Home: A Story of Australian Life*. London: Longman, Brown, Green, Longmans, and Roberts, 1857.

Hughes, W. R. *A Week's Tramp in Dickens-Land*. London: Chapman and Hall, 1891.

The Illustrated London News. Christmas supplement to December 23, 1848.

Linton, Eliza Lynn. *My Literary Life*. London: Hodder and Stoughton, 1899.

"Literature." *The Leader* 402 (December 5, 1857): 1168.

Lucas, Samuel. "Charles Dickens's Christmas Story." *Times* (London), December 24, 1857, 4.

"No Thoroughfare." *The Mask: A Humorous and Fantastic Review of the Month* 1 (February 1868): 14–18. Edited by Alfred Thompson and Leopold Lewis. Published in London, February–December 1868.

Procter, Adelaide A. *Legends and Lyrics, Second Series.* London: Bell and Daldy, 1861.

———. *The Poems of Adelaide A. Procter.* New York: Lovell, 1881.

"The Redeemed Profligate." *Harper's New Monthly Magazine* 10, no. 57 (February 1855): 371–77.

Roberts, Edwin F. *The Christmas Guests round the Sea-Coal Fire.* London: G. Vickers, 1856.

[Sala, George (misidentified as Charles Dickens)]. "What Christmas Is in the Company of John Doe." *Harper's New Monthly Magazine* (December 1851).

The Seven Poor Travellers; or, Life's Faults and Follies: Domestic Dramatic Sketch in Two Acts by G. D. Pitt. Licensed February 9, 1855, for performance at the Pavilion, February 10, 1855. British Library Manuscripts.

The Seven Poor Travellers: Drama in Three Acts, Taken from Mr. C. Dickens' Popular Tale in Household Words. Licensed for performance at the Victoria Theatre, February 5, 1855. British Library Manuscripts.

Shakespeare, William. *The Riverside Shakespeare.* Boston: Houghton Mifflin, 1974.

[Shorter, Thomas.] "Mr Howitt and Mr Dickens." *The Spiritual Magazine* 1, no. 2 (February 1860): 58–62.

Sotheby, Wilkinson and Hodge. *Catalogue of the Original Manuscripts, by Charles Dickens and Wilkie Collins, of* The Frozen Deep, *and* The Perils of Certain English Prisoners, *by Dickens and Collins; Two Poems by Dickens;* The Woman in White, No Name, Armadale, Moonstone, *&c., &c., by Collins; Also a Few Bills of Private Theatricals in Which They Both Took Part . . .* London: J. Davy, 1890.

Southey, Robert. *The Poetical Works of Robert Southey in Ten Volumes.* Boston: Little Brown, 1863.

Thackeray, William. "A Letter from the Editor to a Friend and Contributor." *Cornhill Magazine* (January 1860): inside front cover.

"Tom Tiddler's Ground." *The Queen* 1, no. 16 (December 21, 1861): 313–15.

"The Wreck of the Golden Mary." Review. *The Examiner,* December 20, 1856, 804.

Secondary Sources

Ackroyd, Peter. Foreword to *The Haunted House,* by Charles Dickens, vii–ix. London: Hesperus Press, 2002.

Andrews, Malcolm. *Charles Dickens and His Performing Selves: Dickens and the Public Readings.* Oxford: Oxford University Press, 2006.

Baker, Fran. Introduction to "The Ghost in the Garden Room," by Elizabeth Gaskell. Edited by Fran Baker. *Bulletin of the John Rylands University Library of Manchester* 86, no. 1 (Spring 2004): iii–cxxiv.

Baker, William. *A Wilkie Collins Chronology.* Houndmills, UK: Palgrave, 2007.

Bakhtin, M. M. *The Dialogic Imagination.* Edited by Michael Holquist. Translated by Caryl Emerson and Michael Holquist. Austin: University of Texas Press, 1981.

Barthes, Roland. "The Death of the Author." In *Image, Music, Text: Essays,* translated by Stephen Heath, 142–48. London: Fontana, 1977.

Secondary Sources

Beetham, Margaret. "Towards a Theory of the Periodical as a Publishing Genre." In *Investigating Victorian Journalism*, edited by Laurel Brake, Aled Jones, and Lionel Madden, 19–32. New York: St. Martin's Press, 1990.

Bentley, Nicolas, Michael Slater, and Nina Burgis. *The Dickens Index*. Oxford: Oxford University Press, 1988.

Bodenheimer, Rosemarie. *Knowing Dickens*. Ithaca, NY: Cornell University Press, 2007.

Bolton, H. Philip. *Dickens Dramatized*. Boston: G. K. Hall, 1987.

Bowen, John. "Bebelle and 'His Boots': Dickens, Ellen Ternan and the *Christmas Stories*," pt. 3. *The Dickensian* 96 (2000): 197–208.

———. "Dickens's Umbrellas." In *Dickens's Style*, edited by Daniel Tyler, 26–45. Cambridge: Cambridge University Press, 2013.

Brake, Laurel. "Second Life: *All the Year Round* and the New Generation of British Periodicals in the 1860s." In Mackenzie and Winyard, *Charles Dickens*, 11–33.

———. *Subjugated Knowledges: Journalism, Gender, and Literature in the Nineteenth Century*. New York: New York University Press, 1994.

Brake, Laurel, and Julie F. Codell. Introduction to *Encounters in the Victorian Press: Editors, Authors, Readers*, edited by Laurel Brake and Julie F. Codell, 1–7. Houndmills, UK: Palgrave Macmillan, 2005.

Brake, Laurel, and Marysa Demoor, eds. *A Dictionary of Nineteenth Century Journalism*. Ghent: Academia Press; London: British Library, 2009.

Brake, Laurel, and Aled Jones. *Investigating Victorian Journalism*. New York: St. Martin's, 1990.

Brannan, Robert Louis, ed. *Under the Management of Mr. Charles Dickens: His Production of The Frozen Deep*. Ithaca, NY: Cornell University Press, 1966.

Brantlinger, Patrick. *Rule of Darkness: British Literature and Imperialism, 1830–1914*. Ithaca, NY: Cornell University Press, 1988.

———. *Taming Cannibals: Race and the Victorians*. Ithaca, NY: Cornell University Press, 2011.

Brody, Jennifer DeVere. *Impossible Purities: Blackness, Femininity, and Victorian Culture*. Durham, NC: Duke University Press, 1998.

Bump, Jerome. "Parody and the Dickens-Collins Collaboration in *No Thoroughfare*." *Library Chronicle of the University of Texas at Austin* (1986): 38–53.

Buurma, Rachel Sagner. "Anonymity, Corporate Authority, and the Archive: The Production of Authorship in Late-Victorian England." *Victorian Studies* 50, no. 1 (2007): 15–42.

Callanan, Laura. *Deciphering Race: White Anxiety, Racial Conflict, and the Turn to Fiction in Mid-Victorian English Prose*. Columbus: Ohio State University Press, 2006.

Chadwick, Whitney, and Isabelle de Courtivron. *Significant Others: Creativity and Intimate Partnership*. London: Thames and Hudson, 1993.

Chapman, Anne. "'I Am Not Going On': Negotiating Christmas Publishing Rhythms with Dickens's *Mugby Junction*." *Victorian Periodicals Review* 51, no. 1 (2018): 70–85.

Chapple, J. A. V., and John Geoffrey Sharps. *Elizabeth Gaskell: A Portrait in Letters*. Manchester: Manchester University Press, 1980.

Clemm, Sabine. *Dickens, Journalism, and Nationhood: Mapping the World in Household Words*. New York: Routledge, 2009.

Collins, Philip, ed. *Dickens: The Critical Heritage*. New York: Barnes and Noble, 1971.

———. Introduction to *Charles Dickens: The Public Readings*, edited by Philip Collins, xvii–lxix. Oxford, UK: Clarendon, 1975.

———. "Sala, George Augustus Henry." In *Oxford Reader's Companion to Dickens*, edited by Paul Schlicke, 515–16. Oxford: Oxford University Press, 2000.

Crawford, Iain. "'Hunted and Harried by Pseudo-philanthropists': Dickens, Martineau and *Household Words*." Philip Collins Memorial Lecture. In Mackenzie and Winyard, *Charles Dickens*, 157–73.

Davies, Harold Neville. "The Tauchnitz Extra Christmas Numbers of *All the Year Round*." *Library* 33, no. 3 (September 1978): 215–22.

Davis, Lennard. *Enforcing Normalcy: Disability, Deafness and the Body*. London: Verso, 1995.

Drew, John M. L. *Dickens the Journalist*. New York: Palgrave Macmillan, 2003.

———. Introduction to Mackenzie and Winyard, *Charles Dickens*, v–xxi.

Easley, Alexis. "Authorship, Gender, and Power in Victorian Culture: Harriet Martineau and the Periodical Press." In *Nineteenth-Century Media and the Construction of Identities*, edited by Laurel Brake, Bill Bell, and David Finkelstein, 154–64. New York: Palgrave, 2000.

———. *First Person Anonymous: Women Writers and Victorian Print Media, 1830–70*. Aldershot, UK: Ashgate, 2004.

Ehnenn, Jill. *Women's Literary Collaboration, Queerness, and Late-Victorian Culture*. Aldershot, UK: Ashgate, 2008.

Ellison, David. "The Ghost of Injuries Present in Dickens's *The Signalman*." *Textual Practice* 26, no. 4 (2012): 649–65.

Esmail, Jennifer. "I Listened with My Eyes: Writing Speech and Reading Deafness in the Fiction of Charles Dickens and Wilkie Collins." *ELH* 78, no. 4 (Winter 2011): 991–1020.

———. *Reading Victorian Deafness: Signs and Sounds in Victorian Literature and Culture*. Athens: Ohio University Press, 2013.

Farrell, Michael P. *Collaborative Circles: Friendship Dynamics and Creative Work*. Chicago: University of Chicago Press, 2001.

Ferguson, Christine. "Sensational Dependence: Prosthesis and Affect in Dickens and Braddon." *Literature Interpretation Theory* 19 (2008): 1–25.

Finkelstein, David, and Douglas M. Peers, eds. *Negotiating India in Nineteenth-Century Media*. Basingstoke, UK: Macmillan, 2000.

Fitzgerald, Percy. *Memories of Charles Dickens*. Bristol, UK: J. W. Arrowsmith, 1913.

Forster, John. *The Life of Charles Dickens*. 2 vols. 1872–74. London: Dent/Everyman's Library, 1966.

Foucault, Michel. "What Is an Author?" Trans. Josué Harari. In *The Critical Tradition: Classic Texts and Contemporary Trends*, edited by David H. Richter, 978–88. New York: Bedford St. Martin's Press, 1989.

Fraser, Hilary, Stephanie Green, and Judith Johnston. *Gender and the Victorian Periodical*. Cambridge: Cambridge University Press, 2003.

Furneaux, Holly. "*Household Words* and the Crimean War: Journalism, Fiction, and Forms of Recuperation in Wartime." In Mackenzie and Winyard, *Charles Dickens*, 245–59.

———. *Queer Dickens*. Oxford: Oxford University Press, 2009.

Gasson, Andrew. *Wilkie Collins: An Illustrated Guide*. Oxford: Oxford University Press, 1998.

Genette, Gerard. *Paratexts: Thresholds of Interpretation*. Cambridge: Cambridge University Press, 1997.

Gilbert, Sandra, and Susan Gubar. *The Madwoman in the Attic: The Woman Writer and the Nineteenth-Century Literary Imagination*. New Haven, CT: Yale University Press, 1979.

Glancy, Ruth F. "Dickens and Christmas: His Framed-Tale Themes." *Nineteenth-Century Fiction* 35, no. 1 (1980): 53–72.

———. Introduction to *The Christmas Stories*, edited by Ruth Glancy, xxi–xli. London: Everyman, 1996.

Gregory, Gill. *The Life and Work of Adelaide Procter: Poetry, Feminism and Fathers*. Aldershot, UK: Ashgate, 1998.

Gregory, Melissa Valiska. "Dickens's Collaborative Genres." *Dickens Studies Annual* 41 (2010): 215–36.

Harris, Katherine D. *Forget Me Not: The Rise of the British Literary Annual, 1823–1835*. Athens: Ohio University Press, 2015.

Hollington, Michael. "The Perils of Certain English Prisoners: Dickens, Collins, Morley, and Central America." *The Dickensian* 101, no. 3 (Winter 2005): 197–210.

———. "'To the Droodstone'; or, From *The Moonstone* to *Edwin Drood* via *No Thoroughfare*." *QWERTY* 5 (1995): 141–49.

Holmes, Martha Stoddard. *Fictions of Affliction: Physical Disability in Victorian Culture*. Ann Arbor: University of Michigan Press, 2004.

———. "'Happy and Yet Pitying Tears': Deafness and Affective Disjuncture in Dickens's 'Doctor Marigold.'" *Victorian Review* 35, no. 2 (Fall 2009): 53–64.

———. "The Twin Structure: Disabled Women in Victorian Courtship Plots." In *Disability Studies: Enabling the Humanities*, edited by Sharon L. Snyder, Branda Jo Brueggemann, and Rosemarie Garland-Thomson, 222–47. New York: Modern Language Association, 2002.

Homans, Margaret. *Bearing the Word: Language and Female Experience in Nineteenth-Century Women's Writing*. Chicago: University of Chicago Press, 1986.

Howe, Winona Ruth. "Writing a Book in Company: The Collaborative Works of Charles Dickens and Wilkie Collins." PhD thesis, University of California–Riverside, 1991.

Hughes, Linda K., and Michael Lund. *Victorian Publishing and Mrs. Gaskell's Work*. Charlottesville: University Press of Virginia, 1999.

Isaacs, J. *An Assessment of Twentieth-Century Literature: Six Lectures Delivered in the B.B.C. Third Programme*. Port Washington, NY: Kennikat Press, 1968.

James, Louis. "The Trouble with Betsy: Periodicals and the Common Reader in Mid-Nineteenth-Century England." In *The Victorian Periodical Press: Samplings and Soundings*, edited by Joanne Shattock and Michael Wolff, 349–66. Leicester: Leicester University Press, 1982.

Johnson, Edgar. *Charles Dickens: His Tragedy and Triumph*. 2 vols. New York: Simon and Schuster, 1952.

Jordan, John O., and Robert L. Patten, eds. *Literature in the Marketplace: Nineteenth-Century British Publishing and Reading Practices.* Cambridge Studies in Nineteenth-Century Literature and Culture 5. Cambridge: Cambridge University Press, 1995.

Kitton, Frederic G. *The Minor Writings of Charles Dickens.* London: Elliot Stock, 1900.

Klimaszewski, Melisa. *Brief Lives: Wilkie Collins.* London: Hesperus Press, 2011.

———. "The Contested Site of Maternity in Charles Dickens's *Dombey and Son.*" In *The Literary Mother: Essays on Representations of Maternity and Child Care,* edited by Susan Staub, 138–58. Jefferson, NC: McFarland, 2007.

———. "Examining the Wet Nurse: Breasts, Power, and Penetration in Victorian England." *Women's Studies: An Interdisciplinary Journal* 35, no. 4 (2006): 323–46.

———. "Rebuilding Dickens's *Wreck* and Rethinking the Collaborative." *SEL Studies in English Literature 1500–1900* 54, no. 4 (Autumn 2014): 815–33.

Koestenbaum, Wayne. *Double Talk: The Erotics of Male Literary Collaboration.* New York: Routledge, 1989.

Lai, Shu Fang. "Fact or Fancy: What Can We Learn about Dickens from His Periodicals *Household Words* and *All the Year Round?*" *Victorian Periodicals Review* 34, no. 1 (2001): 41–53.

Laird, Holly. *Women Coauthors.* Urbana: University of Illinois Press, 2000.

Law, Graham. *Serializing Fiction in the Victorian Press.* New York: Palgrave, 2000.

Leary, Patrick. "How the Dickens Scandal Went Viral." In Mackenzie and Winyard, *Charles Dickens,* 305–25.

Leary, Patrick, and Andrew Nash. "Authorship." In *The Cambridge History of the Book in Britain,* vol. 6, *1830–1914,* edited by David McKitterick, 172–213. Cambridge: Cambridge University Press, 2014.

Lehmann, R. C. *Charles Dickens as Editor: Being Letters Written to Him by William Henry Wills, His Sub-editor.* 1912. New York: Kraus, 1971.

Liddle, Dallas. "Salesmen, Sportsmen, Mentors: Anonymity and Mid-Victorian Theories of Journalism." *Victorian Studies* 41, no. 1 (1997): 31–69.

Lohrli, Anne. *Household Words: Table of Contents, List of Contributors, and Their Contributions.* Toronto: University of Toronto Press, 1973.

London, Bette Lynn. *Writing Double: Women's Literary Partnerships.* Ithaca, NY: Cornell University Press, 1999.

Lonoff, Sue. "Charles Dickens and Wilkie Collins." *Nineteenth-Century Fiction* 35, no. 2 (1980): 150–70.

Love, Harold. *Attributing Authorship: An Introduction.* Cambridge: Cambridge University Press, 2002.

Mackenzie, Hazel, and Ben Winyard, eds. *Charles Dickens and the Mid-Victorian Press, 1850–1870.* Buckingham: University of Buckingham Press, 2013.

Masten, Jeffrey. "More or Less: Editing the Collaborative." *Shakespeare Studies* 29 (2001): 109–31.

———. *Textual Intercourse: Collaboration, Authorship, and Sexualities in Renaissance Drama.* Cambridge: Cambridge University Press, 1997.

Maunder, Andrew, and Grace Moore, eds. *Victorian Crime, Madness and Sensation.* Aldershot, UK: Ashgate, 2016.

Secondary Sources

Mays, Kelly J. "The Disease of Reading and Victorian Periodicals." In *Literature in the Marketplace: Nineteenth-Century British Publishing and Reading Practices*, edited by John O. Jordan and Robert L. Patten, 165–94. Cambridge Studies in Nineteenth-Century Literature and Culture 5. Cambridge: Cambridge University Press, 1995.

McGann, Jerome. *A Critique of Modern Textual Criticism*. Chicago: University of Chicago Press, 1983.

McGill, Meredith L. "What Is a Ballad? Reading for Genre, Format, and Medium." *Nineteenth-Century Literature* 71, no. 2 (2016): 156–75.

Michie, Helena. *Outside the Pale: Cultural Exclusion, Gender Difference, and the Victorian Woman Writer*. Ithaca, NY: Cornell University Press, 1993.

Moore, Grace. *Dickens and Empire: Discourses of Class, Race and Colonialism in the Works of Charles Dickens*. Aldershot, UK: Ashgate, 2004.

———. "Swarmery and Bloodbaths: A Reconsideration of Dickens on Class and Race in the 1860s." *Dickens Studies Annual* 31 (2002): 175–202.

Moore, Tara. *Victorian Christmas in Print*. New York: Palgrave Macmillan, 2009.

Mussell, Jim. "Cohering Knowledge in the Nineteenth Century: Form, Genre and Periodical Studies." *Victorian Periodicals Review* 2, no. 1 (Spring 2009): 93–103.

———. "Moving Things: Circulation and Repetition in Victorian Print Culture." Pt. 2 of 5, "Moving Things." December 19, 2013. jimmussell.com/2013/12/19/moving-things-circulation-and-repetition-in-victorian-print-culture-25/.

———. "Repetition; or, 'In Our Last.'" *Victorian Periodicals Review* 48, no. 3 (Fall 2015): 343–58.

Nayder, Lillian. *The Other Dickens*. Ithaca, NY: Cornell University Press, 2011.

———. *Unequal Partners: Charles Dickens, Wilkie Collins, and Victorian Authorship*. Ithaca, NY: Cornell University Press, 2002.

Newsom, Robert. *Dickens on the Romantic Side of Familiar Things: Bleak House and the Novel Tradition*. New York: Columbia University Press, 1977.

Oddie, William. "Dickens and the Indian Mutiny." *Dickensian* 68 (January 1972): 3–15.

Oliphant, Margaret. *Women Novelists of Queen Victoria's Reign: A Book of Appreciations*. 1897. Folcroft, PA: Folcroft Press, 1969.

Onslow, Barbara. *Women of the Press in Nineteenth-Century Britain*. Basingstoke, UK: Macmillan, 2000.

Oppenlander, Ella Ann. *Dickens' All the Year Round: Descriptive Index and Contributor List*. New York: Whitston Publishing, 1984.

Page, Norman. *A Dickens Chronology*. Boston: G. K. Hall, 1988.

———. *Speech in the English Novel*. Atlantic Highlands, NJ: Humanities Press International, 1988.

Park, Hyungji. "'The Story of Our Lives': *The Moonstone* and the Indian Mutiny in *All the Year Round*." In *Negotiating India in Nineteenth-Century Media*, edited by David Finkelstein and Douglas M. Peers, 84–109. New York: Macmillan, 2000.

Patten, Robert L. *Charles Dickens and "Boz": The Birth of the Industrial-Age Author*. Cambridge: Cambridge University Press, 2012.

———. *Charles Dickens and His Publishers*. Oxford: Oxford University Press, 1978.

Perkins, Frederic Beecher. *Charles Dickens: A Sketch of His Life and Works*. New York: Putnam and Sons, 1870.

Peters, Catherine. Introduction to *Hide and Seek*, by Wilkie Collins. Oxford: Oxford University Press, 1993.

———. *The King of Inventors*. Princeton: Princeton University Press, 1991.

Peters, Laura. *Dickens and Race*. Manchester: Manchester University Press, 2013.

———. "'Double-Dyed Traitors and Infernal Villains': *Illustrated London News, Household Words*, Charles Dickens, and the Indian Rebellion." In *Negotiating India in Nineteenth-Century Media*, edited by David Finkelstein and Douglas M. Peers, 110–34. New York: Macmillan, 2000.

———. "Perilous Adventures: Dickens and Popular Orphan Adventure Narratives." *The Dickensian* 94, no. 3 (Winter 1998): 172–83.

Piesse, Jude. "Dreaming across Oceans: Emigration and Nation in the Mid-Victorian Christmas Issue." *Victorian Periodicals Review* 46, no. 1 (Spring 2013): 37–60.

Plunkett, John, and Andrew King. *Victorian Print Media: A Reader*. Oxford: Oxford University Press, 2005.

Poovey, Mary. *Uneven Developments: The Ideological Work of Gender in Mid-Victorian England*. Chicago: University of Chicago Press, 1988.

Pope-Hennessey, Una. *Charles Dickens*. London: Chatto and Windus, 1968.

Prins, Yopie. "Sappho Doubled." *Yale Journal of Criticism* 8, no. 1 (1995): 165–86.

Quirk, Randall. "Some Observations on the Language of Dickens." *Review of English Literature* 2 (1961): 19–28.

Recchio, Thomas. *Elizabeth Gaskell's Cranford: A Publishing History*. Aldershot, UK: Ashgate, 2009.

Rylance, Rick. *Victorian Psychology and British Culture*. Oxford: Oxford University Press, 2000.

Sabey, Brian. "Ethical Metafiction in Dickens's Christmas Hauntings." *Dickens Studies Annual* 46 (2015): 123–46.

Schelstraete, Jasper. "'Literary Adventurers': Editorship, Non-fiction Authorship and Anonymity." In Mackenzie and Winyard, *Charles Dickens*, 147–56.

Schor, Hilary. *Scheherezade in the Marketplace: Elizabeth Gaskell and the Victorian Novel*. Oxford: Oxford University Press, 1992.

Sedgwick, Eve Kosofsky. *Between Men: English Literature and Male Homosocial Desire*. New York: Columbia University Press, 1985.

Shannon, Mary. *Dickens, Reynolds, and Mayhew on Wellington Street: The Print Culture of a Victorian Street*. Farnham, UK: Ashgate, 2015.

Sharpe, Will. "Authorship and Attribution." In *William Shakespeare and Others: Collaborative Plays*, edited by Jonathan Bate and Eric Rasmussen, with Jan Sewell and Will Sharpe, 641–745. Houndmills, UK: Palgrave, 2013.

Shatto, Susan. "Miss Havisham and Mr. Mopes the Hermit: Dickens and the Mentally Ill." Pt. 1. *Dickens Quarterly* 2, no. 2 (June 1985): 43–50.

———. "Miss Havisham and Mr. Mopes the Hermit: Dickens and the Mentally Ill." Pt. 2. *Dickens Quarterly* 2, no. 3 (September 1985): 79–84.

Shattock, Joanne. "*Household Words* and the 'Community of Print' in the 1850s." In Mackenzie and Winyard, *Charles Dickens*, 1–10.

Shattock, Joanne, and Michael Wolff. Introduction to *The Victorian Periodical Press: Samplings and Soundings*, edited by Joanne Shattock and Michael Wolff, xiii–xix. Leicester: Leicester University Press, 1982.

Shenk, Joshua Wolf. *Powers of Two: How Relationships Drive Creativity*. New York: Mariner Books, 2015.

Slater, Michael. *Charles Dickens*. New Haven, CT: Yale University Press, 2009.

———. *The Great Charles Dickens Scandal*. New Haven, CT: Yale University Press, 2012.

Spivak, Gayatri Chakravorty. "Three Women's Texts and a Critique of Imperialism." *Critical Inquiry* 12, no. 1 (Autumn 1985): 235–61.

Stace, Wesley. Introduction to *The Haunted House*, by Charles Dickens, xi–xxi. New York: Modern Library, 2004.

Steig, Michael. *Dickens and Phiz*. Bloomington: Indiana University Press, 1978.

Stillinger, Jack. *Multiple Authorship and the Myth of Solitary Genius*. Oxford: Oxford University Press, 1991.

Stone, Harry, ed. *Charles Dickens's Uncollected Writings from Household Words, 1850–1859*. 2 vols. Bloomington: Indiana University Press, 1968.

———. "Dickens and Interior Monologue." *Philological Quarterly* 38 (1959): 52–65.

———. "Dickens Rediscovered: Some Lost Writings Retrieved." *Nineteenth Century Fiction* 24, no. 4 (March 1970): 527–48.

———. *The Night Side of Dickens: Cannibalism, Passion, Necessity*. Columbus: Ohio State University Press, 1994.

———. "Unknown Dickens." *Dickens Studies Annual* 1 (1970): 1–22.

Stone, Marjorie, and Judith Thompson. "Contexts and Heterotexts: A Theoretical and Historical Introduction." In *Literary Couplings: Writing Couples, Collaborators, and the Construction of Authorship*, edited by Marjorie Stone and Judith Thompson, 3–37. Madison: University of Wisconsin Press, 2006.

Sutherland, John. *Victorian Novelists and Publishers*. Chicago: University of Chicago Press, 1976.

Tambling, Jeremy. "Dickens and Chaucer." *English* 64, no. 244 (2015): 42–64.

Taylor, Jenny Bourne. *In the Secret Theatre of Home: Wilkie Collins, Sensation Narrative, and Nineteenth-Century Psychology*. London: Routledge, 1988.

Thomas, Deborah. *Dickens and the Short Story*. Philadelphia: University of Pennsylvania Press, 1982.

———. "Dickens' Mrs. Lirriper and the Evolution of a Feminine Stereotype." *Dickens Studies Annual* 6 (1977): 154–66.

Tomalin, Claire. *The Invisible Woman: The Story of Ellen Ternan and Charles Dickens*. New York: Knopf, 1990.

Trodd, Anthea. "Collaborating in Open Boats: Dickens, Collins, Franklin, and Bligh." *Victorian Studies* 42, no. 2 (2000): 201–25.

———. "Messages in Bottles and Collins's Seafaring Man." *Studies in English Literature, 1500–1900* 41, no. 4 (Autumn 2001): 751–64.

Uffelman, Larry K. "From Serial to 'Novel': Elizabeth Gaskell assembles *Round the Sofa*." *Gaskell Society Journal* 15 (2001): 30–37.

"Victorian Networks and the Periodical Press." Special issue edited by Alexis Easley, *Victorian Periodicals Review* 44, no. 2 (Summer 2011): 111–213.

Wagner, Tamara S. "Dickens's 'Gentleman for Nowhere': Reversing Technological Gothic in the Linkages of *Mugby Junction*." *Dickens Quarterly* 28, no. 1 (2011): 52–64.

Waters, Catherine. *Commodity Culture in Dickens's* Household Words: *The Social Life of Goods*. Aldershot, UK: Ashgate, 2008.

Whidden, Seth. Introduction to *Models of Collaboration in Nineteenth-Century French Literature: Several Authors, One Pen*, edited by Seth Whidden, 1–16. Burlington, VT: Ashgate, 2009.

———. "Poetry in Collaboration in the 1870s: The Cercle Zutique, 'Le Fleuve' and 'The Raven.'" In *Models of Collaboration in Nineteenth-Century French Literature*, edited by Seth Whidden, 77–90. Burlington, VT: Ashgate, 2009.

Whitmore, Richard. *Mad Lucas: The Strange Story of Victorian England's Most Famous Hermit*. Hertfordshire, UK: North Hertfordshire District Council, 1983.

Wiener, Joel H., ed. *Innovators and Preachers: The Role of the Editor in Victorian England*. Westport, CT: Greenwood, 1985.

Young, Paul. "Economy, Empire, Extermination: The Christmas Pudding, the Crystal Palace and the Narrative of Capitalist Progress." *Literature and History* 14 (2005): 14–30.

Zeigler, Garrett. "The Perils of Empire: Dickens, Collins and the Indian Mutiny." In *Pirates and Mutineers in the Nineteenth Century: Swashbucklers and Swindlers*, edited by Grace Moore, 149–64. Farnham, UK: Ashgate, 2011.

Index